2238973   Co

NOV 26 2013

MACARTHUR IN ASIA

MACARTHUR IN ASIA

The General and His Staff in the
Philippines, Japan, and Korea

Hiroshi Masuda

**Translated from the
Japanese by Reiko Yamamoto**

CORNELL UNIVERSITY PRESS   **ITHACA AND LONDON**

Frontispiece: MacArthur and the Bataan Boys. From center top in clockwise direction: Sutherland, George, Willoughby, Marquat, McMicking, Rogers, Diller, Wilson, Morehouse, Huff, Sherr, Casey, Stivers, Marshall, and Akin. Reproduced with permission of the MacArthur Memorial Library and Archives.

Cornell University Press gratefully acknowledges receipt of grants from the Suntory Foundation and from Toyo Eiwa University that aided in the publication of this translation.

MacArthur by Hiroshi Masuda
Copyright © 2009 by Hiroshi Masuda
All rights reserved.
Original published in Japan by Chuokoron-Shinsha, Inc., Tokyo
English translation rights arranged with Hiroshi Masuda through The Sakai Agency
English translation copyright © 2012 by Cornell University

First published 2012 by Cornell University Press
Printed in the United States of America

Library of Congress Cataloging-in-Publication Data

Masuda, Hiroshi, 1947–
  [Makkasa. English]
  MacArthur in Asia: the general and his staff in the Philippines, Japan, and Korea / Hiroshi Masuda; translated from the Japanese by Reiko Yamamoto.
    p. cm.
  Includes bibliographical references and index.
  ISBN 978-0-8014-4939-0 (cloth: alk. paper)
  1. MacArthur, Douglas, 1880–1964.   2. Generals—United States—Biography.
3. Japan—History—Allied occupation, 1945–1952.   4. World War, 1939–1945—
Campaigns—Asia. I. Title.
  E745.M3M2813   2013
  355.0092—dc23   [B]   2012009130

Cornell University Press strives to use environmentally responsible suppliers and materials to the fullest extent possible in the publishing of its books. Such materials include vegetable-based, low-VOC inks and acid-free papers that are recycled, totally chlorine-free, or partly composed of nonwood fibers. For further information, visit our website at www.cornellpress.cornell.edu.

Cloth printing   10 9 8 7 6 5 4 3 2 1

Contents

Preface and Acknowledgments   vii

1. Encounter with the Philippines   1
Before His Appointment to the Philippines · Army Chief of Staff · From
Quezon's Military Advisor to Commander of the United States Army
Forces in the Far East

2. Origins of the Bataan Boys   9
The Upper Level Group · The Middle and Lower Groups · The Other Group

3. From the Approach of War to the Evacuation from Manila,
October to December 1941   27
Washington before the Outbreak of War · Preparations in Manila before
the Outbreak of War · The Attack on Pearl Harbor · The Attack on Clark
Field · Washington's Modification of the Military Strategy · The Japanese
Military Landing Operation in the Philippines · The Evacuation from
Manila to Corregidor

4. The Fall of Manila and the First Offensive and Defensive Battles,
Early January to Early February 1942   51
The Corregidor Fortress · The Japanese Military Landing on Luzon ·
Withdrawal to the Bataan Peninsula · The Fall of Manila and the
First Bataan Operation · The Good Fight and the Hardships of
MacArthur's Troops

5. Planning the Escape from Corregidor, Early February to
Late February 1942   73
Quezon's Anti-Americanism and Demand for Neutrality · The Evacuation
of Quezon and Sayre · MacArthur's Authorization to Evacuate

6. The Evacuation of MacArthur from Corregidor,
Late February to the Middle of March 1942   93
The Means of Evacuation and the Accompanying Persons · Evacuation
Dates and Route · Evacuation Day · From Corregidor to Tagauayan · From
Tagauayan to Mindanao · From Mindanao to Australia

7. The Second Bataan Operation and the Death March,
Early February to Early May 1942   121
Preparing for Battle · The Battle Unfolds · The Fall of Corregidor · The
Bataan "Death March"

8. From Australia to the Philippines,
March 1942 to October 1944   149

The Beginning of the Counterattack · The Battle in New Guinea ·
Teamwork in MacArthur's Inner Circle · Conflict with the U.S. Navy
Leadership · "I Shall Return"

9. From the Philippines to Japan,
October 1944 to August 1945   169

Control over Leyte Island · Advance toward Manila · Recapture of
Bataan and Corregidor · De-Japanization and Democratization of the
Philippines · The Rise of Whitney · Japanese Surrender · Arrival at
Atsugi Airfield

10. The Demilitarization of Japan,
August 1945 to December 1947   193

The Surrender of Japan and the Beginning of the Occupation · The
Establishment of GHQ/SCAP and the Departure of Sutherland · The
Disarmament of the Japanese Military and the Arrest of War Criminals ·
The Meeting between MacArthur and Emperor Hirohito · Disease and
Food Shortages in Japan

11. The Democratization of Japan,
August 1945 to April 1950   209

The Purge · The New Japanese Constitution · Dissolution of the
Zaibatsu and Land Reform · Educational Reforms · The First
Postwar General Election · Dissolution of the Ministry of Home Affairs

12. Washington's Policy Shift on Japan and MacArthur's
Resistance, January 1948 to June 1950   229

Failure of the Proposal for an Early Peace Treaty with Japan ·
Washington's Review of the Japan Occupation Policy · MacArthur's
Opposition · NSC 13/2 and MacArthur's Resistance · Conflict within
GHQ/SCAP: GS vs. G-2 · The Proxy War for GS vs. G-2: Ashida vs.
Yoshida · The "Cold War" between MacArthur and Washington

13. The Korean War and the Dismissal of MacArthur,
June 1950 to April 1951   249

Outbreak of the Korean War and MacArthur's Appointment as
Commander of the United Nations Command · MacArthur's Directive
for Japan's Rearmament · Secret Activities of Japanese Minesweepers ·
The Sneak Landing Operation on Inchon · China's Entry into War · The
Dismissal of MacArthur · "Old Soldiers Just Fade Away"

Conclusion   275

Notes   287
Bibliography   307
Index   313

Preface and Acknowledgments

The enduring mythology around the figure of Douglas MacArthur (1880–1964) has been sustained in both the United States and Japan. Even a half century after his death, interest in and enthusiasm for MacArthur continue to grow. More than seventy books on MacArthur have appeared in the United States. In contrast, Japanese scholars have written only a few academic studies of MacArthur, although many translations of foreign studies as well as magazine articles have been published. Sodei Rinjiro's *Makkasah's Nisennichi* (MacArthur's 2,000 Days), published in 1974, was the first major Japanese study of MacArthur. This book follows Sodei's, nearly forty years later.

American and Japanese accounts of MacArthur differ in their interests and focus. U.S. studies of MacArthur usually cover the eighty-four years of his life, including his relationship with his family, World War I, his period of service as Army chief of staff, his time as the military advisor in the Philippines, the war between the United States and Japan, the occupation of Japan, and his dismissal during the Korean War. They tend to treat MacArthur's activities in each period evenly and in detail. In brief, the intellectual interest in and the evaluation of MacArthur in his homeland focus not only on his distinguished talent for strategy and extraordinary courage as a commander in dangerous battlefields, but also on his distinguished leadership as a peacetime administrator. He has won respect and credibility as one of the greatest heroes of the twentieth century, who led his nation to a glorious victory.

By contrast, Japanese analysts are likely to concentrate on the five-and-a-half years of the Allied Occupation, the two thousand days when MacArthur administered Japan as the supreme commander for the Allied Powers (SCAP). MacArthur's dignity and authority surpassed those of Showa Emperor Hirohito, and his godlike presence at the peak of General Headquarters (GHQ) awed the Japanese people into silence. As supreme commander MacArthur carried out large-scale and essentially experimental reforms based on the Potsdam Declaration in order to rehabilitate Japan, transforming it from a military state into a democratic and peaceful nation. These reforms covered the Japanese legal system, politics, military affairs, the economy, social affairs, and the educational system, and included specific measures such as the drafting of a new constitution, the dismantling of the Zaibatsu, land reforms, public purges, the organization of labor unions, and the introduction of women's suffrage. Since so many elements of modern Japanese identity originate in the Occupation era, it is undeniable that MacArthur made hugely significant contributions as an administrator. It's a perfectly reasonable assumption that the Japanese Occupation would have been completely different had the supreme commander not been MacArthur. It can be safely said that the occupation of Japan was a MacArthur occupation. The differences in intellectual concerns between U.S. and Japanese accounts of MacArthur reflect the differences in historical experience between the two nations.

Two characteristics of this book should be noted. The first is that it begins not with the occupation of Japan, which is the focus for most Japanese studies, but with MacArthur's service in the Philippines, starting in 1935, ten years prior to the Japanese defeat. The reason for beginning in the Philippines is that MacArthur's experience there constitutes the origins of the Occupation policies he adopted in Japan. Using this longer perspective, the book clarifies parts of the Japanese Occupation that have not been fully explored in previous studies of MacArthur in Japan.

MacArthur had long and close ties with the Philippines, and he developed a deep affection for the Philippine people. Because his father had served as commander of the army of the Philippines in the early twentieth century, MacArthur chose the Philippines for his initial service (as a second lieutenant) after his graduation from the U.S. Military Academy at West Point. Following World War I, he was sent to the Philippines as commander of the Philippine army (at the rank of colonel). From the late 1920s through the early 1930s, he served as field marshal of the Philippine army (as a major general) and U.S. Army chief of staff (as a general), and after retirement in 1935, at the request of President Emanuel L. Quezon he was named military advisor for the organization of the Philippine army. Until his retreat from the Philippines, in March 1942, MacArthur spent more than thirteen years in the Philippines, serving four tours of duty there. During his service he faced the Japanese military threat and the Japanese invasion of the Philippines. He took as his vital mission the tasks of eliminating the pressure exerted by the Japanese southward advance and figuring out how to defend the Philippines once the Japanese invasion had begun.

Shocked by the surprise attack on Clark Field on December 7, 1941, which occurred almost simultaneously with the air raid on Pearl Harbor, MacArthur and his staff abandoned Manila and moved to Corregidor Island, a fortress in Manila Bay. His aim was to hold on to a military base and put up tenacious resistance on the Bataan Peninsula. Against a ferocious attack by some fifty thousand Japanese troops, the eighty-thousand-strong U.S.-Philippine defending force on the Bataan Peninsula was almost overwhelmed. Following orders from President Franklin D. Roosevelt, MacArthur and a few of his staff managed to break through the Japanese siege and escape from Corregidor to Mindanao and on to Australia.

Although this dramatic evacuation strengthened the hero myth of MacArthur, he had deserted his men at the most critical moment of their hopeless fight—a blow to MacArthur's pride that became, for him, the greatest dishonor of his life. His famous phrase "I shall return!" made in a speech to news reporters at the Adelaide railway station in March 1942 while on his way to Melbourne reflected the self-reproach caused by this experience.

Nevertheless this mortification contributed to a firm resolution. MacArthur became determined to avenge his humiliation by attacking the Japanese and completely defeating them as a military power. It was a determination that stemmed not simply from his responsibility as a commander but also from a desire to wipe away his disgrace. Launching a counterattack from Australia and fighting through the Solomon Islands, New Guinea, and Morotai Island, MacArthur's troops successfully landed on Leyte Island in the Philippines in October 1944. He thus fulfilled his "I shall return" pledge. After difficult fighting and many casualties, MacArthur recaptured Manila from the Japanese in March 1945. MacArthur implemented a series of policies for the demilitarization and democratization of the Philippines, including military reforms, administrative reforms, arrests of war criminals and public purges, construction work, and health and welfare policies.

The reforms that MacArthur carried out in the Philippines provided a template for those he would later implement during the occupation of Japan. In effect, Manila was a proving ground for what was later accomplished in Tokyo. It is, therefore, indispensable to examine the Philippine period in order to understand the occupation of Japan.

The second characteristic of this book is its focus on MacArthur's immediate staff, specifically the "Bataan Boys" (or "Bataan Gang"), whose testimony sheds light on MacArthur's personality and achievements. The Bataan Boys were a group of fifteen army officers who, on March 12, 1942, escaped with MacArthur in four torpedo (PT, or Patrol Torpedo) boats from Corregidor Island. Breaking through heavy Japanese defenses, they reached the southern part of Mindanao and after three days of hardship flew to Australia. The escape occurred only three months after the outbreak of the Pacific War.

Although the dramatic escape may have damaged MacArthur's self-esteem, the shared experience of a critical moment strengthened his bond with the Bataan Boys. In this process the Bataan Boys gained an invincible advantage. They formed an inner circle in MacArthur's General Headquarters (GHQ), building a high barrier around him. The mere mention that a particular staff officer was one of the Bataan Boys was often enough to quell opposition. The cordial and steady relationships MacArthur formed with his staff made the Bataan Boys an exclusive and powerful faction, what we might call "MacArthur's court." Because of their influence on Japanese Occupation policy, we need to understand the development of this unique group and the identity of each of its members. However, there are no full studies on the Bataan Boys from inception to dismissal, either in the United States or in Japan. By offering a thorough account of "MacArthur's court," this book fills some unexplained gaps in studies not only of MacArthur but also of the Japanese Occupation.

By analyzing MacArthur's occupation of Japan as a subsequent phase, or perhaps even continuation, of his Philippine administration, this book adds new information to the body of research on MacArthur. Using materials from the State Department and the War Department, and GHQ materials covering the ten years from the outbreak of war until his departure from Japan (1941–51), as well as oral histories of the Bataan Boys and others concerned, I aim to illuminate a distinguished, complex, and versatile personality.

My research on the Occupation began some thirty years ago with a study of the political purge of Ishibashi Tanzan (1884–1973), who, after World War II, served as minister of finance, minister of international trade and industry, and prime minister. I went on to conduct research on the purge of former Imperial Army and Navy officers and on the Japanese rearmament issue and the Japanese Defense Forces. During a quarter century of conducting research relating to the Occupation, I kept away from the difficult figure of MacArthur, because history's ultimate verdicts on his greatness and his complicated traits were still unclear to me. However, during the ten years I spent studying Japanese rearmament issues, I began to feel that the mist obscuring MacArthur was clearing. I was spurred to undertake this study by a visit to the MacArthur Memorial Library in Norfolk, Virginia, after a long interval away, at the moment when I saw a photo panel of the Bataan Boys. The Bataan Boys are widely known by name in Japan, but even though they were deeply involved in the Occupation administration under MacArthur, their lives, roles, and responsibilities, and the details of their leaving Japan were not well known. A thorough study of MacArthur would, I decided, be impossible without researching the Bataan Boys, and I began to collect materials on them.

My personal experience of a trip to the Bataan Peninsula and Corregidor Island in March 2007 helped clear up some of the confusion that surrounds MacArthur and the Philippines during the war years. That trip gave me a sense of the actual distances and environment that I could not gather from books and documents. I experienced the lofty mountain ranges and curved roads of the Bataan Peninsula, the high humidity even before the rainy season, villages that have changed little for decades, the friendly residents, the unexpectedly large expanse of Corregidor, which appears as a mere pinpoint on the map, and the Malinta Tunnel, which was large enough to allow several vehicles to travel abreast. During the trip, walking the same road where U.S. and Filipino prisoners had been forced to march, my imagination went beyond the events that happened more than sixty years ago. What were MacArthur's thoughts as he stayed in the battery-fortified fort at Corregidor? What was the hard-fought field between the United States and Japan like? What were the sufferings of the prisoners who were forced to endure the Death March?

I look forward to the reactions of American readers to this book, which was first published in Japan in 2009. I expect they will differ from those of Japanese readers.

I am indebted to the help and cooperation of many people. First, I extend my deep appreciation to the Japanese pioneers of Occupation studies: Professors Takemae Eiji, Amakawa Akira, and Sodei Rinjiro, as well as members of the Society for the Occupation and Modern History. My research on the Occupation has been fostered in the academic atmosphere of the Society. My debt of appreciation also extends to the late Dr. Hans Baerwald, whose personal experiences during the Occupation provided guideposts for my research while I studied at UCLA. Valuable assistance was provided by Mr. James Zobel, archivist and librarian of the MacArthur Memorial Library. Mr. John R. Heffernan of Reston Indexing and Research helped me collect research materials from the National Archives and Records Administration (NARA). Generous support and appropriate advice from Zobel and Heffernan served to define my basic approach to this book.

I would like to dedicate this book to the late Raymond Aka and the late William Osuga, both of whom were second-generation Americans of Japanese descent. Mr. Aka came to Japan immediately after the war as a soldier and worked in the Government Section of GHQ as an interpreter for Courtney Whitney and Charles L. Kades. After the Occupation ended, he contributed to the development of U.S.-Japan relations through his work in charge of defense affairs at the U.S. Embassy. Mr. Osuga came to Japan immediately after the war, following a severe experience in an internment camp. As an interpreter for the Allied Translation and Interpreters Service (ATIS) under G-2, he worked on the trials of Band C class war criminals. After leaving Japan, he worked at the UCLA Library. Both Mr. Aka and Mr. Osuga were men of a high integrity that is rare among Japanese people today. I pay my respects and express gratitude for their fatherly affection, generous support, and personal encouragement.

Finally, I am grateful to Yamamoto Reiko, who recommended publication of this book in English and contributed generously of her time for the translation. Moreover, I extend my gratitude to Dr. Patricia Sippel, my colleague at Toyo Eiwa University, who helped to realize publication by Cornell University Press and made painstaking efforts to improve the translation from the point of view of a native speaker of English. Without their efforts, this book would not have been completed. I am indebted to Mr. Matsumuro Toru, deputy manager of Chuo Koronsha Press, Mr. Roger Haydon, editor at Cornell University Press, and Ms. Karen Laun, senior production editor at Cornell University Press. Mr. Matsumuro made great efforts in the publication of the original Japanese version, and Mr. Haydon and Ms. Laun kindly offered generous cooperation and editorial guidance that assisted publication in the United States. This book received grants from Toyo Eiwa University and the Suntory Foundation to help defray the costs of publication; I express my gratitude to both organizations.

Every four years a presidential election is held in the United States, and the results of that contest rest in the hands of Americans. Three times MacArthur aimed secretly to become the Republican candidate for president, but his efforts were unsuccessful. If MacArthur had been elected president, what political and diplomatic policies would he have adopted to lead the world? Although his own dream was never realized, McArthur was a person of such charisma as to encourage dreams of greatness in others.

MACARTHUR IN ASIA

FIGURE 1. PT 41 boat used by MacArthur to evacuate from Corregidor. Reproduced by permission of the MacArthur Memorial Library and Archives.

ENCOUNTER WITH THE PHILIPPINES

Before His Appointment to the Philippines

Douglas MacArthur's encounter with the Philippines had complex origins. The first point of contact was through his father, Arthur MacArthur Jr., who attained the rank of lieutenant general in his military career. In June 1899, when Douglas MacArthur was admitted to the U.S. Military Academy, West Point, at the age of nineteen, his father, the military governor of the Philippines, was engaged in the occupation of Manila and the suppression of rebellions following the Spanish-American War. Douglas was captivated by a place in distant Asia where his much-respected father was serving. However, by June 1903, when Douglas graduated from West Point at the top of his class with a grade point average of 98.14, Arthur had been recalled to the United States because of a conflict with William Howard Taft, the civilian governor of the Philippines (and later president of the United States).

Douglas applied to the elite Army Corps of Engineers, and in October he was commissioned as a second lieutenant and assigned to the Philippines. This was his first direct encounter with the Philippines; he was twenty-three years old. He served in the Manila military district, where he was engaged in the improvement of Manila Bay, the construction of fortresses on Corregidor Island, and road construction on the Bataan Peninsula. While stationed in the Philippines, MacArthur became acquainted with a pair of rising politicians, Emanuel L. Quezon and Sergio Osmena, both of whom later became president of the Philippines. He was to maintain a lifelong friendship with Quezon in particular. In later years, after the outbreak of the war with Japan, MacArthur and Quezon would spend several months of great hardship on Corregidor. But MacArthur contracted malaria and, in October 1904, he was forced to return to the United States. His first appointment to the Philippines came to an end after only one year.[1]

It was his father, Arthur, who brought Douglas back to Asia. Dispatched to Manchuria to observe the Russo-Japanese War, Arthur was named military attaché in Tokyo in early 1905 and called Douglas to Japan to serve as an aide. Douglas arrived in Tokyo in October of that same year. He had no notion that forty years later he would govern Japan as supreme commander of the Allied Powers (SCAP). Douglas embarked on an eight-month inspection tour through much of Asia with his family. It was through this family tour that Douglas learned much about various Asian countries; Asia became closer to him than Europe.

After his return to the United States, MacArthur became White House attaché and won quick promotion through his service at the headquarters of the chief of staff. In 1916, Major MacArthur became military attaché to the secretary of the army, where he came up with the idea of a "national guard." On this basis the 42nd Division (the so-called Rainbow Division) was formed. His duties as a press censor helped him realize the importance of mass media while at the same time providing an opportunity for him to gain skills in the use of propaganda—skills that he would demonstrate during the Philippine campaign and throughout the Pacific War. At the age of thirty-six, MacArthur was promoted by the Department of the Army to the rank of colonel, and appointed chief of staff of the Rainbow Division. He could finally experience actual fighting in France, an experience for which he had long yearned.

MacArthur was fearless on the battlefield, leading his troops on the frontline without so much as wearing a helmet. (He may have inherited this trait from his father, who had served valiantly in the Civil War.) Participating in eight battles, MacArthur was injured twice. He won fifteen medals in all and was promoted to brigadier general at the age of thirty-eight, the youngest ever to receive the appointment. MacArthur subsequently commanded an infantry brigade and a division, and for four months in winter 1918 gained valuable administrative experience in the occupation of Germany on the west bank of the Rhine. This experience, too, was a forerunner for his later administrative work in the Philippines and Japan.

After he returned to the United States in April 1919, his glorious career continued. MacArthur was appointed superintendent of the U.S. Military Academy at West Point for three years, during which he reformed an out-of-date organization with the aim of educating modern career soldiers. While there, he married Louise Cromwell Brooks, a belle of the Washington social world. The union, dubbed a "marriage between an admirable soldier and a millionaire," was widely covered in the press. Then in October 1922 MacArthur traveled with his new wife to the Philippines, where he assumed the position of commander of the Manila military district and commander of the Philippine Scouts, a U.S. military organization of Filipino troops. It was MacArthur's second period of service in the Philippines and came after an eighteen-year interval. He was welcomed as "Young General MacArthur" by those who had known his father. The young general, like his elder, rejected racial discrimination, and developed friendly relationships with Quezon, the chairman (later president) of the Upper House, and Quezon's circle of friends. He visited the Bataan Peninsula, located on the other side of Corregidor at the entrance to Manila Bay, and walked some forty miles in order to have a map drawn of the region. After the outbreak of war between Japan and the United States, MacArthur would boast that he knew Corregidor,[2] and it was not an idle boast.

However, the marriage between Louise, who liked to circulate in fashionable society, and MacArthur, who devoted himself to his work, began to unravel, and in 1929 the couple was legally divorced. In January 1925, thanks in part to lobbying by his mother, Mary Pinckney (nicknamed Pinkie),[3] MacArthur was promoted to become the youngest major general in U.S. Army history, at the age of forty-four. In April 1925, MacArthur returned to the United States following his three-year term of service in the Philippines. Thereafter he commanded the corps of two military administrative areas, Washington and Baltimore, and in 1928 led the U.S. team to the Amsterdam Olympics.

In August 1928, three years after his return to the United States, MacArthur was reassigned to the Philippines. His assignment as army commander in the Philippines was a prestigious one, and allowed him to follow in his father's footsteps. MacArthur took great pride in improving the training, pay, and status of the Philippine Scouts, gaining popularity among the local people for his efforts. MacArthur himself looked to these troops as a key to the future defense of the Philippines. His treatment of Filipinos as equals and his cultivation of a friendship with Quezon and persons of influence also won him local popularity. Eventually, MacArthur endorsed the concept of the gradual independence of the Philippines desired by Quezon and others.[4]

But MacArthur struggled with the strategic problem of how to cope with the Japanese threat. In 1904, Washington had adopted War Plan Orange (WPO), which stipulated that in the case of a Japanese attack on the Philippines, the defense line should be pushed back to the Bataan Peninsula and the military line held at Bataan and Corregidor for six months until reinforcements from the United States arrived. Subsequent revisions were developed under the titles WPO-1, WPO-2, and WPO-3, but MacArthur had doubts about all of the Orange Plans, which he considered impractical. U.S. and Filipino troops of just seventeen thousand men would not be able to defend the Philippines. Another problem was an increase in the Japanese population of the Philippines. The number of Japanese sugarcane laborers and businesspeople had been increasing, particularly on Mindanao Island. Quezon and other Philippine business leaders did not recognize this as a threat, believing that the newcomers would attract investment capital, promote business, and revive the stagnant local economy, but their views were not shared by MacArthur.[5]

Army Chief of Staff

In September 1930 MacArthur was ordered to leave the Philippines by President Herbert C. Hoover, and he assumed the post of 8th Army chief of staff with the rank of general. His appointment to general at the age of fifty made him the youngest general on record in the U.S. Army. This was the honor that his father Arthur had dreamed of, but could not achieve. It could be said that the son had cleared his father's deep grudge against the army. Touching her son's four stars, his mother Pinkie whispered that if Arthur had been alive, he would have been delighted.

Nevertheless, the position was by no means easy. Economic depression was affecting the United States, and Congress was demanding deep cuts in the military budget and in the number of army officers. MacArthur responded by appealing to Congress to understand the necessity of national defense. He finally succeeded in getting the military budget passed, and in preventing a reduction in the number of officers. But the so-called Bonus March incident in 1932 cast a shadow over MacArthur's popularity and career. Veterans of World War I and their families assembled in Washington from all over the United States to demand immediate cash payment of the military service bonuses they had been promised. Following President Hoover's order to disperse the crowd, MacArthur fired on about fifteen thousand demonstrators with tear gas. To the end of his life, MacArthur believed this protest had been incited by Communists. With his four-year term as chief of staff extended by one year, MacArthur demonstrated his administrative ability during this long tenure by instituting military reforms and other measures.

Even before leaving his chief of staff post, the fifty-five-year-old MacArthur was preparing a second career, in the Philippines, which was then embarking on a period of great political innovation. In 1934, Congress passed the Tydings–McDuffie Act, which authorized Philippine independence on July 4, 1946, ending forty-eight years of American rule. (U.S. military personnel and bases would remain, and in case of war the U.S. president had the power to place the entire Philippine military under U.S. military control.) In 1935 the Philippines established a commonwealth, or provisional government, to prepare for the longed-for independence. But a fundamental problem remained unsolved: the Japanese threat to the security of the Philippines. Defending a nation of islands posed a difficult challenge. When MacArthur's old friend Quezon begged him to help with the defense of the Philippines, he responded: "The Philippines could be defended if enough men, weapons, money, and time were available."[6] He accepted the job of forming the Philippine army after completing his term as chief of staff.

In considering the background of this career change, we should not ignore the relationship between MacArthur and President Franklin Roosevelt. MacArthur, a political conservative, did not get along with Roosevelt, a Democrat and architect of the New Deal. Roosevelt had served as assistant secretary of the navy from 1913 to 1920, and tended to view the navy preferentially even after his inauguration as president. MacArthur, of course, emphasized the importance of the army. Moreover, Roosevelt reportedly said directly to MacArthur: "Douglas, you are the most excellent general that the country has ever had, but as a statesman you are the worst."[7] An additional issue in MacArthur's transfer to the Philippines may have been his involvement in a lawsuit by a Philippine woman; this, too, may have been a hidden factor in his decision to move to the Philippines.[8]

From Quezon's Military Advisor to Commander of the United States Army Forces in the Far East

On October 1, 1935, MacArthur took up his position as military advisor to Quezon. In compliance with the U.S. legislation that authorized military advisory groups as well as his personal agreement with Quezon, MacArthur accepted a reduction in rank from general to major general. On the other hand, while he maintained his salary level from the U.S. Army, he received a generous allowance and the courtesy title "General of the Army" from the Commonwealth of the Philippines.[9] On this, his fourth and final tour of duty in the Philippines, MacArthur was accompanied by many staff officers from Washington. Among them was Major (later General and President) Dwight D. Eisenhower, MacArthur's junior at West Point, who was to become chief of staff in the Philippines. MacArthur's eighty-three-year-old mother also moved with him. It was during the voyage to the Philippines that MacArthur encountered Jean Faircloth and fell in love with her. She was from an intellectual and wealthy family in Tennessee. She cut short her planned visit to Shanghai and headed for Manila, and Douglas and Jean married two years later.[10]

On November 15, immediately after MacArthur arrived in Manila, the Commonwealth of the Philippines was established with Quezon as the first president and Sergio Osmena as vice president. At Quezon's request, MacArthur initiated a defense plan for the Philippines. Patterned after the citizen-soldier system of national defense in Switzerland, MacArthur's plan aimed to enhance the defensive powers of the Philippine army. Dividing the country into ten military jurisdictions, his plan called for four thousand men to be trained in each jurisdiction every year. American and Filipino officers were to assume responsibility for training at 128 bases that would be built throughout the country. By 1946 there would be forty army divisions comprising a total of four hundred thousand men. The plan also called for a naval force of fifty torpedo boats (the so-called PT boats, for Patrol Torpedo boat) and an air force of about 250 planes. Indispensable to this ambitious plan was financial aid from both the United States and the Philippine government. To that end, MacArthur and Quezon visited Washington in early 1937. MacArthur's aim was to obtain military aid, and Quezon's was to secure the full independence of the Philippines, brought forward from 1946 to 1938. Quezon's request angered Roosevelt; MacArthur's was ignored. From the beginning, the obstacles to obtaining sufficient financial aid were formidable. Furthermore, the Philippine National Assembly, insisting that budget priority should be given to public works rather than strengthening the military, slashed the military budget. At this point, Quezon also vacillated.[11]

Despite these setbacks MacArthur continued military training for Filipinos, while staff officers Eisenhower and Major James Ord labored over the actual defense plans for the Philippines. The United States, as we have seen, had approved its Orange Plan as early as 1904 for use in the case of a war against Japan. The main goal of the plan was to defend U.S. territory in the Pacific from the Japanese threat mainly by using American naval power, and the Philippines was the biggest military staging area. However, after World War I, when Japan secured a mandate over the South Sea Islands (Micronesia), and developed its air capabilities, a defense plan based on naval power became vulnerable. Although MacArthur aimed to secure the military independence of the Philippines in order to develop and expand the Philippine national army, U.S. military aid was indispensable. Eisenhower and Ord developed plans based on MacArthur's thinking, but without military support from the United States it was impossible to avoid the conclusion that their plans were impractical.

Navy Lieutenant Charles Bulkeley (later rear admiral) criticized MacArthur's defense plan, saying, "He was a romantic in the sense that he was in the Wall City [sic], the old city of the Philippines, had his offices there on top of the wall and…he was given the honor and privilege there of training the Philippine Army and call it the militia whatever you want to call it there. Which he preceeded [sic] to do the best he could with the limited forces there and plan for the defense of the Philippines which were not fully carried out."[12]

MacArthur's strategy was to stop an enemy attack at the coastline. But the number of tanks and artillery was limited, the transport system was inadequate—and the national defense budget had been slashed. It was almost impossible to build up land forces, let alone purchase combat planes for the air force and PT boats for the navy. And as long as the Philippines was about to gain independence, the U.S.

Department of the Army had no intention of allotting funds for the defense of the Philippines.[13] Eisenhower, Ord, and others had already dismissed the idea of attempting to defend the Philippines against Japanese attack or indeed defeat any aggressor without outside help. They concluded that as long as there were no funds to build a navy or air force, if the Japanese military did attack, Philippine forces would have to fight a war of attrition until powerful allied forces came to the rescue.[14] Eisenhower in effect disregarded MacArthur's plan.

Adding to the military problems, MacArthur aroused a political controversy. When the Commonwealth of the Philippines was established in 1935, the governor-general, Frank Murphy, became the first high commissioner to the Philippines. MacArthur was at odds with Murphy, perhaps because he himself had wanted the high commissioner position or perhaps because he viewed Murphy as a watchdog for Roosevelt. For his part, Murphy believed that MacArthur was collaborating secretly with Quezon to undermine the terms of the Tydings-McDuffie Act. The problem was alleviated in 1936, when Roosevelt named Paul V. McNutt to replace Murphy as high commissioner. Nevertheless, before leaving his position Murphy warned Washington that the military adviser in Manila was proving increasingly difficult. Perhaps because of this warning, the U.S. regular army division stationed in the Philippines withdrew its cooperation from the military adviser's office.[15]

As MacArthur dealt with these political difficulties, tensions between the United States and Japan mounted. In 1937 the Sino-Japanese War broke out, followed by World War II in Europe in 1939. After France surrendered to Germany in 1940, the Japanese army invaded the northern part of French Indochina (northern Vietnam), and in September 1940 Japan, Germany, and Italy signed the Tripartite Pact. In July 1941 Japan advanced into the southern part of Indochina in order to blockade the Indochina Line, which supported Chiang Kai-shek's administration in Chongqing. On July 26, the U.S. government intensified the pressure on Japan by freezing Japanese assets in the United States and embargoing petroleum imports to Japan. The outbreak of war between the Soviet Union and Germany in June 1941 reduced the German threat to the United Kingdom, while Japan, released from Soviet pressure, was free to continue its southward advance. In the Pacific, on the other hand, the United States adopted a tougher attitude toward Japan.

As U.S.-Japan relations worsened, the defense of the Philippines suddenly assumed urgent importance, and the tensions between Washington and Manila were set aside. Roosevelt established the headquarters of the U.S. Army Forces in the Far East (USAFFE) in Manila. He recalled MacArthur, who had retired from the U.S. Army at the end of 1937, to active duty as commanding general of USAFFE, promoting him from major general to lieutenant general. In making this appointment, Roosevelt was obliged to accept the recommendation of the Army chief of staff, General (later General of the Army) George C. Marshall. On July 26, Roosevelt issued an executive order incorporating the Philippine Scouts into the regular U.S. Army forces. With this order, the formerly separate U.S. forces based in the Philippines and the Philippine Scouts that MacArthur had headed were combined into one force under the command of MacArthur.[16]

Not only was MacArthur saved from political tensions by the sudden worsening in U.S.-Japan relations but with the dramatic changes in the Philippine situation he had secured an opportunity to bask once more in the limelight. Already sixty-one, MacArthur could feel relief and pride in his position and subsequently pushed himself to accomplish the great mission entrusted to him.

ORIGINS OF THE BATAAN BOYS

This chapter moves from MacArthur to the Bataan Boys, the group of fifteen army officers who served under MacArthur, and who escaped from Corregidor Island and the southern part of the Bataan Peninsula on the night of March 11, 1942.

The Bataan Boys can be divided into two groups according to rank, position, and the process of appointment. The first, upper-level group consisted of eight men: Major General Richard K. Sutherland, Brigadier General Richard J. Marshall, Brigadier General Hugh J. Casey, Brigadier General Spencer B. Akin, Brigadier General William F. Marquat, Brigadier General Harold H. George, Colonel Charles P. Stivers, and Colonel Charles A. Willoughby. Except for George, who was killed in an accident in Australia right after the successful evacuation, all played important roles as MacArthur's aides.

The second group consisted of seven men: Lieutenant Colonel LeGrande A. Diller, Lieutenant Colonel Francis H. Wilson, Lieutenant Colonel Sidney L. Huff, Lieutenant Colonel Joseph R. Sherr, Major Charles H. Morehouse, Captain Joseph R. McMicking, and Sergeant Paul P. Rogers. They carried out official and private roles as MacArthur's adjutant, including care of MacArthur's family, or worked as assistants for members of the upper-level group. Sherr died in an air accident during the war.

Although detailed information about the military careers and appointment process for each individual is limited, the following profiles are based on available data. The ages given refer to age at the outbreak of war between Japan and the United States in December 1941.

The Upper-Level Group

Richard K. Sutherland

Major General (later Lieutenant General) Richard K. Sutherland was the most important of MacArthur's aides. In 1938, while stationed with his troops in Tianjin, China, he responded to MacArthur's request to transfer to the Philippines. He was probably chosen to succeed Major James B. Ord, who had died in an air accident. However, when the popular Lieutenant Colonel Eisenhower returned to the United States in late 1939 despite MacArthur's earnest request that he stay, Sutherland replaced him as chief of staff to the military advisor to the Philippine Commonwealth. It was even suggested at the time that relations between MacArthur and Eisenhower had cooled because of Sutherland's ambition to take over Eisenhower's position.[1] In July 1941, when MacArthur returned to active duty and was appointed commander of the U.S. Army Forces in the Far East (USAFFE), Sutherland was retained as chief of staff with the rank of colonel. He was forty-eight years old, thirteen years younger than MacArthur.

Under MacArthur, Sutherland worked hard to develop and strengthen the U.S. and Philippine armies. After the outbreak of war with Japan, he helped lead resistance to the fierce Japanese attacks from his base on Corregidor before escaping with MacArthur to Australia. Subsequently, he continued to support MacArthur on the front lines against Japan, and at the surrender ceremony held on the battleship USS *Missouri* in Tokyo Bay in 1945, Sutherland stood beside MacArthur. He demonstrated outstanding command and executive ability in continuously overseeing MacArthur's troops. As MacArthur's right-hand man, Sutherland has to be placed first on the list of Bataan Boys.

Born in Maryland in November 1893, Sutherland was the son of a West Virginia senator. After graduating from Yale University, he enlisted in the Connecticut National Guard. In 1916, he transferred from reservist to second lieutenant in the regular army. This kind of transfer was rare. In the following year, Sutherland was promoted to captain and fought in the French theater. After the war he completed elite courses at the U.S. Army Infantry School, the Command and General Staff College, and the U.S. Army War College. After serving with the Operations and Training Division of the War Department General Staff, he was placed in command of a battalion of the 15th Infantry in 1937. In 1938 he was promoted to lieutenant colonel. At the end of 1941, he was promoted from colonel to major general as MacArthur's chief of staff.[2]

Sutherland attracted both praise and criticism for his character and personality. Charles A. Willoughby, another Bataan Boy, commented favorably:

> He was a man who was also austere and almost an ascetic type, unusual in this service. He was a secretive, remote person who worked as hard,

if not harder, than anybody else. He was always willing to do it, and he would gradually impose his personality regardless of whether they liked or disliked him. I have given credit to Sutherland in spite of occasional collisions, principally differences of opinions, on specific situations. I've given him credit for indefatigable energy and application to reach the objective. He was brilliant and had a quick perception of the General's wishes, which he passed on with complete clarity in staff meetings. He then pursued particular individuals to see that the plans were executed. I would say, then, that he was almost an ideal chief of staff with a combination of ability and executive vigor.[3]

On the other hand, Sutherland invited criticism for his attempts to control access to MacArthur. Although Sutherland may have been concerned in part to protect the overly busy MacArthur, he was also aiming to strengthen his own authority over the staff. Many of the staff found his coolness difficult. To them he was a distant figure, keeping himself at arm's length. In particular Major General (later General) Walter Krueger, who commanded the 6th Army at the front, and Major General (later Lieutenant General) Robert L. Eichelberger, commander of the 5th Army, had a strong dislike for Sutherland. According to Willoughby, he was seen as the "hatchet man"[4] by members of his staff, attracting antagonism because of his terseness in transmitting instructions. Richard J. Marshall, his deputy (later his successor as chief of staff), was closest to Sutherland and highly commended him as a man of brilliance and mental sharpness, with a straightforward and positive outlook. But when Marshall warned his friend of the criticism directed at him, Sutherland reportedly responded: "Well, Dick, somebody around here has got to be the S.O.B. General MacArthur is not going to be and you certainly aren't going to be, so I guess I'm it."[5]

As chief of staff, Sutherland was both coolheaded and devoted to MacArthur. Because of his loyalty, MacArthur wanted him by his side. In particular, MacArthur depended on Sutherland's ability to manage personnel affairs and exercise strategic and tactical judgment, as well as to conduct confidential communications with Washington. In the latter part of the war, however, Sutherland incurred MacArthur's displeasure because of his affair with an Australian woman, and at the end of 1945, soon after Japan's surrender, he was forced to leave Japan.

Richard J. Marshall

The second person on the list of Bataan Boys was Brigadier General (later Major General) Richard J. Marshall, deputy chief of staff to MacArthur in 1941. He was two years younger than Sutherland. For several months in 1930, he served as a quartermaster for the U.S. Army in the Philippines and at a New Year's reception he met MacArthur for the first time. Years later, in 1938, he received a letter from

Sutherland telling him that MacArthur was looking for a logistics man, and he made up his mind to go to the Philippines. At that time Marshall was stationed in Washington as chief of the transportation division of the office of the Quartermaster General. He moved to Manila in September 1939, immediately after the outbreak of the European war. Although his main duties were in logistics, he was also assigned initially to the training of Philippine military officers. However, when Eisenhower returned to the United States at the end of the year and Sutherland succeeded him as chief of staff, Marshall was named deputy chief of staff. When USAFFE was established in July 1941, he was appointed deputy chief of staff of USAFFE. He was forty-six years old. As the threat of war grew stronger, Marshall sent his family back to the United States. Faced with the decision whether he should return to the United States or stay in the Philippines, Marshall decided to remain in the Philippines in his USAFFE position. Soon after, he was promoted from lieutenant colonel to colonel.

Marshall was born in Virginia in June 1895. After he graduated from the Virginia Military Institute, he attended the Quartermaster School and Army War College. During World War I he met Sutherland in the U.S. Army's 1st Division, became friends with him, and subsequently deepened his friendship. For some twenty years Marshall specialized in logistics, but after his move to the Philippines in 1937 he worked continuously in MacArthur's headquarters, assisting Sutherland as deputy chief of staff and serving as acting chief of staff while Sutherland was absent. After Sutherland retired at the end of 1945, in the early months of the occupation of Japan, Marshall was promoted to chief of staff. He left Japan in May 1946 to become Superintendent at the Virginia Military Institute, his alma mater.

Brigadier General (later Major General) Courtney Whitney commented on Marshall's personality: "Marshall was less aggressive, less dominant than Sutherland. It was perhaps in the nature of his work that persuasion, conference methods and compromise were more essential than brusque decisions of execution."[6] In brief, Marshall did not demonstrate the same kind of outstanding leadership as Sutherland; he was good-natured rather than dogmatic. While following rules carefully, he was able to create good relationships among the staff and, as a result, attracted little opposition.

Hugh J. Casey

Brigadier General (later Major General) Hugh J. Casey assumed overall responsibility in the field of civil engineering, including the building of roads and bridges that were indispensable for troop movements as well as the construction of airfields in the Philippines. He had established a reputation for doing good work and gained MacArthur's trust. He was said to have a good personal relationship with MacArthur and was often seated next to him at meetings and dinners. It was for this reason that Casey was chosen as one of the Bataan Boys and, in terms of achievements, he ranked third, after Sutherland and Marshall.

Casey was born in Brooklyn, New York, in July 1898 to a family of Irish descent. His father, a pumping and heating contractor, died young, leaving Casey to work his way through school. Due to his outstanding academic record, he was accepted at West Point at just sixteen years of age. With the U.S. entry into World War I, Casey completed his studies ahead of schedule and was assigned to the Army Corps of Engineers. Known for his expertise in rivers and harbors, he later made important contributions in the private sector as well. He received a doctorate in engineering while studying in Germany. Beginning in September 1937, at the request of MacArthur, who was then military advisor to the Philippine Commonwealth, Casey conducted hydroelectric generation and flood control projects for the Commonwealth, gaining a high reputation with MacArthur and Quezon for his work. Three years later, at the end of 1940, Casey returned to Washington, where he became chief of the Design and Engineering Section in the Construction Division of the Office of the Quartermaster General. However, in October 1941 he received an earnest request from MacArthur to return to the Philippines as his chief engineer. Casey was forty-three, three years younger than Marshall, and held the rank of colonel.

Casey proved his engineering expertise in the front lines of the Bataan campaign. Immediately after the outbreak of war with Japan, as MacArthur abandoned Manila and fled to Bataan, Casey's demolition corps used dynamite ("Casey Dynamite") to destroy the main roads and bridges ahead of the advancing Japanese. In the first round of the Bataan conflict he used cigar boxes to make explosive devices ("Casey Coffins") against Japanese tanks. On the other hand, he refused MacArthur's order to build a road through the jungle, stating that the task was impossible. Far from being a "yes man" or obeying MacArthur unquestioningly, he spoke his mind frankly, thereby gaining MacArthur's trust. As an engineer, Casey demonstrated a scientific and rational way of thinking that was valued by MacArthur. The following story illustrates the deep connection between MacArthur and Casey. In March 1942, on the second morning of the withdrawal from Corregidor by PT boats, the crew manning machine guns on Casey's boat mistook the PT-41 boat for a Japanese destroyer, and prepared their torpedo, but almost simultaneously Casey stopped them. It happened to be the boat with MacArthur and his family on board. Casey had saved the boat from being hit by mistake.

Following the evacuation to Australia, Casey gained military distinction by his leadership of the engineering units in the subsequent campaigns against Japan.

After the Japanese surrender, he undertook the dangerous task of inspecting the devastated city of Tokyo ahead of the MacArthur's main army, which suggests how much MacArthur trusted him. After working for four years during the Occupation as the chief of engineering sections of USAFFE and the Far East Command, he left MacArthur's service in July 1949 and retired from the army at the end of that year. His greatest achievements as an engineer came during his eight years with MacArthur.[7]

Spencer B. Akin

Brigadier General (later Major General) Spencer B. Akin was the chief signal officer of the Signal Corps, which included the encryption unit. During the war, his team contributed significantly to the successes of MacArthur's army by intercepting and decoding Japanese military communications. He was for this reason referred to as MacArthur's secret weapon. After the outbreak of hostilities with Japan, he wanted to be on the front line in the first round of the Bataan combat, but Sutherland persuaded him to stay in the rear where he focused his efforts on intercepting and decoding Japanese military codes. He also worked on the "Voice of Freedom" radio program that raised the military spirit of the U.S. military and the Philippine people through its three daily broadcasts. These contributions ensured Akin's inclusion in the group of Bataan Boys.

He was born in February 1889 in Greenville, Mississippi. After graduating from Virginia Military Institute in 1910, he was assigned to various locations as an infantry officer and served in World War I. Then he attended the U.S. Army Infantry School Advanced Course, the Air Corps Tactical School, the Command and General Staff School, and the Army War College. Because of the confidentiality of his code-breaking mission, neither the details of his appointments in the encryption unit nor his assignments as MacArthur's signal officer are clear. Fifty-two years old when the war with Japan broke out, Akin was the oldest of the Bataan Boys. He was a plain man but well liked and, except for a conflict with Willoughby, was on good terms with General Headquarters (GHQ) staff.

His activities were particularly valuable after the withdrawal from Bataan. He poured his energy into decoding from the headquarters he set up in Australia while at the same time offering new ideas and exercising strong leadership at the forefront of each operation. For example, having developed a communications station for intercepting enemy radio messages, he learned in advance of the bombing targets planned by the Japanese. He relayed the information to those on the front lines so that they could defend themselves or prepare a counterattack. As a result, the Army Air Forces used the information he supplied to destroy large numbers of enemy aircraft. Akin's intelligence services crossed service boundaries. Information was forwarded to the signal intelligence detachment led by Fleet Admiral William Halsey that coordinated intelligence between the army and the navy.

In March 1943 Akin's team finally succeeded in completely decoding the Japanese communications, giving the Americans access to valuable information regarding Japanese movements. In particular, the team contributed to the success in the leapfrogging operation at Hollandia, New Guinea, in spring 1944. However, Akin's relationship with Colonel Charles Willoughby, who was responsible for information in the intelligence unit (G-2), worsened. Willoughby was reluctant to pass along information necessary for decoding to Akin at the necessary time, and Akin annoyed Willoughby by bypassing him and giving his accurate information directly to MacArthur. The main reason for the conflict was their rivalry with regard to MacArthur.

After the Japanese surrender Akin accompanied MacArthur to Atsugi on August 30, 1945. He was assigned as chief of the Civil Communication Section (CCS) of the General Headquarters of the supreme commander of the Allied Powers (GHQ/SCAP). A year and half later, in March 1947, he returned home, and that same year he was promoted to major general. He served as chief of the Army Communication Bureau dealing with military occupation issues toward Japan until he retired in 1951.[8]

William F. Marquat

Brigadier General (later Major General) William F. Marquat was chief antiaircraft officer on Bataan, but the details of his military career are unclear. Although it is believed that he had a special assignment within MacArthur's army, its content has remained confidential. Marquat's selection as a member of the Bataan Boys was probably based on that special assignment as well as on his work in the antiaircraft corps.

Marquat was born in St Louis, Missouri, in March 1894. After he graduated from a private high school in Seattle, Washington, he worked as a journalist from 1913 to 1917. He enlisted in the Coast Artillery unit as second lieutenant during World War I. For several years after the war he was editor of the automobile section of the *Seattle Times*, but in 1920 he became an army captain and went on to attend the Coast Artillery School, and the Command and General Staff School. In 1938 he took up a staff officer position under MacArthur in Manila and was put in charge of the antiaircraft corps with the rank of major.[9] At the outbreak of war with Japan he was forty-six years old, one year older than Sutherland, and held the rank of brigadier general. After participating in the Bataan campaign, Marquat accompanied MacArthur to Australia. He subsequently served in New

Guinea, the Bismarck Archipelago, and the Philippine campaign, and was promoted to major general. Perhaps because of his quiet personality, he is barely referred to by his companions.

Immediately after the Japanese surrender, Marquat arrived in Japan with MacArthur. As MacArthur's deputy, he worked for a short time to represent the United States in the newly established Allied Council for Japan (ACJ). At the end of 1945, he was appointed second chief of Economic and Scientific Section (ESS), the largest organization in General Headquarters (GHQ), succeeding the first chief, Raymond Kramer, who returned to the United States after only three months in that position. Unfamiliar with economic policy, Marquat depended mostly on the economic advisor Sherwood Fine and other specialists. Fine commented that Marquat was sensitive and considerate, far from the image of a typical soldier. Perhaps because he had not graduated originally from a military academy, he seemed different from other career officers. Fine noted that many years after becoming an officer, Marquat had attended the Command and General Staff School, but he had still seemed to be something of an outsider.[10] Fine's words suggest that, although Marquat was one of the Bataan Boys, he was somewhat isolated from others in the inner circle. Moreover, according to First Lieutenant Cappy Harada, an American of Japanese descent who served as Marquat's aide, Marquat showed great loyalty to MacArthur. Such was his great devotion that he never left the office as long as MacArthur was on duty.[11] He was crazy about baseball, and any talk about the game would cheer him up.

Even after MacArthur's dismissal in 1951, Marquat remained as chief of ESS; he served in that position for six and half years until the end of the Occupation, recording the longest period of service among the Bataan Boys. However, he became well known in Japan not as ESS chief but rather for his association with the so-called M-Fund, which he supposedly oversaw. Why the M-Fund bore Marquat's initial, what the reality of the M-Fund was, or whether indeed the M-Fund ever existed, is unknown to this day. After returning to the United States, Marquat served as chief of the Office of Civil Affairs Military Government (OCAMG) for about three years, from October 1952 until his retirement.[12] Compared with Willoughby, who could not find another position after his retirement from G-2, Marquat's treatment by the U.S. government is worth noting.

Harold George

Brigadier General Harold George had general responsibility for the Far East Air Force in the Philippines. As a result of the Japanese sneak attack on the largest airbase in the Philippines on December 8, 1941, almost all U.S. aircraft at Clark Field were destroyed. George became commander of the Far East Air Force, succeeding Lewis H. Brereton, who left the Philippines after only a brief term of service. George had already gained MacArthur's trust by providing him wide-ranging information and expertise regarding air operations. In fact, it was because of George's efforts that it had been possible to deploy B-17s, the newest bombers, to the Philippines before the outbreak of war.

George was born in Lockport, New York, in September 1892. He enlisted in the New York National Guard, 3rd Infantry, in 1916. In 1917 he was commissioned as a first lieutenant in the Aviation Section of the Signal Corps. After he graduated from the Air Corps Tactical School and the Command and General Staff School, he became a combat pilot, earning the Distinguished Service Medal as an "air ace" during World War I. Later, as director of air operations in the Philippines he was highly praised as a distinguished soldier for his tenacious battles against the Japanese. Although he had begun his career at the lowest rank, George ultimately gained the rank of brigadier general. MacArthur liked him. Casey, who had an especially close relationship with George, wrote: "He was initially in command of the pursuit air force—very conscientious, very active. At one time when we were on Bataan he conferred with me and Commander John D. Bulkeley on a proposal to ship the Air Force pilots to China."[13] This kind of positive thinking, together with his ability to command the air operation, ensured George's inclusion in the Bataan Boys at the age of forty-nine.

In April 1942, soon after arriving in Australia after the evacuation from Corregidor, George was killed when a parachute training aircraft collided with his plane. His funeral was conducted with elaborate ceremony and in the presence of MacArthur and his wife. This was the only funeral that MacArthur attended during the war, suggesting how deeply MacArthur was affected by George's death. George was further honored with the opening of George Field in Lawrenceville, Illinois. Twenty-five thousand people attended the opening ceremony. The airfield was completed in January 1943 and is still in use.[14]

Charles P. Stivers

Colonel (later Major General) Charles P. Stivers was assigned to the personnel section (G-1) of the General Staff, assisting Sutherland, who was chief of staff. In fact, Stivers was Sutherland's right-hand man, and the testimony of various associates suggests that he did most of Sutherland's actual job. In contrast with Sutherland, who had many enemies, Stivers had a warm personality and was skilled at managing human relations, allowing him to compensate for Sutherland's shortcomings. Marshall described him as "a quiet man not given to talk but to great study and research. General MacArthur brought him from Corregidor because he thought he would be the best man on personnel details that he would get anywhere."[15] When he joined the Bataan Boys, Stivers was fifty years old.

Stivers was born in Illinois in 1891. In 1916, after graduating from college in Wisconsin, he enlisted in the army, and after World War I, he was promoted to major. He went on to study at the U.S. Army Infantry School Advanced Course and the Command and General Staff School. In 1936, after graduating from the Army War College, Stivers was assigned to MacArthur's army in Manila, where his orders were to work in G-1 under Sutherland.[16] Willoughby, head of G-2, commented: "Stivers was an amiable, easy-going, reserved type. He was neither given to joviality, ebullience, heavy drinking, or anything like that. He quietly went [on] his way."[17] He returned to the United States before the end of war, probably because of health problems. He retired as colonel in December 1945, after the termination of the war, and in September 1946 he ended his military career as a major general. There is little information about this period of his life.

Charles A. Willoughby

Colonel (later Major General) Charles A. Willoughby had general responsibility for the intelligence section (G-2) of the General Staff. In the wartime Philippines his status and authority did not match those of Sutherland or Marshall, but his influence expanded so dramatically during the occupation of Japan that he and Major General Courtney Whitney, chief of the Government Section (GS) of GHQ, could be said to have divided power between them. He remained close to MacArthur until April 1951, when he followed the dismissed general out of Japan. In this sense it could be said that after Sutherland and Marshall left Japan Willoughby was the leader of the remaining Bataan Boys.

Willoughby's background was unique among his circle of officers. He was born in Heidelberg, Germany, in 1892 to Baron Tscheppe-Weidenback and his American wife, Emma Willoughby. His family moved to the United States in 1910. At the age of nineteen he changed his name, selecting his mother's surname, and became a naturalized U.S. citizen. After graduating from Gettysburg College in Pennsylvania, Willoughby pursued graduate studies at the University of Kansas. He later enlisted in the army, and was commissioned a second lieutenant in World War I, and fought in France. For ten years, from 1921 to 1931, he served as an intelligence officer in South America, and from 1934 to 1935 he was an instructor in the Command and General Staff School. By Willoughby's own account, when MacArthur visited the school as chief of the army general staff, he was intrigued by Willoughby's lecture on military history, which made use of visual aids, maps, and slides. He later told Willoughby that he picked him on the strength of that brief contact at the Command and General Staff School.

Willoughby was proud of MacArthur's statement, and active in finding a post. In 1939 Willoughby took up his new post in Manila.

At first Willoughby was assigned to the logistics section (G-4), and under Major General George Grunert he worked to strengthen the defense line on the Bataan Peninsula. Two years later, in July 1941, when USAFFE was established and MacArthur succeeded Grunert as commander, Willoughby was transferred to G-2 as he had long desired. He was forty-nine at the time. For ten years, until April 1951, he occupied the position of intelligence chief to MacArthur and wielded great authority.[18]

Marshall, who had been a student at the Command and General Staff School, admired Willoughby: "General Willoughby is one of the greatest students of history that I've ever encountered in my service. He had intellectual capacity, and he was very reserved, dignified and formal."[19] But Marshall's was probably a minority opinion among GHQ officers. The more general view was that he had a somewhat strange personality. He spoke like a prima donna. He did not get along with Sutherland. He was not seen by others as a friend and, indeed, had many enemies. During the occupation of Japan, he was involved in some mysterious incidents, but because there was no information on intelligence-related matters, his work remained secret.[20] In fact, after returning to the United States at the time of MacArthur's dismissal during the Korean War, he tried to get a position with the Central Intelligence Agency (CIA), but was turned down. He had a close relationship with Franco in Spain and was famously termed "my lovable fascist" by MacArthur.[21]

In the early occupation of Japan, Willoughby's highly critical stance toward the demilitarization and democratization policies developed by GS under Whitney caused severe conflicts with GS officers. However, after the deepening of the cold war caused the U.S. government to shift its policy to stress Japanese economic autonomy, Willoughby, an ardent anticommunist, strengthened his cooperation with Prime Minister Yoshida Shigeru and exerted great influence on Japanese domestic policies. Willoughby was one of the Bataan Boys who became well known within Japan.

The Middle and Lower Groups

Francis H. Wilson

Lieutenant Colonel (later Colonel) Francis H. Wilson was one of the Bataan Boys because he was MacArthur's military aide as well as Sutherland's. Born in Norfolk, Virginia, in 1894, Wilson joined the United States Army while attending Johns Hopkins University. After serving in an infantry division, he served on the

Mexican border during World War I. Just eighteen days before the attack on Pearl Harbor, he was shipped to Manila and was soon appointed aide to MacArthur; he also served Sutherland. On Christmas Eve in 1941, Wilson and MacArthur went to Corregidor, and afterward withdrew to Australia. After 1944 Wilson was placed in charge of the Officer Candidate School in Brisbane, Australia. After that he helped "close out" American forces and property. Then he served on MacArthur's staff in Japan as Chief of the Historical Section. Returning to the United States after seven years of service abroad, he was chosen to head the Alabama National Guard. In 1953 he retired from the Army as a colonel. Wilson attended the University of Maryland, taking graduate courses in history, earned a master's degree, and became a high school teacher.[22]

LeGrande Diller

Lieutenant Colonel (later Brigadier General) LeGrande Diller, another aide to MacArthur, served for a long time as a press relations advisor. MacArthur's success in attracting public attention both at home and in the Philippines owed much to the skillful information control exercised by Diller under MacArthur's instruction. Because of this service role, Diller can be considered one of the Bataan Boys.

Diller was born in New York State in 1901. After graduating from Syracuse University, he enlisted in the Army Infantry Division. Having served in the Philippines since 1939, Diller met MacArthur for the first time in July 1941. According to Diller's later recollections, MacArthur greeted him warmly before inviting him to become an aide: "You graduated from Syracuse University in 1924.... The class of West Point in 1924 was kind enough to make me the Superintendent of the Academy at that time and an honorary member of the class, so you and I are practically classmates."[23] After a brief hesitation, Diller accepted the position. MacArthur took him by the hand and looked him squarely in the eye and noted that Diller would be "a member of my family now." MacArthur had probably chosen Diller on the basis of his work in the Philippines, but this anecdote indicates MacArthur's psychological skill in controlling his staff.

Diller subsequently served as MacArthur's exclusive aide, particularly in the area of press relations. He took pains to protect MacArthur's prestige and image from damage and was particularly careful to prevent information or rumors unfavorable to MacArthur from leaking out. At the same time, Diller secretly managed MacArthur's private financial assets. In sum, he held two posts concurrently as a private secretary. Throughout the Pacific War, Diller exercised his considerable ability in human relations and encouraged rumors and a public consensus that emphasized MacArthur's heroic status. He accompanied MacArthur at the surrender ceremony on the battleship USS *Missouri* in September

1945. Immediately afterward, he was promoted from aide-de-camp to military secretary and served under MacArthur until June 1947. After a further assignment in West Germany, Diller retired at the rank of brigadier general.[24]

Sidney L. Huff

Lieutenant Colonel (later Colonel) Sidney L. Huff was born in California in 1894. In October 1935 Huff was stationed in Manila as a lieutenant in the United States Navy, assigned to the USS *Black Hawk,* a tender for the destroyer squadron of the Asiatic Fleet. Huff met MacArthur after MacArthur became military advisor to the Philippine Commonwealth in 1935. MacArthur wanted a retired Navy officer to assist with such things as revision of the steamboat-inspection rules. He was keenly interested in Huff's knowledge of motor torpedo boats (which MacArthur arbitrarily referred to as Q-boats instead of as PT boats). He discussed the possibility of importing them from Britain. In 1936 Huff returned to the United States and retired after suffering a heart attack during a golf game with Sutherland. However, MacArthur recalled him to Manila, this time as an army officer. Huff became MacArthur's private aide, and worked on the idea of building a unit of PT boats that would be indispensable for the defense of the Philippines. The episode illustrates MacArthur's keen interest in PT boats. Huff's efforts and forward thinking made possible the dramatic escape from Corregidor in which PT boats were to play an important role. They saved not only MacArthur's life but also the lives of his family and the other Bataan Boys.

Huff was also ordered to assist and look after MacArthur's wife, Jean, and his son, Arthur. His personality and appearance favorably impressed Jean, adding another reason for his inclusion among the Bataan Boys. In 1944, after the evacuation from Bataan, Huff married an Australian woman.[25] Offended by his flamboyant actions at social events, Jean kept away from him and eventually he was removed from his position as MacArthur's aide. Immediately after the beginning of the occupation of Japan, Huff requested permission to return to the United States, but he was persuaded to stay on. He continued as MacArthur's aide until MacArthur's dismissal during the Korean War in 1951. After returning home in 1954, MacArthur asked him to be his aide once more, and he was with MacArthur until he died in 1963.

Joseph P. Sherr

Lieutenant Colonel (later Colonel) Joseph P. Sherr dedicated himself to the most important intelligence work of the U.S. Army, breaking the Japanese secret codes. After secretly working on the Japanese decoding machine, Purple Machine, from the mid-1930s, he succeeded in breaking the codes during the Pacific War in cooperation with the U.S. Navy. Because of the national security implications, the details of Sherr's career have still not been disclosed. Due to his technological expertise, Sherr was selected as one of the Bataan Boys. Moreover, he was selected for evacuation from the Philippines because if he were captured by the Japanese military, the decoding work would be revealed, causing considerable damage to the U.S. side while at the same time bringing advantages to the Japanese.

When Sherr was withdrawn from Corregidor, he carried a decoding machine with him to Australia. Together with Akin, he set it up in the central headquarters in Australia, and continued the secret work. In 1943, while in the Marshall Islands, they finally completed the task of breaking the Japanese military codes. In August of that same year, Sherr was killed in an aircraft accident in India. Because of the confidential nature of his work, his death was not announced to anyone outside his immediate family in Tennessee. Only his wife and Sutherland attended the funeral.[26]

Charles H. Morehouse

Major (later Lieutenant Colonel) Charles H. Morehouse was a military doctor who served as MacArthur's family doctor. He was selected as one of the Bataan Boys, because Jean and young Arthur needed a doctor during the escape from Corregidor by PT boat. Morehouse was born in New York in March 1902. After graduating from medical school and studying in a master's program, he joined the 21st Division in 1928. He subsequently obtained a PhD in medicine from Brown University. Morehouse continued to pursue his studies at high-level medical schools while remaining a medical doctor. It is unclear when and how he took up his position in Manila. While working on Bataan he had a chance to make friends with Casey and Akin and through that connection was selected as MacArthur's medical aide. However, Jean asserted that she first became acquainted with Morehouse in March 1942, at the time of the evacuation from Corregidor. It seems likely that he was summarily appointed as MacArthur's family doctor.

When Morehouse returned to the United States at the end of 1943 and the beginning of 1944, he declared publicly that MacArthur was not interested in politics and had no intention of running for president. Morehouse's statement reflected not MacArthur's true intention but the very opposite and consequently he was dismissed by Sutherland as his aide. In 1947 Morehouse received a PhD from Harvard University and was promoted to the rank of lieutenant colonel.[27]

Joseph D. McMicking

Captain Joseph D. McMicking was a young Philippine army officer of Spanish and Filipino decent. Because he was from an upper-class family and had close

connections with the Philippine elite, he played an important role as an interme-
diary between the U.S. military, including Sutherland and MacArthur, and members of Philippine society. For this reason, he was the only Filipino included among
the Bataan Boys. Jean noted: "Joe McMicking was Spanish, lived in the Philippines
and he was like General Romulo [a member of Quezon's cabinet and the postwar
ambassador to the United States]. I suppose, the General put him in the Army, on
the General's staff, working directly under General Sutherland.... Sutherland was
the one who suggested bringing him out on the PT boat.... He would've been
killed [otherwise]. They [Japanese] killed his family, his mother and all.... He was
a businessman in Manila. He and his wife were great friends of all of us socially."[28]

As the war progressed, however, McMicking clashed with Sutherland, and in
1943 he was released from his duties in intelligence and sent to work in general
affairs. He returned in triumph to the Philippines in 1945 only to learn the shocking news that his entire family, with the exception of his wife, had been killed
by the Japanese. In the postwar years, McMicking established a company that
produced recording tapes and pursued a successful career as an entrepreneur.

Paul P. Rogers

Sergeant (later First Lieutenant) Paul P. Rogers was Sutherland's personal secretary, and later became MacArthur's secretary concurrently. Born in 1920 in
the American Midwest, Rogers enlisted in the army while a student at William
Jewell College in Missouri. In October 1941, just weeks before the outbreak of
war with Japan, he arrived in Manila. His outstanding stenographic skills were
soon noticed and he became personal stenographer and secretary to Sutherland. Indispensable to Southerland, Rogers was the only enlisted man to be
included in the Bataan Boys. He was twenty-two at the time, the youngest in
the group.

After the retreat from Corregidor to Australia, Rogers continued as Sutherland's stenographer and secretary. Since he typed not only Sutherland's important messages but also secret correspondence between the field and the U.S.
homeland, Rogers had detailed knowledge of almost every issue. After he came
to know about the conflicts between MacArthur and Sutherland, he had a nervous breakdown. Moreover, after the retreat from Corregidor, when Rogers saw
Manila in ruins and knew that many of his friends left behind had been captured
or sacrificed their lives, he was overcome with guilt. After the war he returned
home, earned his PhD in economics, and became a university professor. However, he never talked about his war experiences. He accepted a request to participate in the movie *American Caesar,* a televised documentary, but disappeared
during the shooting. He died of cancer in 1991.[29]

The Other Group

In addition to these fifteen members of the Bataan Boys, others who accompanied MacArthur in the escape from Corregidor to Australia were Rear Admiral Francis W. Rockwell and Captain H. James Ray.

Details of Ray's military career and later movements are unclear. Rockwell was appointed as commander of Philippine coastal defense in November 1941, immediately before the outbreak of war with Japan. After hostilities began, because U.S. air power in the Philippines had been destroyed, the Asiatic Fleet under Rear Admiral Thomas C. Hart retreated to the south. But at the end of December the central headquarters moved from Manila to Corregidor and Rockwell was appointed commander of the Philippine navy, with a concurrent position as commander of the 16th Naval District. He moved the navy coast defense force to Corregidor, where he came under MacArthur's command. Working with Ray, Rockwell drew up a plan for an escape by the PT boats in which MacArthur had shown interest. When the plan proved successful, Rockwell gained MacArthur's deep trust. At the time of MacArthur's dismissal in 1951, Rockwell was attached to the headquarters of the Pacific Fleet in Hawaii. He offered his house for MacArthur and Jean to use when they stopped at Oahu Island after leaving Tokyo.[30]

Another of the Bataan Boys was Lieutenant Junior Grade (later Rear Admiral) John Bulkeley, who was widely recognized for his success in leading MacArthur's withdrawal from Corregidor.

He was born in New York in August 1911. In 1941 he was engaged in a program to test the high-speed torpedo boat (or PT) in Key West Florida. The test was conducted in rough waters, and aimed to improve the functioning of the torpedoes and to raise the military capability of other combat systems on the boats such as the .50-caliber machine guns. It was decided that one of the two lieutenant commanders engaged in the testing would be sent to the Philippines. Bulkeley was chosen to go to Corregidor even though it was only eight months since he had returned. In August 1941 Bulkeley headed to Washington, where he received orders to command a motor torpedo boat squadron in the Philippines. Since he was also told to prepare for war, he loaded six PT boats with fuel tanks filled to capacity onto a tanker and conducted training while en route so that they would be ready if war were declared.

When Bulkeley arrived in Manila, MacArthur contended that he needed two hundred motor torpedo boats or PT boats to defend to the Philippines against the onslaught of the Japanese navy. At MacArthur's request he submitted his report on torpedo boats, noting that in addition to the six boats he had brought with him, six more were scheduled to arrive from Hawaii. But they did not arrive before the outbreak of war in December. MacArthur ordered him to conduct basic training for the Filipinos using four of the boats. A captain assigned to the offshore patrol (perhaps Ray) argued that the boats should also be used for attacking purposes. With MacArthur and Hart looking on, the boats led by Bulkeley demonstrated strong offensive power against a light cruiser. Thereafter, the role of the PT boat squadron changed from defense to offense. Based on this record, MacArthur surprised U.S. government and military leaders by successfully using the PT boats to escape from Corregidor. Bulkeley's achievement brought him well-deserved honor.

MacArthur was keen on extraordinary heroism in fighting actions, like Bulkeley's, and rejected a submarine option for his flight from the Philippines. Bulkeley met expectations and, overcoming the challenges, successfully got MacArthur, his family, and the Bataan Boys to Kabacan on the southern island of Mindanao. He subsequently served in the European theater, then returned to the Pacific as a commander of a PT boat squadron. He continued on active duty until 1988 and lived until 1996, the last surviving Bataan Boy.[31]

FROM THE APPROACH OF WAR TO THE EVACUATION FROM MANILA, OCTOBER TO DECEMBER 1941

Washington before the Outbreak of War

At 7:49 a.m. Hawaii time on December 7, 1941, Japan's military attack on the U.S. naval fleet at Pearl Harbor prompted the outbreak of war between the United States and Japan. What kind of plan was being worked out in Washington and Manila for the defense of the Philippines in the weeks before the attack?

On October 8, two months before the outbreak of war, Leonard T. Gerow, chief of the War Plans Division (WPD) of the War Department, wrote a memorandum entitled "Strategic Concept of the Philippine Islands," and submitted it to Secretary of War Henry Stimson.[1] The outline was as follows:

> [1] Japan aspires to control eastern Russia, China and Malaysia. If conditions become favorable, she will resort to war to attain those aspirations....[2] The present deterrents should be maintained and further strengthened by the provision of strong offensive air forces in the Philippines....[3] The Philippine Islands are in the path of any Japanese movement to the south. If Japan should attempt to bypass these islands to the west, her lines of advance and supply will be under constant threat of air bombardment and naval attack....If she moves by the eastern route she must keep east of the Pelews,....her line of advance will then be subject to attack by the United States Pacific Fleet. Even if Japan were successful in by-passing the Philippines, she would still be confronted with the combined aviation of the Associated Powers operating from Britain and Dutch bases....[4] The cost of this operation

would be so great that Japan will hesitate to make the effort except as a last resort. [5] To-day the ground forces have a total strength of approximately 29,000, backed up by the Philippine Army of some 91,000, men now being organized and trained. Reinforcements sent to the Philippine Islands included one regiment of antiaircraft artillery; one battalion of tanks (54 light tanks)....The Army now has in the Philippine Islands, in addition to obsolescent aircraft, nine heavy bombardment and 81 pursuit, of modern type. This force will be further increased before the end of 1941 with 35 heavy bombers, 52 light bombers, and 50 pursuit.

Although the War Plans Division did not dismiss Japanese military power, it relied considerably on the Philippine army and air force to serve as an effective deterrent or defensive force. Moreover, it was surprisingly optimistic about the effectiveness of Allied efforts to deter the Japanese advance southward.

On October 21, General George Marshall, chief of staff of the U.S. Army, prepared a memorandum for President Roosevelt, informing him of the tense situation: "Present garrison or enrouts [sic] 31,000 (12,000 native troops). Critical situation. Japan wavering. Strong air and naval forces on her flank may deter her or wean her from Axis. If Japan moves, forces in position to assist Associated Powers."[2] Then, on November 19, preparing for the worst—the termination of negotiations with Japan—Marshall directed officers attached to the chief of staff to gather information necessary for conducting air raids over Japan. Of particular note, on December 1, Marshall raised the possibility that if war should be declared, the U.S. Army Air Force could attack Japan from military bases around Vladivostok. He wanted to know how and from where MacArthur would attack Japan. On this point, Marshall was strategically dependent on Major General Lewis H. Brereton, commander of the Far East Air Force, who had been dispatched from Washington to assist MacArthur in the Philippines. After Brereton arrived in Manila in November 1941, MacArthur obtained a map that displayed some six hundred targeted industrial sites across Japan, including those connected with steel, oil, and electric power, and the two men discussed the possibility of using air power based in the Philippines to conduct air raids over Japan. They determined that areas in which the steel industry was concentrated and densely populated cities such as Tokyo and Yokohama would be the most effective targets for any bombing. However, MacArthur's conclusion reflected a negative view about bombing Japan: "We are going much too far on the offensive side. The 160 or 170 heavy bombers eventually contemplated for the Army Air Forces in the Philippines is truly a substantial force in view of the strength of the Air Force Combat Command today; however, those two groups (second aviation objective strength) are far from a 'strong air force' in the eyes of the British,

German, or Russians."[3] It can be assumed that Marshall was disappointed by MacArthur's negative assessment.

If an attack on Japan was considered impractical, there was no other choice than to commit to a defense of the Philippines. On the morning of November 26, Marshall held an important conference in the Washington office of the chief of staff with Gerow as well as Major General Henry H. Arnold, head of the Army Air Corps, and Colonel Thomas T. Handy and Colonel Charles W. Bundy, who were both from WPD. Marshall explained that: "the President and Secretary of State feel the Japanese are dissatisfied with the conferences in Washington and will soon cut loose. While both the President and [Secretary of State] Mr. [Cordell] Hull anticipated a possible assault on the Philippines, General Marshall said he did not see this as a probability because the hazards would be too great for the Japanese."[4] An immediate problem was what instruction should be given to MacArthur: "He should be told that the negotiations have bogged down and that if war cannot be averted, the United States at least does not desire to commit the first overt act; however, General MacArthur should not be required to refrain from acting, particularly as to reconnaissance....General Gerow stated that it is to defend the Philippine Archipelago, to support the Navy and to attack threatening Japanese convoys."[5]

Marshall thus anticipated the opening of hostilities with Japan, but he dismissed almost entirely the possibility either of an invasion of the Philippines or an attack on Pearl Harbor. Admiral Harold R. Stark, chief naval officer, agreed with Marshall. What then did the top levels of the Army and Navy view as the primary targets of invasion? As they stated in a November 27 memorandum to the president entitled "Subject: Far Eastern Situation": "If the current negotiation end [sic] without agreement, Japan may attack: the Burma Road; Thailand; Malaya; the Netherlands East Indies, and the Philippines....Recent Japanese troop movements all seem to have been southward."[6] However, as long as U.S. forces remained on Luzon, they believed, it would be difficult for Japan to make a direct attack either on Malaya or on the Netherlands East Indies. In this situation, according to Japanese prediction, Burma or Thailand could be invaded with little resistance and would become the target of a Japanese invasion. However, both Marshall and Stark held to the optimistic analysis that any attack on Burma would be hard and would end in failure.

Stark and Marshall recommended to the President that in the case of a Japanese advance into Thailand, Japan should be warned by the U.S., the British, and the Dutch governments that advance beyond specified lines might lead to war; "prior to the completion of the Philippines reinforcement, military counter-action should be considered only if Japan were to attack or directly threaten the United States, British, or Dutch territory as above outlined."[7] The recommendation was accepted, and on December 1 the United States, the British Commonwealth, and the Netherlands East Indies issued their warning: "In view of the vital interests of the United States, and of the British Commonwealth and the Netherlands East Indies, the movement of any Japanese expeditionary force into waters in close proximity to the Philippine Islands or into the China Sea south of latitude ten degrees north, will of necessity be considered a hostile act directed against the governments concerned."[8] Ironically, this was the same day on which the Japanese emperor presided over an imperial conference that decided to declare war against the United States, Great Britain, and the Netherlands. In contrast to the Japanese, the Washington summit hesitated to take any counteraction and, instead, continued their wait-and-see attitude. They did not anticipate that Japanese attacks on Hawaii and the Philippines were almost at the countdown stage. The U.S. Army's mistaken conviction that existing Philippine forces could contain the Japanese advance southward is surprising. In this sense, Roosevelt and Hull had more accurately anticipated the situation: believing that Japan might attack the Philippines.

Preparations in Manila before the Outbreak of War

What was the military situation in Manila in the months leading up to the outbreak of war? On August 1, 1941, MacArthur, who assumed Command of U.S. Army Forces in the Far East (USAFFE) days after its establishment on July 26, authorized an increase in the defense forces of the Philippines. His order was based on a WPD recommendation that Marshall signed on July 31. From that point onward a tremendous number of men and supplies poured into the Philippines. By November, after the New Mexico National Guard was added, the U.S. Army garrison had increased to 31,095 (including twelve thousand Philippine Scouts). In addition, there were ten reserve divisions of the Philippine Army, comprising some one hundred thousand men.[9] During this time, however, MacArthur dismissed Major General George Grunert, commander of the U.S. Army in the Philippines, who had contributed much to the building up of the Philippine defense forces. He moved Grunert's senior officers into his own staff and had them conduct a thorough training of Philippine officers. Quite a few army officers felt dissatisfied and mistrusted MacArthur because of his treatment of Grunert.[10]

On October 28 MacArthur sent an optimistic report to Marshall, outlining the military situation in the Philippines and noting proudly that, because morale in the Philippine Army was exceptionally high, training had progressed beyond expectations. Furthermore, he requested a revision of the Rainbow-V operation plans that the War Department had developed to reinforce the defense of the Philippines.

The Rainbow plans had been drawn up in June 1939, each based on a different military scenario. They were distinct from the original Orange Plan and other color-coded war plans that outlined potential U.S. strategies. Of the five, Rainbow-II was the most aggressive in envisaging military operations in the Pacific. However, under the crucial circumstances of French defeat and Britain's possible surrender, the United States considered the European theater more serious and important for its own national security than the Asian theater. In November 1940, Stark and Marshall recommended to Roosevelt a strategy of offense in the Atlantic and defense in the Pacific, should the United States enter the war. Thus the emphasis shifted from Rainbow-II to Rainbow-IV, which envisaged a separate war. This shift implied a defensive posture in which the fleet would be kept in Hawaii and no naval reinforcements would be sent to the Philippines. In April 1941 the Joint Chiefs of Staff (JCS) and Secretary of Army Stimson acknowledged the shift to Rainbow-V, the most defensive of the five options.[11] Their intention was to stabilize the European defense line by dispatching U.S. forces either to the eastern Atlantic, Africa, or continental Europe, and to initiate offensive operations in collaboration with the Allies to defeat both Germany and Italy. Until success in the European operation against the Axis made the dispatch of additional forces to the Pacific possible, the United States would maintain a defensive strategy against Japan in the Pacific.

MacArthur disagreed with this shift to Rainbow-V, arguing that it was based on an outdated concept of defense at the entrance of Manila Bay. He recommended the adoption of a new plan that sought to secure the defense of the whole archipelago and the Philippine coast by strengthening Philippine military power. MacArthur was tenaciously pushing a military strategy that Eisenhower's staff had earlier judged to be too difficult.

When Brereton arrived in Manila in early November, he brought a letter from Marshall authorizing the revision of Rainbow-V as proposed by MacArthur. Based on this authorization, MacArthur established the North Luzon Force and the South Luzon Force in the north, and the Visayan-Mindanao Force in the south. The North Luzon Force (about twenty-eight thousand men), under the command of Major General Jonathan M. Wainwright, consisted of three Philippine army divisions (the 11th, the 21st, and the 31st), the 26th Cavalry (Philippine Scouts), and the 45th Infantry Battalion of the U.S. Army. Its mission was to defend the whole northern area of Manila, including Lingayen Gulf and the Bataan Peninsula. The South Luzon Force (about sixteen thousand men) consisted of the 41st Division and the 51st Division of Philippine Army and the U.S. Army field battery. Under the force's commander, Brigadier General George M. Parker Jr., its mission was the defense of the southern part of Manila.[12]

In October 1941, Colonel Hugh J. Casey, who had returned to his job as chief of civil engineers, reviewed the situation in the Philippines as follows:

> Nothing had been done in the way of improving any of the armament or other military facilities in the Philippines. They were just on sort of maintenance basis. But shortly before I arrived, the decision had been made to actually and aggressively increase the defenses.
>
> Many troop units were organized to be sent out to us in the Pacific. Additional armament, guns, and other equipment were on order and would be sent out. Additional air units were scheduled to come, and that of course meant the building of additional airfields and their improvement. The signal facilities were also scheduled to provide radar protection and so on, and preparations for all of this were under way at that time.
>
> When war broke, it had not been accomplished. I think if we had had three or four months more before the war actually broke, we'd have been in a much better position for defense. But as it was, we were sort of in the initial phase of defense reinforcement when the war did break.[13]

Later events would show that, as Casey observed, MacArthur's Philippine defense system was not ready for the outbreak of war with Japan.

The Attack on Pearl Harbor

On November 24, MacArthur received a radiogram from Rear Admiral Thomas C. Hart, commander in chief of the Asiatic Fleet. It conveyed information and a warning from Stark: "Chances of favorable outcome of US-Japan negotiations are very doubtful. This situation together with statements of Japanese government and movement of their naval and military force intimate in our opinion that surprise aggressive movement in any direction including attack on the Philippines or Guam is a possibility."[14] Subsequently on November 27, MacArthur received a radiogram from the War Department: "Prior to hostile Japanese action you are directed to take such reconnaissance and other measures as you deem necessary....Should hostilities occur, you will carry out the tasks assigned in revised Rainbow Five, which was delivered to you by General Brereton. Chief of Naval Operations concurs and request [sic] you notify Hart."[15]

On the same day, MacArthur conferred with Hart and High Commissioner Francis B. Sayre. According to John Jacob Beck's book, *MacArthur and*

Wainwright, MacArthur told them "in reassuring terms that the existing align-ment and movement of Japanese troops convinced him that there would be no Japanese attack before the spring."[16] Brigadier General Clifford Bluemel, com-mander of the 31st Division of the Philippine army, also testified that at the beginning of November MacArthur had predicted that it would be not the Tojo cabinet but its successor cabinet that might commence hostilities.[17] Bluemel's testimony makes it clear that MacArthur had no expectation of a Japanese sur-prise attack. On November 28, MacArthur radioed confidently to Marshall that "everything is in readiness for conduct of successful defense."[18] Despite Arnold's warning that the Philippine air bases should be protected, MacArthur responded indifferently on December 6: "All Air Corps stations here on alert status."

Neither the army in Manila nor army and navy leaders in Washington pre-dicted the Japanese attack that occurred in December 1941. Moreover, MacAr-thur's officers had no specific battle plan. Clearly, they can be faulted for pride and carelessness. Casey later explained:

> In the ordinary sense of preparation for war, you didn't feel any sense of hysteria or concern. I think they had the attitude, which all of us felt, that if anything was going to happen in connection with Japan, they were going to hit the Philippines first because Hawaii was a far distance away. I think they probably felt that the warning would come from [*sic*] attack out in the Philippines rather than on their doorstep.[19]

For this reason, the confidential telegram sent from Washington to Manila dated December 7, 1941, came as a shock to MacArthur: "Sixty Japanese carrier borne dive bombers attacked airfields and Pearl Harbor, Oahu, at eight a.m. damaging hangers and planes on ground. Three US battleships reported sunk and three others seriously damaged. Second air raid at eleven a.m. Six transports were reported in Japanese forces. Reports of attacks on Wake and Guam all air attacks made with bombs torpedoes and machine guns. First objectives seem to be air and naval installations and shops."[20]

How did MacArthur and his staff react to the emergency? John Beck elo-quently described the reaction in Manila. Here is a summary of events based on Beck's detailed accounts.[21]

When Hawaii was attacked, Major General Richard K. Sutherland, MacAr-thur's chief of staff, Brigadier General Richard J. Marshall, deputy chief of staff, and Colonel Hugh J. Casey, chief of engineers, were asleep at No. 1 Military Plaza. Soon after 3:00 a.m. on December 8, Brigadier General Spencer B. Akin woke up Sutherland, and told him that Pearl Harbor had been bombed by Japanese air force planes. Sutherland telephoned MacArthur on a private line to tell him about the attack. "MacArthur repeated incredulously 'Pearl Harbor!'" At 3:55 a.m.

MacArthur received confirmation of the attack through Admiral Thomas C. Hart, commander in chief of the Asiatic Fleet. Hart had just received a message from Admiral Kimmel, commander in chief of the Pacific Fleet at Pearl Harbor.

At 5:00 a.m., MacArthur's staff was "alerted and assembled" at No. 1 Calle Victoria. MacArthur ordered American and Filipino troops to take assembly positions. He took steps to bring the Philippine Constabulary and Civilian Emergency Administration, made up of volunteer guards in every city, town, and barrio, under military control. Major General Lewis H. Brereton, commander of the Far East Air Force, visited headquarters at 5:00 a.m. Since MacArthur was in conference, he requested Sutherland to give permission to launch an air attack with B-17 bombers against Japanese airfields in southern Formosa. Agreeing with the plan, Sutherland told Brereton that MacArthur would give permission for the daylight attacks. Leaving headquarters, Brereton waited for MacArthur's order.

At 7:30 a.m. MacArthur received a second radiogram from the War Department: "Hostilities between Japan and the United States, British Commonwealth and Dutch have commenced. Japanese made air raid on Pearl Harbor this morning December 7th. Carry out tasks assigned in Rainbow-V. In addition cooperate with the British and Dutch to the utmost without jeopardizing the accomplishment of your primary mission of defense of the Philippines." At 7:55 a.m. there was a telephone call from Gerow to MacArthur. Gerow asked, "Have you been attacked?" MacArthur replied, "Not at all." But he said: "A Japanese bombing squadron was reported, but turned back thirty miles from the coast. That was last night between 11:30 and 12:00 p.m. our time." In his message to Marshall, he said: "Our tails are up in the air."[22] He had received little information from the navy.

When MacArthur first heard of the Pearl Harbor attack, he was confident of U.S. military victory. In his reminiscences, however, MacArthur frankly wrote: "I learned, to my astonishment, that the Japanese had succeeded in their Hawaiian attack."[23] The Japanese attack was clearly beyond his expectations.

The Attack on Clark Field

Four hours after the telephone call that alerted him to the attack on Pearl Harbor, MacArthur received another shock: the news that Japanese aircraft had launched a sudden attack on Clark Field Air Base near Manila. At 8:30 a.m. on the morning of December 8, 1941, he received reports that a group of high-flying planes had been observed north of Clark Field, and all B-17s were ordered airborne. However, at 8:50 a.m. Sutherland telephoned Brereton and instructed him to hold off on the planned bombing of Formosa. Just thirteen minutes later Sutherland was notified that the Japanese planes north of Clark Field were approaching. Brereton visited Sutherland immediately to inform him that, if Japanese aircraft succeeded in attacking Clark Field, it would be impossible to use the B-17 in an offensive operation. Again, he requested authority to carry out the offensive before Clark Field was attacked. Just before 10:10 a.m. Sutherland summoned Brereton to inform him that MacArthur had decided to send a reconnaissance mission to Formosa before the offensive. A coded message was dispatched recalling all airborne B-17s to Clark Field for refueling and for briefing on the probable mission. Three of the bombers were to be dispatched to Formosa for reconnaissance and the remainder would follow later on bombing missions.

At 11:00 a.m., Sutherland informed Brereton by telephone that an order to bomb Formosa might be issued. Fifty-five minutes later, at the direction of General MacArthur, Sutherland telephoned Brereton again to request a report on air operations being planned for the following two hours. However, at 12:35 p.m., while the pilots who were going on the reconnaissance mission were being briefed (and the rest were at lunch), a group of Japanese bombers and fighters flying at altitudes of more than twenty thousand feet launched a surprise attack on Clark Field. Ironically, although a radar system was being installed at Clark Field at the time of the Japanese attack, it did not work because the warning system had not been set up. By 1:37 p.m., when the bombing and strafing stopped, half of the planes of the Far East Air Force had been destroyed. Of thirty-five B-17s, just seventeen remained. Also destroyed were fifty-three P-40s and three P-35s, along with twenty-five or thirty miscellaneous aircraft. As many as eighty servicemen had been killed and 150 wounded. The Philippine air force was destroyed, and it was widely reported that Clark Field had become another Pearl Harbor. On December 9, Japan's *Asahi* newspaper reported extensively on a glorious military success in Hawaii and the Philippines and the shooting down of one hundred enemy aircraft in the Philippines.

From this time on, the strategy of using air power to defend the Philippines from invasion changed radically. Brereton and MacArthur took responsibility for the calamity at Clark Field. At 3:50 they discussed the disaster at the headquarters of USAFFE. MacArthur held a conference at 5:30 with High Commissioner Francis B. Sayre. When Sayre entered MacArthur's office, the general was pacing the floor and Sayre could see by the expression on his face that he was deeply troubled. MacArthur described the tragedy in his *Reminiscences:* "We were exposed by fierce attack of (Japanese) 307 army aircraft, 444 Navy aircraft, total 751 of them. The ratio of our disadvantage was 7 to 3.[24] At 11:45 a.m. a report came in of an overpowering enemy formation closing in on Clark Field. Our fighters went up to meet them, but our bombers were slow in taking off and our losses were heavy. Our force was simply too small to smash the odds against them."[25]

There are, however, considerable errors in this account. First, the number of Japanese navy aircraft that attacked Clark Field included 106 army bombers and 85 Zero fighters, 191 in all. Second, the USAFFE at that time was composed of the 4th Mixed Unit, the 19th Bombers, the 24th Pursuing Force, the 27th Bombers; at five military bases including Clark Field, a total of 249 aircraft were stationed, including 35 B-17 bombers, 18 B-18As, 9 A-27s, 12 B-10Bs, 107 P-40 E fighters, 16 P-26As, and 52 P-35As.[26] U.S. air power in the vicinity of Clark Field was by no means inferior in size; and the number of the Japanese aircraft given by Mac-Arthur was exaggerated.

One particularly serious problem was MacArthur's disregard of Brereton's operational plans in the lead-up to the attack on Clark Field. Having been informed of the attack on Pearl Harbor, Brereton had rushed to headquarters at five in the morning and suggested to Sutherland that eighteen B-17 bombers should be launched for an air strike against Japanese transportation vessels around Formosa. Even before his arrival in Manila, Brereton had conferred in Washington about conducting air raids over Japan and had also been considering an operation against the Japanese military in Formosa. MacArthur, however, ignored Brereton's proposal and withheld his permission. Later MacArthur claimed: "I know nothing of any interview with Sutherland, and Brereton never at any time recommended or suggested an attack on Formosa to me. My first knowledge of it was in a newspaper dispatch months later. Such a suggestion to the Chief of Staff must have been of a most nebulous and superficial character, as there was no record of it at headquarters."[27] From the account given above, it is clear that MacArthur could not have been entirely ignorant of the proposed attack on Formosa. His later comments were perhaps an attempt at self-justification.

Captain Benson Guyton, who at the time commanded an antiaircraft battery at Corregidor, later testified that he learned about the attack on Pearl Harbor at about three in the morning, and the attack on Clark Field around noon. Believing that blame lay with MacArthur rather than Brereton or Sutherland, and refusing to blame the antiaircraft regiments stationed at Clark Field, he said:

> Since I was commanding an antiaircraft battery of which I thought I knew a little, my condemnation went toward the antiaircraft regiments who were assigned the job of protecting Clark Field. I have talked to many of the people there; they could not open fire until they got the order from their regimental commander, and they never got it....But ten days before the war started I was delegated authority to fire at anything that flew over the island. Now, Corregidor was an entirely different type of fortified position from what Clark Field was, and our planes

were prohibited from flying over Corregidor. So we didn't have to worry too much about the identification of aircraft, and they at Clark would have had a problem.

I have talked to several of the B-17 pilots, and it was my understanding that all of them were of the opinion that MacArthur kept them from bombing Formosa. When the Air Corps got the word that Pearl Harbor had been bombed, they immediately fueled their planes, loaded them up with bombs, and reported to MacArthur that they were ready to take off and bomb pre-determined targets on Formosa. MacArthur told them that they couldn't do it; they were to confine their activities to reconnaissance.... I would say that somewhere between 90% and 100% of the B-17 pilots and co-pilots that I talked to blamed this on MacArthur.[28]

Casey, on the other hand, held Brereton responsible for the Philippine disaster. He claimed that, although MacArthur had issued orders to Brereton to remove all B-17s from Clark Field to Del Monte Airfield in Mindanao, Brereton had not followed the order. Casey recalled hearing Sutherland talking on the phone to Francis M. Brady, Brereton's chief of staff, and he asked: "Why the hell weren't they down there [in Mindanao] and we want them moved?"[29] If those planes had been removed, they would not have been destroyed. According to Casey, the night before Pearl Harbor, Air Force personnel in Manila gathered for a big celebration. They were going to move the planes within the next day or so. Casey blamed Brereton's disregard of the order to move the planes for the disaster at Clark Field. MacArthur's aide Sidney L. Huff, who would later become one of the Bataan Boys, shared this view.[30]

Certainly Brereton should be blamed for the lack of air defense at Clark Field during the lunch break on December 8 and for his failure to carry out MacArthur's order, communicated through Sutherland, to move all B-17s out of Clark Field. It was inexcusable that only sixteen aircraft had been moved to Del Monte Airfield by the time of the Japanese attack. On the other hand, it is also true that MacArthur was overly hesitant in responding to Brereton's strong request to conduct air raids on Japanese airfields in Formosa. Although one might argue that Washington had issued an order to refrain from air strikes, conducting reconnaissance only, MacArthur's own immediate, on-the-spot error of judgment on the day of the attack exerted a profound influence on events. His stance amounted to a failure to implement the revised Rainbow-V operation plan that he himself had requested.

Japan thus followed its great military success at Pearl Harbor with consecutive victories in the Philippines. Japanese army air force planes attacked Tuguegarao Air Field in the northern part of Luzon and Baguio Barracks in the central area, while Japanese navy air force planes attacked Clark Air Field and Iba Air Field near Manila. Two days later, Nichols Field and Nielson Air Fields were bombed. This three-day sequence of attacks almost annihilated U.S. air power in the Philippines. Fierce assaults were directed not only at the U.S. air bases but also at the U.S. naval base located at Cavite on Manila Bay. Fortunately the Asiatic Fleet under the command of Rear Admiral William A Glassford retreated rapidly to safer areas in the south and thus avoided destruction.[31]

Under the circumstances, MacArthur decided that Brereton would withdraw the 19th Bombardment Group that he commanded to Australia and Dutch-held Java. MacArthur wrote later that it was Brereton who recommended the withdrawal. Brereton stated that he had recommended to MacArthur that he remain and fight but that MacArthur decided that he should withdraw. The discrepancy between the two statements is considerable. MacArthur was perhaps indebted to Brereton because of the mistake he had made at Clark Field. Or perhaps MacArthur disliked Brereton because of his close relationship with Marshall, and wanted to move him away. MacArthur certainly appreciated the leadership of General Harold H. George, Brereton's successor: "Back in the Philippines, our fighters, with the greatest persistency and many successes, under the brilliant leadership of General Harold H. George, maintained the unequal struggle before succumbing to inevitable attrition. George's final strike in Subic Bay, sinking an enemy transport with reinforcements aboard, was made with his last four planes."[32] Later George became one of the Bataan Boys. On December 10, responding to a telephone call from Major General Henry H. Arnold, the chief of Army Air Forces, Brereton explained that he had tried to do everything in his power "to get authority to attack Formosa on December 8 but the policy toward Formosa had been relegated to a 'strictly defensive attitude' by higher authority."[33]

The destruction of the U.S. Army Air Forces at Clark Field was the gravest defeat that MacArthur had ever experienced. If the attack at Pearl Harbor meant the destruction of the U.S. Pacific Fleet, the bombing of Clark Field meant the destruction of the U.S. Far East Air Force. The Pacific bulwark connecting Hawaii with the Philippines had crumbled. The defeat in the Philippines was regarded as MacArthur's defeat, and it left an indelible stain on MacArthur's brilliant military career. However, MacArthur continued to repudiate all responsibility for the outcome and in his *Reminiscences* directed criticism at Washington and the Navy:

> Actually, the ultimate usefulness of our air arm in the Philippines had become academic because of the crippling of the American fleet at Pearl Harbor. We were operating under the provisions of a basic plan known as Rainbow-V. It provided that our supply lines—sea lanes—should be kept open by the Navy, and our ground forces should hold out for from four to six months. The Pacific Fleet would then move in with massive force,

escorting relieving ground troops. The Navy, being unable to maintain our supply lines, deprived us of the maintenance, the munitions, the bombs and fuel and other necessities to operate our air arm....The stroke at Pearl Harbor not only damaged our Pacific Fleet, but destroyed any possibility of future Philippine air power.[34]

In further criticism of the navy, MacArthur argued that the decision making had been irresolute and overly optimistic:

Although Admiral King[35] felt that the fleet did not have sufficient resources to proceed to Manila, it was my impression that our Navy deprecated its own strength and might well have cut through to relieve our hard-pressed forces. The Japanese blockade of the Philippines was to some extent a paper blockade....American carriers, having escaped destruction at Pearl Harbor, could have approached the Philippines and unloaded planes on fields in Mindanao....They had broken the Japanese code and knew the location of their ships. There was a great reservoir of Allied naval power in the Atlantic Ocean and Mediterranean Sea. A serious naval effort might well have saved the Philippines, and stopped the Japanese drive to the south and east.[36]

Finally, MacArthur directed his criticism at the highest levels of U.S. government leadership:

A top-level decision had long before been reached that the Atlantic war came first, no matter what the cost in the Far East. President Roosevelt and Prime Minister Churchill, in a Washington conference after the Japanese attack on Pearl Harbor, reaffirmed a policy to concentrate first on the defeat of Germany. Until victory was won in Europe, operations in the Pacific would be directed toward containing the Japanese with the limited resources available. General Marshall, the Army Chief of Staff, supported this policy. Unhappily, I was not informed of any of these vital conferences and believed that a brave effort at relief was in the making.[37]

Since the principle of "Europe First," while maintaining a defensive policy in the Pacific, had been clarified in the Rainbow-V document, it was impossible that MacArthur did not know about it. MacArthur appears to have been stressing that he had been right, and others—including Roosevelt, Marshall, and Stark—were wrong. Although it is true that Marshall and Stark had minimized the possibility of a Japanese sneak attack, MacArthur, too, had almost no expectation of the Pearl Harbor or the Clark Field attack. In this sense, he shared the responsibility for the defeat. MacArthur did not hesitate to use stubborn insistence or outright falsehood to deny his responsibility and transfer the blame to others.

Washington's Modification of the Military Strategy

Due to the defeats in Hawaii and Manila, the army and navy leaders in Washington were forced to modify their military operation plans. On December 11, 1941, Admiral Stark dispatched to Marshall a confidential document entitled "The Dangerous Strategic Situation in the Pacific Ocean." The main points of the document read as follows:

1. The destruction or disabling of the United States battleships and cruisers in the raid on Oahu permits this Japanese naval force to concentrate its entire attention on the offensive.... Japan is currently attempting to capture Midway and Wake for use as air and submarine bases.

2. The offensive operations in the Mid-Pacific are: 8 or 9 battleships, including the most recent construction; 5 or 6 aircraft carriers; 12 to 14 heavy cruisers, about 8 light cruisers; 30 to 50 destroyers of the newer types; about 40 submarines, 50 to 60 troop transports and cargo vessels, with various special types such as minelayers, patrol craft, etc.

3. Opposed to this formidable Fleet the United States has 3 large aircraft carriers; about 10 heavy cruisers; 3 or 4 light cruisers; about 35 destroyers; and about 13 or 14 submarines, some of which have departed the Hawaiian Area on offensive tasks. Shorebased in the Hawaiian Islands, in addition to the garrison of troops, are about 30 patrol bombers, 10 or 15 Army heavy bombers, some medium and light Army bombers; about one squadron of Navy dive bombers; 40 Army pursuit planes; and several Navy fighters.... They are vulnerable to attack.... The antiaircraft gun defenses of Oahu are inadequate.

4. It is apparent that insufficient airplanes and vessels remain available to insure detection of another surprise air raid. If such an attack develops, the pursuit aviation and antiaircraft gun defenses are inadequate to prevent the destruction of practically all the remaining shorebased aviation, additional severe damage to the naval and merchant vessels in port, and severe damage to the Navy Yard and power, fuel, and water facilities. Reserve stocks of food on Hawaii are estimated at from 45 to 60 days,

5. It seems improbable that Japanese landing operations on Oahu could be successful in capturing the island. It is easily possible, however, for the undefended islands of Hawaii, Maui, Molokai, and others to be occupied by Japanese troops. The Japanese strength in naval vessels is such that the U.S. Pacific Fleet which remains intact could not prevent landings on the undefended islands.

6. ...
7. Once [the Hawaiian islands are] captured, and with the Pacific Fleet greatly reduced in strength, the West Coast Alaska, and the Canal, as well as coastwise and trans-Pacific shipping, would be subject to heavy raids.
8. Every resource of the United States in ships, troops, aircraft, and material, should be considered available for use in this emergency.[38]

In light of these instructions, this document proposed further measures such as reinforcement of army strength on the Hawaiian Islands, the concentration of all transport and cargo vessels on the U.S. West Coast, the removal of army and navy aircraft and food supplies to Hawaii, the laying of mines off the Hawaiian harbor entrances, and the use of small aircraft for regular monitoring.

Marshall opposed Stark's recommendations, noting in his written response the following day that "the present situation also makes mandatory dispositions that will insure protection of the Panama Canal and of certain critical establishments and regions in Continental United States that are now exposed to the possibility of immediate air raids."[39] In fact, the WPD wrote in its December 21 draft analysis of the situation: "Japan has achieved important initial successes. She has undisputed control of the Western Pacific and can strongly dispute control of the Eastern Pacific. Her position in Thailand, Malaysia and the Philippines is now such as to seriously threaten the territories of the Associated Powers in the Southwestern Pacific and block further aid to China via the Burma Road."[40] This analysis was quite different from that of the U.S. Navy.

Writing from a broader perspective on December 16, the War Department had, as mentioned above, communicated an encouraging message to MacArthur: "The strategic importance of the Philippines is fully recognized and there has been and will be no, repeat no, wavering in the determination to support you. The problem of supply is complicated by naval losses in the Pacific but as recommended in yours of December fourteenth bomber and pursuit reinforcements are to be rushed to you."[41]

Although the War Department's words must have raised MacArthur's expectations, events were to prove them false. In Washington President Roosevelt convened a conference with Stimson, Marshall, Knox, and Stark to discuss the issue of sending aircraft carriers to the Far East as requested by MacArthur. Stark opposed using aircraft carriers to supply airplanes to the Philippines, claiming that such a move would reduce the striking power of the fleet. As a compromise, Marshall suggested a plan for getting aircraft to the Philippines without the use of aircraft carriers.[42] However, failing to obtain cooperation from the navy, he eventually decided to change the base for counterattack from the Philippines to Australia. This change was to have the effect of forcing MacArthur into a war of attrition against the Japanese.

The Japanese Military Landing Operation in the Philippines

While Washington was unable to firm up support for MacArthur's troops, the Japanese military advanced its operations from the initial stage of gaining control of sea and air space to the more concrete stage of amphibious landings on the Philippine Islands. On November 6, 1941, Lieutenant General Homma Masaharu, former commander of Japanese forces on Formosa, had been appointed commander of the 14th Army of Firipin Koryakugun (the Philippine Operational Force), a new formation of sixty-five thousand troops drawn from the 16th and the 48th Divisions and the 65th Brigade. On November 10 General Sugiyama Gen, Army chief of staff, briefed Homma on the proposed Philippine operation. According to the briefing manual, the operational purpose of the 14th Army was to destroy the enemy and the main enemy bases in the Philippines. The operational strategy was for the 14th Army to land on Luzon Island in cooperation with the navy, capture Manila immediately, and occupy important positions across the Philippines. The first step in the invasion was to launch an air strike by the 5th Air Group to destroy U.S. air power on Luzon Island, and then to make a landing at Lingayen Gulf by the 48th Division (comprising three infantry regiments, one reconnaissance regiment, one mountain regiment, one field artillery regiment, one engineer regiment, and two tank regiments), in order to destroy the enemy in the central part of Luzon and capture Manila. At the same time, the 16th Division (three infantry regiments, one hunting regiment, one field artillery regiment, and one engineer regiment) was to land at Lamon Bay and attempt to capture Manila by attacking from southern Luzon.[43]

The Japanese military's strategic operational plan for the Philippines differed from its planning for the Malaya operation. In contrast, Japanese plans for invading the Philippines were to first destroy enemy air power and then use advance forces to occupy the air fields in northern Luzon as a military outpost. Fighter planes and bombers would be immediately sent to provide air cover for the main military forces as they attempted a landing at Lingayen Gulf on the northwestern coast of Luzon, and at Lamon Gulf in the southeast. Both groups would then advance on Manila and capture it. This was the operational strategy that the headquarters of the Army Chief of Staff had long been planning. While the Japanese navy, focused on a southward advance, had traditionally emphasized confrontation with the U.S. Navy, the army had disregarded the Philippine and U.S. Army forces. In comparison with the planning for Malaya, plans for the Philippine operation appear to have been completed in a somewhat relaxed mood.[44]

From November 24 through November 27, a Japanese operational meeting held in Taipei set the timing for the landing at Lingayen Bay at around fifteen days from the beginning of the operation. Lieutenant General Maeda Masami, chief of staff of the 14th Army, requested that, since the battle would be against the United States, and not the Philippines, the staff should issue specific orders prohibiting the plunder or burning of private houses. On November 27 in negotiations conducted in Washington, the U.S. side presented its so-called Hull Note, which demanded that Japan withdraw from China and Indochina. The Japanese interpreted its harsh conditions as an indication that the United States had already decided on war against Japan. At an imperial conference held on December 1, the imperial decision was announced to wage war against the United States, the countries of the British Commonwealth, and the Netherlands. The opening of hostilities was set for December 8 (Japan time), one week later. General Terauchi Hisaichi, commander of the Southern Army, issued orders to each southern detachment including the 14th Army to stand ready to begin operations.[45]

Operational preparations for the 14th Army proceeded as planned, and by the morning of December 7, the army and air advance forces were ready for departure. The 48th Division, well known as one of Japan's few mechanized forces, was made up of sixteen thousand men. Among the advance forces, the Tanaka and Kanno troops had shipped out from Kaohsiung, Formosa, on November 27, and by early December had assembled at Maco in the Pescadores. Following training exercises for landing, the unit landed between December 10 and 20 on Aparri and Binuangan in the northern part of Luzon, and then on Legaspi in southeastern Luzon. Under Homma, a forty-three-thousand-strong main force, including the 48th Division, the 5th Squadron, and fleets under the direct control of the army, spent a considerable time in assembling and boarding, but it advanced southward, escorted by the 3rd Fleet, with seventy-six transport vessels and nine navy transports. On December 21, the entire group reached the Lingayen Gulf. On the other hand, the 16th Division, comprising seven thousand men who were also part of the main force, set sail from Amami Ohshima in the Ryukyus in twenty-four transport vessels. Although it encountered a typhoon and strong winds, there was no interference by U.S. planes or submarines, and the group proceeded southward, arriving at Lamon Gulf in the southeastern part of Luzon on December 24.

The U.S. and Filipino forces that opposed the Japanese advance comprised approximately 150,000 men in total. There were 30,000 men in the main force, which consisted of three infantry regiments, and two field artillery regiments of the US. Filipino forces, plus one infantry regiment, one cavalry regiment, two tank regiments (with fifty-four M3 tanks each) two field artillery regiments, and one coastal artillery regiment. In addition there were 120,000 men in ten Philippine army divisions of 75,000 (7,500 each division) and one constabulary force. Numerically, the U.S. and Filipino forces thus had an overwhelming advantage,

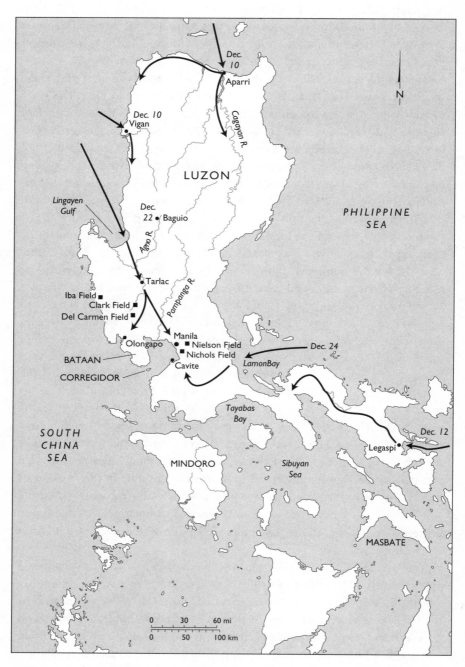

MAP 1. The Japanese invasion of Luzon, December 10–24, 1941

but each Philippine division had equipment problems, including tanks and artillery that had never been adequately tested. Immediately after the outbreak of war, the Japanese 14th Army was informed that the main U.S. and Filipino forces (five divisions each) had assembled in the middle of Luzon to prepare for a counteroffensive against the Japanese landing operation at Lingayen. One group, consisting of the 41st and 51st Divisions, was deployed at a strategic point in southern Luzon to confront the expected overland movement of Japanese forces from Lamon Bay through Batangas Bay. The report also stated that the 5th flight group belonging to the 11th Japanese navy carrier fleet had made air strikes on both the Clark and Iba air bases. More than one hundred aircraft were successfully downed or burnt on the ground, but thirty fighter planes and about ten large bombers had survived the Japanese attack.[46]

Early in the morning of December 22, the right wing of the Japanese 48th Division began a landing to the south of Agoo on the Lingayan Gulf and soon occupied the area. The left wing began a landing nearby in the Aringay area and by the end of the morning the forces were assembled. One of the soldiers who participated in the landing of the left wing reminisced:

> We were landing before the enemy. The sea was rough, but before day-break we gathered on the deck in full military uniform. Although we had all been chatting until that moment, no one spoke now but simply waited for the order. The sea was dark and the waves seemed high.... The order was given and we began our move to the boats. Climbing down the rope ladder, we had to think of the height of the waves and jump into the boat carefully, so as not to get injured. Thanks to our landing training, we could all move safely into the boat, and the boat moved away from the ship. Gunfire could be heard. It grew fiercer.... As our third group approached the shore, the boat was hit two or three times by high waves and sank. With the help of the engineers who jumped in the water to help us, all members were able to land safely.... The first and second groups had a difficult time. Although we tried to support them, many lost their lives.[47]

Another soldier wrote: "Separating from the transport ship, we advanced 500 meters and at a point just before 100 meters from the shore, put on life jackets. Carrying our rifles above our heads, we jumped into the ocean, and barely surviving the shower of gunshots, reached the shore."[48]

Having successfully completed their landing, both units began the march toward Manila, 250 kilometers (156 miles) to the south. Ueshima Yoshio, commander of the left flank unit, ordered his troops to advance with no less speed than the motorized 48th Division and along the way he organized them as a bicycle unit to speed up their movement. They reached their destination of Tarlac, some 100 kilometers (62.5 miles) away, ahead of the 48th Division, and defeated the enemy after a few hours of fierce fighting. The average daily 22 kilometer (13.75 mile) advance of the bicycle unit was said to have surpassed the achievement of the Nazi "blitzkrieg." The main body of the right flank unit drove out several hundred U.S. and Filipino forces equipped with tanks that had been defending the Rosary area, and occupied it. Another group advanced southward from Agoo along the coast. Near Saint Thomas they encountered U.S. and Filipino forces, heading north with fifteen tanks, and defeated them before resuming their southward advance. The 16th Division from the south landed at Lamon Bay on December 24 without encountering resistance and headed toward Manila, 150 kilometers (93.75 miles) to the west.[49]

Approximately twenty-eight thousand U.S. and Filipino forces were stationed in the northern Luzon area under the command of General Jonathan Wainwright; some sixteen thousand were stationed in the southern Luzon area, under the command of General George Parker. They were no match, however, for well-trained Japanese troops. As soon as civilian militia troops among the U.S. and Filipino forces saw Japanese troops, they began to run away. Around December 29, the main Japanese forces advanced to Cabanatuan, one hundred kilometers north of Manila, and the 16th Division reached Saint Thomas, sixty kilometers to the south. Around that time Japanese air reconnaissance revealed that the main U.S. and Filipino forces had retreated in the direction of Bataan.[50] However, the Japanese army did not see any great significance in this information.

The Evacuation from Manila to Corregidor

How did MacArthur's army respond to the Japanese landing operation? In the weeks before the attacks on Hawaii and the Philippines, MacArthur had successfully pushed for the modification of the "Manila Bay as Fortress" defense strategy stipulated in the Orange and Rainbow plans, into a positive defense of the entire Philippine Islands. Washington had authorized the shift. This modified approach had been further transformed into a strategy of repelling the Japanese attack on the Philippine coastline. But the U.S. Asiatic Fleet had retreated in the face of Japanese attacks, making it easy for the Japanese advance parties to land. MacArthur's strategy was rendered unrealistic. He was forced to plan his withdrawal from Manila to the Bataan Peninsula, even though such a move would mean a return to the Orange and Rainbow-V plans he had criticized as out-of-date. As early as December 12, three days after the first Japanese landing on the Philippines, MacArthur advised Manuel Quezon, president of the Philippine Commonwealth, to prepare for the worst by getting ready to move to Corregidor. MacArthur's plan was to assemble all military forces under his control on the Bataan Peninsula, transfer his headquarters from Manila to Corregidor, and declare Manila an open city.[51]

On December 17, MacArthur sent Lieutenant Colonel Sidney Huff to convince Quezon that he should transfer the seat of the Philippine government from Manila to Corregidor. According to Huff, Quezon could choose: either leave Manila with the military or be captured by the enemy. After several days of discussion, MacArthur ordered Huff to tell Quezon that MacArthur wanted to go to Corregidor with Quezon. He also ordered Huff not to leave until Quezon had accepted the idea. At 5:00 p.m. that same day Huff visited the tuberculosis-stricken Quezon at his residence and talked carefully for several hours. Since Quezon, however, still hesitated to leave the city, Huff took him to Manila in a car with its lights off, so that he could talk with MacArthur in person. He pulled in to the rear entrance of the hotel where MacArthur was waiting to avoid public attention and speculation. The time was 9:00 p.m.[52]

MacArthur pointed out to Quezon that it was unwise to keep the North and South Luzon Forces scattered across the island. His plan was to concentrate his army on the Bataan Peninsula and on Corregidor where he was determined to fight until the end. Quezon reportedly asked: "Why would I have to go to Corregidor in that case? The military defense of the Philippines is primarily America's responsibility and not mine. I have already placed every Filipino soldier under your command."[53] He argued further: "Were I to go to Corregidor, my people would think I had abandoned them to seek safety under your protection. This I shall never do." MacArthur responded that it was not merely a question of running away. He reminded Quezon of their previous agreement "to declare Manila an open city to avoid the destruction of the city and save the lives of its populace." When Quezon still hesitated, MacArthur revealed his true thinking: that it was his duty to prevent the head of the Commonwealth from being captured by the Japanese. Quezon concluded the discussion by promising that he would convene the Council of State to hear their views on the very next day.[54] According Huff's later recounting, fifteen minutes later MacArthur commended Huff for his efforts and expressed confidence that all would be well.[55] Quezon had probably used his remaining minutes with MacArthur to confirm his agreement to move.

On December 22, MacArthur sent a radiogram to the War Department with the following content: "Major enemy effort in strength estimated at eighty thousand to one hundred thousand men of four to six divisions. I have available on Luzon about forty thousand men in units partially equipped.... When forced to do so I shall release Manila and the metropolitan area by suitable proclamation in order to save civilian population. I will evacuate the high commissioner and the government to Corregidor. I intend to hold Corregidor."[56] Stimson, who saw the message, was reminded of MacArthur's tendency to overestimate his military strength. Marshall replied to the radiogram on the same day: "Your proposed line of action approved. We are doing our utmost to organize in Australia to rush air support to you. The convoy arrived there last night with seventy planes aboard.... Three B-24 planes departed yesterday. Three B-17s leave today via same route and three B-17s and B-24s alternate each day thereafter to total of eighty heavy bombers.... President has seen all of your messages and directs navy to give you every possible support in your splendid fight."[57]

On December 24, MacArthur informed Marshall by radiogram of the steadily deteriorating situation: "On north front bitter fighting continues. The pier area of Manila has just been bombed by the enemy.... I am evacuating this afternoon the high commissioner and the commonwealth government. I will subsequently issue the following proclamation: 'in order to spare the metropolitan area from the possible ravages of attack either by air or ground, Manila is hereby declared an open city without the characteristics of military objective.'"[58]

On the same day MacArthur read routine military reports at his headquarters at Calle Victoria and held discussions with his commanders and staff officers. With Sutherland he discussed operational problems; with Marshall, his deputy chief of staff, he discussed the transfer of supplies to Bataan and the bombing of strategic sites before the Japanese advance; with his chief engineer, Casey, he discussed replenishing supplies at the front, the destruction of bridges and power facilities, and power generation. At 11:00 a.m. Sutherland announced to members of the staff that they would be leaving that night to establish a headquarters on Corregidor. Marshall was ordered to remain in Manila until the last moment in order to maintain contact with forces in the field, and to coordinate the withdrawal of the North and South Luzon Forces to Bataan. He was also ordered to expedite the movement of supplies to Bataan and to destroy supplies that could not be moved in order to prevent the Japanese from making use of them.[59]

During this time Huff prepared Quezon's luggage, sending a series of cautions to Sayre and his family, and—at MacArthur's urgent request—preparing a Christmas present for Jean. Late in the afternoon Huff was sent to get Jean and Arthur and Ah Cheu, his son's Cantonese nanny. He would recollect that Christmas Eve as follows:

> I got a light truck with a Filipino driver and, to avoid attracting attention, drove to the rear of the hotel.... Jean was just finishing packing. She had put almost nothing of herself into her own suitcase, but used it to take as much food and clothes as possible for Arthur.... [From a closet] she pulled out the brown coat with a small fur collar that she had

worn on her wedding trip four years before. Then, at the last moment she came across the General's many decorations and medals in a glass case, as well as the gold baton of field marshal presented to him by the Philippine Government. She couldn't bear to leave them behind, so she scooped them up and dumped them into a Manila Hotel bathroom towel and dropped them in a suitcase.[60]

Huff carried the suitcase to the car, and squeezed in Arthur's tricycle as well. Jean took a last look around, telling Castro, the house boy, to take care of everything because they would be back soon. Her eye fell on a small bronze vase that had been given to MacArthur's father by the emperor of Japan at the time of the Russo-Japanese War (1904–5). At its base were Arthur MacArthur's name and date of presentation, and the notation that it was a gift from the emperor. Half smiling, Jean said: "Maybe when the Japanese see it, they will respect our home."[61] She took her son's hand and asked, "Ready to go to Corregidor, Arthur?" They were heading to the elevator when the siren sounded.

Jean's recollection echoed Huff's:

> At four o'clock Castro and Sid Huff came up for us....We went down the back elevator. He didn't want to upset people, you know, they saw us going or anything. And I can remember Castro standing there and kind of holding on to my hand and he wanted so to go with us and he was almost in tears. And the only thing I can remember was I said,....General had talked to him that morning telling him that he must stay in the apartment, the penthouse, and do what the Manila Hotel told him to do....So I left him there. The other boys had gone. But Castro stayed....He [Arthur] was so confused, you know, and he said, 'Mummy, I think I've seen enough of Corregidor.'"[62]

That meant he wanted to go home, but Jean said he couldn't.

At the pier, the small steamer *Don Esteban* was waiting. Already about one hundred staff were on board, but the steamer could not leave until dark for fear of Japanese attacks. Jean let Arthur play on the deck. At 6:00 p.m. the USAFFE staff began to board. At 8:00 p.m., MacArthur and Sutherland boarded and the ship pulled away from the pier. "At 11:00. p.m., the Don Esteban tied up at Corregidor's North Dock after a 26 mile voyage."[63] Two days later, on December 26, Manila was declared an open city.

THE FALL OF MANILA AND THE FIRST OFFENSIVE AND DEFENSIVE BATTLES, EARLY JANUARY TO EARLY FEBRUARY 1942

The Corregidor Fortress

Formed in the shape of a salamander, Corregidor Island occupies an area of about 7.8 square kilometers (4.86 square miles), about one-twelfth the size of Manhattan. The distance from the head-shaped section in the east to what might be seen as the salamander's tail in the west is about 6.3 kilometers (3.93 miles), while at its longest point it is just 2.1 kilometers (1.3 miles) from north to south. Geologically, the island is composed mainly of volcanic rock. It is located some 41.6 kilometers (26 miles) from the west coast of Manila City and 3.2 kilometers (2 miles) from the southern tip of the Bataan Peninsula. Because of its position at the entrance to Manila Bay, it was historically a strategically important island, used by the Spanish from the eighteenth century as a customs post and to prevent attack by pirates. After the late nineteenth century Spanish-American War in which MacArthur's father had participated, the island was gradually reinforced. In 1922 the Malinta Tunnel was completed and the entire island took shape as a U.S. military base. At the time MacArthur's headquarters moved there from Manila, the so-called Topside, at some 200 meters above sea level, had fifty-five huge coastal artillery guns, three to 12 inches in diameter, to defend the island from enemy invasion from the South China Sea. To the south of Corregidor, small islands such as Fort Drum, Hughes, and Frank also played a defense role.

On December 24, 1941, MacArthur's group moved to Corregidor and spent Christmas Eve in the Malinta Tunnel at a place called Bottom Side. The tunnel, which was to house MacArthur's General Headquarters, was in the shape of a semicircle about thirty-five feet wide, one hundred feet long, and twelve feet high. The walls and ceilings were made of natural limestone, the floor of rough cement that had been imported from Japan.[1] The tunnel was wide enough for two cars to pass abreast. On both sides many smaller tunnels branched out laterally. About thirty officers and enlisted men worked there. One third of the lateral tunnels were occupied by air officers and the adjutant general, with modest staff groups. Another third was occupied by the section heads of personnel (G-1), intelligence (G-2), operations (G-3), and supply (G-4), together with their assistants. Chief of Staff Richard K. Sutherland, his secretary Sergeant Paul P. Rogers, and MacArthur's two aides, Lieutenant Colonel Sidney Huff and Lieutenant Colonel LeGrande A. Diller occupied the final third of the tunnels. MacArthur's private quarters were located at the inner back. There were also a hospital, rest quarters, and a magazine for ammunition storage.

On somewhat elevated land above the tunnel was the so-called Middle Side. The upper center of the island formed the Topside, where officers were quartered and the guns on a hill guarded Manila Bay. On Christmas Day 1941, the day after his arrival, MacArthur moved to the Topside house of Major General George F. Moore, the harbor defense commander. MacArthur ordered Huff to travel back to Manila and bring some of MacArthur's documents that had been left behind as well as the Colt .45 that MacArthur had carried in World War I, an old campaign hat, and a bottle of Scotch from MacArthur's apartment. Huff crossed the bay at night in a torpedo boat to escape enemy air strafing, dashed around the empty streets of Manila, and the next day, during an intense air bombardment, he returned to Corregidor. He also brought some baby food for young Arthur. These events occurred a few days before the Japanese took over Manila.[2]

On December 29, at 11:45 a.m., the air raid alarm sounded on Corregidor. The Japanese were finally attacking the island, with eighteen midsized bombers and ten dive-bombers: they knew that MacArthur had fled there from Manila. As the bombs fell, the noise was tremendous and the ground shook. From his Topside quarters, MacArthur walked into the yard to count the number of planes. A direct hit on the house landed in MacArthur's bedroom and shattered the whole building. Fragments flew across the yard, and MacArthur ducked behind a hedge. A Filipino sergeant, Domingo Adversario, took off his own helmet and held it over MacArthur's head. A steel splinter hit the helmet and wounded Domingo in the hand. Huff later recounted that that the bombing continued for three hours and 57 minutes,[3] although Japanese reports gave the time as forty minutes. Topside was in splinters. The *Asahi Shimbun* covered the bombing, reporting that in repeated attacks by the Japanese air force MacArthur had been wounded in the right shoulder by a shrapnel splinter.[4]

Meanwhile, led by Colonel Francis H. Wilson, Sutherland's adjutant (and later one of the Bataan Boys), Jean hurried to a designated shelter in the tunnel with three-year-old Arthur, Ah Cheu, and Benny, their Filipino driver. Jean wore a hel-met, sandals, and a cotton dress since she had no slacks with her. Wilson put a helmet on Arthur to wear as he ran. When the bombing was over, the stairs they had used were gone. Jean said later that she could not remember how she got back to MacArthur. The next day MacArthur moved the family to a small house on Bot-tom Side, about a mile away to the east. The families of President Quezon and High Commissioner Francis B. Sayre were living in this neighborhood. Beds had been set aside in the tunnel for MacArthur and his family, but both MacArthur and Jean refused to sleep inside the tunnel. Huff described conditions there as follows:

> MacArthur would be standing in the entrance of the tunnel, watching them come. Everybody on the staff tried to persuade the General to keep away from the entrance or at least to wear a helmet during raids. He paid no attention to us. We put up big telephone poles, strung with cables, along the approach to the tunnel to prevent suicide bombers from crashing the entrance....He was standing with his hands jabbed into his hip pockets and his pipe jutting aggressively from his jaw, look-ing up at a bomber that had missed its mark.[5]

During air raids Jean would take Arthur and Ah Cheu for the one-and-a-half–minute ride to the tunnel and drive back to the house where MacArthur stayed. When the air raid was over, she would drive Arthur and Ah Cheu back from the tunnel to the house. Sometimes she would go through that routine three or four times in a single night. She would not leave the general alone. Later she remarked that the time spent on Corregidor was the longest part of the war for her. Those three months seemed longer than the three years she was to spend in Aus-tralia. Arthur quickly adjusted himself to life on Corregidor and did not seem to mind the bombs. As days passed, and stretcher bearers carried the wounded to the hospital inside the tunnel, Jean and Ah Cheu worried about the boy and tried to shield him from scenes that might frighten him, but Arthur was not afraid. He got along with everybody, from the Chinese tailor who made MacArthur's cloth-ing to Quezon himself. Within several weeks of arriving on Corregidor, Arthur was idolized by the army nurses.[6]

Why did MacArthur repeatedly expose himself to danger by refusing to wear a helmet during raids? He explained the reason as follows: "There was nothing of bravado in this. It [to watch the weaving pattern of the enemy's formation] was simply my duty. The gunners at the batteries, the men in the foxholes, they too were in the open. They liked to see me with them at such moments."[7] It is unclear whether MacArthur was convinced that bombs would never hit him, or whether he was willing to risk death. But it is clear that due to his bold, even reckless behavior, his staff was deeply devoted to him.

Meanwhile MacArthur was probably displeased by the series of radiograms sent by George C. Marshall, Army chief of staff, in Washington, to encourage him. A radiogram dated December 24, 1941, indicated that development of strong U.S. air power in the Far East based in Australia might provide MacArthur with an opportunity to counterattack. Another, dated December 26, emphasized that Major General George H. Brett was preparing for the operation in Australia, and Washington was trying hard to reinforce air power in the Far East. It urged MacArthur to cooperate with Brereton in undertaking the plan, even though Brereton had left Manila after failing to get along with MacArthur.[8] MacArthur may well have been annoyed at such urgings.

Another situation aroused his displeasure. On December 26, the Asian Naval Fleet under Rear Admiral Thomas C. Hart left Manila to join the fleet to the south. On December 21, immediately before the Japanese main forces landed at Lingayen Gulf in the northwest of Luzon Island, MacArthur sent a radiogram to Washington, requesting a naval demonstration in order to limit the enemy's capacity for unhindered bombardment. The Navy responded in the negative. Disappointment with the responses of both the navy and the air force appears to have aroused an uncontrollably gloomy feeling in MacArthur.

Later MacArthur noted with sarcasm that it was several months after the fall of the Philippines before the Navy initiated a brave counterattack toward the west. On December 26, the rest of the fleet under the command of Admiral Francis W. Rockwell moved to Corregidor. MacArthur wrote critically: "The crux of the problem lay in the different interpretation given to local problems by Admiral Thomas C. Hart, the naval commander, and myself....Apparently, he was certain that the islands were doomed and made no effort to keep open our lines of supply. In addition to his refusal to risk his ships in resisting the landing made on Luzon, he made no effort to oppose the Japanese blockade."[9]

On the other hand, MacArthur praised Rockwell's ability and cooperative approach as well as the vigorous actions of his troops: "The naval wireless station on Corregidor, the experienced 4th Regiment of Marines, three gunboats, three minesweepers, six PT boats, and a few other craft, all under Admiral Rockwell, then passed to my command."[10] Because of his ability, Rockwell joined as a member of the Bataan Boys and participated in the flight from Corregidor.

The Japanese Military Landing on Luzon

MacArthur saw Japanese operations as follows. First, he considered that the December 10, 1941, landing at Aparri in the north and Vigan on the northwest coast, followed by the December 12 landing at Legaspi in the south, were preliminary actions aimed at scattering and confusing his men. Therefore, he held back his main forces in readiness for the main Japanese attack. On December 22, when a huge invasion force in three transport echelons entered Lingayen Gulf, northwest of Manila, MacArthur recognized the troops as the 14th Army commanded by Lieutenant General Homma Masaharu. "It [the strategy] was obvious he [Homma] sought to swing shut the jaws of a great military pincer, one prong being the main force that had landed at Lingayen, the other the units that had landed at Atimonan [on Lamon Bay, to the southeast of Manila]. If these two forces could effect a speedy junction, my main body of troops would have to fight in the comparatively open terrain of central Luzon, with enemy to the front and to the rear."[11] Realizing the disadvantages for his troops, MacArthur needed to deceive the Japanese in order to smash the enemy. He made an immediate decision to withdraw all of his forces to Bataan and barricade them there. This strategy was not new. It was none other than a version of the Orange Plan or the Rainbow V plan that MacArthur himself had previously criticized as impractical. He was thus abandoning his own strategy to vanquish the enemy at the Philippine coast. He was not ashamed of this shift, nor did he make any excuses. He did not call attention to it, acting as if nothing had happened.

Immediately MacArthur made the following plan for defense. The 1st Corp under the command of Jonathan M. Wainwright would fight a war of attrition by pulling back defense lines into the central broad plain at the top of the Bataan Peninsula. Then, under the protection of this war of attrition, the 2nd Corps under Brigadier General Dwight F. Jones, as well as the Manila unit and all units on the south and central plains, would withdraw to Bataan, where they would be able to hold out against the superior airpower, tanks, and artillery of the Japanese. After all units had safely withdrawn to Bataan, MacArthur strategized as follows:

> The main line of resistance would run from Moron, on the coast of the China Sea, to Abucay on the shore of Manila. If this line was breached, we could drop back to a reserve line some seven miles to the rear. A third line crossed the Marivales [sic] Mountains, the highest part of the peninsula. Still further to the rear, Corregidor, separated from Bataan by two miles of water, would serve as the supply base for the Bataan defense and deny the Japanese the use of Manila Harbor, even though they had the city of Manila itself.[12]

According to MacArthur, this four-stage defense plan was possible because of his "intimate knowledge of every inch of the bewildering area,"[13] and he was confident of controlling his whole force.

How did the Japanese respond operationally? As of December 27, the Japanese 14th Army Headquarters had accumulated the following information about the enemy. First, four or five divisions of the U.S. and Filipino forces in central Luzon had tried to prevent the Japanese from landing, but the main force of the 11th Division was annihilated between Bacnotan and San Fabian on the Lingayen Gulf. The main force of the 71st Division with some tanks and cavalry units was annihilated around Rosario; the main force of the 91st Division was totally destroyed near Pozorrubio and Binalonan; and the 31st Division around Iba and San Marseilles was retreating toward Mariveles. Second, the movement of the U.S. and Filipino forces in Manila was unknown, but some had fought in the battle of the northern Agno River against Japanese troops who landed in the Lingayen Gulf, and apparently sustained extensive damage. Third, the headquarters of the U.S. Army in the Far East (USAFFE) had escaped from Manila to Corregidor on December 24. Fourth, U.S. and Filipino forces could for the time being expect no reinforcements from the American mainland.

After assembling the above information, Japanese military headquarters concluded that U.S. and Filipino forces might fight a war of attrition from their military base of the Corregidor fortress and the Bataan Peninsula. However, the Japanese decided to follow their original plan, destroying the U.S. and Filipino forces rapidly in order to take Manila and then moving forward to Cabanatuan, in central Luzon north of Manila.[14] This decision was the first step in a crucial misjudgment by the Japanese.

Two days later, on December 29, interrogation of the captured chief of the 1st Battalion of the U.S. 21st Division revealed that U.S. and Filipino forces were emphasizing the Tarlac-Cabanatuan line between Lingayen Gulf and Manila. So long as they held this defensive line, U.S. and Filipino forces would be able to hold Manila, but if it were broken, the Japanese believed, they would probably withdraw to Bataan. The Japanese, however, did not yet realize that their enemy had already decided on a withdrawal from Manila. Moreover, after learning on December 27, through an intercept of a San Francisco broadcast, that Manila had been declared an open city, Tokyo headquarters informed the Japanese command in the Philippines and urged caution. The Japanese knew that the U.S. and Filipino forces were concentrating their military provisions at Cabcaben and Mariveles in the southern part of Bataan and that their headquarters was moving to Mariveles. The military command finally realized that the majority of U.S. and Filipino forces were retreating to the Bataan Peninsula.[15]

Thus the course of a war that had been based on the assumption of combat with U.S. and Filipino forces focused on the capture of Manila was clearly changing. As the Japanese military headquarters reviewed its ongoing operations, Akiyama Monjiro, chief of staff officer of the air force, insisted that the main forces should dash into the Bataan Peninsula and capture the enemy on the run. But Maeda Masami, chief of staff, and other staff officers opposed such a policy change on the grounds that to do so would be to neglect duties assigned by the Imperial General Headquarters in Tokyo and the Southern Army. Homma made a final decision to concentrate the main forces on the occupation of Manila. In the discussion, the air corps insisted that the U.S. and Filipino forces heading for the Bataan Peninsula should be attacked; the 48th Division, too, repeatedly recommended bombing the Calumpit Bridge to block the enemy's progress. Nevertheless, the final decision was to send all troops into Manila to help the 48th and 16th Divisions in their attack on the city. Although the command knew that most of the U.S. and Filipino forces around Manila were retreating to the Bataan Peninsula through San Fernando, staff officers believed that a powerful force remained to defend the city and anticipated battle there.[16] This was a second grave miscalculation on the Japanese side.

The "dash to Manila" order sealed the fate of much of the Japanese force. Without thoroughly examining the enemy's movements, an operational decision was made to attack Manila swiftly in accordance with the plans of the Imperial General Headquarters and the Southern Army. This decision gave U.S. and Filipino forces time to avoid a decisive battle in the Manila area and to flee to Bataan.

The Japanese finally accomplished their goal, occupying Manila on January 1, 1942, but the expected fierce battle did not take place and most of U.S. and Filipino forces escaped to Bataan. Lieutenant General Tsuchihashi Yuichi, commander of the 48th Division, expressed his bitter regret, but it was too late. Thereafter, the Japanese were to struggle with consecutive defeats. After the war Nakayama Motoo, a high-ranking staff officer, recalled the situation as follows:

> About December 29, searching from the air, we learned that a large number of the U.S. and Filipino forces were retreating to Bataan. But we expected they would change their courses and proceed toward the sea lane through Bataan. Therefore, we did not give much consideration to the possibility that they would stop at Bataan and try a serious resistance there.... If the U.S. and Filipino forces were going to withdraw to Bataan, we should have just let them go. The occupation of Manila would become easier. Since a cornered rat is dangerous, it would have been unwise to hinder the enemy from running away.[17]

The Japanese thus believed that MacArthur's army would not stay on Bataan but would flee overseas. If they were trying to escape overseas, then they might as well be allowed to do so. Based on no evidence, this was astonishingly subjective thinking, and it constituted a third major Japanese misjudgment.

The Nendo Sakusen Keikaku Saiko (Details of the Annual Operational Plan) prepared by the general staff office in 1937 stipulated particular operational instructions to be followed in the case of a U.S. military withdrawal to Bataan.

However, the Dai 14 Gun Sakusen Yoko (14th Army's Military Operation Plan) compiled at this time made no mention of a retreat by U.S. and Filipino forces. Sejima Ryuzo, staff officer of the Imperial General Headquarters, later wrote: "The Manila strategy was so influential both at home and abroad that its value in war leadership was greatly emphasized. Moreover, there was an overwhelming anticipation that a decisive battle would take place in northern Luzon. Thus, the question was whether the 14th Army's mission was to destroy the enemy main forces or to accomplish the capture of Manila. In the end, capturing Manila became the main objective."[18]

Even on December 30, 1941, the Japanese leadership adhered to its fixed operational strategy, unable to determine whether the troops remaining in Manila or those retreating to Bataan were the main enemy forces. This uncertainly brought great fortune to MacArthur and his forces. At the same time, the Japanese 16th Division, which was militarily weak and not expected to perform well, swept northward in a great offensive advance after landing in the south. Its success was due to the U.S. and Filipino force's tactical withdrawal.[19]

Withdrawal to the Bataan Peninsula

MacArthur was thus successful in misleading the Japanese. Retreating step by step, his forces bought time so that men and supplies could be assembled at the peninsula. Two points were key. One was preventing the Japanese from using important military facilities and munitions in Manila. Colonel Hugh J. Casey was placed in charge of this job. After December 24, when all troops had left Manila, Casey led a small demolition squad in blowing up the gigantic Pandacan oil installation, blasting facilities at Fort McKinley and Nichols Field, burning warehouses along the Manila waterfront, destroying bridges, power plants, and radio stations, and dynamiting the boilers of two dozen locomotives in the Manila Railroad yard. It is estimated that at least fifteen million dollars' worth of property was destroyed. After completing his dangerous mission at about 3:00 a.m. on January 1, 1942, the day before Manila fell, Casey left the city by launch for Corregidor. He was the last USAFFE staff officer to leave the city. The second key point was ensuring that military units and munitions could cross Calumpit Bridge. Located directly south of San Fernando, the bridge marked the intersection of the road running from northern Luzon to Manila and the road leading to Bataan. It was such an important strategic point that the Japanese 48th Division would surely aim to bomb it. After returning to Corregidor and confirming that the Luzon South Force had crossed the Calumpit Bridge safely and had moved into Bataan, Casey ordered his demolition engineers to dynamite the bridge to prevent the Japanese from crossing. The bombing was carried out at 6:15 a.m. on January 1, 1942.[20]

The Japanese military was astounded by Casey's tactics of destruction. One report read as follows:

> The destruction of the bridges, especially those to the south of Agno river done by the U.S. and Filipino forces was thorough and ingenious. Hundreds of large and small bridges had been blown up, but these actions affected very little on the progress of the Japanese troops, because side-roads, and railroad bridges were available and engineering and road construction units could repair much of the damages. The demolition of the Calumpit Bridge, however, was a different story. The last U.S. and Filipino forces, including the 51st Infantry Regiment and the 51st Division, passed over the bridge at 5:00 a.m. and at 6:15 a.m. the bridge was completely blown up.[21]

On the early morning of New Year's Day, another member of MacArthur's staff arrived at Corregidor after a dangerous journey: Richard J. Marshall, deputy chief of staff, who was responsible for logistics and had commanded transport missions in Manila until immediately before the Japanese took the city. No rescue boat arrived. But he narrowly escaped death because of a providential delay in the Japanese advance. Accompanied by Sutherland, Marshall reported to MacArthur, and received the general's congratulations before leaving on January 5 to establish a communications center in the Mariveles mountain range for the intended military headquarters in Bataan. With the work completed, Marshall was able to maintain close telephone communication with Sutherland and update him on the military situation there.[22]

Following Marshall's extraordinary efforts, the U.S. and Filipino forces used all forms of available transportation, including commercial buses, trucks, cars, trains, and boats to move goods, ammunition, equipment, and medical supplies to Bataan. MacArthur wrote: "Day and night, General Parker, acting as a guard, fended off the pressing enemy." He continued: "Wainwright quickly developed a pattern of defense to cause the maximum of delay to the enemy. He would hold long enough to force the Japanese to take time to deploy in full force, when he would slowly give way, leaving the engineers under the leadership of General Casey to dynamite bridges and construct roadblocks to bar the way. Again and again, these tactics would be repeated. Stand and fight, slip back and dynamite. It was savage and bloody, but it won time."[23] MacArthur took pride in the strategy, claiming: "The success of this operation enabled the assembly and reorganization on Bataan of the bulk of my forces, and made possible the subsequent defense of the peninsula. No trained veteran divisions could have executed the withdrawal movement more admirably than did the heterogeneous force of Filipinos and Americans." MacArthur argued that, as long as he controlled Corregidor and Bataan, the Japanese would not be able to make use of Manila: "Its use would be denied the enemy. He might have the bottle, but I had the cork." He thus emphasized his own military superiority and justified his declaration of Manila as an open city.

Even the historian Michael Schaller, who is relatively critical of MacArthur, praises the speedy and successful movement of supplies and men:

> Previously, MacArthur had ordered supplies put in forward depots. Now the defenders scurried to recover as much as they could before the Japanese overran them. Regular American army units (including the Philippine Scouts) prevented the retreat from becoming a rout. By early January, about 80,000 soldiers, 26,000 civilians, and substantial amounts of material reached Bataan.[24]

Nevertheless, the reality was not as admirable as both MacArthur and Schaller described it. William Manchester criticized MacArthur's handling of the situation:

> He was still convinced that the main Japanese thrust would come at Lingayen, and he was right. His error lay in waiting for the blow to fall before withdrawing into the Bataan peninsula.... Major General Jonathan Wainwright, who led his North Luzon Force, and who ... believed their only hope lay in prompt retirement into the peninsula. But he [MacArthur] hesitated. In the opinion of Harold K. Johnson, then a lieutenant in the 57th Infantry and later a chairman of the Joint Chiefs [of Staff (JCS)], MacArthur's decision to oppose the Lingayen landing was "a tragic error." While the General was motoring around Luzon in a dusty old Packard sedan, encouraging Filipinos to fight where they stood, he could have been supervising the shipment of supplies, which would be desperately needed later, into Bataan. One depot alone, at Cabanatuan on the central Luzon plain, held fifty million bushels of rice—enough to feed U.S. and Filipino troops for over four years. The failure to move it was a major blunder, one which must be charged to MacArthur's vanity.[25]

Lieutenant Benson Guyton, commander of one of the antiaircraft batteries on Corregidor, believed that the failure to transfer supplies caused a shortage of shells for counterattack. He noted that many soldiers complained about the failure to move munitions and provisions from the warehouses in Manila to Bataan and Corregidor.[26]

MacArthur himself commented proudly: "I have always regarded my decision as not only my most vital one of the Philippine defense campaign, but in its corollary consequences one of the most decisive of the war."[27] His high self-appraisal derived from three factors: first, the series of Japanese strategic mistakes based on mistaken preconceptions by the Japanese 14th Army Headquarters; second, the ambitious political maneuvers of Japan's Imperial General Headquarters and the Southern Army Headquarters, who desired to highlight the capture of Manila for propaganda purposes as a success following on that of Pearl Harbor; and finally, the heroic efforts of field commanders and their soldiers in withdrawing to Bataan in accordance with the Orange Plan and Rainbow V strategy, which MacArthur had once criticized and then revived.

The Fall of Manila and the First Bataan Operation

On January 3, 1942, the Imperial General Headquarters in Tokyo announced that, on the afternoon of January 2, the Imperial Army Philippine Capture Corps had occupied the capital city, Manila, and that they had gone on to attack the enemy at Corregidor and Bataan. The Japanese had captured Manila with little resistance, and it seemed to the Japanese military command that the operation in the Philippines had achieved its objectives. Having abandoned Manila and fled into the dead end of the Bataan Peninsula, the U.S. and Filipino forces were fated for surrender or annihilation. The Japanese occupation of the entire peninsula was imminent. The city of Manila had fallen into chaos after the withdrawal of U.S. and Filipino forces and police, with refugee uprisings, frequent arson, and the looting of shops. However, the arrival of Japanese troops on January 2 placed a brake on the disorder. On January 3, all of Manila's thirty-five hundred Japanese residents, including Japanese embassy personnel, were safely rescued. A soldier of the 16th Division who had arrived with one of the early groups on January 1, wrote: "All the Japanese residents had been confined to the Nippon Club. They welcomed us with tears in their eyes. I, too, felt as if I had returned to the homeland."[28]

Although Japanese forces had accomplished the capture of Manila earlier than expected, taking only ten days after landing in northern Luzon, they had not completed their mission. They had occupied a major location but had not achieved the more important goal of destroying the enemy. By contrast, U.S. and Filipino forces had succeeded in evacuating to Bataan without sustaining serious damage. As MacArthur boasted, the Japanese navy did not realize the complete control of Manila Bay for which it longed. Manila Bay is a fine natural harbor, about sixty kilometers (37.5 miles) wide, formed in the shape of a ring with a small opening

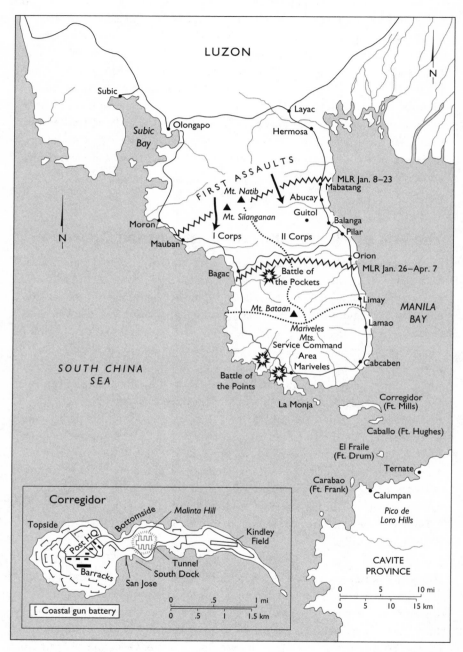

LUZON

Subic

Subic
Bay

Olongapo

Layac

Hermosa

FIRST ASSAULTS

Mt. Natib

Abucay

MLR Jan. 8–23
Mabatang

Moron

Mt. Silanganan

I Corps

Guitol

II Corps

Balanga
Pilar

Mauban

Bagac

Battle of
the Pockets

Orion

MLR Jan. 26–Apr. 7

Mt. Bataan

Limay

MANILA
BAY

SOUTH CHINA
SEA

Mariveles
Mts.
Service Command
Area
Mariveles

Lamao

Cabcaben

Battle of
the Points

La Monja

Corregidor
(Ft. Mills)

Caballo (Ft. Hughes)

El Fraile
(Ft. Drum)

Ternate

Carabao
(Ft. Frank)

Calumpan

Pico de
Loro Hills

CAVITE
PROVINCE

0   5   10 mi
0   5   10   15 km

Corregidor

Topside

Bottomside

Malinta Hill

Post HQ

Kindley
Field

Barracks

San Jose

South Dock

Tunnel

[Coastal gun battery

0   .5   1 mi
0   .5   1   1.5 km

MAP 2.   The campaign on Bataan, January–April 1942

to the west as its entrance. Corregidor Island lies in that entrance. Some forty kilometers (25 miles) to the east of the entrance to the bay is the city of Manila. To the west is the Bataan Peninsula, about fifty kilometers (31.25 miles) long and thirty kilometers (18.75 miles) wide. Much of the peninsula is covered with dense forests. In the northern half lies the Natib Massif, and in the south the Samat Massif. It was here on the Bataan Peninsula that some eighty thousand U.S. and Filipino forces were now stationed. However, 14th Army Headquarters speculated that most of the U.S. and Filipino forces had already been destroyed, with no more than two or three divisions surviving. As one staff officer, Imoto Kumao, later testified, "We knew nothing of MacArthur's strategy and the actual conditions in Bataan."[29]

The 14th Army Headquarters decided to attack MacArthur's forces in Bataan, and began its preparations. On the evening of January 2, however, the headquarters of the Southern Army in Tokyo ordered the 5th Air Squadron to move to Thailand, and the 48th Division to transfer out of 14th Army so that it could be used in the Netherlands East Indies. This transfer order caused confusion within the 14th Army Headquarters, and conflict among the Imperial General Headquarters, the Southern Army, and the 14th Army Headquarters. Imoto recalled the mood at headquarters at that time:

> The staff judged that the enemy had no fighting power left. From the beginning, in disregard of the order, the staff had no thought of using the entire power of the entire 14th Army to handle the Bataan situation because they had no knowledge about topography nor history of the Spanish[-American] War. It was decided to carry out the transfer order as decided in November of the previous year. This, however, resulted in an unfortunate situation for the 14th Army. It was left with about 7,000 men in the 16th Infantry Division and another 7,000 in the 65th Brigade as the core of the ground forces and just 70 aircraft in the 14th Air Squadron. The Japanese military used this residual force to begin the so-called "first Bataan combat."[30]

The force assigned as the advance party was the 65th Brigade under Lieutenant General Nara Akira. The brigade had been formed temporarily in the southern Honshu and Shikoku areas of Japan for the purpose of defending occupied areas. Its organization, equipment, and combat ability were far inferior to those of an ordinary field force. Most of the soldiers below officer level were conscripts. Each unit had only a few motorized goods wagons and no transportation units. Before Nara left for Formosa, Homma had informed him that the brigade's assignment would be security. Clearly, the group was not prepared for the battlefield. The Army Headquarters estimated the number of U.S. and

Filipino forces who had fled to the Bataan Peninsula and Corregidor Island at twenty thousand to thirty thousand, but in fact the number was about eighty thousand plus twenty-six thousand refugees. Based on this miscalculation, the attack at Bataan was entrusted to the 65th Brigade, which carried rifles but had almost no artillery. This Japanese underestimation of enemy forces meant that the ensuing battle proved difficult.[31]

The 65th brigade began its operation on January 9, 1942, replacing the 48th Division near San Fernando. It attacked U.S. and Filipino forces at their front base, but resistance was so fierce that the Japanese advance was blocked and Japanese forces were defeated. One soldier of the 9th Regiment described the situation as follows:

> The terrible fact was that the firepower of the brigade consisted of old-style artillery only, and there were no more than six machine guns in each battalion. We in the 9th Regiment feared the worst because the 48th Division, which had been scheduled to fight with us, suddenly disappeared, leaving us to fight with an elderly troop of senior reservists. In any case, we thought that all we had to do was destroy an almost defeated enemy. First, on January 9 the 65th Brigade attacked the enemy camp on Mt. Natib. It was an area of thick jungle. It was an encampment strongly constructed and surrounded by a wire fence. Furthermore, at the front of the defense line, gun sights were adjusted in advance, and 15-centimeter [5.85 inch] howitzers fired at our troops accurately and continuously. We were astounded that there the bullets were fired without pause. Even after we ran into the jungle, we were sprayed with bombs, leaving us nowhere to flee to. We learned afterwards that directional microphones had been set up here and there so that targets could be set accurately. We heard that the enemy had used this area as a training area for defense maneuvers before the war. Without any geographic knowledge, there was no possibility of our winning on the enemy's home ground.[32]

Of necessity, the Japanese army sent about five thousand men who had been stationed in Manila for relief, but the enemy camp did not waver. At the end of January, two infantry battalions in the 16th Division made another landing on the west coast of the southern Bataan peninsula to attack from behind the enemy positions, but they too were defeated to the last man. Another Japanese infantry regiment was rescued immediately before annihilation. The 65th Brigade's casualties included 10 percent of the officers killed, and an additional 15 percent were injured. Ten percent of noncommissioned soldiers were killed, and another 18 percent were injured. A quarter of the total attacking force were killed or injured. The reminiscence of the 9th Regiment soldier continues:

> Our Takechi unit cut its way through the jungle to provide the side attacking force for the brigade under Nara's command, but we could advance no more than 100 meters per day. Attacked by mountain leeches, we slept straddled across the forks of trees. Supplies dropped from the air to alleviate the food shortages were caught in the jungle canopy and never reached the ground. I dreamed often of eating potatoes until my stomach was full. At the end of January we finally managed to break through the barricade on Mt. Natib, and headed for the second enemy encampment on Mt. Samat. But we suddenly met fierce resistance and, after losing two thirds of our men, we were forced to retreat. At that time, blueprints of the enemy encampment were found in the underground storage below the Manila city offices. It was said that our military leaders turned ashen at the discovery and the decision was made to suspend our operation.[33]

The Daihonei Rikugunbu Senso Shido Han, or War Operations Department of the Imperial General Headquarters, wrote in its operation diary for January 15: "The attack in the Bataan area is going worse than expected. It will be left to the judgment of future historians who is to blame, the highest commanding division or the 14th Army."[34]

On February 8, one month after the fierce campaign had begun, Homma suspended the Bataan operation until the arrival of substantial reinforcements. This marked the end of the first battle of Bataan.

The Good Fight and the Hardships of MacArthur's Troops

How did U.S. and Filipino forces continue the fight? On January 1, 1942, MacArthur sent a message to the War Department: "Covering forces on the Porac-Guagua line and vicinity of Olongapo. First defensive position Abucay-Mauban, second position generally along Pilar-Bagac road, rear boundary Limay-paysawan. In this position I intend to accept decisive battle."[35] On January 5, the army headquarters was established on Bataan under Marshall's leadership to report on the combat situation on Bataan to Corregidor headquarters. On the morning of January 10, acting on Casey's advice, MacArthur traveled from Corregidor to Bataan for the first time to inspect the various positions. He was accompanied by Sutherland, Marquat, and Huff. On January 15, MacArthur encouraged his officers and assured them that help was on the way from the United States, thousands of troops and hundreds of planes having been dispatched. MacArthur had already received a letter from the Japanese general command warning of attacks and demanding surrender. Propaganda leaflets dropped over the front line urged U.S. and Filipino soldiers to give up.[36]

Their warnings ignored, the Japanese began a full-scale attack. MacArthur wrote:

> In headlong attacks of unabated fury they tried to break the 20-mile Peninsula de Fengo line from Abucay to Mauban. But our intimate knowledge of every inch of that bewildering area paid off. Our artillery, accurately placed in concealed positions for interdiction and flanking fire, completely stopped the bull-like rushes with such heavy slaughter as to leave their infantry, in spite of its great superiority in numbers, baffled and infuriated. They concentrated first on Abucay, our eastern anchor, and for a fleeting moment penetrated. But our counter attack promptly threw them out.…Constantly, fresh Japanese troops arrived by transport to replace the enemy's losses.…In all, nearly 100,000 replacements kept their original strength intact.[37]

The Japanese pressure forced MacArthur's troops to give ground, withdrawing to the second defense line from Orion west to Bagac. The Japanese tried to storm this line, but were stopped.

It cannot be denied that MacArthur's troops fought a good fight. The engineering corps led by Casey made extensive use of the so-called Casey Dynamite to block the Japanese advance by blowing up bridges and roads. When Japanese tanks pushed forward, they suffered from such devices as "Casey's Coffin," designed as an antitank mine, and "Casey's Cookie," a bamboo stick stuffed with dynamite, nails, and broken glass, some with time fuses, that worked effectively as hand grenades.[38] Another factor that helped MacArthur's troops take the advantage was the Japanese decision to change its frontline troops from the competent 48th Division to the militarily inferior 65th Brigade.

The situation on the battlefront was favorable, but for the U.S. and Filipino forces the food situation had become serious. On January 17, MacArthur reported on the increasing gravity of the situation in a radiogram sent to the War Department. He identified the refugee problem as one cause of the food shortage, criticizing the Japanese army for intentionally driving refugees across the Bataan line in order to worsen shortages: "The Japanese had craftily furthered this movement by driving the frightened population of the province of Zambales, just north of Bataan, into our lines knowing full well we would feed them—a humanitarian measure which cut deeply into our food stocks."[39] In fact, however, the Japanese mistakenly estimated U.S. and Filipino forces at no more than twenty or thirty thousand and had not expected that more than twenty thousand refugees would be added. Rather, as MacArthur suggested in a comment quoted above, his own failure to manage the transportation of indispensable supplies when evacuating from Manila was a more significant cause. MacArthur never referred to this point; rather he explained food shortages by focusing on the inhumane attitude of the Japanese military. What is conspicuous here is not so much the adroitness of the Japanese military as the adroitness of MacArthur's public relations.

On Corregidor, as well, food shortages were serious. Paul Rogers, the only noncommissioned officer to evacuate from Corregidor with MacArthur in March, left a detailed diary in which he recorded:

> December 30; Damned Japs hit our water tanks and mixed the salt water with the fresh water. It surely tastes awful. I have missed dinner for the past three days.
> January 1; Water supply is critical.
> January 17; Seriousness of food shortage. Lack of rations here.[40]

Bulkeley, who led the successful withdrawal of MacArthur's party from Corregidor, testified that "there were no provisions for sustaining us such as food allowances there or provisions there from the navy there. We had to live off the country....One of our officers managed to capture a live wild pig....We roasted this pig, and this was for 111 men and the men were almost frantic....We scrounged rice, coconut meat, copra, and anything we possibly had."[41] Due to deficiencies in vitamin A, the gun crews suffered from night blindness, so manning coastal artillery at night was a problem.[42]

The MacArthur family experienced the same hardship as ordinary soldiers. Jean described her meals: "Army rations—whatever everybody else was eating and like that. But I remember the Quezons had brought some food over for themselves. They had some canned stuff."[43] The Japanese forces set up artillery on the Cavite naval base to the south of Manila. Between 8:00 a.m. and noon, barrages of four-inch shells were sprayed over Corregidor. During this time of the day, solar reflection made it impossible for the U.S. and Filipino artillery crews to spot the flashes of the enemy guns. Air raids intensified, and in a repeat air raid on January 6, thirty men were killed or injured by one direct hit. The Japanese bombers came over in perfect formation at a twenty-thousand-foot elevation. Since U.S. antiaircraft artillery could reach only seventeen thousand feet, it was difficult to shoot the Japanese down. Inside Malinta Tunnel the moaning of the wounded could be heard at all hours. Quezon, who suffered from tuberculosis, became increasingly ill, and at night his hacking cough echoed through the tunnel. He could not sleep without a morphine injection administered by a medic. During his first eight weeks on the Rock, MacArthur lost about twenty-five pounds. He wrote: "At the end they were subsisting on less than a thousand calories a day."[44]

If there was any reaction in Washington, however, it came only in the form of encouragement. Roosevelt wrote: "My personal and official congratulations on the fine stand you are making. All of you are constantly in our thoughts. Keep up the good work. Warmest regards."[45] Secretary of War Stimson's message was: "Your reports and those of press indicate splendid conduct of your command and troops. The president and Secretary of War and quite evidently the entire American people have been profoundly impressed with your resistance to Japanese endeavors."[46] Of course, Marshall, too, expressed encouragement and admiration. His message of January 23 read: "The magnificent fight of American and Filipino soldiers under your dynamic leadership already has become an epic of this war and an inspiration to the nation. The successes of your troops and your name headline the news of the day."[47] For several months after the outbreak of war, no one in Washington criticized MacArthur for the defeat by the Japanese of his air forces at Clark Field. Whereas Admiral Husband E. Kimmel was held responsible for the Pearl Harbor attack and dismissed, nothing comparable occurred in MacArthur's case. It would not be surprising if MacArthur had feared being held accountable, but the Washington leadership expressed deep admiration for MacArthur's efforts in the defense of the Philippines.[48]

In fact, from January 1942 something that can be described as a "MacArthur craze" had been sweeping across the United States. Messages of encouragement were delivered to MacArthur. Many state legislatures passed "gratitude of the state" resolutions. According to Schaller, this response reflected the drama created by MacArthur's dramatic press releases. The anti-Roosevelt press tried to make use of the drama to promote MacArthur, describing him as the "Lion of Luzon" and "Hero of the Pacific," bravely facing the Japanese enemy alone. Cities and towns throughout America renamed bridges, streets, and buildings in honor of the general. Marshall's statement had been no exaggeration: from January through May, there was not a day on which newspapers and radios failed to report MacArthur's heroic resistance in the Philippines. During its three months on Corregidor MacArthur's headquarters issued 140 press releases: most of the articles were written by MacArthur himself. Almost all referred to MacArthur, appearing to suggest that he had launched his own fierce attack on the Japanese and had thwarted all of Tokyo's war plans. None of the front-line units or officers were trusted to make their own reports. MacArthur and his press officer, LeGrande A. Diller, emphasized only positive aspects, and their newspaper releases often reported victories in fictitious battles.[49]

Nevertheless, as the situation worsened, MacArthur became increasingly frustrated, and he vented his displeasure on Washington. In the middle of January he realized that help would probably not arrive. His characteristic paranoia emerged and he began to suspect that top figures in the Roosevelt administration and military were scheming to bring him down. Rogers, who handled the confidential correspondence with Washington, wrote in his diary:

> January 8; The appoint[ment] of [Major General George] Brett as deputy cinc [commander in chief] in the Far East has stripped MacArthur of anything but his stars. The center of action for the U.S. Army is in Australia. The Philippines are a side issue. America First. The President of the U.S. is sacrificing his own citizens to save the British.... Mac to Marshall urging steps to secure more aggressive and resourceful handling of naval units in this area.
>
> January 13; [Field Marshal Archibald] Wavell appointed Supreme Commander, Brereton deputy S.C. and [Admiral Thomas C.] Hart supreme naval commander of the ABDA [American-British-Dutch-Australian] Area. Damn all politicians including Roosevelt.
>
> January 18: radio speech—"definite change in Philippine situation in 72 hours." What does that mean?
>
> January 23; Radio MacA to Agwar [Adjutant General, War Department]. Enemy has settled down to attrition because of his unopposed command of the sea. Our losses have been heavy—35% of our forces. We will soon be forced to withdraw to our final positions here. Stand will be made to destruction. MacA praises the conduct of his troops. "There have never been troops who have done so much with so little." He laid it to the charge of Washington to keep our fame and glory alive. In case of his death he recommends General Sutherland as his successor.[50]

Ceasing to ask for rescue after his radiogram of January 17, MacArthur himself explained the critical situation as follows:

> I regrouped my forces on Bataan into two corps. The North Luzon Force now became the I Corps under the command of General Wainwright and occupied the left perimeter, and the II Corps, formerly the South Luzon Force under the command of General Jones came under the command of General Parker, and held the right. The troops dug trenches, and the scratched artillery units were immediately organized for countermeasures against the overwhelming enemy forces. The 4th Marine Regiment, which was under the control of the Navy, was not

committed to the heavy fighting on Bataan, being held in reserve for the actual defense of Corregidor.[51]

Already on January 13, in a secret radiogram sent to the Adjutant General's Section (AGWAR), MacArthur acknowledged the difficulty of the campaign, noting, as Rogers had observed, that due to the heavy fighting, losses during the campaign would mount to 35 percent. He pessimistically assumed that a withdrawal all the way back to Corregidor would be necessary. Anticipating the worst, he requested that Sutherland be appointed as his successor in case of his death. On January 24, he reported to Washington: "In Luzon the enemy has landed fresh troops in the Subic Bay Area and is attacking in force along my left and along the coast at many points. His coastal thrusts are covered by Navy warships and air forces. I am counter attacking these landings…I am doing everything possible along this line. In Visayas and Mindanao no change."[52]

In early February, MacArthur sent a long radiogram, his most important to date, to Roosevelt. He began:

> The condition of the Philippines has reached such an almost hopeless stage that I believe that definite action is imperative.…After nine weeks of fighting not even a small amount of aid has reached us from the United States. Help and assistance have been sent to other belligerent countries, viz: the NEI [Netherlands East Indies], Australia, Ireland England and possibly others.…The British and American Navies, the two strongest fleets in existence, have seemingly pursued a strategy that excludes any attempt to bring aid to the Philippines. Consequently, while perfectly safe itself, the United States has practically doomed the Philippine nation to almost total extinction in order to secure a breathing space.[53]

Suggesting the possibility of surrender, MacArthur did not hesitate to express his anger and resentment.

Even more than the suffering of battle itself, MacArthur's forces were tormented by disease and starvation. Philippine soldiers began to flee the battlefield. Casey described the difficulties frankly:

> Rations were short; we were on half-rations on Bataan. We had a light breakfast, a light supper, but no lunch. And our ammunition supplies and other supplies were dwindling. We had an outbreak of malaria. We had no quinine nor atabrine, and the troops were getting weakened with hunger and disease. My headquarters was very busy with continuous inspection of defense installations and making suggested changes.[54]

On January 27, Wainwright, who commanded the left perimeter, requested that Sutherland dispatch Marshall in order to discuss the withdrawal of the left and right front lines. On February 7, Wainwright sent a discouraging report to MacArthur: "I have spoken to generals, officers and men, and I have not found a single one who did not believe that very soon the American Navy and American planes are going to arrive and turn the tide of war in our favor....I wonder if those men knew that help is not coming within a reasonable time....I wonder, I repeat, how long their morale and will to fight would last."[55]

Meanwhile, in Washington, the deputy chief of staff of the War Plans Division, Dwight Eisenhower, who had served as chief of staff under MacArthur for five years, and afterward in charge of the Philippine theater under Marshall, wrote in his diary on January 19: "I prepare about six cables a day. In many ways MacArthur is as big a baby as ever. But we've got to keep him fighting."[56] On January 23, he wrote: "Today, in a most flamboyant radio, MacArthur recommends successor in case of 'my death.' He picked Sutherland, showing that he still likes his boot lickers." On January 29, he observed: "MacArthur has started a flood of communications that seem to indicate a refusal on his part to look facts in the face, an old trait of his. He has talked about big naval concentrations."

Eisenhower's diary entries indicate the general evaluation of MacArthur in Washington. But Washington was obliged to rescue MacArthur from his difficult situation. This was a dilemma shared by Roosevelt, Stimson, Marshall, and Eisenhower, and, in the end, there was no alternative but to convince MacArthur to escape from Corregidor.

PLANNING THE ESCAPE FROM CORREGIDOR, EARLY FEBRUARY TO LATE FEBRUARY 1942

Quezon's Anti-Americanism and Demand for Neutrality

Manuel L. Quezon, president of the Philippines, originally declined MacArthur's request that he withdraw from the capital. Caught off guard by MacArthur's message, he protested: "My own first duty is to take care of the civilian population and to maintain public order while you are fighting the enemy."[1] MacArthur's real intention was to make sure that Quezon was not captured and, thus, to prevent the Japanese from using the head of the Philippine government as a symbol of their glorious triumph. In this sense, Quezon was an important American political hostage who should not be handed over to the Japanese. Looking at *Hito Koryaku Sakusen* (Operation to capture the Philippines) the documentary collection prepared by Japan's National Institute of Defense Studies,[2] however, one finds no reference to any operation targeting Quezon. However, since Prime Minister Tojo Hideki was to propose independence for the Philippines soon thereafter, one can assume that finding a way to get Quezon on their side was a major concern for the Japanese. Accepting MacArthur's request, however, Quezon evacuated from Manila to Corregidor with his wife, two daughters, and a son. The movement of the head of state meant that the capital of the Philippines had moved from Manila to a small island, about one-third the size of Manhattan Island.

On December 27, 1941, the *Asahi Shimbun* covered Quezon's message with the headlines "Imperial Army Advances to Manila," "U.S. Headquarter Starts

Withdrawal," and "Philippine Government Announces Removal of Government Facilities."[3] Quezon's announcement confirmed that the Philippine government had moved from Manila on MacArthur's recommendation, and that Quezon himself would continue to lead the government from Corregidor in cooperation with the U.S. commander of the Far East. Moreover, the paper noted that, using his emergency powers, the president would reduce the number of cabinet members from nine to four in order to strengthen presidential authority. Even at this stage, the Japanese side was not aware that MacArthur's party had removed to Corregidor.

However, the health of Quezon, who suffered from tuberculosis, steadily deteriorated, affected by air raids and bombardments, insufficient food rations and hunger, and, above all, frustration and disappointment that the hoped-for relief was not arriving from the United States. In the daytime he needed a wheelchair, and at night morphine was indispensable to ease his coughing. Quezon's illness was more serious than that of anyone on Corregidor, with the exception of wounded soldiers.

Under these distressing circumstances, Quezon made some political decisions. The first concerned the disposal of the national treasure brought from Manila. On January 11, 1942, John K. Davis, the treasury advisor to High Commissioner to the Philippines Francis B. Sayre, asked Washington whether Philippine cash and certificates of credit transferred from the Manila Bank to Corregidor should be destroyed or sent to the United States so as not to fall into Japanese hands. On January 16, Army Chief of Staff George C. Marshall conveyed to Quezon through MacArthur that he had reached an agreement with the Department of the Treasury not to allow Philippine treasure to fall into enemy hands. With the permission of the Department of the Treasury, Sidney L. Huff, MacArthur's aide, put millions of dollars into a barrel, poured gasoline in, and set the money on fire. The numbers on each dollar bill were recorded. Seeing the smoke, the Japanese on Cavite turned their guns in that direction. On the night of February 4, ten million dollars' worth of gold and silver bullion brought from Manila were transferred out of the island by the submarine *Trout*.[4]

Quezon's second political decision concerned the payment of a special award to MacArthur and some of his immediate aides. On January 3, Quezon issued his Secret Executive Order No.1, by which $640,000 was withdrawn from Commonwealth funds on deposit in the United States for payment to MacArthur ($500,000), Chief of Staff Richard K. Sutherland ($75,000), Deputy Chief of Staff Richard J. Marshall ($45,000), and Huff ($20,000). Six weeks later MacArthur accepted the money. The special payment was for services rendered by MacArthur as military advisor during the period from July 1941, when he was recalled to active duty as major general (later general), through December 1941. As such it was in violation of army rules. Why did Quezon make this payment at this particular time? Historian Michael Schaller makes the following interpretation: "As soon as they took Manila, Japanese military authorities called upon Filipino officials to remain in their jobs. The conquerors promised early independence as a reward for collaboration.... Shocked by the collaboration of so many of their friends, Quezon and MacArthur both sought a way to reaffirm their allegiance to each other."[5] However, the reason for the payment was probably not so simple. Sergeant Paul P. Rogers, Sutherland's secretary and stenographer, left a detailed record on the background to the payment, which will be explained later in this chapter.

Quezon's third political decision resulted in his sudden and anti-American demand for neutrality and early independence. At least three factors formed the background to this decision. First, on January 7, Japan established a puppet administrative regime with Jorge B. Vargas, Quezon's former secretary, as its head. Second, on January 21, Prime Minister Tojo Hideki made a policy speech to both houses of the Japanese Diet in which he announced the possibility of conditional Philippine independence: "With regard to the Philippines, in the future, so long as the Philippine people understand the true intentions of our Imperial Government and cooperate with the Japanese project of establishing the Greater East Asia Co-prosperity Sphere, the Imperial Government of Japan will gladly grant the honor of independence to them."[6] Third, responding to the Japanese announcement, on February 6 General Emilio Aguinaldo, Quezon's political antagonist, made an impassioned plea to MacArthur through a radio broadcast from Manila. He urged MacArthur to end the resistance and to surrender in order to avoid further deaths among the Filipino people and further destruction of the Philippine Islands.[7]

Quezon was particularly irritated by Aguinaldo's anti-American and anti-MacArthur radio broadcast, because he realized that its pro-Japanese stance would have a big influence on non-elite Filipinos. More serious was the negative attitude of Washington. Sitting in a wheelchair as he listened to American radio broadcasts, Quezon was enraged to learn that a large consignment of relief material as well as military forces was being sent to Europe. Worried about Quezon, MacArthur sent Chief of Intelligence Section (CIS) Charles A. Willoughby, a fluent speaker of Spanish, to soothe him. But Quezon's resentment toward the United States could not be softened. He told MacArthur that he was seriously considering turning himself over to the Japanese. MacArthur explained that the Japanese would never allow him to be the master of Malacanan Palace. Quezon ignored that argument and expressed his strong desire that the Philippine people should cooperate with Japan and that Filipino soldiers at the front should abandon the U.S. forces and surrender to the Japanese. After thorough consideration, however, Quezon gave up his original idea of placing himself at the mercy of the Japanese and settled instead on a second proposal: to end the war in the Philippines and call for the acknowledgment of Philippine neutrality by both the United States and Japan. Calling a meeting of his skeleton cabinet, Quezon read a message addressed to President Roosevelt in which he severely criticized U.S. war policy. Vice President Sergio Osmena and MacArthur's adjutant Manuel A. Roxas questioned Quezon's stance, but as Quezon threatened to demand their resignations, they reluctantly assented.[8]

In Washington on the afternoon of February 8, Secretary of War Henry L. Stimson, reading Quezon's letter via MacArthur, was at a loss. Army Chief of Staff George C. Marshall was also shocked. Quezon wrote that from a military point of view, unless there was immediate support from the United States, he could not save the soldiers now fighting gallantly. All soldiers in the field had been animated by the belief that U.S. help would be forthcoming. But that help had not been realized, and the Philippine people had suffered death, misery, and devastation. On the following morning, Quezon's second plea via MacArthur reached Stimson:

> I feel that the elements of the situation here can be composed into a solution that will not reduce the delaying effect of our resistance here but which will save my country from further devastation as the battle ground of two great powers....The government of the United States under the McDuffie-Tydings Law is committed to grant independence to the Philippines in 1946, and the same law authorized the president to open negotiations for the neutralization of the Philippines. On the other hand, the Japanese government has publicly announced its willingness to grant the Philippines her independence. In view of the foregoing I propose the following: that the United States immediately grant the Philippines complete and absolute independence; that the Philippines be at once neutralized; that all occupying troops, both American and Japanese, be withdrawn by mutual agreement with the Philippine government within a reasonable length of time; that neither country maintain bases in the Philippines; that the Philippine Army be immediately disbanded, the only armed forces being maintained here to be a constabulary of modest size; that immediately upon granting independence the trade relations of the Philippines with foreign countries be a matter to be determined entirely by the Philippines and the foreign countries concerned; that American and Japanese civilians who so desire be withdrawn with their respective troops under mutual and proper safeguards. It is my proposal to make this suggestion publicly to

you and to the Japanese authorities without delay and upon its acceptance in general principle by those two countries that an immediate
armistice be entered into here pending the withdrawal of their respec-
tive garrisons.[9]

Sayre echoed MacArthur in his support for Quezon: "If the premise of President Quezon is correct that American help cannot or will not arrive here in time
to be availing, I believe his proposal for immediate independence and neutral-
ization of the Philippines is the sound course to follow."[10] MacArthur, further,
emphasized the dire situation of the troops in his report on the military situation:

> The troops have sustained practically 50% casualties from their origi-
> nal strength. Divisions are reduced to the size of regiments, regiments
> to battalions, battalions to companies. Some units have entirely dis-
> appeared. The men have been in constant action and are badly battle
> worn. They are desperately in need of rest and refitting. Their spirit
> is good but they are capable now of nothing but fighting in place on a
> fixed position. All our supplies are scant and the command has been on
> half rations for the past month.[11]

MacArthur thus reported that the military situation had reached a desperate
stage. Hinting at eventual surrender, MacArthur implicitly communicated that
Quezon's legitimate consideration of the possibility of neutrality was inevitable.

In his *Reminiscences,* MacArthur criticized the absence of a broad policy perspective in Washington:

> Those that had dictated the policies of the United States could not have
> failed to see that this is the weakest point in American territory. From
> the beginning they should have tried to build up our defenses. As soon
> as the prospects looked bad to me, I telegraphed President Roosevelt
> requesting him to include the Philippines in the American defense pro-
> gram. I was given no satisfactory answer.
>
>   "How long are we going to be left alone? Has it already been decided
> in Washington that the Philippines front is of no importance and that,
> therefore, no help can be expected here in the immediate future, or at
> least before our power of resistance is exhausted?"[12]

While criticizing Washington policy makers, MacArthur also defended Quezon
for having to write Roosevelt demanding that the United States should grant
immediate independence to the Philippines and that Philippine neutrality should
be recognized by a protocol between the United States and Japan. On the other
hand, MacArthur justified his own position in words pitched carefully enough

that they could easily be used to support either side: "I remonstrated with Quezon as best I could against the proposals involved, and said bluntly I would not endorse them, that there was not the slightest chance of approval by either the United States or Japan."[13] There is no evidence to indicate whether MacArthur had actually attempted to persuade Quezon.

Washington recognized that the situation was serious. Roosevelt, Stimson, Marshall, and other top leaders were shocked by Quezon's series of demands for the early independence and neutrality of the Philippines, and they were clearly offended. They labeled Quezon as no different from a traitor, and they were annoyed at MacArthur's implicit support for him. Stimson, especially, thought Quezon's demand was impractical and that MacArthur's report on the military situation was much worse than it was portrayed in Quezon's message.

Eisenhower's diary entries recorded the Washington atmosphere. On January 29 he wrote: "He [MacArthur] has forwarded (probably inspired) letter from Mr. Quezon; statement (Quisling) from Aguinaldo; he complains about lack of unity of command, about lack of information. He's jittery!"[14] On February 3: "Looks like MacArthur is losing his nerve. I'm hoping that his yelps are just his way of spurring us on, but he is always an uncertain factor." On February 8: "Another long message on 'strategy' to MacArthur. He sent in one extolling the virtues of the flank offensive. Wonder what he thinks we've been studying for all these years. His lecture would have been good for plebes. Today another long wail from Quezon. I'll have to wait though, because it is badly garbled. I think he wants to give up." On February 9: "Spent the entire day preparing drafts of president's messages to MacArthur and Quezon. Long, difficult, and irritating. Both are babies. But now we'll see what happens. Tonight at 6:45 I saw the president and got his approval to sending [sic] the messages."

In the White House, Roosevelt, Stimson, and Marshall, together with Admiral Ernest J. King, newly appointed to head the War Plans Division, and Harold R. Stark, former head of the War Plans Division, met to discuss the U.S. government response. Late in the afternoon of February 9, two top-secret messages were sent to MacArthur. The first, entitled "The Far East Situation," was sent from Roosevelt to MacArthur through Stimson. Clearly rejecting Quezon's proposal of February 8, it communicated the president's firm intention to keep American forces in the Philippines while at the same time mentioning the evacuation not only of Quezon and his cabinet but also of Sayre and MacArthur with their families. The second message, from Marshall to MacArthur, contained Marshall's comments on Roosevelt's response to Quezon. In particular, with regard to Quezon's request that his proposal should be made publicly to the authorities of both the United States and Japan, he explained to MacArthur that Roosevelt would make no public statement directly or indirectly on the matter. He also urged MacArthur to finalize an evacuation plan by submarine for Quezon without delay. It is not certain whether MacArthur confirmed the correspondence, but the next day he dispatched another radiogram to Washington to discuss Philippine independence.[15]

Quezon was disappointed at Roosevelt's flat refusal. He dictated his resignation as president of the Commonwealth to his secretary, and said he would sign it in the morning. It was Osmena who persuaded Quezon to reconsider, arguing that if he persisted in resigning, history might judge him as a coward and a traitor, and that if he took his family to Manila, his daughters might be raped by Japanese soldiers. Quezon reconsidered, and then wrote to Roosevelt through MacArthur that he comprehended the basic reason for Roosevelt's decision and would accept it.[16] The issue was not raised again.

As a result of this confusion, Washington condemned Quezon as a traitor and strongly urged MacArthur to get Quezon to evacuate from Corregidor.

The Evacuation of Quezon and Sayre

According to the U.S. official record, a proposal to evacuate Quezon from Corregidor had already been raised in the radiogram sent from Marshall to MacArthur and dated December 31, 1941.[17] In it Marshall reported that Roosevelt, Stimson, and the resident commissioner of the Philippines in Washington had discussed Quezon's evacuation to the United States. If MacArthur and Quezon agreed, he proposed asking the U.S. Navy for help.

Marshall's coded radiogram reached MacArthur late in the afternoon of January 1, 1942. Before consulting Quezon himself, MacArthur held a conference with Sutherland, Marshall, Huff, and Willoughby. All agreed that the best course of action was for Quezon to remain on Corregidor. MacArthur then met with Quezon. Sayre followed Quezon into the meeting room. MacArthur read aloud Marshall's radiogram to Quezon, and then his draft reply to Marshall in which he recommended that Quezon stay on Corregidor. After a long silence, Quezon asked for time to discuss the matter with Vice President Osmena and other staff. He then sent a reply to Washington through MacArthur that fell within the parameters of MacArthur's draft response: "The evacuation of President Quezon is deemed by me to be too hazardous to attempt. This garrison is now beleaguered in Bataan and Corregidor. The only means of egress is by air or submarine, both fraught with great danger in view of complete control of sea and air by the enemy."[18] Marshall's offer had been turned down.

On January 11, the State Department instructed that "steps be taken to prevent President Quezon and, presumably, High Commissioner Sayre, from being captured by the Japanese."[19] On January 18, a message came from Roosevelt's

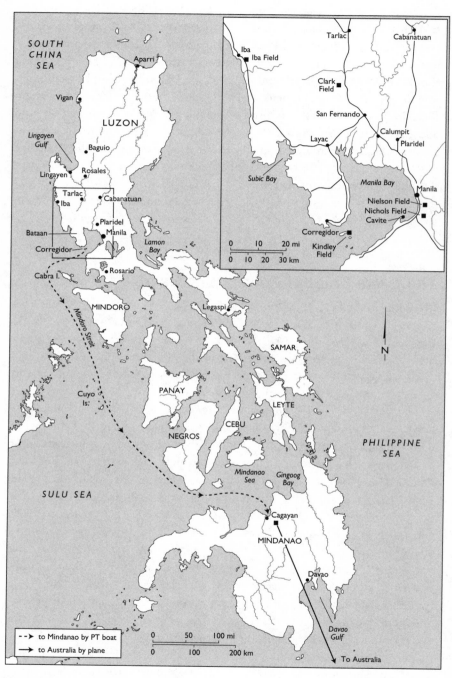

The map contains the following labels:

SOUTH CHINA SEA

Aparri

Vigan

LUZON

Lingayen Gulf

Baguio

Rosales

Lingayen

Tarlac
Iba

Cabanatuan

Bataan

Plaridel
Manila

Corregidor

Lamon Bay

Cabra I.

Rosario

MINDORO

Legaspi

Mindoro Strait

SAMAR

N

Cuyo Is:

PANAY

LEYTE

CEBU

NEGROS

PHILIPPINE SEA

Mindanao Sea

Gingoog Bay

SULU SEA

Cagayan

MINDANAO

Davao

Davao Gulf

To Australia

- - ▶ to Mindanao by PT boat
——▶ to Australia by plane

0   50   100 mi
0   100   200 km

Inset map:

Tarlac

Cabanatuan

Iba
Iba Field

Clark Field

San Fernando

Calumpit

Plaridel

Layac

Subic Bay

Manila Bay

Manila

Nielson Field
Nichols Field
Cavite

Corregidor

Kindley Field

0   10   20 mi
0   10   20   30 km

MAP 3.   The escape from Corregidor

staff, urging MacArthur to reconsider seriously the question of Quezon's evacuation from Corregidor.[20] There is no evidence that MacArthur replied. From his point of view, even if Quezon was in poor health and had limited actual authority, evacuation of the president from his own country would not only affect the morale of the soldiers but strike an immeasurable blow at the entire Philippine people. There was a possibility that the severely strained battlefront would simply weary of the war. Recognizing this situation, the Washington leadership maintained close communication with Sayre while at the same time being forced to pay careful and respectful attention to MacArthur's opinion and dignity.

On January 27, Secretary of State Cordell Hull sent the following message directly to Roosevelt:

> It is the consensus of opinion among the officers of the three Departments who have been giving this matter special consideration that all concerned should keep in mind the question of the desirability that President Quezon and his family and Mr. Osmena not fall into the hands of the Japanese; and that, as the military situation develops, consideration be given to the question of possible need for and possible nature of further messages to Mr. Sayre, General MacArthur, and Admiral Hart on that subject. It is my understanding that General Marshall and Admiral King will keep in close touch with each other regarding the situation and this problem.[21]

It was not until February 2 that MacArthur's response on this matter reached Marshall. The Bataan military situation was about to worsen, causing MacArthur to hint at surrender. He wrote to Marshall: "In case of ultimate loss of Bataan and consequent siege of Corregidor, the question arises as to the ultimate preservation of President Quezon and his family Vice President Osmena and the immediate members of the commonwealth cabinet."[22] For the evacuation of Quezon's group, MacArthur urged the use of submarine rather than air transportation, and asked that the specific plans be arranged from Washington. MacArthur also communicated Quezon's wish that he be evacuated to the United States. At this point MacArthur finally moved away from his originally negative attitude toward evacuation.

Marshall replied on the same day as follows:

> The President and his advisers feel that if and when military considerations no longer call for continued presence of President Quezon and other Philippine officials, the evacuation of Quezon and family, of Osmena and of other such officials will become desirable.
> The question whether any of those persons and whether any other persons including Mr. Sayre and family, Mrs. MacArthur and son, and

other Americans, shall at any time be evacuated will be for your decision in the light of the military situation, the feasibility and hazard of the operation of evacuation and wishes of individuals concerned.[23]

The message reflected Washington's delicate effort not to damage MacArthur's fragile self-esteem.

On February 9, Roosevelt replied through Stimson to MacArthur:

If the evacuation of President Quezon and his cabinet appears reasonably safe they would be honored and greatly welcomed in the United States. They should come here via Australia. This applies also to the High Commissioner. Mrs. Sayre and your family should be given this opportunity if you consider it advisable. You yourself, however, must determine action to be taken in view of circumstances. Please inform Sayre of this message to you and to Quezon.[24]

On the same day Marshall again contacted MacArthur, seeking his help in settling the details of the submarine evacuation plan for Quezon: "I should like to be advised so as to arrange so far as possible for a safe and speedy trip to the United States."[25] Taking advantage of Quezon's neutrality declaration, MacArthur tried to extract from Washington the reinforcements and concessions that he had long desired, but Roosevelt flatly refused. MacArthur may have felt as frustrated as Quezon did.

MacArthur sent a response to Washington on February 11. Noting that he had communicated Roosevelt's message to Quezon and Sayre, he wrote: "If opportunity presents and can be done with reasonable safety and of course with their own consent I will evacuate the members of the Commonwealth Government the High Commissioner and Mrs. Sayre and their son. I am deeply appreciative of the inclusion of my own family in this list, but they and I have decided that they will share the fate of the garrison."[26] MacArthur thus agreed to the evacuation of Quezon and Sayre with their families, but conveyed a firm refusal to evacuate himself and his family. His stubborn resolve may be interpreted in part as revenge against Roosevelt for his flat refusal of Quezon's and MacArthur's appeals. One can detect here a clash over face, or a clash of wills, between Roosevelt and MacArthur.

On February 16, MacArthur informed Marshall that Quezon and his cabinet desired to establish the seat of the Commonwealth not in the United States, but in unoccupied portions of the Visayan Islands, located between Luzon and Mindanao islands in the central Philippines. He also noted that, in accordance with Roosevelt's wishes, they intended to put up a fierce resistance against the Japanese. With regard to the evacuation, they would travel by water and at night. But in the case of a Japanese attack, it was possible they would remain in the safety of Mindanao. MacArthur emphasized that, even if Washington opposed the plan, he intended to carry it out, and he requested authority to utilize a submarine within the next three or four days. Since it seemed difficult to evacuate Quezon's and Sayre's party at the same time, he had scheduled Quezon's evacuation first, followed by Sayre's. Marshall agreed immediately to these proposals.[27]

The evacuation of Quezon and Sayre from Corregidor was thus decided. Quezon and MacArthur moved quickly to make the final arrangements. On February 13, MacArthur learned in a secret communication from Quezon that there were silver currency and other assets left in the vault at Corregidor. (According to Rogers, MacArthur knew the location of the vault, so he probably already knew the secret.) Reporting this information to Washington, MacArthur noted that he would take measures to prevent the silver currency from falling into the hands of the enemy. After receiving acknowledgment from Roosevelt the following day, MacArthur reported to Washington on February 17: "The Philippine Government has delivered to the United States Navy the following: 1 small case marked G-11 containing 5 small bars of gold bullion, 1 bar of silver bullion, and various other pieces of gold and/or silver bullion; 264 small bars of gold bullion; 630 bags containing 1,000 pesos each."[28] However, Roosevelt promised MacArthur and Quezon that he would never announce this fact publicly, and what actually happened to these assets remains unclear.

On February 15, just before the transfer of the assets, MacArthur restarted procedures, held pending since January 3, to receive his $500,000 special payment from Quezon. He requested that Chase National Bank and Trust Company, New York, withdraw $500,000 from the general assets it held for the Commonwealth of the Philippines and transfer it to the account of Douglas MacArthur at the Chemical National Bank and Trust Company, New York. In addition, he requested the following transfers: $75,000 to the credit of Richard K. Sutherland; $45,000 to the credit of Richard J. Marshall; and $20,000 to the credit of Sidney L. Huff. The transfer documents bore the signatures of Quezon and Secretary of Finance José Abad Santos.[29] At this point, MacArthur had not yet agreed to his own evacuation and that of his family from Corregidor, and in Washington there was a sense of urgency, focusing on how to persuade him to evacuate after Quezon and Sayre. A matter of precise timing linked the two delicate problems of MacArthur's own evacuation and the transfer of Philippine assets.

Two questions arise in this regard. Why did MacArthur receive such a large special payment from Quezon at this time? Why did Quezon decide to hand over the remaining Philippine assets to the United States via MacArthur at this time?

The key point is the relationship between Marshall's December 31 recommendation for Quezon's evacuation and MacArthur's January 1 refusal. As a result of the conference held with his aides before meeting Quezon, MacArthur had prepared the draft of a response in which he noted that it was too dangerous for Quezon to evacuate from Corregidor. He then asked for Quezon's agreement. Following a long silence, Quezon conferred with other government officials before deciding to follow MacArthur's recommendation. Nevertheless, Quezon's long silence indicated that his agreement did not come from the heart; his agreement was reluctant at best. Quezon had opposed leaving the capital, Manila. He was battling serious illness on Corregidor. As a virtual political prisoner, however, he had no alternative but to rely on MacArthur. The objective situation meant that he could not reject MacArthur's plan. In this situation, Quezon's offer of a large sum of money to MacArthur several days later may be interpreted as coming from the recognition that he and MacArthur were bound together by fate; the payment was an insurance premium to secure the safety of Quezon's top officials. An alternative interpretation might suggest that the payment was a political maneuver to help Quezon negotiate a more advantageous outcome for himself. Paul P. Rogers, Sutherland's secretary and stenographer, concluded that Quezon's offer was a defensive action against the anti-Quezon powers who had opposed his military plans.[30]

Washington subsequently finalized the plans for Quezon's evacuation. In the process, three points became crucial: first, the timing of the evacuation; second, the method of evacuation; and third, the destination. As far as the timing was concerned, January was considered to be too early and April too late because of expected battles. From the viewpoint of the campaign schedule, the period from late February to early March, when the enemy's offensive power would be temporarily weakened, was judged to be the most appropriate time for Quezon's withdrawal. However, Quezon's sudden demand to the United States for neutrality moved the planning forward, and the evacuation was set for the middle of February. With regard to the method of evacuation, Quezon's illness had a complicating influence. His personal doctor disapproved of submarine travel, but travel on a surface vessel carried the danger of capture or death at the hands of the Japanese military. In the end, Quezon chose the submarine option, and the date of the U.S. submarine's arrival at Corregidor was set as the departure date. Regarding the destination, a final decision proved elusive. Although Washington originally welcomed Quezon to the United States and Quezon favored the idea, the destination was later changed to the Visayan Islands or Mindanao Island. It is unclear what discussions were conducted between Quezon and his officials, or between Quezon and MacArthur. MacArthur may have thought that if Quezon remained in the United States, he might be politically constrained by Roosevelt. Therefore, using the pretext of directing the guerrilla campaign against Japan, MacArthur may have decided it was better to keep Quezon in the middle of the southern part of the Philippines, where he could control him more effectively.

Quezon's last and most dependable resources were Philippine government assets that were transferred to the U.S. Navy at this time,. They formed an indispensable fund that he would need during his life in exile and he wanted to leave the details vague. Roosevelt understood and, in accordance with MacArthur's request, canceled any obligation to make the transfers public.[31]

The evacuation plans for Quezon and Sayre were finalized by February 17. On February 19, the U.S. Navy submarine *Swordfish* broke through the Japanese blockade to reach Corregidor. On February 20, Quezon left the island, accompanied by four family members and several of his cabinet members. Roxas, who had gained MacArthur's trust, remained. (Later, he was arrested by Japanese forces, and was forced to cooperate with the puppet government of José P. Laurel, but he did not abandon his hope for liberation by the United States.) Three days later, on February 23, eleven people, including three members of Sayre's family, left Corregidor and headed for Australia.[32] Jean MacArthur and Ah Cheu were the only women who remained on the island.

MacArthur's Authorization to Evacuate

On January 27, 1942, MacArthur's evacuation from Corregidor was discussed at a conference in Washington. After consulting with Marshall and Admiral Ernest J. King, Hull recommended to Roosevelt that in addition to Quezon and Sayre, consideration should be given to evacuating MacArthur as well. Roosevelt, however, did not shift from his position that the decision should be left to MacArthur.[33]

As noted, it was on February 2 that MacArthur's attitude regarding Quezon's evacuation changed from negative to positive. Marshall did not miss this opportunity to press MacArthur: "The question whether any of those persons including Mr. Sayre and family, Mrs. MacArthur and son, and other Americans, shall at any time be evacuated will be for your decision in the light of the military situation."[34] Marshall's message posed a new problem for MacArthur.

MacArthur remarked in his *Reminiscences*:

> General Marshall had suggested that Mrs. MacArthur and Arthur be evacuated by submarine. The tactical picture was worsening almost minute by minute; this might be the last opportunity for sure deliverance of the two human beings dearest to me. The Quezons implored me to agree; they and the Sayres planned to leave at once. It was one of the desperate moments of my life, but even before I spoke to Jean I knew the answer....I answered Marshall's sympathetic suggestion; "I and my family will share the fate of the garrison."[35]

Jean recalled that MacArthur called her to his office and showed her Marshall's message. Her response was firm: "I'm just not going. I said, just thank whoever it was—I think it was the President. Thank him and tell him I appreciate it, but that Arthur and I stay with you. I made the decision."[36] The recollections of both MacArthur and Jean were both inaccurate. In fact, it was not at this time, but a week later, that MacArthur made the statement that he and his family would share the fate of the garrison when he responded to a similar suggestion from Roosevelt.

On February 4, Brigadier General Leonard T. Gerow, assistant chief of staff of the War Plans Division (WPD), raised the possibility of evacuation again in a secret radiogram and suggested new responsibilities for MacArthur:

> Your possible movements should your forces be unable [sic] longer to sustain themselves in Bataan and there should remain nothing but the fortress defense of Corregidor. Under these conditions the need for your services there might be less pressing than at other points in the Far East.
>
> There seem to be but two possible courses of action: the first is that you, at least initially, proceed to Mindanao. How long you would remain there would depend on the good you might do toward stimulating guerrilla operations in the Visayas and Mindanao, especially if our blockade running operations now under way meet with fair success and the Japanese threats at the Malay barrier are checked. From there you could later proceed south to resume command of the United States forces in the Far East. The alternative would be for you to proceed south direct without pause in Mindanao.
>
> Measures now progressing should soon provide, unless seriously interrupted, comprehensive service of supply in Australia and an active U.S. air force of five bomber and four pursuit groups in the NEI [Netherlands East Indies]....No record is being made of this message within the War Department and I have arranged that your reply labeled personal to General Marshall for his eye [sic] only will come directly from the decoding clerk to me with no copy retained and no other individual involved.[37]

It was clear that Washington was showing sensitive consideration toward MacArthur.

MacArthur, however, had no intention of accepting such proposals. On February 8, the same day Homma ordered a temporary halt to the Bataan offensive, MacArthur attempted an enormous challenge to Washington. His aim was to obtain the long-sought assistance and military reinforcements from the United States by pushing forward discussion of Philippine neutrality and early independence. Roosevelt's response of February 9 shattered MacArthur's expectations. MacArthur, along with Quezon, had lost the political game. Moreover, Roosevelt suggested that a means of evacuation should be offered not simply to Quezon and his family but also to Sayre and MacArthur and their families. Roosevelt's formal suggestion was as follows:

> I authorize you to arrange for the capitulation of the Filipino elements of the defending forces, when and if in your opinion that course appears necessary and always having in mind that the Filipino troops are in the service of the United States. Details of all necessary arrangements will be left in your hands, including plans for segregation of forces and the withdrawal, if your judgment so dictates, of American elements to Fort Mills [on Corregidor]. The timing also will be left to you....I therefore give you this most difficult mission in full understanding of the desperate situation to which you may shortly be reduced.[38]

Now it was MacArthur's turn to turn down the offer. Although he had agreed with the evacuation of Quezon and Sayre, on February 11 he wrote that "I am deeply appreciative of the inclusion of my own family in this list but they and I have decided that they will share the fate of the garrison." Rejecting the recommendation to surrender and boldly proclaiming his choice of a loyal death, he added: "My plans have already been outlined in previous radios [radiograms]; they consist in fighting my present battle position in Bataan to destruction and then holding Corregidor in a similar manner. I have not the slightest intention in the world of surrendering or capitulating the Philippine elements of my command."[39] Rather than bravery, MacArthur's stance probably reflected his sense of dignity and pride toward Roosevelt.

Subsequently, however, MacArthur was forced to accept the difference in status between himself and those in Washington. On February 14, Marshall wrote: "Regarding decision that your family will not be evacuated, I think it very important that you have in mind the possibility that some later situation might require duty from you that would compel separation from them under circumstances of greatly increased peril." He added: "I am anxious that you do not overlook this particular possibility of poignant embarrassment to you personally."[40] Marshall's words pointed to the logical weakness in MacArthur's position, and probably had the effect of altering his thinking. It was on February 13 that Quezon had secretly raised the matter of treasury assets to MacArthur, and MacArthur had passed the information on to Washington. Both MacArthur and Quezon had requested that Roosevelt keep the matter completely secret and, understanding the implications, Roosevelt agreed to their request the following day. Rogers kept a record of a meeting held between MacArthur and Sutherland at Malinta Tunnel on

February 13. His interpretation was that Quezon and MacArthur had reached an agreement and Sutherland had put it in writing: "Quezon raised the matter with MacArthur and asked that MacArthur put the document in final form. Or, it may be believed that MacArthur and Sutherland prepared a document and presented it to Quezon for signature."[41]

On February 15, MacArthur conveyed to Roosevelt his gratitude for the president's consent to secrecy regarding the Philippine assets and, at the same time, requested that Chase National Bank and Trust Company, New York, transfer the $500,000 cash payment offered by Quezon on January 3 through the War Department. Stimson authorized payment on the same day and instructed the bank to initiate procedures for payment.[42] What was the meaning of this smooth flow of agreements?

Schaller comments that MacArthur's change of attitude was closely related to Roosevelt's blunt refusal of Quezon's demand for Philippine independence. He notes that while the $500,000 was being processed for payment into his account, MacArthur requested from Roxas a loan for more than that amount:

> Pending confirmation of the transfer, MacArthur asked Manuel Roxas, Quezon's aide, to loan him 1.2 million pesos worth over a half million dollars. (He returned this after the transfer was confirmed.) Of all the honors and awards he received, this was the only one the general kept secret. Besides implying that he knew about the legal complications, MacArthur's convoluted behavior suggested he did not intend to "share the fate of the garrison."[43]

Schaller's analysis contains both correct and incorrect elements. He is correct in noting that there was a close connection between MacArthur's acceptance of the cash and Roosevelt's rejection of Philippine independence. He is also correct in the conclusion that MacArthur had no intention of sharing the fate of the garrison and that, in fact, evacuating from Corregidor was already in his mind. On the other hand, Schaller's analysis does not clarify how the tacit agreements between MacArthur and Quezon, and between MacArthur and Roosevelt (or Stimson), were made.

Rogers explained why MacArthur postponed the implementation of Quezon's January 3 Executive Order No. 1 (the payment to MacArthur and others) until February 15: "MacArthur had served as Chief of Staff under the Roosevelt administration, knew Stimson and Roosevelt, and was acquainted with the probable course of events which must follow receipt of such a dispatch from Corregidor at a time when both these men were still quivering from the shock of Quezon's proposal to neutralize the Philippines."[44] Since MacArthur's strong sense of caution made him alert to the possibility of being brought to account

before a court-martial or other legal authority, he avoided immediate acceptance of the money and calculated a more advantageous timing. Regarding that
timing, Rogers speculated that MacArthur seized the moment when shock at
Quezon's demand for neutrality had caused both Stimson and Roosevelt to
waver, but this explanation does not sit right. Although it is no more than speculation, one might guess that, since a person facing death would not require a
large sum of money, Roosevelt, Stimson, and Marshall regarded MacArthur's
request for $500,000 as a clear indication that he had chosen not honorable
death with his family on Corregidor but, rather, survival on the island of Mindanao or in Australia. Along with the handling of the Philippine assets, the large
payment to MacArthur could be seen as an exchange for MacArthur's acceptance of evacuation from Corregidor. For this reason, even though Roosevelt
and Stimson could have prevented this legally questionable action, they gave it
their tacit approval.

Still, questions remain. First, although there is clear documentation concerning the procedures for transferring the funds, there is no record of their actual
deposit into MacArthur's accounts. Probably Roxas, who remained in Corregidor and was a liaison officer between MacArthur and Quezon, played some kind
of role. Rogers revealed the following interesting exchange:

> Late in January Diller had given me several pages to copy. They were
> lists of MacArthur's security holdings with names and amounts. Diller
> warned me several times that this was a matter of MacArthur's personal
> finances and made me state that I would make just one copy and no
> more. When I finished the task, Diller was waiting by my side to take
> the copy and asked again whether I had made more than one copy. I was
> irritated because Diller seemed to challenge my integrity.[45]

Again, Rogers wrote in his diary entry for February 13: "Executive Act #1 of
the Philippine Commonwealth grants General MacArthur fifty [sic] thousand
dollars US currency, and three officers sums forty-five thousand, forty thousand,
and twenty thousand each. God! I would like to be a general."[46] Eventually, the
issue of the payment, like that of the disposal of Philippine assets, was consigned
to a gray zone from which the details have never been recovered.

Second, why, among MacArthur's aides (those who would become the Bataan
Boys), were Sutherland, Marshall, and Huff selected to receive payments, but
Willoughby, for example, was not? According to Rogers, "Willoughby was never a
member of the Military Mission. He joined MacArthur's Headquarters USAFFE
in November 1941 long after the Military Mission had been dissolved." Therefore,
he was not entitled to receive the cash award.[47] But Willoughby had played an
important role as Spanish-English translator between Quezon and MacArthur,

which might have qualified him for an award. His eccentric personality may have been an obstacle.

Given these considerations, one might say that the ensuing communications between Corregidor and Washington assumed a ritualistic character. On or around February 15, Marshall informed MacArthur that "the President directs that you make arrangements to leave Fort Mills and proceed to Mindanao.... From Mindanao you will proceed to Australia where you will assume command of all United States Troops.... You are authorized to take with you your Chief of Staff, General Sutherland."[48] On February 21, the day after Quezon left Corregidor, Marshall informed MacArthur that "the President is considering advisability of ordering you to Mindanao to continue your command of the Philippines from that locality" and "the Secretary of War and I desire your views on the above."[49]

Regarding this communication, MacArthur wrote in his *Reminiscences:*

> On February 21st—Arthur's fourth birthday—Marshall notified me that the President was considering ordering me to Mindanao to set up a new base of operations for the defense of the southern part of the Philippines. The same day the cabinet in Canberra had requested my immediate assignment to Australia as commander of the newly formed Southwest Pacific Area. When [Australian] Prime Minister [John] Curtin's recommendation reached the White House, President Roosevelt personally sent me a message to proceed as soon as possible to Mindanao. There I was to do what I could to buttress defenses, then go on to Australia.[50]

MacArthur, however, had no intention of giving up his poker game with Washington. He described his own thinking and the situation within his camp and the Philippines as follows:

> My first reaction was to try and avoid the latter part of the order, even to the extent of resigning my commission and joining the Bataan force as a simple volunteer. But Dick Sutherland and my entire staff would have none of it. They felt that the concentration of men, arms, and transport which they believed was being massed in Australia would enable me almost at once to return at the head of an effective rescue operation. They also suggested that I might seek to delay my departure. For two days I delayed a final decision. Finally, I answered the President in a message that warned of the results that might follow the failure to adequately sustain the Philippines. Because of the very special confidence the Filipino people and army had in me, my sudden departure might set

off a collapse at the Filipino defenses. I therefore requested authorization to delay my departure.

"Please be guided by me in this matter," I concluded. "I know the situation here in the Philippines and unless the right moment is chosen for so delicate an operation a sudden collapse might result. These people are depending upon me now, any idea that might develop in their minds that I was being withdrawn for any other reason than to bring them immediate relief could not be explained."[51]

MacArthur's personality is well reflected in his conviction that he had the full trust of all Filipinos and in his unhesitating declaration that without him the Philippines would collapse.

On February 24, MacArthur sent a reply to Marshall in which he expressed his gratitude for Marshall's suggestion. MacArthur's message was immediately communicated to Roosevelt:

I am deeply appreciative of the confidence in me....It is my studied opinion however the immediate movement directed is too sudden and abrupt in that it may result at this time in collapse in the Philippine area with ensuing adverse effect on the entire theatre before the means are available for counter offensive action from Australia....I am of the opinion that during the initial stages of that organizational effort I can better accomplish the aims of the president as set forth in your radio by temporary delay in my departure. This would not prevent any immediate reorganization that you may have in mind nor my reassumption of command of the troops in the Far East at this time;...I earnestly hope that you accept my advice as to the timing of this movement. I know the situation here in the Philippines and unless the right moment is chosen for this delicate operation, a sudden collapse might occur which would carry with it not only the people but the government. Rightly or wrongly these people are depending upon me now not only militarily but civically and any idea that might develop in their minds that I was being withdrawn for any other purpose than to bring them immediate relief could not be explained to their simple intelligence....Please be guided by me in this matter.[52]

That one man on the small island of Corregidor, located in a corner of the Philippines, should hold such grand illusions about holding the fate of the land and people of the entire Philippines in his hands suggests something of MacArthur's sense of self.

One who predicted MacArthur's arrogant response was Brigadier General Eisenhower, assistant chief of staff, who wrote in his diary as follows:

February 22

ABDA [American, British, Dutch and Australian] area is disintegrating. We have concocted a message to MacArthur directing him to start south to take command of Australian area, etc. I've always been fearful of this plan. I think he's doing a better job in Bataan than he will anywhere else. (Draft of message went to FDR.)

February 23

Message to MacArthur was approved by president and dispatched. I'm dubious about the thing. I cannot help believing that we are disturbed by editorials and reacting to "public opinion" rather than to military logic. [Edwin] "Pa" Watson [U.S. Army general and military advisor to Roosevelt] is certain we must get MacArthur out, as being worth "five army corps." He is doing a good job where he is, but I'm doubtful that he'd do so well in more complicated situations. Bataan is made to order for him. It's in the public eye; it has made him a public hero; it has all the essentials of drama; and he is the acknowledged king on the spot. If brought out, public opinion will force him into a position where his love of the limelight may ruin him.

February 24

MacArthur says, in effect, "not now." I think he is right. This psychological warfare business is going to fall right into the lap of WPD, principally for the reason that no one else will lead with his chin. We'll probably take it on.[53]

Eisenhower's predictions proved to be correct. On February 25, Marshall wrote to MacArthur that the president had carefully considered MacArthur's views and had ordered that the time and method of departure would be left entirely in the general's hands. Moreover, the Department of the Army (Marshall) had directed Major General George H. Brett in the Melbourne, Australia, headquarters to dispatch bombers to Mindanao at a time to be ordered by MacArthur. MacArthur, of course, had no quarrel with these arrangements and on February 26 informed Marshall that he was satisfied with them.[54] In this last tactical maneuver, MacArthur had defeated Roosevelt, and had secured himself a free hand in deciding the time and method of his evacuation.

THE EVACUATION OF MACARTHUR FROM CORREGIDOR, LATE FEBRUARY TO THE MIDDLE OF MARCH 1942

The Means of Evacuation and the Accompanying Persons

On January 27, 1942, having obtained the agreement of high-ranking army and navy officers, Secretary of State Cordell Hull suggested to Roosevelt that he should urge MacArthur to evacuate from Corregidor. On February 2, taking advantage of the shift in MacArthur's view on Quezon's evacuation, Army Chief of Staff George C. Marshall additionally proposed that MacArthur's wife and son and one "other person" (presumably MacArthur) should be added to the evacuation group. This proposal failed, and on February 4, Leonard T. Gerow, chief of the War Plans Division under Marshall, secretly asked Roosevelt to consider MacArthur's "movement"[1] to Mindanao or Australia. On February 9, Roosevelt indirectly urged MacArthur to evacuate, offering as a nominal reason the need to prepare for a counterattack in the south. On February 15 and again on the night of February 21, Marshall insisted that MacArthur should make a clear decision, referring to a presidential order and citing the name of Secretary of War Henry L. Stimson.

Through these twists and turns, MacArthur came to accept the evacuation of himself and his family, but it is not clear when he made the final decision. Historian William Manchester put the date at the day after the staff meeting of February 23:

> When the officers had gathered, the General read the President's message to them and said that he faced an impossible dilemma. If he disobeyed Roosevelt he faced a court-martial. If he obeyed, he would des-

ert his men. Therefore he intended to resign his commission, cross to Bataan, and enlist as "a simple volunteer."

They protested. All week the island had been buzzing with rumors that a great relief expedition was assembling in Australia. Obviously, they argued, MacArthur was being sent there to lead it back before the garrison's food and ammunition would be exhausted....Torn, MacArthur dictated a draft of his resignation anyhow. At Sutherland's suggestion he agreed to sleep on it. In the morning the prospect of a great counteroffensive seemed more substantial, and he radioed Roosevelt, agreeing to go but asking that he be permitted to pick the right "psychological time."[2]

Although it is not known who attended this staff meeting, with the exception of Sutherland, Manchester's account is probably correct regarding the date and time of the meeting and the content of the discussion. But it is likely that MacArthur had already decided to evacuate before the meeting, probably on February 13, the day he received the $500,000 cash award from Quezon, or perhaps immediately before. (Rogers guessed that it was on February 9, the day he received the president's order.) One might expect that a large sum of money was not necessary for a person who had made up his mind to die, sharing the fate of his volunteer garrison. However brave he might have been, MacArthur was familiar with the severe situation on Corregidor. In order to survive, he had no choice other than to escape. Neither MacArthur nor Manchester wrote about the cash award or the disposal of Quezon's assets. However, in working out financial arrangements for himself and his family, MacArthur clearly considered, first, the means of evacuation; second, the members of the evacuating group; and third, the timing and the route.

Concerning the means of evacuation, MacArthur replied to Marshall on February 24: "With regard to the actual movement I deem it advisable to go to Mindanao by combined use of surface craft and submarine and thence to destination by air."[3] Two days later, on February 26, he called for two submarines to be dispatched to Corregidor by the Department of Navy.[4] Both in Washington and in Corregidor, the use of submarines was emphasized. However, MacArthur was thinking of using not submarines but PT boats. Huff testified as follows:

> Washington obviously expected us to go by submarine as others already had gone. That's what I expected too. In fact, it hadn't entered my mind that we would go any other way. Furthermore, all of those on the list with whom I talked—and I talked with almost all of them then or later—not only assumed we would go by submarine but definitely wanted to do it that way....

I listened with surprise, because I hadn't thought about trying to get through the enemy blockade by torpedo boat and I doubt that any of the others had considered that idea. But, as he talked, it was obvious that the General preferred the PT boats to a submarine. I'm not sure why, but it was almost as if he suffered a touch of claustrophobia. He had, I remembered, shown the same attitude by refusing to sleep in the underground tunnel, and I felt he instinctively disliked the idea of being cooped up.[5]

The observation that MacArthur's choice of PT boats can be attributed to claustrophobia is interesting, but the true explanation is probably that MacArthur understood the PT boats and evaluated them highly. His defense plan for the Philippines relied on hundreds of PT boats for naval power. MacArthur was convinced that to defend the long Philippine coastline and the nation's seven thousand small islands, speedy and small boats would be the most effective means. At that time, no one shared his idea. First Lieutenant John D. Bulkeley, who was about to break through the enemy lines by leading four boats of the 3rd Motor Torpedo Boat Squadron, stated:

> The only boats that could ever make it out would be a high speed boat like a PT boat there which we did....
>
> PT boats were used because MacArthur decided that...as being the one and only way he could get [out], achieve complete surprise with Japanese forces which were surrounding him and intending to capture him....It's the genius of the man that no one ever expected that the torpedo boats would make a break-out....They had floating mines, they, we had mine fields. It was a very dangerous thing to go out of that bay, look out of that harbor and no one ever expected it.[6]

It was an idea so extraordinary that even an expert on PT boats like Bulkeley was amazed. Another reason for MacArthur's decision was that getting to the destination by submarine would have taken forty-eight hours—two whole days—longer than by PT boat. Bulkeley concluded that only with high-speed vessels like the PT boats would evacuation have been possible.

As it turned out, the decision may have saved the lives not only of MacArthur but also of his family and all the members of the Bataan Boys. If MacArthur had chosen the seemingly safe option of the submarines, it is doubtful they would have reached Mindanao. Had the Japanese fleet noticed them and sunk them or had there been any accident along the way, MacArthur's heroic legend would have been terminated. His foresight, free of any stereotype of common sense, was the deciding factor in securing the group's safety.

Once the use of PT boats had been decided, the navy's cooperation was of the utmost importance. On March 4, one week before the departure, MacArthur revealed the president's secret order for evacuation to Rear Admiral Francis W. Rockwell, commander of the 16th Naval District. MacArthur asked Rockwell and Colonel Harold G. Ray to join the group. Next, MacArthur approached Bulkeley, who was expected to lead the escape. Huff came to see Bulkeley and asked whether he would join him in a run down to Puerto Princesa on the island of Palawan, about five or six hundred miles to the south. Bulkeley amazed Huff by answering that he did not mind at all. Bulkeley told Huff what he had in mind: "I was completely self-confident in my abilities and the abilities of the boats there and what we could do, and we knew our navigation well. No problem at all. At that time I guessed MacArthur and others were planning to make a break-out and they were going to use my boats. Of course, this is a feeling operation [an operation to feel me out about the idea] as far as I was concerned."[7]

Next MacArthur himself approached Bulkeley, summoning him to the north dock in order to award him the army's Distinguished Service Cross. That afternoon MacArthur came down to the dock with Jean, Sutherland, and several other generals. After presentation of the award, MacArthur asked Bulkeley to take him and Jean on a short cruise. Bulkeley had them board PT boat no. 41 and conducted a cruise for about thirty minutes. Realizing what the boat was capable of, Jean was reassured. At this point, Bulkeley remarked later, he knew what was happening.

To avoid attention, MacArthur called Bulkeley to his quarters that night. Jean said that Bulkeley looked like a pirate. Living on board like an ordinary sailor, he had an unkempt moustache and wore a crash helmet. But MacArthur liked this kind of unconventional person. According to Bulkeley, MacArthur took him to a deserted field so that no spies or anyone else could hear them talking and said: "My plans were to make a break-out. I had direct orders from the President of the United States, to a third time actually, to break-out and to go to Mindanao, and then to Australia, at least at the very latest by the 15th of March."[8] When Bulkeley replied that he saw no problem, MacArthur made up his mind to evacuate from Corregidor in PT boats.

Chief of Staff Richard K. Sutherland was already secretly engaged in the selection of personnel to accompany MacArthur. This process marked the moment that the Bataan Boys were born. Beside MacArthur's wife and son, Roosevelt and Marshall had given permission for Sutherland alone to join the evacuation but MacArthur was determined to use a free hand in the selection of individuals as well as in determining the time of departure. In the end, Roosevelt and Marshall were obliged to give tacit approval to MacArthur's desire for a group of no fewer than twenty-one persons. MacArthur justified the selection in his *Reminiscences:* "My first care was the selection of those who were to accompany me. Besides my family, there were seventeen servicemen. They were chosen because of their anticipated contribution to the liberation of the Philippines and largely formed the subsequent staff of the Southwest Pacific Area."[9]

Indeed, as explained in chapter 2, fifteen army officers accompanied MacArthur, including eight upper-ranking officers from MacArthur's headquarters and seven middle- and lower-ranking support officers. Two navy officers brought the total to seventeen. Leaving aside Rear Admiral Francis W. Rockwell and Captain Herbert J. Ray of the navy, the fifteen army officers were Sutherland, chief of staff; Brigadier General Richard Marshall, deputy chief of staff; Brigadier General Hugh Casey, chief engineer; Brigadier General Spencer Akin, chief signal officer; Brigadier General William Marquat, chief antiaircraft officer; Brigadier General Harold George, aircraft officer; Colonel Paul Stivers, personnel officer; and Colonel Charles Willoughby, intelligence chief. In addition to these higher ranking officers, the group included Lieutenant Colonel LeGrande Diller and Lieutenant Colonel Sidney Huff, both aides to MacArthur; Lieutenant Colonel Francis Wilson, aide to Sutherland; Lieutenant Colonel Joseph Sherr; and Major Charles Morehouse, MD. Captain Joseph McMicking, who acted as liaison officer on Philippine matters, and Sergeant Rogers, typist and stenographer for Sutherland, were also included.

After MacArthur informed a very limited number of officers of the president's order on February 24, Sutherland informed each selected member privately and with MacArthur's consent. Rogers, who knew the content of important correspondence with Washington, noted his own selection for evacuation in his diary for February 24: "I will be with Sutherland."[10]

At least three other persons discussed the process of their selection. Casey stated:

> I was on Bataan all the time. I'd make a trip over to Corregidor at night, check up on the engineer situation over there—utilities and reconstruction of the bombed, damaged utilities, and so on—and also on our small airfield that we had up at Corregidor, engineer problems such as that. It was then that I was told by General Sutherland that I was to accompany the group....We sensed that it was impossible to hold out forever. We knew that we were not going to get any major reinforcements. But we thought that this would be an opportunity for General MacArthur and the staff—going down to Australia—whereby we'd have access to planes and forces, in that way we felt that we had a great chance of getting reinforcements back into the Philippines, hopefully rescuing our command before the situation was completely lost.[11]

Casey thus believed that evacuation offered the best possible chance for survival.

Huff also testified regarding his selection: "I believe it was that night that Sutherland advised me officially of the messages and of MacArthur's decision to go. He then gave me a list of the staff officers and one sergeant—the General's secretary—who were selected to make the trip."[12] That list, in Sutherland's handwriting, remained in Huff's possession.

Diller was the third person to leave us observations on his selection:

> One evening we had dinner with the General [MacArthur] and General Sutherland and I walked back from the General's quarters up on topside and outside the tunnel, General Sutherland said, "let's stop and smoke a cigarette," which was normal, we didn't smoke inside and then he looked all around like a detective and I wondered what was going on. He said, "the General's leaving for Australia next Tuesday and you're going with him." That was the only time I really got weak in the knees during the war. I was scared many times but that time I got weak all over because here was a complete change in my philosophy and plans for the future.[13]

Jean and four-year-old Arthur, as well as Ah Cheu, were included. MacArthur talked about that decision from a humanistic viewpoint: "Another excuse for angry criticism was the fact that Ah Cheu, the Cantonese nurse, went out with us....Ah Cheu had been with us since Arthur's birth. Because of her relationship to my family, her death would have been certain had she been left behind."[14] Huff supported MacArthur's way of thinking: "Perhaps MacArthur realized that this might be a point of criticism, but at the same he had considered the fact the nurse, as an alien, was under bond to him and that he was legally responsible for her. With this in mind—as well as her faithful service to the family—he decided it was his duty to include her. Once he had reached that decision, he carried it out without regard for what people might say."[15] Thus, a total of twenty-one persons—MacArthur and three household members, fifteen Bataan Boys, and two navy officials—were selected for evacuation.

Evacuation Dates and Route

MacArthur communicated with Army Chief of Staff George C. Marshall in Washington regarding the date of departure. In an important reply to Marshall dated February 24, MacArthur accepted the order to move to Mindanao or to Australia but requested that decisions on the date and method be left to him. On February 25, Marshall told MacArthur that the president understood his request and would give him complete authority. The president had noted, however, that any concrete plan would depend on clarification of the date and time. It was in his reply of February 26 that MacArthur suggested, for the first time, that the date of departure might be around March 15. Marshall notified George H. Brett, a commander in Melbourne, and ordered him to arrange long-distance bombers to be sent to Mindanao with that date in mind.[16]

With the evacuation date thus firming up, attention turned to the evacuation route. After receiving a direct order from MacArthur to use the PT boats, Sutherland called in Bulkeley, Ray, and Huff, and told them to work out the details of the trip in great secrecy. Huff wrote about their differences of opinion:

> Nobody was given a hint of our plans....Even the crews of Bulkeley's boats didn't know where they were going or why until the last minute....Rockwell and Ray were experienced Navy men, of course, but they, on the other hand, were not PT boat experts.
>
> My own experience with the Q-boats [PT boats] I had built for the Philippine Navy had convinced me that, on a long trip, it would be best to travel in single file or in follow-the-leader formation. In that way, the first boat would break the path and the others could skim along in its wake and avoid the powerful wash rolled up by these speedy craft. Rockwell and Ray, however, felt that since we might have to fight our way out, it would be best to go in a diamond formation, with the boat carrying General MacArthur at the tail end of the diamond. My protests were brushed aside, although I insisted that such a formation would make the going very rough even on a calm sea.[17]

On the other hand, Bulkeley and Rockwell agreed that the best route would be "to go far out to sea, fifty miles out to sea, not going down in the passageway where the Japs would expect us to go and probably be waiting for us and block, but way out to sea where it would be very hard to find us."[18] Furthermore, Bulkeley wrote proudly: "There was no radar in those days so they'd have to site us by the old eyeball and that's a little bit hard to do. That we did, and the plans were made and I got my operation orders and so forth there. I was in command of the expedition and MacArthur made that perfectly clear that no army general and certainly no navy rear admiral was going to tell me how to do it. And that's fine." Huff added: "On the first night we would go to one of the Cuyo Islands, a group of dots on the map northwest of Mindanao. We would hide there during the daylight hours and, if possible, continue the following night to Mindanao. Just as a precaution, a submarine was ordered to come into the Cuyos on the second morning to pick us up there if, for some reason, we could not make the last leg of the journey by torpedo boat."[19]

Departure was rescheduled from March 18 to March 11. Explaining the reason for the change later, Huff referred to the full moon. The original date of March 18 was close to the full moon: "In order to take advantage of a very thin moon, it was absolutely necessary to go in the dark of the moon, because the PT boats running at high speed left a wide, frothy wake that could be seen by enemy aviators even at night."[20]

After discussion, the details of operation order for MacArthur's party were set on March 10, 1942, as follows:

From: The Commandant, SIXTEENTH NAVAL DISTRICT
To: The Commander, MOTOR TORPEDO BOAT SQUADRON THREE

Subject: Operation Order

Enclosures: (A) ANNEX "A". (General Instructions.)
(B) ANNEX "B". (Alternate Plans.)
(C) ANNEX "C". (Embarkation Plan.)
(D) ANNEX"D". (Enemy Information.)
(E) ANNEX "E". (Copy of dispatch to PERMIT)

1. MOTOR TORPEDO BOAT SQUADRON THREE is to be used for the transportation of a party of twenty one passengers to a southern port which will be designated later. Enemy air and surface activity is to be expected along the route.
2. The party will embark in accordance with ANNEX "C" on March 11, in time to rendezvous at Turning Buoy at 2000. Proceed to sea via swept channel and arrive TAGUAYAN ISLAND about 0730 March 12. Anchor close to lee shore (West side) and disembark party for the day. Re-embark at 1700 and proceed to designated port, arriving not later than 0700 March 13. Disembark party and proceed as instructed under separate orders. If any boat breaks down she will transfer passengers and proceed independently or transfer all personnel and scuttle ship if necessary.—last boat in column is designated to go alongside disabled boat.
3. Take fuel for five hundred and ten miles (510). And food for five (5) days. (x) Use zone minus nine time.
   Rendezvous: Tagauayan Island, Piedra Blanca Island, Cagayan. Same as for relief sub.
4. See enclosures for detailed instructions and alternate plans.

F. W. ROCKWELL

ANNEX "A" GENERAL INSTRUCTIONS

1. ENEMY ACTION

(a) If MOTOR TORPEDO BOAT SQUADRON THREE contacts enemy at night, evasion tactics will be used unless discovered and attacked, in which case senior boat turn away; others attack, seek day hide-outs at discretion and proceed Point Dog as practicable.

(b) If day hide-out is discovered by enemy surface craft (with threat of investigation), the squadron will get underway immediately, scatter, and attempt to draw the enemy to northward or westward before attacking. Undamaged boats return if practicable for re-embarkation of passengers by dusk, otherwise proceed CAGAYAN (MINDANAO) as practicable.

(c) If practicable, one boat will be sent ahead to reconnoitre hide-outs before landing are [sic] made.

(d) MTB [PT boat, or motor torpedo boat] doctrine will obtain insofar as cruising and attack formations are concerned.

ANNEX "B" ALTERNATE PLANS

Plan 1. If, due to enemy air or surface attack on first leg, MTBRON THREE is unable to reach TAGAUAYAN ISLAND prior daylight, they will proceed to nearest hide-out available (probably DIGABAITO ISLAND—Culion Group) and make best of way to Cagayan on second and third nights.

Plan 2. It is decided that entire party will remain on board during daylight instead of disembarking. Flag Boat will post lookout and signalmen to warn of approaching surface vessel. On receipt of such information, all boats may be directed to scatter to the westward and rendezvous later at designated point and time.

Plan 3. If, due to enemy air or surface attack on TAGAUAYAN, insufficient MTB's remain available for reembarkation, party will be re-assigned and any who are forced to remain will be picked up by the PERMIT at daylight March 13.

Plan 4. If, due to delay on second leg, MTB's are unable to reach CAGAYAN by daylight, proceed nearest hide-out and continue following night.

Plan 5. In case other plans fail and it becomes necessary to employ the services of either PERMIT or the relief submarine (SNAPPER), orders will be issued through General Sharpe [sic; Sharp] via COMSIXTEEN (NPO) giving instructions as to when and where submarine is to make rendezvous, using Point FOX as reference point. If possible, an MTB or other tender will meet the submarine at the designated rendezvous—if at night this boat will show side lights for one minute at intervals of ten minutes, and an all round white light for thirty seconds at intervals of every ten minutes.

ANNEX "C" EMBARKATION PLAN

1. Boats and passengers will be in the following locations at times designated, expedite loading, and shove off in ample time to make rendezvous at 2000.

PT-41 (Lt. Bulkeley)—North Dock at 1930
PT-34 (Lt. Kelly)—Passengers embark in "Como" at North
PT-35 (Ens. Akers)—Dock at 1800, proceed Sisiman Cove.
PT-32 (Ens. Schumacher)—Quarantine Dock (Mariveles) at 1915.

2. Passengers have been assigned as follows:

PT-41 Gen. MacArthur (and 3), Maj. Gen. Sutherland, Capt. Ray, Lt. Col. Huff, Maj. Morhouse.
PT-34 Rear Adm. Rockwell, Brig. Gen Marshall, Col. Stivers, Cpt. McMicking.
PT-35 Col. Willoughby, Lt. Col. Diller, Lt. Col. Wilson, Mstr. Sgt. Rogers.
PT-32 Brig. Gen. Akin, Brig. Gen. Casey, Brig. Gen. Marquat, Brig. Gen. George, Lt. Col. Sherr.

ANNEX. "D" ENEMY INFORMATION

1. Enemy troops are reported to be in possession of the following localities:
   LUZON. BATANGAS, SORSOGON.
   MINDORO. PORT GALERA, CALAPAN. Occupation may extend as far south as BONGABONG on the East Coast.
   MASBATE. MASBATE, AROROY.
   MINDANAO. ZMBOANGA, DAVAO.
   JOLO. JOLO.
2. Enemy surface vessels have been reported operating in the following areas in addition to northern Luzon and the vicinity of localities noted above:
   a. South and East coasts of Mindoro. A destroyer was reported anchored in the lee of AMBULONG Island some days ago.
   b. Between Southwest NEGROS and Southwest Panay.
   c. Shelling of the following cities has been reported:
   CEBU. CEBU.
   NEGROS. DUMAGUETTE.
   MINDANAO. SURIGAO, NASIPIT, BUGO.
3. Considerable air activity has been reported in the Visayan area. Apparently ferry flights are being made from FORMOSA to MANILA, thence to DAVAO. En route these planes search the interior waters of the Archipelago. The LEGAZPI was strafed in PALAUAN BAY (MINDORO); CAGAYAN (MINDANAO) was bombed. Present practice would seem to be for the planes to locate the vessel, then have the surface vessels capture

them. The REGULUS was last reported in tow of a Japanese destroyer in the lee of AMBULONG Island.

4. Enemy surface activity in the Subic Bay area is increasing. Varying numbers of enemy war vessels up to cruiser type are reported daily, as well as merchant vessels. They usually arrive in the morning and depart in the late afternoon. Our patrol vessels have been unable to locate them after dark, hence it is not known whether these vessels are the same ones that have been reported acting in the southern PHILIPPINES or whether convoys are stopping regularly in Subic Bay to load men and materials for return to Japan.[21]

Evacuation Day

During the time of preparation, Corregidor sustained waves of bombings and artillery fire almost daily from the Japanese. Rogers communicated the harshness of the attacks in his diary:

> February 6. Japs shelled Corregidor for about 3 hours. 100 hits on Fort Drum [a small island to the south of Corregidor]. Artillery action on front. Reported landings of reinforcements false....
>
> February 14. Artillery fire from Cavite....
>
> February 16. Heavy artillery fire from Cavite and increased along the front. Fort Frank's outside water supply destroyed. Being supplied by barge from Fort Mills....
>
> February 17. Increased artillery fire upon all fronts and on Harbor forts....
>
> February 22. Enemy's forces have been greatly reduced by casualties which will necessitate many reinforcements before he can hope to attack and attempt to destroy us....
>
> March 2. Cities in south shelled by Jap cruisers and destroyers.... I walk to Middle Side in the evening. Boy! Am I brave?...
>
> March 4. I'm lonesome and hungry. Dam [sic] it!...
>
> March 5. Java fallen. Malaria bad in Bataan. God pity the hospitals when the rainy season begins....
>
> March 9. Traded my watch for a hunk of chocolate. It was worth it. No activity on the fronts. I am becoming a regular rapscallion.[22]

Bulkeley, too, described the desperate situation: "Corregidor was being bombed every afternoon by anywhere from fifty to seventy-five bombers coming down from Formosa, heavy bombardments. At the same time the Japanese on Batangas, or on Bataan there near the Cabcaben naval shipyard had set up long-range guns, and they were bombarding Corregidor. It was just a matter of time. Yes, the situation was desperate there. The end was coming, everyone knew it there unless relief came from the United States and that was hopeless."[23]

In addition to the Japanese bombardments by air and land, psychological stress from hunger and fatigue brought the Corregidor headquarters and defense force to the limits of endurance. Information regarding MacArthur's secret evacuation plan began to leak out. Since inclusion in the plan or not was a matter of life or death, it is not difficult to imagine that all of the defense force felt nervous about the course of events. In fact, whether selected or not, their state of mind was complicated. Diller confessed:

> It was a very difficult time because when General Sutherland told me that we were going to leave Corregidor, I was very much surprised and sworn to secrecy. It was very difficult because I had many close friends on Corregidor, I couldn't say good-bye to them, I couldn't tell them I was leaving. Apparently there was a leak somewhere because several of them came up and gave me letters and said I know you're going, don't deny it, please mail this when you get out. And I couldn't say anything and it was a very difficult time. Of course, I was hoping that the General could get out so that he could organize a force to come back and relieve the Philippines which was probably the only hope for the Philippines and Corregidor but it was difficult to leave our friends.[24]

MacArthur, too, was sensitive about the situation:

> My detractors would have seized on any selection as an opportunity for further criticism. Virulent stories gained currency and grew with the telling. One, widely retailed with apparent relish, suggested that seriously ill American nurses had been left on Corregidor so that the PT boats could transport furniture (one version included the piano) from my Manila Hotel apartment. The fact is that no member of that group who left the Rock, including myself and the members of my family, was allowed more than one suitcase. There was no other baggage of any kind.[25]

Jean learned of the evacuation plan from MacArthur just a few days before departure. Despite her normally strong memory, she later claimed to have forgotten the precise date. Still she probably sensed something unusual much earlier in the planning. She spent the days before departure busily helping Huff secure supplies for those on the four PT boats. She recalled: "Sid [Huff] went to the quartermasters and got these great big bags. We went into the tunnel where the supplies were. We went into this dark place,...and filled up these four bags with K rations and everything in case something happened to us on those PT boats....I didn't know whether I even told Ah Cheu and Arthur what was doing....All I did was just fill them up and then Sid had charge of getting them secreted.[26] Huff's testimony was as follows: "I had another scrounging job to do in order to provide enough food for passengers and crews for ten days. Jean helped me with the food problem, quietly transferring canned goods to the General's quarters in the tunnel, where we had four duffel bags, one for each boat. For more than a week we collected food in small quantities and Jean carefully divided it among the four duffel bags."[27]

On March 10, the day before departure, Major General Jonathan M. Wainwright, who headed the left wing of the defense force on Bataan, was called in to Corregidor, where he was informed of MacArthur's evacuation plan. He was greatly shocked. Wainwright had been a freshman when MacArthur was a senior at West Point, and the senior-junior relationship between the two men was absolute. Wainwright had achieved popularity among noncommissioned officers as head of the class of 1906. MacArthur directed Wainwright to hold Bataan until he returned. Jean later recalled of Wainwright: "The General always called him Jonathan—he was the only person in life that called Wainwright—Jonathan. Everybody called him "Skinny" including me. He was always very formal with me—Mrs. MacArthur....I said, I'm never going to call you "Skinny" anymore, because you won't call me Jeanne [sic]—that was last conversation I had with him."[28] Having been entrusted to replace MacArthur in charge of the mission, Wainwright was soon promoted from major general to lieutenant general. But he was to spend no less than three years, from the fall of Corregidor in May 1942 to the defeat of Japan, as a prisoner in Manchuria. This was the moment that sealed his fate.

On March 11, the day of departure, Huff later wrote: "MacArthur told me to have the four-star license plates taken off his automobile and put in our luggage. We may not be able to replace them in Australia....I had to have three staff automobiles driven into the tunnel to load our duffel bags and other luggage....Some of us said good-by quietly to close friends. It was a tense and unhappy and uncomfortable few minutes. Nobody said much. Nobody asked many questions."[29]

MacArthur recalled the day as follows:

> It was 7:15 on the evening of March 11th when I walked across the porch to my wife. "Jean," I said gently, "it is time to go." We drove in silence to the South Dock, where Bulkeley and PT-41 were waiting; the rest of the party was already aboard. Shelling of the waterfront had continued intermittently all day. I put Jean, Arthur, and Ah Cheu on board, and then turned slowly to look back.
>
> On the dock I could see the men staring at me. I had lost 25 pounds living on the same diet as the soldiers, and I must have looked gaunt and ghastly standing there in my old war-stained clothes....

Darkness had now fallen, and the waters were beginning to ripple from the faint night breeze. The enemy firing had ceased and a muttering silence had fallen. It was as though the dead were passing by the stench of destruction. The smell of filth thickened the night air. I raised my cap in farewell salute, and I could feel my face go white, feel a sudden, convulsive twitch in the muscles of my face. I heard someone ask, "What's his chance, Sarge, of getting through?" and the gruff reply, "Dunno. He's lucky. May be one in five."

I stepped aboard PT-41. "You may cast off, Buck," I said, "when you are ready."[30]

At eight in the evening Bulkeley released PT-41 from the north dock and headed toward the deep darkness of the bay. A statue of MacArthur now stands near the wharf from which he departed.

From Corregidor to Tagauayan

Bulkeley later described the PT boats used in the evacuation as follows:

The boats we had out there were seventy feet long. They had three pocket marine engines. We could make fifty-two to fifty-five knots which is over sixty miles an hour. They carried four torpedos, very deadly indeed here. They carried four fifty-calibre machine guns for air protection there. We also had some Lewis guns at the short end. We carried a crew of two officers and seven men. They were made not out of plywood as commonly supposed but they were made out of mahogany diagonally planked and with canvas in between and so forth. They were very, very powerful boats there at that time.[31]

Although indeed powerful, the four PT boats had received such long and hard use that they would have problems on the way, as we shall see. Nevertheless, their effectiveness lay in their attacking power, including the ability to make such high speeds that they could overtake the Japanese cruisers and destroyers and the total of sixteen torpedoes [four each] that they carried. In addition, each carried ten drums of fifty-gallon high-octane gasoline.

Three of the four boats assembled at Corregidor's north dock. Eight persons, including MacArthur and his family, Sutherland, Ray, Huff, and Morehouse were on board the flagship Boat No. 41, with Bulkeley as captain. Boat No. 34 had four persons, Rockwell, Marshall, Stivers, and McMicking, together with Lieutenant Robert B. Kelly as captain. Boat No. 35 also had four persons, Willoughby, Diller, Wilson, and Rogers, together with Ensign A. B. Akers as captain. The remaining members, Akin, Casey, Marquat, George, and Sherr, together with V. E. Schumacher as captain, boarded Boat No. 32 at Mariveles in the south of the Bataan Peninsula. Departing at roughly the same time, the four boats came together a little way out to sea.

Bulkeley, who acted as leader of the entire group, later described the first night of the evacuation as follows:

> We've got to get through the mine fields. And we got through our own mine fields, no problem. I knew them like the back of my hand, but we also probably had Japanese floating mines to contend with to block us in and we had to go through the business there of very quietly at the same time slowly and at the same time seeing or spotting those mines and fending them off so, we'd not hit them. This we did. We're in column formation. One boat right after the other. I headed south to the Lubang Island there where in order to go around they make an inrun [sic; end run] around the Japanese blockade and ships there, which we did, and we may have been detected, I'm not sure about that, but fires were lighted on the island there which may have been a signal to indicate [to] the blockading ships that we were, had been sighted, the break-out was occurring. There we cranked on high speed, rough seas the whole way which was a real, a real factor for us there in making a safe passage there and we went at 33 knots the entire way down.[32]

MacArthur's observation was somewhat different: "On the run to Cabra Island, many white lights were sighted—the enemy's signal that a break was being attempted through the blockade. The noise of our engines had been heard, but the sound of a PT engine is hard to differentiate from that of a bomber, and they evidently mistook it."[33] In any case, the diamond formation of the boats was broken and each moved in a different direction.

MacArthur's account of what followed indicated even more heightened tension:

> The sea rose and it began to get rough. Spiteful waves slapped and snapped at the thin skin of the little boats; visibility was becoming poorer.
>
> As we began closing on the Japanese blockading fleet, the suspense grew tense. Suddenly, there they were, sinister outlines against the curiously peaceful formations of lazily drifting cloud. We waited, hardly breathing, for the first burst of shell that would summon us to identify ourselves. Ten seconds. Twenty. A full minute. No gun spoke; the PTs rode so low in the choppy seas that they had not spotted us.

Bulkeley changed at once to a course that brought us to the west and north of the enemy craft, and we slid by in the darkness. Again and again, this was to be repeated during the night, but our luck held.[34]

As for the other PT boats, Diller wrote that No. 35 quickly encountered problems: "We were guided through the mine field and out into the open.... I was reminded of the Kentucky Derby, 'there [*sic*] off' and win, lose or draw here we were, we were on our way, we went out into the China Sea. And there was some difficulty with gasoline, gas was not filtering properly, so we all got separated. We were planning to sail in a diamond formation but we got separated."[35]

Rogers, who was in Boat No. 35, wrote of being separated from the others after a smooth night:

> We crossed from Corregidor to an isolated inlet on Bataan where we boarded three Navy torpedo boats. The fourth boat had left earlier in the day. As it began to grow dark, the engines were warmed up and we roared across Manila Bay, past Corregidor and the other fortified islands out into the night. I sat aft on the deck and watched the other boats as we raced over the sea in echelon. The first night's ride was relatively smooth; even then the boat raised quite a spray and I was soaked through to the skin as I stood on deck. Early in the morning the boats were separated and daylight found our boat some fifty miles from the appointed rendezvous. We cruised along until about nine o'clock and finally anchored off a small island.[36]

Casey described the confusion on board Boat No. 32: "We proceeded through the night, with blackout because the Japanese controlled all the intervening waters. Our boat, which was the last, during the night conked out with motor trouble. We fixed it up. Having lost distance, we restarted with maximum speed. Again, the motors failed, but finally we got them going."[37]

By late into their first night, the boats had lost their diamond formation and each boat was heading separately for Tagauayan, where they expected to regroup.

Huff felt anxious about the problems on MacArthur's boat:

> After we passed the Apo Islands the spray wet the magnetos on our engines and we had to stop to dry them off. Similar troubles beset the other boats, and in the darkness we could not keep in contact. It seemed many hours to me before the eastern sky began to show light, and when the sun came up we were a sorry-looking crew. But that wasn't the half of it. The island we were supposed to reach at dawn, which was around

seven o'clock, was nowhere in sight. In fact there was nothing in sight—no friendly boats and, fortunately, no unfriendly boats or airplanes.[38]

MacArthur, too, wrote of his stress during this incident:

> The weather deteriorated steadily, and towering waves buffeted our tiny, war-weary, blacked-out vessels. The flying spray drove against our skin like stinging pellets of birdshot. We would fall off into a trough, then climb up the near slope of a steep water peak, only to slide down the other side. The boat would toss crazily back and forth, seeming to hang free in space as though about to breach, and then would break away and go forward with a rush. I recall describing the experience afterward as what it must be like to take a trip in a concrete mixer. The four PTs could no longer keep formation, and by 3:00 a.m. the convoy had scattered. Bulkeley tried for several hours to collect the others, but without success. Now each skipper was on his own, his rendezvous just off the uninhabited Cuyo Islands.[39]

How did MacArthur's family fare on the trip? According to Huff, "Arthur and Ah Cheu, his Chinese amah, were seasick again almost as soon as we set out, and Jean was nervous. Spray began flying over the boat and some of it drifted down into the cockpit where she and the General had again seated themselves on the mattress on the deck."[40] As the boat lurched, Ah Cheu and Arthur became violently ill, so Jean moved them to the bottom of the boat, where there were two little rooms. Jean later described the situation: "The noise was terrific on those boats. . . . I stayed with the General. I never left the General. We sat in the bow, and the General sat in one chair and I sat in another chair—facing each other. . . . They [the PT boats] couldn't have any communication with each other. Because the Japanese would have picked it up. It had to be dead silence. . . . I don't remember eating a mouthful on that boat."[41] Jean had a light gown and dress, a coat over the dress, little straw shoes that were popular at the time, and some bedroom slippers.

Despite damage, the fourth boat, No. 32, with Akin and Casey on board advanced toward the rendezvous point. Casey recounted:

> Then early the next day, just as dawn was breaking, we were approaching a little spit of land and our commander looked back and through his scope saw this vessel approaching us. He shouted, "A Japanese destroyer is headed down on us." . . . "Shall we oppose?" . . . "We certainly will." So he [Akin] got out a knife and personally cut the lashings that held the drums of gasoline on the deck. We needed this extra fuel to get to where

we were going. He dumped those overboard; the crew manned our
machine guns, got our torpedoes ready to function; and he kept observing with his glasses this approaching boat. Suddenly he said, "That's not
a Japanese destroyer. That's one of our boats." Well, it happened to be
the boat with General MacArthur and his family on it, and we were getting ready to sink them to the bottom of the drink.[42]

The episode on Casey's boat suggests that MacArthur was an unusually lucky
man. His boat speedily dodged the drums of gasoline dumped by Boat No. 32 and
came up alongside. After MacArthur and Casey had a short talk, Casey moved to
MacArthur's boat and continued to the destination. When they reached Tagauayan finally, they found that No. 34, with Marshall on board, had already arrived,
but No. 35, carrying Willoughby and others, was missing. The three boats waited
for No. 35, camouflaged to avoid discovery by the enemy. At the same time, they
awaited the arrival of a submarine that could, if necessary, take MacArthur and
his family to Australia.[43]

From Tagauayan to Mindanao

Huff described the stay on Tagauayan Island on March 12, 1942, as follows:

Bulkeley wouldn't let anyone but a lookout go ashore on the island—
which was deserted, except for a lean and hungry dog—because if we
were spotted by an enemy plane, our boats would have to make a run
for it, abandoning the lookout. We gave No. 32 a little of our gasoline,
refueled and then had hot cakes for breakfast. They tasted wonderful!
But after sitting around on the deck for a while, the General began to
get restless. He was fearful that we would fail to make connections with
the other boats if we waited too long and that the whole trip might be
jeopardized. "What would you think of trying to go on to the rendezvous island by daylight?" he asked Capt. Jimmy Ray, chief of staff for the
16th Naval District, who was on our boat.

Neither Ray nor Bulkeley nor anyone else could do more than point
out that there was always a chance of running into enemy ships and
that, because our engines were faulty, we might not be able to outrun
them. On the other hand, if we remained in the cove, we might be seen
by an enemy plane and, in any event, we were going to disrupt our
schedule.

Finally, MacArthur consulted with Bulkeley, who was willing to
take a chance and said, "Well, let's go."...We waited there for darkness,

arousing fear that it [No. 35] was lost with Brig. Gen. Charles Willoughby, Lt. Col. L. A. Diller and others aboard.[44]

MacArthur and Rockwell discussed switching to the submarine, and MacArthur
asked for Casey's advice on whether to proceed by submarine or to continue
further in the same boat. Casey was surprised at MacArthur's question, because
he was a man of decision, and he usually never asked anyone for suggestions or
advice. Casey urged him to continue on, and MacArthur agreed.[45] It was decided
that Boat No. 32, which had discarded its fuel, would remain at Tagauayan until
the submarine arrived from Australia. (It arrived there later and the Navy crew
got safely to Australia.) When Rockwell expressed his conviction that the seas
would be calmer, Bulkeley disagreed. Bulkeley proved correct. Late in the afternoon (Manchester gives the time as 2:30 p.m., but other accounts differ) but
before dark, boats No. 34 and 41 set off. The crew originally assigned to No. 32,
namely Akin, Casey, Marquat, George, and Sherr, were divided between Nos. 34
and 41. No. 34, with Rockwell and Marshall on board, took the lead, with MacArthur following on No. 41. Bulkeley decided on this order out of consideration
for MacArthur's safety. Big waves washed over the boat, drenching the crew. But
Jean and MacArthur sat in the chairs on deck all night. Jean recalled: "I never
undressed, I don't remember ever taking my clothes off. I don't remember anything about any of that. I don't remember even getting my teeth brushed or
anything....We could see a Japanese cruiser shelling the southern islands of the
Philippines. We saw them....I can remember lying there and looking up at the
stars....I thought we're going to be hit."[46]

Soon after departure, they came across a Japanese ship. This was a hazardous
moment. MacArthur recalled: "I gave the order to move out southward into
the Mindanao Sea for Cagayan, on the northern coast [of Mindanao]....The
night was clear, the sea rough and high....Once more, huge and hostile, a
Japanese warship loomed dead ahead through the dark. We were too near
to run, too late to dodge. Instantly we cut engines, cleared for action—and
waited. Seconds ticked into minutes, but no signal flashed from the battleship
as she steamed slowly westward across our path. If we had been seen at all, we
had been mistaken for part of the native fishing fleet. Our road to safety was
open."[47]

Huff's description was, however, different from MacArthur's:

> He [Bulkeley] knew she was a Japanese cruiser, traveling at an angle that
> would intercept us. It was still daylight, but there was at least a chance
> that the enemy had not sighted us. Bulkeley made a sharp turn and
> put on full speed in order to change our course and avoid getting any
> closer to the cruiser. They never did sight us, but for the next fifteen or

twenty minutes, until the sun went down with tropic suddenness, we
were plenty nervous. Or at least I was. The General was lying back on
the mattress and didn't say anything, although both he and Jean heard
the crew's conversation and knew what was up.[48]

Casey's recollection was different again: "[We] proceeded that afternoon before
dusk instead of waiting for the darkness of night. Shortly before dark we looked
ahead and here was a Japanese cruiser, this time a real cruiser, headed east as we
were headed south. We swerved over to the west, hoping we would not be recognized; maybe they would figure we were two Philippine fishing boats. In any case,
the cruiser proceeded on and its commander missed a wonderful opportunity to
capture General MacArthur and his staff."[49] According to Bulkeley's testimony,
the Japanese cruiser traveled north until about six miles ahead, and then suddenly changed its direction to the south.

Each of these accounts differs from the others. MacArthur described the
enemy ship as a warship, while Huff and Casey called it a cruiser. In describing the group's response, MacArthur emphasized: "We cut engines, cleared for
action—and waited." In contrast, while one stated that the boats headed west and
the other south, both Huff and Casey wrote that they fled immediately. Moreover, while all accounts agree that the situation was extremely difficult, it cannot
be denied that MacArthur overstated the dangers. Still, we can confidently say
that the group's survival in the face of such a threat offers further evidence that
MacArthur attracted good luck.

Bulkeley noted that Jean's attitude deserved the highest praise: "Mrs.
MacArthur was one of the bravest women I've ever come across....She came up
out of the cockpit where she had been with General MacArthur, took one look
at it [the Japanese cruiser], never showed the slightest sign of panic or fear. I
felt that it could have been the death of all of us at that time if they had sighted
us."[50] Probably referring to the situation after the tension had been relieved,
Jean recalled:

> We went all that night....They put a mattress and the General was
> lying on the mattress and I was lying on the mattress. Ah Cheu and
> Arthur still in the bunk down below, still sea sick. Somebody brought
> me up—one of the enlisted men, I suppose—one of the naval—a little
> thermos bottle full of hot chocolate or hot cocoa. And I turned it—the
> thing was so rough that it fell over all on top of me and all on top
> of the little mattress we were on. I had a flashlight and I started with-
> out realizing—I almost turned the flashlight—and Bulkeley yelled at
> me....The one dress that I had was soaked. That left me with just
> one dress.[51]

Huff wrote that he was awakened by a voice saying, "Sid." MacArthur couldn't sleep and wanted to talk. Jean seemed to be asleep. He described the scene:

> That began a couple of the strangest hours of my life up on deck.... What had happened, I soon realized, was that he had had time to think back over our defeat in the Philippines and he was now trying to analyze it and get it all straight in his mind.... He talked about the program he had drawn up for preparing the Philippines to defend themselves by 1946.... He remembered his differences with Washington.... It was two o'clock in the morning when he stopped thinking out loud. Then he added, "Sid, if we ever get to Australia, the first thing I'm going to do is to make you and Diller full colonels. Good night."[52]

Huff became a full colonel on MacArthur's first day at his office in Australia. Having survived a major threat and moving one stage closer to his final destination, MacArthur was too animated to sleep.

Before daybreak on Friday, March 13, the two boats changed direction, turning eastward in the Sulu Sea and entering the Mindanao Sea. By sunrise they were already behind schedule. They needed to arrive at the north side of Mindanao Island before dark. At 6:30 a.m. they came close to Mindanao Island, near a Del Monte pineapple plantation. Immediately afterward, one of the lookout crew on Boat No. 34 confirmed lights on Cagayan Point. As the harbor came into view, the crew watched intently for Japanese warships, but no ship was flying a Japanese flag. At 7:00 a.m., after thirty-five hours of sailing, Boat No. 41, with Bulkeley at the helm, took the lead in entering the waterway and dropping anchor at the pier. Boat No. 34 followed. Seventeen of the original twenty-one members had thus safely completed 560 long miles of travel. Bulkeley and his crew on Boat No. 41 had accomplished their goal of evacuating MacArthur.

At the pier, Brigadier General William F. Sharp, commander of the southern district, was waiting with an infantry unit. MacArthur called together the officers and enlisted men from both PT boats and spoke to them with emotion: "It was done in true naval style. It gives me great pleasure and honor to award the boats' crews the Silver Star for gallantry for fortitude in the face of heavy odds."[53] Bulkeley recalled that MacArthur said to him: "You have taken me out of the jaws of death and I shall not forget it."[54] MacArthur also used the phrase, "I shall return," which would later become one of his most memorable expressions; Bulkeley found his words short and sweet. Shaking hands with Bulkeley, MacArthur said in a small voice: "You'll take your orders from General Sharpe [*sic*] here and conduct a defensive warfare against the empire of Japan, against all, in all waters north of Mindanao."[55] Impressed by the honor, Bulkeley later observed: "As a little bit of an aside here, that made me commander-in-chief of the Pacific at that time with four boats left."

And what was the fate of Boat No. 35, which had gone missing with Willoughby, Diller, Wilson, and Rogers on board? Rogers described their survival:

> About three in the afternoon a two-masted sailing vessel was sighted running a course that would bring her across our stern. Glasses were broken out and the boys tried to make out the Japanese ensign. They have a very appropriate name for it. Not being able to make out any colors we got under way, prepared our guns for action and swung out around the ship.... [The] boat turned out to be a fishing vessel. One of the natives raised both hands while another ran below and came back with small American and Filipino flags which he waved in the air.... About six p.m. we took off for the rendezvous to meet the other boats.... My intention was to stay dry, but we ran into heavy seas, water started leaking down into my bunk from the decks which were continually running water, and, as a climax, boat's bouncing me up and down on my bunk caused it to break down.... By that time it was nearly morning and I went up topside and stayed there. We cruised into our destination something around noon after slowly following the coastline for five hours, anxiously watching for any enemy aircraft. Anyhow, none came along and the trip ended with everyone happy.[56]

All twenty-one members of the evacuation group thus successfully reached Mindanao from Corregidor.

From Mindanao to Australia

While MacArthur was making his desperate escape, Washington and Australia watched the course of events. On February 26, 1942, Chief of Staff George C. Marshall had already informed George H. Brett, commander of the United States Army Forces in Australia (USAFIA) based in Melbourne, that MacArthur's arrival in Mindanao would probably be around March 15. Marshall ordered Brett to dispatch three long-range bombers to Mindanao. Two days later, Brett responded to Marshall that he understood the secret mission. On March 6, Marshall notified MacArthur that Brett was waiting for his arrival in Australia. On March 10, one day before MacArthur's departure from Mindanao, Marshall sent, with Roosevelt's permission, the following directives to Brett: first, MacArthur was expected to land in Australia on March 17, but until that time Brett was to keep the matter strictly secret; second, within one hour of MacArthur's arrival Brett was to call upon the Australian prime minister or some other high-level official to report that the general had come on the president's orders and was assuming command of all U.S. Army forces in Australia; third, Brett should propose that the Australian government nominate MacArthur as supreme commander of the Southwest Pacific Area and recommend that the nomination be submitted simultaneously to London and Washington; and, fourth, Brett should arrange to turn command of U.S. Army forces in Australia over to MacArthur as soon as practicable after his landing, and should report to MacArthur as his deputy in command of the air forces. On March 12, Brett responded that all preliminary arrangements had been completed.[57]

However, when MacArthur arrived at Mindanao, he found that preparations were still incomplete. Sharp told him that, although four bombers had been sent from Australia for his arrival on Mindanao, two did not arrive and another had crashed into the bay. The remaining bomber had arrived safely but, because it was old and in bad condition, it had returned to Australia before MacArthur's party had arrived. MacArthur was enraged. At 11:25 p.m. on March 13, he telegrammed General Marshall that the group had arrived at Mindanao and at the same time criticized Brett:

> I have made hazardous trip successfully by naval motor torpedo boat to Del Monte Mindanao. In order to expedite movement I did not await submarine. Upon arrival discovered that Brett had sent four old B RPT B-seventeens of which only one arrived and that not repeat not fit to carry passengers due to inoperative supercharger. Failure of three planes to arrive not repeat not due to enemy action. The other plane took off for return trip before my arrival. Am informing Brett but request you inform him of group to be transported and order him to dispatch suitable planes if on hand, otherwise that you make such planes available to him. Am accompanied by my wife and child and fourteen officers, Admiral Rockwell and his chief of staff. The best three planes in the United States or Hawaii should be made available with completely adequate and experienced crews. To attempt such a desperate and important trip with inadequate equipment would amount to consigning the whole party to death and I could not accept such a responsibility. Am in constant communication with Corregidor and request reply to that station in usual manner. I am continuing to function in command of all forces in Philippines. My presence in Del Monte should be kept completely secret and every means taken to create belief that I am still in Luzon. Pursuant your order I did not inform Brett of mission and it would appear that he was ignorant of importance unquote.[58]

MacArthur thus criticized Brett as "ignorant" of the importance of the evacuation. Noting MacArthur's anger, Casey commented: "MacArthur felt that Brett
was operating more on sort of a peacetime administrative basis rather than, say,
under the wartime atmosphere that prevailed under combat conditions up in the
Philippines."[59] Casey concluded that the nondelivery of the bombers impacted
badly on the later relationship between MacArthur and Brett. Although relieved
to learn of MacArthur's safe arrival at Mindanao, Marshall was presumably disturbed that the planes were not ready. On the following day, March 14, Marshall
directed Brett to send three of his best B-17s immediately to Mindanao, and to
give this mission precedence over any other.[60] But Brett had difficulty making
secret arrangements with the Australian side and took his time.

What was the situation of MacArthur's group in Mindanao? After arriving at
Cagayan on March 13, they advanced under Sharp's guidance to Del Monte, five
miles away, and had breakfast at the clubhouse. Huff later recalled the wonderful
fresh pineapples, the first fresh fruit available since Manila, and said he ate three.
Jean, who had barely eaten on the PT boat, claimed that she would remember the
pineapple as long as she lived. Nevertheless, Cagayan, where they were staying,
was not safe. Rogers wrote: "We were apprehensive as to what would happen if
news of the General's being there leaked out. The Japanese could have scored a
major victory by wiping out that party of seventeen; it included some of the best
men in the allied armies."[61] In fact, the group saw Japanese aircraft flying over
them many times.

While Jean, Arthur, and Ah Cheu were resting in a small house, a Filipino sergeant acting under Sharp's orders led them to a dirty underground tunnel. The
three had to crawl on their knees through the dirt. Although it was an air raid
shelter, Jean never wanted to go there again. She told Sharp that they would stay
in the house under any circumstances and Sharp assented. Suddenly, a Filipino
woman appeared and asked to speak to Jean. She had had walked twenty-five
miles to ask for news of her son, who was fighting on Bataan. Jean, of course,
could not tell her anything, but the presence of the woman indicated that word
of MacArthur's supposedly secret stay on the island had already been leaked.
Suspecting that she might be a spy, Sharp held the woman at Del Monte until
MacArthur's departure, but Jean learned later from Willoughby that there had
been no problem.[62]

Three days later, on March 16, MacArthur received a message that the three
bombers would come not from Darwin as originally planned but from Batchelor
Field further south. Jean heard MacArthur saying that the pilots did not know
the Del Monte airstrip. In fact, one of the planes, flown by Major Richard H.
Carmichael, failed to make the landing on the short runway, and was forced to
turn back. The dangerous landing required great courage. When the other two

planes approached, it was necessary to guide them down through the darkness using car headlights. Both planes managed to land at around 8:00 p.m. The group hurried to leave that same night. Jean described the situation: "We got in a car and went down to the runway. There were only two planes—so what we had had to be gotten rid of. I had one little suitcase and I had my nightgown in it. I didn't have a pocketbook—I didn't have anything. And then we got there—got down to the field."[63] Jean recalled a young lieutenant standing at the steps of the plane they were to board. MacArthur put his hand on the young man's shoulder and said something. The boy replied that he would do his best to get him through. After helping to balance the overloaded aircraft, MacArthur sat right behind the pilot, so that he would be protected in case of a crash. Again, Jean recalled: "We took off after midnight and it was a big moonlight night....Arthur and Ah Cheu and I were lying on a mattress on the floor. There was one sort of a seat or chair there. So that was where the General sat."

MacArthur gave a vivid description of the four-hour flight to Australia:

> We would be flying over enemy-held territory, relying on darkness to help us evade Japanese patrols. Over Timor, we were spotted and they came up after us. But we changed course from Darwin, where they figured we would land, and came in at Batchelor Field, 40 miles to the south, just as they hit the Darwin field...."It was close," I remarked to Dick Sutherland when we landed, "but that's the way it is in war. You win or lose, live or die—and the difference is just an eyelash."[64]

Jean remembered that as they landed at Batchelor Field, she could see no hangars, just some tents scattered around. After everyone got off the plane, the crew members were decorated; MacArthur spoke to each in turn. Jean remembered: "I went over and I can remember talking to that young lieutenant and he looked about ten years older than he had the night before. But I thanked him for getting us through and they were all promoted immediately."[65]

Batchelor Field was not secure, however. Word had been received that twenty-five Japanese bombers were headed there. MacArthur's group hurried aboard the DC-3 aircraft prepared by Brett and flew about one thousand miles to Alice Springs in central Australia. They stepped out into a blast of stiflingly hot, dry air in a big airfield that conjured up images from a Western movie set. Pushed beyond endurance by the terrible shaking of the aircraft, Jean refused to board a plane for the final stage of the trip to Adelaide in South Australia and insisted on taking a train. But the weekly passenger train had left the previous day. Brett, who had already organized travel by air, had to make arrangements for a special train to take the group to Adelaide the following day. They stayed overnight at an old, rickety, and primitive hotel, bothered day and night by swarms of flies.

Brigadier General Patrick J. Hurley, who had served as U.S. ambassador to New Zealand, arrived in a chartered plane to take MacArthur's group to Melbourne. Jean, however, turned down the offer, so the MacArthur family, Sutherland, Huff, and Morehouse remained in Alice Springs while the others flew to Melbourne in Hurley's plane. Around noon on March 18, MacArthur and those who had remained with him boarded a train consisting of two wooden coaches pulled by a small locomotive and headed for Adelaide, located a thousand miles to the south across the desert. Huff described the trip as follows: "It was near the end of the Australian summer,... There was nothing we could do but sit and look out the windows, and it gave us a chance to relax and get some rest."[66] According to Huff, Jean knew this train trip would be best for MacArthur. It was the first time he had really slept since Pearl Harbor. ⁻

Meanwhile, a grand ceremony was being prepared to mark MacArthur's arrival in Australia. The plan had been initiated by Washington to make sure that MacArthur's withdrawal from Corregidor was not regarded as a "loser's flight," since such a perception might be used to reinforce Axis propaganda. It was thus necessary to present MacArthur as a general in triumph. It was hoped that this would heighten morale among all troops and, by extension, rouse public enthusiasm in the United States. Needless to say, such staging offered a heaven-sent opportunity for a man of conspicuous self-confidence such as MacArthur.

On March 17, the day MacArthur survived Japanese bombardment to land at Batchelor Field, the War Department made the following announcement: "General MacArthur arrived in Australia by plane today. He was accompanied by Mrs. MacArthur and son, and by his Chief of Staff General Sutherland, General George of the Air Corps and several other staff officers. He will be the Supreme Commander in that region, including the Philippines, in accordance with the request of the Australian Government."[67] On the same day Roosevelt cabled to naval personnel:

> MacArthur and a small staff arrived in Australia by air today. Since Prime Minister of Australia as well as New Zealand had proposed a United States supreme commander in that region, suggesting Brett, I had instructed Brett immediately on MacArthur's arrival to propose the latter officer to Mr. Curtin as Supreme Commander in Australia.... Mr. Curtin enthusiastically accepts MacArthur. They urge immediate joint press release to avoid leak. This I think highly important if Axis propaganda attacking MacArthur's departure from the Philippines is to be forestalled. Therefore I authorized a press release at ten thirty a.m. Washington time announcing MacArthur's appointment as Supreme Commander in that region.[68]

In other words, the political rationale for MacArthur's appointment as supreme commander, as Marshall indicated on March 17, was that it was made in accordance with the Australian government's request and for the purpose of deflecting Axis propaganda regarding MacArthur's evacuation from the Philippines. Marshall directed, further, that announcements of the evacuation should stress that U.S. military headquarters had been "transferred" rather than "withdrawn."[69]

It is clear from the above account that both Roosevelt and Marshall viewed MacArthur's arrival in Australia in political rather than military terms and paid particular attention to mass media strategy. Since MacArthur had also become thoroughly familiar with media tactics even before his appointment as commander, he understood their considerations. On March 20, after a seventy-hour trip that extended over three days, he arrived at Adelaide Station, where a crowd awaited him. Responding to press requests, he commented: "The President of the United States ordered me to break through the Japanese line and proceed from Corregidor to Australia for the purpose, as I understand it, of organizing the American offensive against Japan, a primary object of which is the relief of the Philippines. I came through and I shall return."[70] Although MacArthur uttered the expression, he later claimed: "I spoke casually enough, for the phrase 'shall return' seemed a promise of magic to the Filipinos."[71] It is hard to believe that a man so proficient in media manipulation chose his words casually. The words "I shall return" were to become, as MacArthur later wrote, powerful as magic.

MacArthur took a gorgeous express train, and arrived at Spencer Station in Melbourne at 9:57 the next morning. MacArthur felt satisfied. As the train pulled into Melbourne cheering thousands lined the station in a tumultuous welcome. MacArthur and the Bataan Boys had covered three thousand miles on their eleven-day trip. They had not "run away," but they had relocated successfully.

THE SECOND BATAAN OPERATION AND THE DEATH MARCH, EARLY FEBRUARY TO EARLY MAY 1942

Preparing for Battle

The first Bataan offensive, which started on January 9, 1942, inflicted heavy casualties on the Japanese 65th Brigade and on February 8, Homma Masaharu, commander of the 14th Army, ordered a cease-fire. The Japanese had clearly underestimated the U.S. and Filipino forces. Following the cease-fire, operational conflicts emerged among the 14th Army Headquarters, the Southern Army, and the Imperial General Headquarters.

Within the 14th Army Headquarters there were three competing proposals regarding the next move. The first was to make sufficient preparations for resuming the attack on Bataan, at the same time moving to stabilize the security of Luzon and the south-central area of the Philippines by defeating any remaining enemy there. The second was to barricade enemy troops on Bataan and wait until starvation forced them to surrender. The third was to continue the attack on Bataan. The first proposal had majority support at the 14th Army Headquarters; the second was supported by Maeda Masami, chief of staff of the 14th Army, and a few others; the third had the backing of just one person, Colonel Nakayama Motoo of the operations staff. By the middle of February, Homma had decided to blockade Bataan, as suggested by Maeda. Maeda, who was well informed about the Philippines, concluded that, in addition to the difficulty of launching an assault on the forts around Manila Bay, including Corregidor, the steep hills on the Bataan Peninsula made a sudden attack difficult. His was a rational plan that would avoid a headlong attack, blockade U.S. and Filipino forces, and wait until a deterioration in the enemy's fighting powers forced them to surrender. The plan was based on the estimate that enemy provisions would not last half a year.

In contrast to Army Headquarters, the Southern Army stressed the need to continue a fully committed attack on Bataan, even though the weakened 14th Army would need time to complete the operation. The Southern Army believed that the Bataan operation could not be successfully completed by leaving the main enemy forces intact while attacking the remainder in other areas of the Philippines. Lieutenant Colonel Arao Osakatsu, chief of the operations staff, traveled to Manila to persuade the 14th Army Headquarters to accept and implement the third proposal suggested by Nakayama. The Imperial General Headquarters in Tokyo, however, broadly agreed with the 14th Army Headquarters proposal of resuming the attack after completing adequate preparations. In sum, the 14th Army supported containment; the Southern Army wanted to continue the attack; and the Imperial General Headquarters supported advancing preparations. The three proposals remained separate and consensus was never reached.

On February 20, right before Maeda was to travel to Saigon to explain the Bataan blockade and surveillance plan to obtain agreement of the Southern Army, he was dismissed from his position as chief of staff. Maki Tatsuo, chief of operations staff, and Inagaki Seiji, chief of logistics support, were transferred because they shared Maeda's opinion. The *Kimitsu Senso Nisshi* (Secret War Diary),[1] a record of the daily operations of the Imperial General Headquarters, noted on February 16, 1942, that an inspection of the southern region had revealed a problem with the Bataan operation: the frontline forces had a tendency to emphasize discussion on administrative control over the areas they would occupy after the battle. On February 17, it reported that, three days after his appointment as group leader, Lieutenant Colonel Tsuji Masanobu had flown to the front in high spirits to lead the revival of the Bataan operation. This record shows that the policy direction of the Imperial General Headquarters and the staff changes in Army Headquarters were closely related. In the end, it was the third proposal, that of continuing the Bataan campaign, that took effect. Major General Wachi Takaji, Homma's close acquaintance, was appointed to Maeda's position.[2]

After the initial suspension of the Bataan operation, it was finally decided to resume the attack. Learning from the failure of the first Bataan battle, the Imperial General Headquarters felt keenly the need to strengthen its military power in the Philippines and make other preparations for attack. As a result of discussions with the Southern Army, it reached an informal decision on February 8 to dispatch the 4th Division to the Bataan front. At the same time, artillery and bombing capacity was increased, and plans were made to transport supplies and provisions that the 14th Army would need for the attack on the U.S. and Filipino positions. By this time, Burma and the Philippines were the only southeastern Asian countries that remained outside Japanese control, and both the Imperial General Headquarters and the Southern Army had turned their attention to the Philippines. Although the 14th Army had been assigned only supplementary operations since the outbreak of war, it was finally receiving the military power necessary to become a proper attacking force.

At the beginning of March, the Japanese found in the U.S. barracks in Manila the U.S. Army disposition map of the southern Bataan Peninsula. Judging from the battles already fought, it was clear that the U.S front lines and various facilities were roughly the same as shown on the map, and the map was thus an effective tool for planning the next attack on U.S. and Filipino forces. Meanwhile, the 14th Army realized the cause of failure in the first Bataan battle; they had not been well trained in attacking a fort located in a particular topography. Therefore, after the suspension of operations, the 16th Division and the 65th Brigade carried out specific training to prepare for the next operation. The newly arrived 4th Division and Nagano task force underwent the same type of training, which was monitored by troop commanders and staff officers.[3]

Meanwhile, in Bataan, the U.S. and Filipino force responded to the retreat of Japanese frontline troops by having each unit advance separately. In particular, they worked to strengthen their main camps at the foot of Mt. Smat and in the eastern district and to reorganize weak units. It seemed to the Japanese that, from the middle of February onward, the bombardment had gradually subsided and they felt that the enemy's fighting spirit was fading. On hearing the sound of grain being ground and pounded at night, they captured and interrogated a Filipino scout to learn what was happening. They found out that U.S. and Filipinos forces were restricting food supply to about half the normal ration and the troops were suffering from hunger. Nevertheless, all Filipino prisoners insisted their comrades were not surrendering; those from the Baguio Military Academy especially had a strong spirit of attack. The Japanese struggled to persuade them but, even though Filipino prisoners were shown newspaper articles published in Manila about defections, they refused to believe that the surrender was real, suspecting the articles were propaganda. Moreover, all of them rejected propaganda broadcasts directed at U.S. and Filipino forces. The Japanese deemed that the Philippine military leadership still exercised powerful control over their troops and that they would resist to the end—they would not surrender in response to propaganda. The Japanese concluded, therefore, that they had no alternative but to renew the attack. Furthermore, since malaria, amoebic dysentery, and dengue fever were rampant in the Bataan Peninsula, U.S. and Filipino forces, like the Japanese, had to pay attention to the struggle with disease as well as to the battle against the enemy.[4]

For the U.S and Filipino troops confined to the Bataan Peninsula, the spread of disease was not the only cause of distress. As provisions ran out they began to suffer from starvation. The inflow of military men and refugees into Bataan and the failure to bring in enough supplies were the main problems. With the possible fall of Bataan in mind, MacArthur had ordered food stocks to be sent to Corregidor, making the situation on Bataan even worse. Moreover, following his inspection of Bataan at the beginning of January, MacArthur had remained confined to his Corregidor fortress. The fact that he never visited Bataan thereafter damaged the fighting spirit of the soldiers. Imagining him living comfortably in his underground base at Corregidor, angry soldiers referred to MacArthur as Dugout Doug and ridiculed him in an insulting military song. Worried about the situation, Casey traveled frequently from Corregidor to Bataan and inspected the front lines during his visits. But MacArthur and the other staff officers on Corregidor rarely visited Bataan, which Casey regretted.[5]

MacArthur could not fail to be aware of the derision directed at him. After he received the evacuation order from Roosevelt on February 21, he wrote in his *Reminiscences* that he had tried for three weeks to resist pressure from Washington: "I began seriously to weigh the feasibility of trying to break through from Bataan into the Zambales Mountains, to carry on intensified guerrilla operations against the enemy."[6] However, since the Japanese elite divisions had been withdrawn from Bataan and nearby Philippine islands at this very time, pressure on the U.S. front line suddenly weakened. According to his later recollection, MacArthur radioed to Marshall that they were perhaps moving into a war of attrition, but received a firm response: "Marshall responded with the information that the situation in Australia called for my early arrival."[7] As a result, he began to prepare for departure. U.S. government records show that MacArthur did indeed send a telegram on February 27: "The enemy contour has now been definitely fixed as a semicircular defensive position....Every indication that we are entering upon a phase of positional warfare of indecisive character."[8] Less certain, however, is MacArthur's claim that he was evacuated from Corregidor because of pressure from Washington and the Japanese suspension of hostilities. Whether or not the soldiers on Bataan were persuaded is open to doubt. One cannot avoid the sense that MacArthur was attempting defensive self-justification.

Captain LeGrande A. Diller remarked: "The Japs were too strong for us, we were too far away, so we all felt that the end was going to come. Sid Huff, who was my best friend, and another Aide to the General noticed that the General carried a 32 pistol in his hip pocket and he commented on it and the General said, 'they're never going to take Douglas MacArthur alive.'... I decided that that was probably the best solution."[9]

Early in March, at the same time as he advanced plans for evacuation with his family and the Bataan Boys, MacArthur worked on a contingency plan for the Philippines. He informed Washington that if President Manuel L. Quezon and Vice President Sergio Osmena should be captured by the enemy, Major Manuel A. Roxas, who had been appointed unofficial advisor to the president in the previous month, would be named president. At this point, Roxas was still MacArthur's adjutant and, although the position lacked substance, he was a representative of the Philippine Commonwealth. In other words, MacArthur was thinking of establishing a puppet government headed by Roxas in place of Quezon. Another of MacArthur's schemes was to request that Washington promote Brigadier General Albert M. Jones, commanding officer on Bataan, to major general, and Colonel Lewis C. Beebe, who led the infantry, to brigadier general. The reason was that both men had performed outstanding service in the preceding three months and their promotions would be important in rebuilding the U.S. and Filipino military force. The promotion to lieutenant general of Major General Jonathan M. Wainwright, who took over MacArthur's command in the peninsula, was carried out not in response to a request by MacArthur but was initiated by decision makers in Washington.[10]

U.S. and Filipino forces achieved brilliant results in their military operations against the Japanese. On March 4, MacArthur reported to Washington: "We made a surprise air attack on Olongapo and Subic Bay destroying the following vessels: one of twelve thousand tons one of ten thousand tons one of eight thousand tons and two motor launches."[11] On March 5, he wrote: "In yesterdays highly successful surprise attack at Subic Bay we had no air losses from action. It is believed his dead run into thousands."[12] Regarding Quezon, who had already evacuated from Corregidor, MacArthur's radiogram quoted Quezon's message: "The following message is for President Roosevelt from President Quezon quote have visited some provinces Visayan group. People loyal to the end and morale fine unquote."[13]

Responding on the Japanese side, all units of the 4th Division, for which the 14th Army was waiting expectantly, left Shanghai in late February and arrived at Lingayen Gulf between February 27 and April 3. Preparations for an all-out attack were gradually falling into place. In advance of the campaign, an order was issued on March 6 to blockade the entire Manila Bay area in order to discourage the enemy force, and the navy cooperated in carrying out the command. By the end of March, the blockade was basically accomplished. Investigations carried out by the Japanese military after the offensive revealed that this naval blockade had a serious physical and psychological impact on the U.S. and Filipino force. They were now almost completely cut off from the outside world and from outside supply units, and their provisions declined rapidly.[14] In fortuitous timing,

MacArthur and his group evacuated from Corregidor just as the blockade of Manila Bay was beginning.

MacArthur's departure naturally affected the morale of U.S. and Filipino forces. The Japanese noticed that shelling from the U.S. and Filipino troops had decreased and felt that their fighting spirit was weakening. On March 20 and 21 dozens of soldiers surrendered in the Bagac area. The Japanese did not learn of MacArthur's evacuation until March 18, a week after he had left. The "Jyoho Kiroku Dai 17 Go" [Intelligence Record No. 17], dated March 18, 1942, stated that "General MacArthur, Commander of the U.S. Army Forces in the Far East, escaped to Australia with Chief of Staff Sutherland and was appointed Commander of the U.S. Army Forces in the Western Pacific. Major General Jonathan Wainwright of the U.S. Army Forces in North East Luzon took the place of MacArthur. High Commissioner Sayre fled to the homeland."[15] The *Asahi Shimbun* covered the news of MacArthur's flight on March 19.

By the time the Japanese learned of MacArthur's evacuation, the group had already reached Australia. Even though a commander's retreat reflected a cowardly attitude according to Japanese traditional culture, the 14th Army and the Imperial General Headquarters were responsible for not considering the possibility that MacArthur might retreat by PT boat rather than by submarine. Although MacArthur's brave actions surpassed Japanese expectations, it cannot be denied that Japanese forces had not paid enough attention to the movements of the enemy. Allowing MacArthur to simply slip away had a negative impact on the Japanese war situation. Japan had lost an opportunity for victory.

The Battle Unfolds

Although the 14th Army steadily advanced preparations for a second offensive operation, the Imperial General Headquarters adopted a cautious attitude. According to his later testimony, Hattori Takushiro, chief of the 2nd Department of the Imperial General Headquarters, felt irritated that the Bataan situation had been affected by poor strategy. Concluding that the situation was untenable because the 20th Infantry Regiment was in trouble and the operations schedule had collapsed, he decided on an attack after making adequate preparations such as deploying artillery.[16] Hattori proposed that all members of his unit discuss new offensive measures. His original plan was to restrict the front line of attack to no closer than four kilometers [2.5 miles] from the enemy's position and to focus on bombardment to break through the enemy's line. He dispatched Lieutenant Colonel Imoto Kumao to the front to give instructions in accordance with the plans of the Imperial General Headquarters. The 14th Army struggled to get the naval air unit to cooperate. On March 23, the commanding officers of each unit assembled at San Fernando, and Commander Homma offered words of inspiration: "The fate of the entire war depends on success in this battle. I expect great efforts by all officers and soldiers.... The enemy commander has retreated from Corregidor and the morale of the enemy soldiers has collapsed."[17] On March 29, the 14th Army set April 3 as the date for the attack, and the command station was transferred from Fernando to Orani at the base of Bataan Peninsula. Preparations for the offensive were complete.

The operation began on the morning of April 3 with an artillery bombardment. The line of battle, powerful by Japanese military standards, consisted of three regiments, each equipped with ten 240mm [about 9.5 inch] howitzers, ten 155mm [6.1 inch] cannons, and other heavy artillery. In addition to the artillery bombardment, the 22nd Flying Squadron conducted air raids across the area. Because the air power of the U.S. and Filipino force had already been largely destroyed, Japanese air squadrons could reinforce the ground operations at will. With air and ground forces consolidated in this second Bataan operation, the 14th Army overpowered U.S. and Filipino troops on the northwestern foot of Mt. Samat. Taking advantage of this success, the Japanese decided to change their schedule and break through the enemy position all at once. The 65th Brigade and the 4th Division continued their attack.[18]

One of the Japanese soldiers who had arrived from China in the middle of March testified as follows:

> Immediately after the Japanese side was badly hit in the first Bataan battle, we arrived as reinforcements at the front.... They had dug trenches and were all sheltering there, unable either to advance or retreat. We arrived as reinforcements to find them in this situation. The commanding officer welcomed the battle-tested subordinates, all of us veterans of the war in China. He looked at our faces and, tears flowing, spoke words of welcome: "Ah, I can sleep soundly from tonight." From then on, we began preparations for the second Bataan offensive.... Because daytime movements would make us enemy targets and we wanted to keep our planning secret, we marched only during the night. The 4th Platoon of the 1st Company in the 1st Battalion continued its night marches as usual, but their movements were hurried...and we felt something strange and different in the mood. Since we were proceeding in pitch darkness, we each attached a white cloth to our backpacks, using the cloth to gain an indication of the way forward. For some reason or another, the 4th Section got separated from the main platoon. Later, they realized that this was the first day of the second Bataan offensive.[19]

A journalist who was accompanying the troops reported:

> On April 3, the anniversary of the accession of Emperor Jimmu [the first
> emperor, before Christ], with preparations complete, a full attack began
> at two in the afternoon.... [I] arrived at Kitano tactical command posi-
> tion, near Mt. Natib around noon.... First, at two in the afternoon, some
> tens of Arawashi aircraft roared in turn at high speed into the airspace
> above the enemy's position and repeatedly bombed enemy targets. As
> though in response, hundreds of our heavy artillery that were cover-
> ing positions throughout the jungle could be heard opening fire all at
> once and the enemy's reinforced camp was completely bombarded. For
> a while, the whole area was enveloped in smoke, but to this horror, so
> great that even the mountains of Bataan changed, the enemy was com-
> pletely silent. At this point, a signal bomb blasted with a roar high into
> the azure sky. The infantry at the front, which had been waiting to know
> whether to move forward now or later, rose at once and swept forward,
> aiming for the enemy's camp. The tank corps trampled over the enemy's
> positions while the roar of engines resounded all over.[20]

Well prepared for this battle, the Japanese army had become a greater threat.
Casey recalled: "We knew that they were excellent at it [jungle fighting]. We sort
of felt that with their experience in China and having been a fighting machine,
having been well trained and equipped, we expected that they would be."[21] Bulkeley's comment was similar: "The Japanese navy having an experience in China
for five years would overwhelm anything we had. We could not fight a naval sea
battle at that time and win."[22]

U.S. and Filipino forces were driven back. They resisted actively on the first day
of the Japanese attack, but their positions were taken over by the Japanese one by
one. Washington, however, ordered Wainwright to resist resolutely. On March 24,
Marshall repeated the president's order and attempted to energize Wainwright:
"This protracted resistance eclipses in importance any other obligation we now
have in the Philippines.... Gradually a world wide line of opposition has been
cemented to oppose those nations that are now attempting to destroy the liberty and freedom of governments and individuals."[23] Wainwright responded on
March 26: "While fully realizing the desperate conditions that are fast developing
here because of shortage of supplies due to the effectiveness of the hostile blockade, I pledge myself to you to keep our flag flying in the Philippines as long as an
American soldier or an ounce of food and a round of ammunition remains."[24]

Nevertheless, the Japanese attacks would not allow U.S. and Filipino forces to
effectively resist. On April 4, the day after the Japanese attack, MacArthur sent
a coded radiogram to Wainwright, ordering that under no condition should

the command be surrendered. On April 5, Wainwright had to return to Bataan to make a firsthand assessment of the situation with Major General Edward P. King Jr. and Major General George M. Parker Jr., who were commanding the frontline forces. On April 7, Wainwright and Brigadier General Lewis C. Beebe, deputy chief of staff, discussed the desperate situation with Brigadier General Arnold J. Funk. Finally, on April 8, a series of important messages regarding Bataan unfolded. In a radiogram sent to Marshall, Wainwright reported on the situation: "Our troops have been subsisted [*sic*] on 1/2 to 1/3 rations for so long a period that they do not possess the physical strength to endure the strain placed upon the individual in an attack....The enemy increased his strength in the pocket, continued the attack, and placed heavy artillery fire on our position....As days passed our troops began getting weaker from their continued exertions."[25] On the same day, MacArthur, too, communicated with Marshall, advising him that the situation was critical: "It is apparent to me that the enemy has driven a wedge between the I Corps and the II Corps and is still advancing. In view of my intimate knowledge of the situation there, I regard the situation as extremely critical and feel you should anticipate the possibility of disaster there very shortly."[26] MacArthur was writing as though he were still directing operations on Bataan.

Again, on April 8, Eisenhower wrote a memorandum to Marshall:

1. There are now 7,500 tons of food at Cebu. Three (3) submarines have gone into Corregidor and another is due tomorrow. One additional submarine is believed to be enroute from Australia. The Commander-in-Chief of the United States Fleet has directed the release of submarines for ferrying food from Cebu to Luzon.

2. One food ship has left Hawaii April 3 and a submarine loaded with medicine left Hawaii April 7....

3. The latest report from General MacArthur shows only seven (7) heavy bombers are in commission...Nine additional bombers are being flown to Australia.[27]

Although Eisenhower's report indicated that Philippine relief actions were ready, everything was too late.

Finally, on April 8, Deputy Chief of Staff Joseph T. McNarney examined the reports from Wainwright and MacArthur, and submitted his own proposal to Marshall: "It is obvious that the situation on Bataan has deteriorated to a marked degree....Please note particularly General MacArthur's estimate and conclusions."[28] He pointed out that the President's instructions, issued in the form of a dispatch to General MacArthur on February 9, needed to be modified, saying: "It is possible that in the literal execution of these orders General Wainwright may be tempted to carry them through to an illogical extreme.... [It] is possible that greater latitude in final decision should be allowed him."[29]

On the basis of these communications, Marshall and McNarney prepared a message to be sent from the president to Wainwright that in effect allowed him to surrender:

> I have read your message number 734 of April 8 and I am keenly aware of the tremendous difficulties under which you are waging your great battle. The physical exhaustion of your troops obviously precludes the possibility of a major counter stroke unless our efforts to rush food to you should quickly prove successful....I am modifying my orders to you as contained in my telegram to General MacArthur dated February 9 and repeated to you on March 23. My purpose is to leave to your best judgment any decision affecting the future of the Bataan garrison. I have nothing but admiration for your soldierly conduct and your performance of your most difficult mission and have every confidence that whatever decision you may sooner or later be forced to make will be dictated only by the best interests of the country and of your magnificent troops.[30]

Stimson, too, acknowledged that Wainwright would be forced to surrender and wrote an encouraging message: "In this critical hour I have nothing but praise and admiration for the conduct of yourself and your troops in a desperate situation."[31]

On April 5, the *Kimitsu Senso Nisshi* described the Japanese Army's successful advance: "At three in the afternoon of April 3, the advance began. Breaking through the enemy front line, the troops were successful beyond expectation owing to our confidence that thorough preparation and the air force reinforcements would bring victory."[32] On April 9, the 4th Division started from the Lamao River at seven in the morning, and at around one in the afternoon the tank troop burst into Mariveles. The main force continued their advance, reaching the northeastern area of Mariveles around five o'clock. The 16th Division, including the Nagano task force, also set out from the river at seven in the morning, and pursued U.S. and Filipino troops who were retreating along the roads to Lamao, Cabcaben, and Mariveles. The leaders of this group reached Mariveles by midnight. At six in the morning of April 9, as the Nagano task force pursued the enemy en route to Cabcaben, a military messenger carrying a white flag arrived and conveyed the message to the troop's leader that Major General King, commander of the garrison force in Bataan, was ready to surrender. The troop leader ordered King to surrender in person. After requesting that the 14th Army send a staff officer, he continued his advance to Cabcaben. On the way, at about eleven o'clock, he came across King, accompanied by his staff officers. At this point, Nakayama arrived and demanded the unconditional surrender of the entire U.S. and Filipino force. But King refused on the grounds that areas outside Bataan Peninsula were out of his control. With the surrender of King and his staff officers, the U.S. and Filipino force lost a key commander and systematic resistance came to an end. From this day on, soldiers and officers came in one by one, amid the disorder and confusion, to surrender.

One Japanese soldier remembered the military situation as follows: "Advancing into the Bataan mountains, we found the march easy because of the effort of the engineering corps in building a road through dense forest from the west to the east coast. The roar of the artillery sounded closer. The second Bataan offensive was different from the first in that the positions at Samat were destroyed by daily air raids and bombardments. Enemy soldiers and officers came to surrender one after another."[33]

The Japanese army never expected officers to surrender.

> The commanders were pleased and surprised. They had assumed that the U.S. and Filipino force would link with the Corregidor fortress in the surrounding positions around Mariveles to make a strenuous counterattack. It was thought that this territory would necessitate a difficult field attack as experienced in Lushun. Preparations for such an attack would surely require considerable time and a large stock of munitions. Since the supply route from Cabcaben to Mariveles was open to view from Corregidor, it was difficult to work out a way of attacking effectively. Moreover, it was necessary to work out a strategy for attacking U.S. and Filipino forces on the west coast that had incurred no bombing damage. Since security on Luzon Island had gradually worsened, there was no possibility of an easy battle. Under these difficult circumstances, the surrender of King and the troops' surrender was a stroke of luck for the Japanese army.[34]

Thus did the second Bataan offensive come to an end. On April 9, Wainwright reported: "The Japanese attack on Bataan peninsula succeeded in enveloping the east flank of our lines, in the position held by the II Corps. An attack by the I Corps, ordered to relieve the situation, failed due to complete physical exhaustion of the troops. Full details are not available, but this situation indicates the probability that the defenses on Bataan have been overcome."[35] Washington confirmed the report. On the same day McNarney communicated the content of Wainwright's message to Marshall:

> General hostilities Bataan ceased when white flag passed through front lines. General King required to confer with Japanese general at ten on

morning April nine. At seven night of ninth he had not returned nor were results of discussion known. Japanese now in southern Bataan with guns implaced to fire on Corregidor. Wainwright cannot reply to fire because of presence of his troops. Renewed air attack on Corregidor. Heavy bombing with no serious results.[36]

On the same day, McNarney sent a message of encouragement to Wainwright: "The president again expressed his satisfaction of Wainwright's conduct in the performance of his mission and stated that he understood that whatever decision Wainwright had been forced to make had been dictated by the best interest of the country. The President expressed his hope that Corregidor would be held."[37]

Following the surrender on April 9 of Major General King, commander of II Corps on the eastern front, Major General Albert M. Johns, commander of the western front, surrendered on April 11. The second Bataan offensive was over.

The Fall of Corregidor

While the Japanese army pursued its second offensive in Bataan, it also made intermittent air strikes on Corregidor from March 24 onward. After the fall of Bataan on April 9, it set up artillery along the southern coast of the peninsula and began shelling in earnest the Corregidor fortress located twelve to sixteen miles away. The *Asahi Shimbun* published consecutive updates: "Corregidor Bombed" (April 3), "Corregidor Fort Faces Last Stage" (April 12), and "Corregidor Cannon Fire Silent" (April 13). Wainwright was monitoring the situation as well: "Southern Bataan occupied by enemy field Artillery in force which keeps Corregidor under constant fire. Terms given King unknown. No communication with Bataan. We still hold Corregidor."[38] According to a U.S. Navy report, forty to fifty days of provisions were available.[39] Corregidor still had staying power.

The well-fortified island of Corregidor had a weak point, however. As Casey later explained, "Corregidor had been built as a major permanent fortification, provided with heavy seacoast artillery and whatnot. But similar to the situation down at Singapore, its artillery, guns, and armament and so on were pointed to an attack from the sea. Their defenses were against a naval force coming in from [to] Manila Bay, and not from an operation over on Bataan. It was the same situation in Singapore, where they were protected against a sea offensive but not against an attack from the land."[40] Just as the Japanese had taken Singapore by attacking from the land, so they now concentrated their shelling of Corregidor not from the water but from the air and the land. Captain Benson Guyton, who was on Corregidor, recalled that the shelling intensified starting the day after Bataan fell.

Shells accurately reached the inside of the trenches and he woke to find shrapnel from the exploding shells flying over his bunk. Guyton recalled that, after being in the tunnel for several days, the men became afraid to go outside; they called the fear "tunnel fever." He also stated that, on Corregidor, as on Bataan, the name Dugout Doug was used pejoratively to refer to MacArthur. Finally, Guyton noted that after the fall of Bataan everyone became fearful, realizing what was in store.[41]

By early May, the garrison force on Corregidor had become desperate. On May 2, the Japanese shelled the island for five hours, firing as many as thirty-six hundred shells. One shell broke through a thick concrete wall and hit the ammunition magazine directly, setting off a huge explosion in the camp. Asked by Marshall to report frankly on the morale and mood in Corregidor, on May 4 Wainwright acknowledged the decline in morale:

> Beginning 29 April (Emperor's birthday) the fire of hostile artillery increased in intensity and has continued at that tempo to present date. The hostile bombing has been relatively ineffective but artillery fire from large caliber guns (240 MM) has resulted in destruction of large percentage of coast defense and beach defense artillery and small arms. Continued bombardment has resulted in about 600 casualties since April 9, and has lowered morale of troops. Morale is difficult to maintain at best because troops have been constantly under or subject to air or artillery attack since December 29.... Enemy is planning to launch an assault against Corregidor. He has prepared a large number of motor boats on which weapons are mounted and has also constructed a large number of smaller boats to be used in transporting troops. I have nothing on which to base an estimate of present hostile troops strength on Luzon.... In my opinion the enemy is capable of making an assault on Corregidor at any time. The success or failure of such an assault will depend entirely on steadfastness of beach defense troops.[42]

On reading Wainwright's report, Marshall realized that the fall of Corregidor was imminent and drafted a letter from the president to Wainwright. On the following day, May 5, an emergency communication was sent from Roosevelt to Wainwright:

> During recent weeks, we have been following with growing admiration the day by day accounts of your heroic stand against the mounting intensity of bombardment by enemy planes and heavy siege guns. In spite of all the handicaps of complete isolation, lack of food and ammunition you have given the world a shining example of patriotic fortitude and self-sacrifice.... The calm determination of your personal leadership in

a desperate situation sets a standard of duty for our soldiers throughout the world. In every camp and on every naval vessel soldiers sailors and marines are inspired by the gallant struggle of their comrades in the Philippines....You and your devoted followers have become the living symbols of our war aims and the guarantee of victory.[43]

Wainwright responded to the president's encouragement in a message sent after seven in the evening on May 5 (Washington time):

I am without words to express to you Mr. President my gratitude for and deep appreciation of your great kindness. We have all done our best to carry out your former instructions and keep your flag flying here as long as humanly possible to do so—at 10:30 PM May 5th the enemy effected a landing here following such terrific air and artillery bombardment of the beaches during the past 7 days that the beach defensive organization was completely obliterated and a great many weapons were destroyed. As I write this at 3:30 AM [on May 6, Philippine time] our patrols are attempting to locate the enemy positions and flanks and I will counter attack at dawn to drive him into the sea or destroy him. Thank you again Mr. President for your wonderful message which I will publish to my entire command.[44]

Immediately before Wainwright's message was sent, all documents stored in Tunnel A, together with forty thousand U.S. dollars, two million Philippine pesos, and all other cash deposits were destroyed.

The 10:30 p.m. attack on May 5 to which Wainwright referred was launched by about five thousand men of the select Kitano corps, who landed some time after 11:00 p.m. on the northeastern side of Corregidor. Breaking down fierce resistance, they had taken complete control of the island by about noon on May 6. One Japanese solder who participated in the attack later recalled:

On the night before the Corregidor landing, a touch of sadness came over me as I thought that perhaps just tonight or tomorrow remained of my life....Thinking of my homeland, I made a secret farewell and wrote my last messages. Our unit boarded the landing craft and under brilliantly shining stars headed for the Corregidor shoreline. The enemy spared no time in discharging illumination fire and tracer bullets, which flew at us from the fortified island. Although I could see that if we raised our heads above the landing craft, we would be shot into the ocean, I had no fear of death. Upon landing on the island, we found that the beach was covered with coal tar and our swords were caught in the stickiness. We spent the night hiding in a cave and the next morning began our attack on the enemy's fortified positions. During the attack, some American soldiers suddenly appeared, waving white flags for surrender. Colonel Sato Gempachi, chief of the 61st Regiment, recognized their actions and suspended fire. Soon afterwards, however, there were more gunshots, so Sato disregarded the previous surrender signal and resumed the attack. Finally, we captured the entire island of Corregidor.[45]

At 2:23 a.m. on May 6 [Philippine time], Wainwright requested Marshall to convey a message to the President: "It is with broken heart and head bowed in sadness but not in shame that I report to your Excellency that I must today go to arrange terms for the surrender of the fortified Islands of Manila Bay—Corregidor (Fort Mills) Caballo (Fort Hughes) El Fraile (Fort Drum)."[46] Just after noon that day, Wainwright raised the white flag to the Japanese army. In just half a day, the Japanese army had captured Corregidor and had taken many U.S. and Filipino soldiers prisoner. At around five in the afternoon, Wainwright met Homma at Cabcaben to discuss surrender terms. Homma declared that he would not accept the surrender unless it included all American and Filipino troops in the whole archipelago including Mindanao. Wainwright was obliged to go back to Corregidor to reconsider the surrender of all troops. On the night of May 7, Wainwright used the radio to order the entire U.S. and Filipino force in the Philippines to surrender. One army journalist described the historic U.S.-Japanese negotiation as follows: "At around ten in the morning [of May 5], I was at the army command center at Limay when I heard that Commander Wainwright of the U.S. and Filipino force, who had asked to surrender, would soon arrive at Cabcaben. I hurriedly drove there with other journalists and newsreel cameramen. In a small house standing alone on the roadside near the burnt-out village of Cabcaben, a historic meeting was held between Commander Homma and Lieutenant General Wainwright... Through the Manila KZRH radio station, Lieutenant General Wainwright broadcast the surrender to all U.S. and Filipino forces in the Philippines."[47]

Even after the broadcast, however, problems remained. On May 7, Wainwright explained to Major General William F. Sharp, commander of the Mindanao district, the process that had led to the announcement:

> General Homma declined to accept my surrender unless it included the forces under your command. It became apparent that the garrison of those forts would be eventually destroyed by aerial and artillery bombardment and by infantry supported by tanks, which have overwhelmed Corregidor....I decided to accept in the name of humanity his proposal and tendered at midnight, night of 6–7 May, 1942, to the Senior

Japanese officer on Corregidor, the formal surrender of all American and Philippine Army Troops in the Philippines. You will, therefore, be guided accordingly and will repeat, will surrender all troops under your command both in the Visayan Islands and Mindanao to the proper Japanese Officer.[48]

Although Sharp had already ordered each island to make its own decision, on receiving Wainwright's message he ordered the commanders of Cebu, Negros, Leyte-Samar, Verueia, Agusan, and Bohol islands to cease all operations at once: "You will raise a white flag and await the approval of my staff officer who will make the terms of the negotiation for surrender of the forces under you. This is imperative and must be carried out in order to save further bloodshed."[49]

Not all commanders accepted this order. Colonel Albert F. Christie, who was defending Panay Island, questioned whether Sharp had the authority to order him to surrender: "[I] doubt his authority to order any such thing. To satisfy me I must have MacArthur's okay otherwise it may be treason. I do not see even one small reason why this unit should be surrendered."[50] On May 11, communicating from Melbourne, MacArthur criticized Wainwright and ordered Sharp to withdraw the order: "Orders emanating from General Wainwright have no validity. If possible separate your force into small elements and initiate guerrilla operations. You of course have full authority to make any decision that immediate emergency may demand. Keep in communication with me as much as possible. You are a salient and resourceful commander and I am proud of what you have done."[51] MacArthur was thus ordering the continued resistance on which Christie had insisted. Because of this lack of consensus among the commanders, the surrender conditions could not be met, producing a situation that would surely affect the treatment of prisoners. MacArthur's "remote control" from Australia had become a source of difficulty. Wainwright already feared that the failure in communication would result in tragedy.

On May 11, Sharp issued a strict order to Christie:

> Your message in reply to my clear message cannot be accepted....I again direct repeat direct you hoist white flag and cease all operations against the Japanese Army at one [sic]. Neither Wainwright nor my surrender has been accepted as yet and unless you and all other commanders comply with my orders at once, active operations will be resumed. I am sending Lt. Col. Thayer by plane to you with written instructions and he will explain the situation in detail. I am in communication with MacArthur and he is advised of my actions which have been ordered by Wainwright. You will reply immediately to message indicating your compliance and actions.[52]

Christie, however, replied on the following day with a restatement of his own view and a direct rebuttal of Sharp's order:

> Your radio surrender of my forces sounds totally unnecessary and for me to comply tends to treason without sanction of WD through MacArthur. Can surrendering of one island automatically do same for others that are in good order.... [Such action] cannot be understood by my simple stolid soldiery....I strongly urge you have the approval of the WD through MacArthur explaining that even if everything else is wrong my forces are intact and capable....I certainly intend to consult with Chynoweth, my immediate commander before any action. In this delicate situation please do not issue me any peremptory orders.[53]

Sharp responded to Christie on the same day, this time in a softer tone: "I have the highest regard for your courageous and resolute stand in carrying out the original mission of maintaining centers of American resistance in these islands. However developments of the war make such actions utterly impracticable....I have pledged the surrender of all forces in the Visayan and Mindanao as ordered by my commanding General. I likewise expect to carry out my orders in this matter."[54] When this message, too, failed to move Christie, Sharp sent an order on May 19 that brooked no further opposition: "You are under my command and accordingly will surrender yourself and troops as I have previously directed. Chynoweth has already complied. Acknowledge this message and state actions taken at once repeat at once."[55] On the same day, Christie conveyed his intention to comply faithfully with the order to surrender. The commanders of all Philippine islands had finally accepted the surrender.

How fully Washington grasped this last-minute confusion is unclear, but Eisenhower, who had been promoted to major general in the War Plans Division, recorded his sympathy for Wainwright and ridicule for MacArthur in his diary entry for May 6: "Corregidor surrendered last night. Poor Wainwright! He did the fighting in the Philippine Islands.... General MacArthur's tirades, to which TJ [Captain T. J. Davis, MacArthur's aide] and I so often listened in Manila, would now sound as silly to the public as they then did to us. But he's a hero! Yah."[56]

The Bataan "Death March"

The two Bataan offensives extending over a full four months had supposedly concluded with a resounding victory for Japan. But the history of the Bataan campaign culminated not with the military outcome but with the notorious Death March that followed. Although not all of the facts have been clarified even today, the Bataan Death March, like the Nanjing Massacre, has become a symbol of the inhumane behavior of the Japanese military in World War II. How did such a horrifying episode take place?

Let us first examine MacArthur's flat opposition to the surrender of U.S. and Filipino troops. MacArthur later asserted that, had Washington temporarily reinstated him to the command position in the Philippines, allowing him to lead the remaining troops in guerrilla warfare, "the dreadful 'Death March,' which followed the surrender, with its estimated 25,000 casualties, would never have taken place."[57] He blamed Washington for its failure to accept his request for reinstatement. MacArthur learned in 1943 of the Death March and details of atrocities suffered by survivors from three American soldiers who escaped from a Japanese prison camp with the help of a local guerrilla group and were later brought to Brisbane by a U.S. submarine. Shocked, he ordered that the following statement (which he probably composed personally) be issued to the press: "I feel intensely disgusted with barbaric atrocities toward war prisoners that an unbelievable report proved. These atrocities certainly infringe the sacred military commandment, and left indelible stains on Japanese military faith."[58] Since Washington, however, forbade the release of any details about atrocities against prisoners of war, neither the soldiers' account nor MacArthur's prepared statement were made public. MacArthur suggested a possible reason in his *Reminiscences*: "Perhaps the Administration, which was committed to a Europe-first effort, feared American public opinions would demand a greater reaction against Japan."[59] Here, too, MacArthur's tendency toward paranoia appears. Why Washington suppressed the story, and whether or not MacArthur's analysis was accurate, are both unknown.

What did those who experienced the Death March testify about the atrocities? Tens of thousands of soldiers suffered the march, and so many stories could be told. Among them, Lester I. Tenney, a volunteer soldier assigned to the 192nd Tank Battalion, had a particularly difficult experience. Tenney was forced to walk the 100 kilometers (62.5 miles) from Mariveles to San Fernando. Then after a train journey and a further 12 kilometer (7.5 mile) walk, he finally reached Camp O'Donnell. Tenney's story reads as follows:

> That morning of April 10, the Japanese marched us to the main road, a distance of about half a mile.... For our group the Bataan Death March began at kilometer marker 167, about two miles east of Mariveles.... If only we had heeded General King's message to save some vehicles for moving our forces to another location, if we had not destroyed all of our trucks, maybe we would have been able to ride to prison camp.... A few of the American prisoners ended up riding all the way to our first prison

camp, Camp O'Donnell.... The entire road was now nothing more than potholes, soft sand, rocks, and loose gravel. Walking on this terrain for short distances would have been bad enough, but walking for any long distance or for any extended period of time was going to be a painful and difficult experience. We started our march in columns of fours, with about ten columns in a group. By the end of the first mile we were walking, not marching, and not in columns at all but as stragglers.... Those who left without a canteen had no means of getting water, even if it was available. Those who left without a cap or headpiece walked in the broiling hot sun.... The Japanese guards also began hollering at us in Japanese, which we did not understand. Because we did not respond to their commands as fast as they thought we should, they started beating us with sticks that they picked up from the side of the road.... After four or five hours of this constant harassment and beating and of being forced to march in their poor physical condition, many of my fellow prisoners just could not go another step without rest; but the guards did not allow us to rest under any circumstances.... In order to live, we had to go in our pants.... On the second day of the march I saw a Japanese truck coming down the road. In the back of the truck were guards with long pieces of rope that they whipped toward us marching men. They tried to hit any prisoner who was not marching fast enough.... I watched a Japanese soldier finish eating rice from his bento box (mess kit) and fish from a can he had just opened. He had about two spoonfuls of fish left in the can and as he turned in my direction, he looked me in the eye and pushed the can toward me.... I had not eaten in almost two days, and I was hungry, tired, and demoralized. Without a moment's hesitation, I took the can.... Although there were many free-flowing artesian wells located in and around Bataan, the Japanese had no set policy on giving water to us prisoners. Some of the guards would let a few men go to a well for water but would deny others the same benefit.... Each day on the march we trudged along like zombies. We walked from 6:30 in the morning till 8:00 or 9:00 at night. Most of the days we would get a few minutes' rest when the Japanese changed guard; otherwise it was hit and miss regarding a rest period.... Due to the poor road conditions, our deteriorating health, the lack of food and water, and our overall defeatist attitudes, we were able to walk only about a mile, or two at the most, for every hour on the march. With the added constant screaming and the beatings by the Japanese guards, we could merely trudge along the road at a snail's pace.... Finally, on the fourth day, as we entered the town of Balanga [in the northeast of the peninsula, between Mariveles and San Fernando],

Filipino civilians stood along the sides of the road, throwing various food items to us.... These Filipinos' gestures lifted our sunken spirits to a new high. Suddenly, we heard shots ring out from somewhere in the middle of our marching group.... The Japanese soldiers were shooting at them for offering food to us prisoners.... I did not have to watch it any longer to have another indelible memory of Japanese barbarism.... Many of the Filipino prisoners on the march with us broke away and ran with their countrymen.... When nighttime finally came we were herded into a large warehouse.... We were so tightly packed together that we sprawled on each other.... That night, the human waste covering the floor from those who had dysentery caused many others to contract this killing disease. The stench, the sounds of dying men, and the whines and groans of those too sick to move to the back of building became so unbearable.... We found three large kitchen pots, each containing rice. Those men without a mess kit received one ball of rice about three inches in diameter.... After the hunger of these last four days, we relished the food, however sparse.

We walked for several more days and often right into the night as well. Only twice were we offered food and water, and then very little of each.... It took two more days to reach the barrio of Orani, a distance of about 15 miles. During these two days we again went without food or drinking water. Along the route, we witnessed more of the same kind of treatment we had seen the first four days.... Finally, exhausted and barely able to stand, we were forced to continue the double-time march until we entered the city of San Fernando, about two kilometers (1.25 miles) away.... We marched to the local railroad station, where we were told to rest. In the distance we could just see a group of boxcars being pulled by an old engine. We sat for about an hour along the railroad trucks before the train finally chugged its way into the little station.... We were herded onto small railway boxcars. Cars were jammed with eighty to one hundred men. We had to take turns just to sit down because there was not enough room for all of us to sit at the same time.[60]

Japanese soldiers' testimonies provide a striking contrast with those of their prisoners. Kawanami Tichi and Ban Hachizo of the 9th Infantry Regiment of the 16th Division recalled:

At dawn, American soldiers bearing white surrender flags emerged from the mountain. Our 4th Unit had a total of 13 Japanese men, but hundreds or thousands of enemy American soldiers were swarming down the mountain. Viewing the scene, we were extremely surprised. They had been disarmed, so they had no weapons, but they tried to put us in a good mood by giving us candies, tobacco, or chocolate. As the surrendered Americans advanced in line, we divided them into groups of about 300, with one Japanese soldier assigned to each group. As noted above, there were just 13 of us Japanese soldiers. Those 13 escorted the surrendered Americans.

Anyway, since we were escorting them back, our job was to transfer them to the battalion headquarters, but we had no idea where the headquarters were. So we simply led them back the way we had come. Each Japanese soldier was leading close to 300 Americans, so if they attacked us from the rear, that would be it; there would be nothing we could do. If the numbers had been reversed, we might have killed them easily, while there were just 13 of them. Only because we had become separated from the main troops in the previous night's battle were we in this strange situation. We ourselves had eaten nothing since the previous night. How could we feed hundreds or thousands of surrendered soldiers? We were relieved when we finally reached the headquarters and could hand over the prisoners. The headquarters were taken aback to see such a large number of surrendered soldiers, and had no idea what to do with them. My guess is that they were moved from the battalion headquarters to the regiment headquarters, from the regiment headquarters to the brigade headquarters, and then from the brigade headquarters to the division headquarters. This would have taken three days. They would have walked for three days in intense heat, with no food or water. Some would have died; others would have suffered from disease. There were no trucks to carry captives. What followed was the so-called Bataan Death March. Commander Homma was sentenced to death and executed for the march, but we never thought of such a thing at the time.[61]

Kotani Teruo, who was in the artillery regiment, offered very similar testimony:

> I participated twice in the transfer of captives. About 15 Japanese soldiers accompanied about 500 captives. Since there was no surrender in the Japanese army, we were surprised to see so many captives appear. We had no system in place for accepting them. We ourselves had no food or water. Their condition was terrible, but so was ours. We had only one canteen of water left, so we were going without food and water. There was a lot of malaria and the captives died in numbers. Because there were no cars we had to walk as well. Food, water, and malaria were three problems for the Japanese army and the captives alike.[62]

The chief of staff of the 14th Army, Wachi Takaji, testified as follows:

> Both friend and foe were troubled by malaria, and in addition many people succumbed to dengue fever and dysentery. All were exhausted. There were 50,000 captives from the U.S. and Filipino force, but an additional 20,000 to 30,000 civilians fled from Bataan with the soldiers, making a total of nearly 80,000 captives. Most of those who had hidden in the mountains suffered from malaria or other diseases. We had to move them to the rear because the military operation on Corregidor continued.
>
> The captives walked all the way from the front line to San Fernando. The Japanese soldiers who escorted them also walked. While the captives each had one water canteen to carry, we Japanese walked with knapsacks and guns on our backs. Because the entire journey was 60 kilometers [37.5 miles] and took four or five days to walk, the soldiers straggled rather than marched. The reason was utter fatigue. Despite the southern location, it became chilly at night. The Japanese soldiers made fires and, after cooking meals, gave the captives food before eating themselves. We ate together. Passing news reporters sometimes offered food. If possible, we should have transported the captives in trucks, but there was little likelihood that the poorly equipped Japanese army would be able to supply trucks. There were not even enough trucks for the next operation, on Corregidor. Let me repeat that we did not abuse them. If you want to call this a death march, you should listen to the testimonies of the escorting Japanese soldiers who experienced it along with the captives.
>
> On the way many of them died, but that was mostly from malaria. Another factor was the prisoners were used to moving by trucks rather than by marching. In other words, there was a difference between a mechanized and non-mechanized military. That does not mean I am proud of being non-mechanized. After arriving at San Fernando, they were transferred by train to Camp O'Donnell in central Luzon. After arriving there, many prisoners died, perhaps because they had finally let down their guard. I felt deeply sorry when I heard that news. After the fall of Corregidor, I hurried to Camp O'Donnell as the representative of Commander Homma to offer flowers to the spirit of the deceased unknown soldiers and to hold a memorial service on behalf of the Japanese army. Moreover, Commander Homma released the Philippine captives. In any case, the Japanese army did its best under difficult circumstances. After the war, however, Lieutenant General Homma was held responsible for the Bataan Death March and shot by firing squad.[63]

A war correspondent attached to the Japanese army described the circumstances of the surrender of American and Filipino force as follows:

> From the mountains, valleys and jungles, enemy soldiers came out with their hands raised, filling the roads and towns. Discarding their weapons, they carried their eating utensils carefully, but little else. We felt sympathy for those dirty and grimy American and Philippine soldiers, thin and unshaven and weakened by half a year of fierce attacks. The prisoners were organized by our men into groups of 50 or 60 before moving in a long formation to the prisoner camp. Intermingled with the prisoners were increasing numbers of refugees, including young mothers carrying children affected by malaria fever and sons encouraging sick old women. These refugees whose skin color was the same as ours were all exhausted and on the verge of death. We turned back to the headquarters at Balanga, where we reported the situation in detail. We received medicines, food, and other necessary goods and set up first-aid stations in several locations along the road to offer food and physical examinations. In addition, officers were dispatched to the Manila headquarters to discuss how to deal with the emergency measures. Moreover, Ozaki Shiro and others were sent several times to Manila to appeal for as much relief as possible. We also contacted the Red Cross through the Philippine administration to ask for emergency help. Finally, many supplies were sent from Manila. Tens of thousands of refugees were revived from the brink of death and returned to their villages.[64]

Among U.S. Navy documents is a report of an interview held in April 1942 with a U.S. Army recruit who had fled from Bataan to Corregidor. The report includes the following statement: "Some were captured but they could easily escape more than once. The Japanese treated war prisoners with no atrocities. The prisoners' camp site was unknown, but more than 2,000 of the wounded were evacuated from Bataan to the back of Japanese front line."[65] This soldier asserted that there were no atrocities in the Bataan March.

A document dated October 1, 1945, entitled Hito Homen Furyo Kankei Chosahyo [Investigation Concerning Prisoners in the Philippine Area] offers an interesting view of the Bataan situation. The document offers information in two contrasting sections: the first, on the upper half of the page, is Beikoku Kogi no Yoten [A Summary of U.S. Charges]; the second, on the lower half of the page, is Teikoku Seifu Kaito no Yoten (A Summary of Japanese Government Reaction). Concerning Furyo no Kogun Yuso Shuyo (The transfer, march, and accommodation of prisoners), the United States had five main complaints: (1) their forced march of ninety miles as far as Camp O'Donnell in spite of exhaustion, disease, and injury; (2) the neglect of nursing care for the wounded and others who fell behind; (3) the lack of food rations for thirty-six hours after arrival at the camp, and being forced to stay outdoors for three days; (4) the refusal of medical help by American and Filipino doctors and nurses and a 25 percent death rate; (5) the armed robbery of shoes, canteens, and watches during the march. In response, the Japanese response was: (1) there was no security immediately after the Bataan occupation; (2) transportation facilities had been destroyed; (3) due to the U.S. military's scorched earth policy, food and medical supplies had been destroyed; (4) because of the current military situation, the Japanese army was also short of food and medical supplies; (5) no preparations had been made for the unexpectedly large number of captives.[66] The charges and responses reflected considerable differences between the United States and Japanese sides.

If we summarize this evidence, four miscalculations by the Japanese army become clear. First, the Japanese estimated the number of U.S. and Filipino troops in Bataan at between twenty-five thousand to thirty-five thousand, but in fact there were twelve thousand U.S. troops, sixty-five thousand Filipino troops, and twenty-five thousand refugees, making a total of 102,000—three or four times the Japanese estimate. Second, the Japanese assumed that the captives were in good health, but the reality was quite the opposite. The rations of U.S. and Filipino forces had been reduced to as little as eight hundred calories per day in the final four or five days. The troops ate rice and a small spoonful of C rations, an emergency military field ration of food intended for use under combat conditions and consisting of specially prepared and packaged meats. All troops at the front ate only two meals a day, and on occasion they ate snakes, monkeys, and iguanas. For this reason, many suffered from scurvy, beriberi, and malaria, and many had already lost the strength to march.[67] Third, the Japanese army was disciplined by *senjinkun,* or battlefield discipline, to consider *gyokusai,* or glorious death, as right and to reject the option of becoming a prisoner. They did not expect the enemy to surrender. Moreover, since the Bataan surrender happened just before the scheduled battle at Corregidor, the Japanese had no system for dealing with the prisoners and had difficulty figuring out how to manage them. Fourth, the unexpectedly early surrender of the U.S. and Filipino force meant that the Japanese were unable to make preparations regarding food, accommodation, or transportation for the prisoners. Since the Japanese themselves were suffering from a shortage of provisions and transportation, they were obliged to make the captives walk to an area where it would be easier to provide for them.

In addition, one needs to consider Japanese psychology and nationalism. The contempt for Americans that derived from the notion of *kichiku beiei,* or "American and British as demons and brutes," together with deep animosity over the wounding and killing of their comrades by U.S. and Filipino forces in the Bataan campaign, prompted inhumane, cruel, and atrocious conduct. Such surges of irrational feeling may be difficult to avoid after heavy combat at any time and place.[68] This is the background to the Bataan Death March, which caused the death of no fewer than 1,522 U.S. soldiers and twenty-nine thousand Filipinos as of August 1, 1942.

It should be noted, moreover, that prisoners taken after the fall of Corregidor did not experience anything like the Bataan Death March. After the fall of Corregidor on May 6, the surrendered U.S. and Filipino troops were sent to Manila by boat, then to Camp Cabanatuan by train. Guyton recalled:

> We got the word, "Destroy your equipment. We surrender at noon."
> Nothing happened all that day, but the next morning some Jap officer
> came up and told us to go down to Bottom Side to the 92nd Garage
> area....We were just herded into an area like a bunch of sheep and pretty
> much stayed in that area for about three weeks, during which time the
> Japs would frequently come in and take people out on work details to
> pick up scrap metal and things like that. I caught on pretty quick; that
> was a good thing to do because you could go out and find food in fox-
> holes and places like that....I don't think anybody was dying from lack
> of food. You could get water, and somebody could find food for you....
> After a couple of weeks I was put on a ship and I thought I was going
> to Japan, but we went across Manila Bay and were booted off the gang
> plank in about four feet of water. We paraded through the streets of
> Manila into Bilibid, the old Spanish prison, where I stayed a couple of
> weeks. Then I was put on a train and went up to the town of Caba-
> natuan.[69]

According to Guyton's account, not only did prisoners from Corregidor avoid a forced march but their general health was also better than that of the Bataan prisoners. Their condition was by no means as desperate when they arrived at their prison camp destination. In terms of nutritional levels, there were differences between occupied areas.

Finally, as MacArthur pointed out, it was not until one year and nine months after the incident occurred that the mainland U.S. press reported the shocking experiences of the Bataan Death March.[70] On January 28, 1944, the *New York Times* covered the story on its front page under the headline "5200 Americans, many more Filipinos die of starvation, torture after Bataan."[71] Based on the accounts of the three survivors, it reported the horror of the "march of death" and described in detail the conditions of the prisoners, skeletally thin, in Camp

O'Donnell: that twelve thousand people were forced to march in the intense heat with no food supply and died or were buried alive, and they were walking skeletons. On the following day, January 29, the newspaper published on its third page a photograph of MacArthur taken on August 4, 1943, with Lieutenant Colonel William E. Dyess and the other two survivors.

Following the publication of these accounts, the expression "Death March," like "Remember Pearl Harbor," became an anti-Japanese slogan, symbolic of Japanese brutality. MacArthur, in particular, never forgot the anger he experienced at the inhuman abuses carried out against his comrades. However, it is likely that the bitter memory of his own humiliating escape from Corregidor lay at the bottom of his deep anger. The fact that he had abandoned his men to flee from the enemy was a deep blow to MacArthur's brilliant military career and pride. It was a record that he would have liked to erase, and this personal bitterness may have produced a multiplier effect that reinforced his outrage about the Death March.

The repercussions of the Death March played out in Japan immediately after the war. MacArthur was firmly determined to bring Homma, commander of the 14th Army in the battle of Bataan, to justice as a war criminal. Landing at Atsugi Airfield on August 30, 1945, MacArthur ordered Brigadier General Eliott R. Thorpe, chief of the Counter Intelligence Corps (CIC), to arrest Homma, who had been moved to the reserves three years earlier. Homma was arrested at Niigata Harbor and escorted to Tokyo by an officer of the Special Higher Police (the so-called Tokkō) in civilian clothes. Detained at Sugamo prison, Homma was required to sign the charge and specification document prepared by Colonel Alva C. Carpenter, chief of the Legal Section (LS) of GHQ. The document listed forty-two crimes. Article 13, in particular, stated: "From about 9 April 1942 to about 27 April 1942 there was conducted the infamous 'Death March of Bataan' which was a series of Death Marches in which approximately 10,500 American and approximately 74,800 Filipino prisoners of war were forced to march distances ranging from 60 to 120 kilometers (37.5 to 75 miles) from Bataan to San Fernando although transportation was available and was to have been used under the terms of the surrender agreement, during which time the following atrocities were committed."[72] Article 1 detailed large and small charges. It stated that, in spite of MacArthur's open city declaration, the Japanese army bombed the city of Manila by air, destroying public buildings and killing and injuring many residents. It stated further that Japanese army officers committed abuses, such as deliberately refusing to provide food, clothing, and medicines to the sick from Bataan. Homma was probably surprised at the content of the document.

Homma was brought before a tribunal but, as in other cases, his death sentence had been decided beforehand. On February 11, 1946, in a case of victors' justice,

Homma was pronounced guilty and sentenced to death by hanging. The defense filed an appeal with the U.S. Supreme Court, but the court refused to intervene. The case was entirely left in MacArthur's hands, and the revenge drama thus came to an end. MacArthur wrote in his *Reminiscences:* "Not a word of the atrocities practiced by its soldiery was published in Japan itself, and when the truth came out after the surrender, it shocked the fine sensibilities of the Japanese public as much as it did those of the Americans and their allies."[73] MacArthur thus characterized the series of war-related judgments, including the judgment on Homma, as the product of "the fine sensibilities of the Japanese public." It is true that it was not until the postwar era that the Japanese public learned many facts about the conduct of the war, but it is doubtful whether the individual action of MacArthur aimed at washing away the humiliation he and his subordinates had suffered can be turned into a general human reaction. Ongoing verification through historical research is necessary to determine the appropriateness and adequacy of such an evaluation.[74]

FROM AUSTRALIA TO THE PHILIPPINES, MARCH 1942 TO OCTOBER 1944

The Beginning of the Counterattack

After arriving in Australia in the middle of March 1942, MacArthur was for a while deeply despondent. The large-scale military force that he believed would be awaiting his arrival in Australia did not exist. He found only one poorly trained U.S. division stationed there, one Australian division, and an air force of some 250 obsolete aircraft; total manpower was no more than twenty-five thousand. The main Australian army had been dispatched to North Africa and the Middle East, leaving no homeland defense force to resist the Japanese. As its sense of crisis intensified with the growing prospect of a Japanese attack, the Australian government repeatedly requested its military to send the main forces home immediately, but the request had not yet been realized. The plan to return to the Philippines with military reinforcements, which had been the rationalization for evacuating from Corregidor, had crumbled. Furthermore, following the surrender of the U.S. and Filipino force at Bataan in early April, reports arrived of Wainwright's surrender at Corregidor in early May. Although MacArthur had ordered all-out resistance from the frontline troops, Wainwright had disregarded his order and, with Washington's approval, had decided to surrender. MacArthur was enraged by this decision, but there was nothing he could do from far-away Australia.[1]

Following its attack on Pearl Harbor, the Japanese military had in a mere half year succeeded in taking most of Southeast Asia and the western Pacific. It had overwhelmed Guam, the Gilbert Islands, and Wake Island in the Pacific, consecutively occupied the cities of Hong Kong, Manila, Saigon, and Singapore, and advanced to New Britain, Bougainville, Malaya, the Netherlands East Indies, Thailand, Burma, and the Philippines. Forced to make significant withdrawals, the five Allied Powers, namely the United States, Britain, the Netherlands, Australia, and New Zealand, were desperate to recoup their losses. Following a large-scale Washington review of strategy against Japan, the Combined Chiefs of Staff (CCS) of the United States and Britain divided the vast Pacific war theater into two areas: the Southwest Pacific Area (SWPA), which included the Philippines, Dutch East Indies, Australia, and New Guinea, and the Pacific Ocean Area (POA), which included the rest of the islands in the Pacific. On March 30, Admiral Chester W. Nimitz, commander of the Pacific Fleet, was named commander of the POA, and MacArthur was appointed commander of the SWPA. It was as though two heroes, of the army and the navy, were being placed in competition so as to develop a proper resistance strategy against Japan.

Since MacArthur believed that command of the Pacific theater was his sole responsibility, he was angered by the dual appointment. He even suspected that Washington had tricked him into the assignment, and his mistrust of Washington increased. In fact, far from being unfair to MacArthur, Roosevelt and the army and navy leadership had already made preparations to transfer large amounts of arms and ammunition as well as troops to Australia. Moreover, after consulting with British prime minister Winston Churchill, Roosevelt decided to transfer two of the three Australian divisions fighting in North Africa back to Australia and place them under MacArthur's command. In fact, two divisions of the U.S. Army arrived in Australia in April, the 5th U.S. Army Air Force was formed in September, and the 7th U.S. Fleet was placed under MacArthur's command. All three Australian divisions returned from the Middle East. With these reinforcements, the military situation was turning favorable.

It was under these circumstances that MacArthur became commander of SWPA, which could be called the united military front of the Allies, on April 18, 1942. His first action was to dismiss Major General George H. Brett, commander of the U.S. Army Air Forces in Australia, whose unsatisfactory management of aircraft during the withdrawal from Mindanao to Australia had roused MacArthur's anger. Brett wanted to retain his position, but MacArthur did not consider him. As staff officers of the newly established SWPA, he appointed Richard K. Sutherland and the other fifteen Bataan Boys who had escaped with him from Corregidor. In addition, MacArthur appointed Brigadier General Stephen J. Chamberlin as chief of G-3 in charge of operations, Colonel Lester J. Whitlock as chief of G-4 in charge of supply and logistics, and Colonel Burdette M. Fitch as adjutant general (AG) in charge of the administrative section. As chief of the

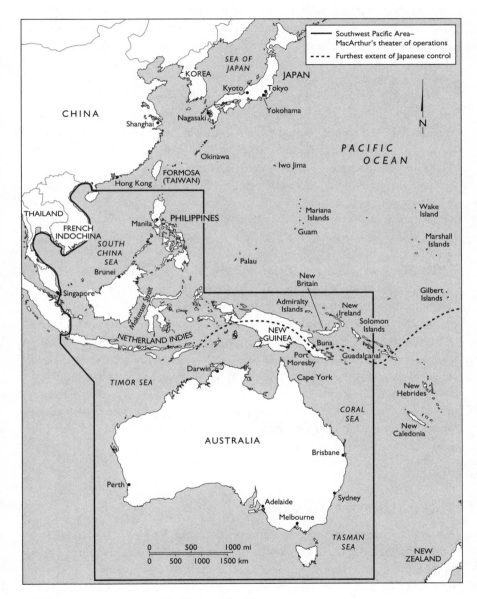

MAP 4. East Asia and the Western Pacific

Civil Intelligence Section (CIS) he named Colonel Elliott R. Thorpe, who was later to compete with Charles A. Willoughby of G-2. Together with the appointment of Brigadier General Harold H. George, who was responsible for the air force units but died later that month in an accident, and Major General George C. Kenney, who moved from commander of the Allied Air Force to succeed Brett as commander of the 5th Air Force, these assignments were to produce new relationships in the headquarters.[2]

Under MacArthur's command, SWPA consisted of allied ground troops, air force, and naval units. The allied ground troops, under the command of Australian General Thomas Blamey, included the 1st, 2nd, 3rd, 6th, and 7th divisions of the Australian army and the 41st and 32nd divisions of the U.S. Army. The allied air force under Kenney's command consisted of two American heavy bomber groups, two middle bomber groups, three battle aircraft groups, and a few Australian, Dutch, and Indian troops. The allied fleet, under the command of Vice Admiral Herbert F. Leary of the U.S. Navy, had two Australian heavy cruisers, one light cruiser, one American heavy cruiser, and many air-defense destroyers.

The immediate and imperative problem MacArthur confronted was the reconstruction of the defense system of Australia. He aimed to change the defeatism that dominated Australia's 7.4 million people to a mood of optimism. Specifically, MacArthur abandoned the Australian defense plan, which aimed to protect a line that stretched from Brisbane in the middle of the eastern coast to Adelaide in the south. He moved the defense line well forward into eastern New Guinea where he planned to stop the Japanese army in the rough mountains of the Owen Stanley Range. His strategy moved the defense line to a position north of Australia's borders. On July 20, 1942, he moved his headquarters from Melbourne to Brisbane, eleven hundred kilometers (687.5 miles) to the north. The offensive operation was under way.[3]

The Battle in New Guinea

Admiral Yamamoto Isoroku, the commander of the Japanese Combined Fleet who had achieved brilliant military results at Pearl Harbor, was planning Operation FS, the second stage of Japanese military strategy. This involved the capture of Fiji, Samoa, and New Caledonia and, after using control of this section of the western Pacific to help block sea and air transportation routes between Australia and the United States, an attack on Australia itself. Since the military base that the Japanese had established at Rabaul on the island of New Britain, east of New Guinea, had already sustained air attacks by Allied aircraft flying from

Port Moresby in New Guinea, Operation FS was launched in March 1942. The 18th Army, consisting of the 20th, 41st, and 51st divisions under the command of Lieutenant General Adachi Hanazo, landed near the New Guinea towns of Lae and Salamaua and soon occupied them. Moreover, with the cooperation of the navy, which had completed its takeover of the Netherlands East Indies, it took control of the western part of New Guinea in April before proceeding to the Port Moresby operation.

The intelligence group in Hawaii's 14th Naval District and the Station CAST of the Office of Naval Intelligence that had moved from Corregidor to Australia had, however, broken the Japanese naval code. Responding in April to the Japanese moves, the U.S. Army confirmed that the Imperial General Headquarters was about to begin a new operation. This was the Port Moresby Operation (Operation MO), which aimed to transport some five thousand troops to launch an invasion. If the Japanese were successful, not only would the northern and eastern parts of Australia (which are directly south of the Port Moresby area) be threatened by Japanese forces but the anticipated counterattack by MacArthur would become a lot more difficult.

On May 8, MacArthur assured Roosevelt that at the present time a Japanese attack on India was unlikely. Rather, he emphasized that, having taken Corregidor, the Japanese army would now use two divisions and all its air power stationed in the Philippines to attack New Guinea and the supply route between Australia and the United States. MacArthur's view was quite different from that of Churchill, who believed that the Japanese would attack India. MacArthur proved to be correct. The Japanese placed priority on the advance south to New Guinea, not west to India, but the Japanese army and naval leadership underestimated MacArthur's ability to build a defense line at Port Moresby.[4]

Having established a forward base at Rabaul, on May 3, 1942, the Japanese military began a large-scale landing operation on New Guinea, using three aircraft carriers. Since the U.S. command in Australia had learned of Japanese movements from the breaking of their codes, it immediately dispatched two carriers to the Coral Sea, located between Port Moresby and northeastern Australia, to strike the Japanese fleet and the convoy. May 8 marked the height of the Battle of the Coral Sea, the first ever battle between aircraft carriers. The Japanese light carrier, *Shoho,* which was escorting the convoy, sank, but the Americans also suffered losses: the USS *Lexington,* a large fleet carrier, as well as a refueling tanker and a cruiser. Comparing the losses, the sinking of the *Lexington* gave the Japanese a tactical victory but the Allies won strategically by forcing the Japanese to suspend the Port Moresby invasion and withdraw. After a series of losses to the Japanese, this outcome helped restore the U.S. Navy's confidence. Moreover, the suspension of the Japanese operation to cut the supply line between the United

States and Australia bought MacArthur's forces, who were defending eastern New Guinea, valuable time to prepare a counterattack.

The Japanese high command, however, did not give up its ambition to seize Port Moresby. Seaborne invasion was abandoned in favor of a more difficult over-land drive across the Owen Stanley Mountains. In August, three months after the Battle of the Coral Sea, the so-called Nankai Task Force of the 18th Army landed at Basabua on the east coast of New Guinea, and marched some 360 kilometers (225 miles) over the 3,000 meter (9,842 feet) mountains of the Owen Stanley Range in order to seize Port Moresby by attacking from the rear. The Nankai Task Force, with difficulty, reached a location that allowed a view of Port Moresby, but it had to abandon the attack and turn back because of a shortage of supplies and ammunition. From this point began the downfall of the Japanese army.

Meanwhile, the Battle of Midway, which was to have a major influence on the outcome of the Pacific War, took place from June 5 through June 7. The battle took place in part in response to the daring air raid conducted on April 18 against major cities such as Tokyo, Yokohama, Nagoya, and Kobe by sixteen B-25 bombers dispatched from the carrier USS *Hornet* under the leadership of Lieutenant Colonel James H. Doolittle. The so-called Doolittle Raid shocked Japanese military leaders, who had been confident of the security of mainland Japan. Yamamoto planned to intercept American attacks and wipe out all of the U.S. carrier fleet that had survived the attack on Pearl Harbor. The Japanese Combined Fleet, consisting of 350 vessels, launched an attack on Midway Island. However, the main aircraft carriers, *Akagi, Kaga, Soryu,* and *Hiryu,* were sunk in massive air attacks by the U.S. mobile task force that was waiting for the Japanese fleet. With the loss of so many highly trained pilots, the Japanese were defeated. The Japanese were subsequently defeated in the Battle of the Solomon Sea, fought in three phases from August to November, and thereafter lost both air and sea supremacy to the Americans. The power relationship between the United States and Japan that had prevailed since the opening of hostilities was about to be reversed.[5]

On the U.S. and Australian side, four airfields were constructed at Port Moresby to secure an advance base for the counteroffensive against Japan, through the efforts of Brigadier General Hugh J. Casey, a Bataan Boy and chief of the engineering unit, and the cooperation of many Australians. At the beginning of October, MacArthur and his staff moved to Port Moresby; in November, he established an advance base. From there he launched a counteroffensive operation aimed at annihilating the Japanese army in the Buna, Gona, and Salamaua areas of northern New Guinea. This was MacArthur's first counteroffensive aimed at his return to the Philippines.

Informed that the Japanese Nankai Task Force was withdrawing in the direction of Buna, MacArthur adopted a bold enveloping strategy: one unit pursued the enemy from behind; a second infiltrated from Milne Bay in the east; and a third was dispatched to Wanigela Airfield, southeast of Buna. A fierce back-and-forth battle ensued, but MacArthur's three-dimensional strategy using the army, navy, and air force proved effective. From the end of 1942 through the beginning of 1943, the Japanese army lost its fighting power, suffering forty-five hundred losses in the Owen Stanley Range and eight thousand in the Buna area. The victory of the U.S. and Australian side in January 1943 marked the end of the first half of the New Guinea (Papua) campaign. At the time of victory, MacArthur commended twelve officers for their courage, efficiency, and precision: General Thomas Blamey, Lieutenant General George C. Kenney, Lieutenant General Edmund F. Herring, Lieutenant General Robert L. Eichelberger, Major General Richard K. Sutherland, Major General George A. Vasey, Brigadier General Charles A. Willoughby, Brigadier General Ennis C. Whitehead, Brigadier General Kenneth N. Walker, Brigadier General George F. Wootten, Brigadier General Kenneth W. Eather, and Royal Australian Air Force Group Captain William H. Garing.

The victory in eastern New Guinea was a major turning point for MacArthur and the U.S. and Australian forces. The Japanese army retreated westward along the north cost of New Guinea. U.S. and Australian forces overtook the retreating Japanese army, landed at key points and attacked them from the front. In the subsequent key battles of Salamaua (Jan.–Aug. 1943), Finschhafen (Sept.–Dec. 1943), Aitape (June–Aug. 1944), and Vial Island (June–Aug. 1944), Japanese forces were crushed by the overwhelming power and air and sea supremacy of the U.S. and Australian forces.[6]

Teamwork in MacArthur's Inner Circle

The General Headquarters of the Southwest Pacific Area (GHQ/SWPA), established in Australia, consisted mainly of the Bataan Boys who had offered firm support to MacArthur since Corregidor. However, as the GHQ moved to Melbourne, Brisbane, and then Port Moresby, new members from the United States and Netherlands East Indies were recruited to serve as staff officials and commanders of combat troops; and so personal relationships within the headquarters changed. Naturally, these changes had an impact on the organization of MacArthur's team and on the conduct of the war. Who were the new members, and what kind of influence did they exert?

MacArthur himself favorably commented on three people, Chamberlin, Kenney, and Eichelberger. Regarding Chamberlin, who became operations officer, MacArthur wrote: "[He was] a sound, careful staff officer, a master of tactical detail and possessed of bold strategic concepts. He was a pillar of new strength." He praised Kenney as commander of the Allied Air Forces: "Of all the brilliant air commanders of the war, none surpassed him in those three great essentials of combat leadership: aggressive vision, mastery of air tactics and strategy, and the ability to exact the maximum in fighting qualities from both men and equipment."[7] Regarding Eichelberger, who would become commander of the 8th Army, MacArthur commented: "He was a superintendant of the United States Military Academy at West Point, and was already noted for his administrative ability. He proved himself a commander of the first order, fearless in battle, and especially popular with the Australians."[8]

How did their colleagues evaluate the three? Regarding Chamberlin, Casey, for example, noted: "General Chamberlin was both later a perfect chief of staff and initially a perfect head of the Operations Division of our headquarters. I think, considering the problems we had in our theater, with the difficulties of undeveloped terrain and distances, the problems of supply, and the problems of logistics, I think by reason of his background and his prior experience in the field of logistics, that qualified him even more for the important post as chief of the Operations Division. I think he had fine insight into all of the problems, and he coordinated personnel and staff and his agencies excellently."[9] Roger O. Egeberg, who served MacArthur as adjutant, testified: "Chamberlin was G-3, the wheel horse. Chamberlin had all the facts and all of the picture of any given operation right in his mind. While a lot of it was on paper, without Chamberlin it was hard to bring it to life. Chamberlin could be counted on. He worked harder than almost anybody else. He's a man of modesty, honesty, extreme loyalty— devoted to his job and the people he worked for. I would think that MacArthur both respected and admired him."[10] Chamberlin was the third highest-ranking officer in the GHQ hierarchy, next to Sutherland and Richard J. Marshall. Even Willoughby, who was noted for his acerbic comments, underscored MacArthur's high evaluation of Chamberlin: "He was a first-class performer and was appreciated by his colleagues. He had a pleasant personality and was rather restrained in his language and reactions. I rate him highly."[11]

About Kenney, Egeberg wrote: "General George Kenney was able, confident, aggressive, buoyant in temperament…. [MacArthur] soon approved of him wholeheartedly, for General Kenney acted with swift effectiveness."[12] Sutherland's secretary and stenographer Rogers noted that Kenney was careful not to disturb the favorable relationship between MacArthur and Sutherland: "Kenney, of course, was MacArthur's frequent visitor and companion but he was equally close to Sutherland. Kenney spent a great deal of time with MacArthur, but he was careful to preserve a comparable relationship with Sutherland."[13] Kenney and Chamberlin, though both new appointees, successfully made their way into

MacArthur's inner circle, and through their high capabilities gained MacArthur's esteem.

Eichelberger, by comparison, had a less favorable reputation. Casey saw him as a man of ambition:

> Eichelberger was, as I say, referred to as the "Lightning Joe" type....General Eichelberger had ambitions to be the senior commander in the Pacific. He was, I felt, jealous of General Krueger, especially in the early phase when Sixth Army was conducting most of the operations....I know he was disappointed, too, when hostilities ended, that General MacArthur didn't return home, because I think he had a strong ambition to be the senior commander over all the forces there, rather than the commanding general of Eighth Army under General MacArthur as Supreme Commander.[14]

Willoughby, too, compared Eichelberger unfavorably with General Walter Krueger: "Krueger was a hard-nosed professional who came up from the ranks....He came from the bottom up....He was a first-class commander and senior one."[15] By contrast: "Eichelberger was for many years the secretary of the General Staff in Washington. That was a powerful position and a position which helped him to make friends in the political field....He was good-looking, smooth, polished, and socially just the thing for Washington." In addition to the personality contrast between the self-made adventurer and the man who was a shrewd man-about-town, there was an underlying contrast between the 6th Army, which was a practical combat troop, and the 8th Army, which acted in a secondary, relief role, and was probably created by MacArthur as an occupation army. In general, the Bataan Boys were severe with regard to Eichelberger and generous with regard to Krueger. MacArthur, in fact, declared Krueger to be the most distinguished military commander in U.S. history and requested Chief of Staff Marshall to assign a post to him. As a result, the 6th Army Headquarters was established in SWPA in February 1943. By contrast, Eichelberger was engaged in the occupation of Japan, but when he returned home after three years, he began to criticize MacArthur's administration of the occupation from Washington.

What did the newcomers think of MacArthur and the Bataan Boys, and how did they evaluate GHQ as a military organization? Kenney later expressed a number of severe criticisms.[16] First, "MacArthur is prone to make all his decisions himself, depending only upon his immediate staff." Second, "One of the perquisites of command, the coordination of the three Services (army, navy and air force) in a combined effort, is absolutely neglected." Third, "Commanders are not conferred with prior to either major or minor decisions. Lack of command and staff meetings results in directives impossible to interpret and orders issued without the help of those who must carry them out and should presumably have the most specialized knowledge of the subject." On this point, Kenney said he heard similar opinions from Admiral Herbert F. Leary and from Blamey, general of the Australian army. Fourth, "MacArthur has not a full appreciation of air operations, nor is there any officer on his Staff sufficiently conversant with air operations to have the ability for proper planning." Kenney concluded: "General MacArthur has a wonderful personality when he desires to turn it on. He is, however, absolutely bound up in himself. I do not believe he has a single thought for anybody who is not useful to him." Regarding the relationship between GHQ and the fighting units at the front, Kenney noted several points of discontent: promotions of officers were unfairly restricted by GHQ; there were no relief units; and living conditions were very poor. These points of dissatisfaction made coordination between GHQ and the front difficult, because, in Kenney's opinion, everything was decided by GHQ officials who had no appreciation of conditions at the front.

Kenney's criticisms were directed particularly at Sutherland: "General Sutherland is primarily an egotist with a smattering of knowledge pertaining to air operations....He is arbitrary in his attitude and often renders decisions in the name of the C-in-C [commander in chief] which it is felt the C-in-C has never had an opportunity to discuss. He is officious and rubs the majority of people (with the exception of his own staff) the wrong way, thereby creating a great deal of unnecessary friction."[17] Kenney concluded that Sutherland was a bully. He noted, moreover, that among staff other than Sutherland, abilities were uneven. Marshall, Willoughby, Marquat, and Casey tended to see themselves as important but they were "yes-men" controlled by Sutherland. Exceptions were Spencer B. Akin, a signals officer, as well as Chamberlin and Lester J. Whitlock (G-4). Kenney noted that Charles P. Stivers might have performed well had there been proper supervision.

Whereas Kenney criticized the staff from the viewpoint of an air officer, Admiral Arleigh A. Burke, who was in command of the destroyer squadron in the Solomon Sea (and was later deputy chief of staff of the Far East Navy and chief of Naval Operations), pointed to the defects of MacArthur and GHQ from a naval perspective: "MacArthur was a great tactician, and he was a great strategist, but not as great as he thought he was. He didn't know everything. Particularly he didn't know about naval forces. He didn't know the maneuverability and flexibility of fast naval warfare."[18] Regarding the conflict between MacArthur and Nimitz, Burke noted both the difference in personalities and the difference in basic attitude between the army and the navy: "When a navy commander would turn over to another naval commander a group of ships and say, 'You can have these for two weeks,' he meant two weeks. He didn't mean two weeks and one day....When Nimitz turned over some of his forces to MacArthur for certain period of operation, MacArthur never wanted to give them back....He just said the circumstances changed....So there were arguments over that."[19] Burke continued: "The biggest weakness of MacArthur was that he didn't know the facts because the staff wouldn't tell him the facts. They would make decisions and announce, 'this is what the 'Old Man' says.'"

Interwoven with various complex human relationships, MacArthur's GHQ was taking shape as a distinctive inner circle.

Conflict with the U.S. Navy Leadership

While the SWPA under MacArthur's command was turning to the offensive in New Guinea, the POA under Nimitz had in August 1942 won a victory in the Solomon Sea and, launching a successful landing on Guadalcanal in the Solomon Islands, was broadening its deadly combat against the Japanese. In October, the U.S. fleet commanded by Admiral Thomas C. Kinkaid engaged in a fierce battle around Henderson Air Base on Guadalcanal against a vanguard of the Japanese navy led by Vice Admiral Kondo Nobutake and fought against Vice Admiral Nagumo Chuichi's mobile force in the ocean north of Guadalcanal and Santa Cruz. The Japanese won a tactical victory, sinking the U.S. aircraft carrier *Hornet* and shooting down seventy-four aircraft, but they suffered a strategic defeat thereafter in the Battle of Midway, losing one hundred aircraft and many well-trained pilots. In November, furthermore, the Japanese suffered a crushing defeat in the third phase of the Battle of the Solomon Sea. In February 1943, they withdrew from Guadalcanal and a battle that had lasted half a year came to an end. As a result, sea and air supremacy shifted from Japan to the United States, and Australia was liberated from any real threat of invasion.

Meanwhile, MacArthur and Admiral Ernest J. King, chief of Naval Operations and commander in chief of the U.S. Navy Fleet, disagreed sharply over the leadership and strategy of the war against Japan. MacArthur believed that operations should be unified under his command and emphasized that the offensive against Japan should consist of the capture of New Guinea and the Philippines followed by an assault on the Japanese main islands. King, on the other hand, argued that the more effective route to the Japanese mainland was to advance north from the Caroline Islands in the central Pacific to the Marianas.

After the end of the Guadalcanal campaign in March 1943, the Joint Chiefs of Staff (JCS) called the chiefs of staff of both MacArthur and Nimitz to a strategy meeting in Washington. However, the two sides simply repeated their assertions and the meeting achieved no more than a confirmation of near-term operation plans. Following this strategy meeting, a U.S.-British summit and a U.S.-British chiefs of staff conference were conducted in Washington in May, but there, too, the conflict between MacArthur and King was a matter of concern. It was feared that the two commanders in charge of prosecuting the war who were split on basic strategy would make future operations impossible. At this point, Roosevelt and Churchill came up with a compromise plan. The advance to Tokyo would be by two routes: the southwestern Pacific route suggested by MacArthur, from New Guinea to the Philippines, Formosa, and Japan, and the central Pacific route favored by King, from the Gilbert Islands to the Marshall Islands, Caroline Islands, Mariana Islands, and then to Japan. MacArthur vigorously opposed the adoption of dual routes, but the decision was not reversed.

Reluctantly, MacArthur ordered an area group consisting mainly of Admiral William F. Halsey's South Pacific Forces (later the 3rd Fleet) to head for Bougainville Island off New Guinea. Unlike Admirals Kinkaid, King, and Thomas C. Hart, Halsey had maintained a good relationship with MacArthur. MacArthur gave him the highest praise: "I liked him from the moment we met, and my respect and admiration increased with time. His loyalty was undeviating, and I placed the greatest confidence in his judgment. No name rates higher in the annals of our country's naval history."[20] Meanwhile, MacArthur led the SWPA forces directly under his command to the north coast of New Guinea and went on to land at New Britain as part of his step-by-step advance on the Philippines. MacArthur described his strategy, popularly called "leapfrogging," as follows: "It was the practical application of this system of warfare—to avoid the frontal attack with its terrible loss of life; to by-pass Japanese strong points and neutralize them by cutting their lines of supply; to thus isolate their armies and starve them on the battlefield."[21] He added, with customary self-praise: "This decision enabled me to accomplish the concept of the direct-target approach from Papua to Manila." Indeed, the adoption of this adroit strategy allowed the U.S. and Australian military, which had already gained sea and air supremacy, to gradually break down the Japanese hold on New Guinea and the Solomon Islands as they approached their objective, the Philippines.

By contrast, the Japanese army in the Pacific was gradually forced to withdraw. On April 18, 1943, Admiral Yamamoto Isoroku flew to the Solomon Islands to inspect and encourage Japanese troops. His plane was shot down by U.S. fighter planes because Americans had broken the Japanese codes. Washington kept the incident secret to preserve the decoding advantage, but the Japanese were shocked by Yamamoto's death. In September they reached the decision to reduce the defensive lines in accordance with the Senso Shido Taiko (War Instruction Outline). In response, MacArthur's army did not allow the offensive to slacken, and at the end of October made a fierce attack on Rabaul, Japan's last base in the region. Japanese air power at the base was destroyed and New Britain was almost overwhelmed. In February 1944 MacArthur's forces took the Admiralty Islands. In April he landed at Hollandia and Aitape in central New Guinea and in May opened a fierce battle with the Japanese on Wake Island, off the northwestern coast of New Guinea.

Egeberg later described MacArthur at that time. At the end of February, following the taking of the Admiralty Islands and on the night before MacArthur was to land on the northern coast of New Guinea with large-scale navy support, he was called to MacArthur's cabin at around 1:30 a.m. Egeberg found MacArthur in a state of agitation. He moved about in his nightclothes, emotionally recalling his years at West Point, his first assignment to the Philippines, and the dangers he had faced in the Philippines and during World War I. After about thirty minutes he gradually calmed down and suddenly said he wanted to go back to sleep.[22] Even MacArthur could not remain calm ahead of the landing operation. Huff confirmed Egeberg's observation that MacArthur's pattern was to vent his heightened emotions by talking uninterruptedly about his past experiences until he returned to normal.

Early next morning MacArthur and Egeberg went ashore in a landing craft. MacArthur, wearing khaki pants and open-necked shirt and his gold-braided military cap, stood straight, without attempting to protect himself from enemy attack. Those accompanying him had to hold themselves erect. Leading the way, MacArthur approached the bodies of two Japanese soldiers who had just been killed to check their rank and equipment. At that moment he showed his instinctive respect for fighting men. When MacArthur and Egeberg returned to the *Phoenix* cruiser, MacArthur scolded Egeberg for not wearing his officer's cap. MacArthur said that the braided cap was his trademark; since soldiers recognized it, he had to wear it and would keep on wearing it. He suggested, however, that Egeberg should wear a helmet from that time on because of the risk in landing.[23] Egeberg recalled that he was overwhelmed by MacArthur's fearless and daring attitude.

Egeberg recalled that sailors on the ship lined up for MacArthur's autograph, and he kept signing until evening. Although MacArthur had resolved not to drink during the war, he was so pleased with the successful landing that he talked about it and about Jean over a rare glass of bourbon. He claimed that the reason he had given up alcohol was the burden of his responsibility for the lives of all the officers in the southwest Pacific. With regard to MacArthur's everyday habits, Egeberg recalled that he ate in his cabin, accompanied usually by his adjutant and sometimes by Kenney and Egeberg. On one occasion he said that he would eat in the officers' mess, but then hesitated and the meal did not take place. Egeberg explained that MacArthur hesitated because he was uncomfortable and shy.

"He enjoyed eating with people he knew well,... but to sit down with a group of people that he didn't know bothered him very much. He felt responsible for the conversation" in the officers' mess. Egeberg, as a medical officer, commented that MacArthur was excessively self-conscious.[24]

Egeberg recalled the setting when he attended briefings for the April Hollandia landing:

> Twelve or fifteen of his officers were there, primarily from G3 [operations]. Among three or four rows of chairs, General MacArthur sat in the middle of the front row with General Sutherland on one side of him and General Stephen Chamberlin, his G3, on the other. Younger officers made the presentations of the options; the older ones enlarged on them, asked questions, and joined the more junior officers in attacking or defending the various plans....He never took a vote on the briefing issues, but asked questions, probed, threw in new possibilities, always ended by thanking the group, and then continued his weighing of possibilities, alone or sometimes with General Sutherland. On several occasions with me as silent audience he talked in the following vein.... We can attack at A or we can attack at B. If we do B, which I think we are more likely to carry off, the enemy has at least three alternatives. They can do X, Y, or Z. Now if the enemy does X, we could do A-prime or B-prime. If the enemy does the Y maneuver, we can do C-prime and should the enemy do Z we could perform D-prime and possibly E-prime....He would carry this scenario of our moves, and the Japanese responses to each of the possibilities and ours in return, all in his head in a period of an hour or more while we were driving, or perhaps just sitting. He pursued the alternatives much as in chess.[25]

Egeberg's description illustrates one of the distinctive characteristics of the MacArthur headquarters.

In the end, the Hollandia landing was successful, and MacArthur set up a base there. On the other hand, the attack on Biak was particularly difficult, so much so that heavy fighting continued for as long as two months. Adopting a different strategy, the Japanese no longer tried to repel the assault on the beach, where they would become cannon fodder for the Americans. Instead, they had foxholes dug in mountains and valleys in the rear, and there they tried to defend themselves from the assault of the Allies and to ambush enemy attackers. This strategy was later successfully applied in the battle at Iwo Jima. With the exception of Biak, MacArthur's army was able to take Wake Island and Noemfoor at the very western tip of New Guinea and other smaller islands up to Sansapor. In just three months MacArthur had succeeding in taking control of the entire twenty-four hundred kilometer (fifteen hundred miles) northern coast of New Guinea. On August 30 the headquarters was moved to Hollandia.[26]

In competition with MacArthur's forces, those under Nimitz also advanced successfully. Their capture of Makin and Tarawa in the Gilbert Islands in November 1943 was followed in February 1944 by landings on Kwajalein and Jalutt in the Marshall Islands where seven thousand members of the Japanese defense garrison were killed. They subsequently bombed the large Japanese naval base on Truk, destroying forty-three ships and 270 planes. In June, U.S. forces landed on Saipan in the Mariana Islands. Since the Japanese naval fleet had been defeated in June 1944 in the Battle of the Philippine Sea, the Japanese forces on Saipan were isolated; in July, thirty thousand troops of the Japanese garrison were killed and many Japanese residents committed suicide. The same fate awaited the defense garrisons at Tinian and Guam. Shocked by the fall of Saipan, the center of defense for the Japanese military, the Tojo cabinet collapsed. The Japanese mainland was now within range of U.S. B-29 planes and air strikes over Japanese large cities began.[27]

At this point, in June 1944, the JCS began to consider the invasion of the Japanese main islands. King proposed suspending MacArthur's campaign to recapture the Philippines and to attack Japan immediately after taking Formosa. Army Chief of Staff Marshall and Major General William H. Arnold, chief of the U.S. Army Air Forces, indicated their support for the proposal. MacArthur, however, opposed the plan vehemently, arguing that bypassing the Philippines to attack Formosa directly was not permissible from a strategic point of view. The conflict between MacArthur and King concerned military strategy, but it was also influenced subtly by a different and political factor: the presidential election campaign scheduled for the fall of 1944 and the possibility of MacArthur's candidacy.

MacArthur's heroic activities in the Pacific had had the effect of pushing forward his name as a powerful potential presidential candidate. Senator Arthur H. Vandenberg, a conservative Republican, took the initiative for the campaign. While affecting detachment, MacArthur, too, was inwardly waiting for an invitation to become a candidate. After he wrote a long letter to Vandenberg implying his willingness to run, supporters set to work. Their scenario for success was to bypass the primaries and have MacArthur nominated as presidential candidate at the Republican convention. However, a House representative from Nebraska publicized his correspondence with MacArthur in which MacArthur criticized the New Deal. With the public airing of opinions that he had wanted kept secret, MacArthur issued a statement on April 30, 1944, expressing his view that a supreme commander on the front lines should not run in the presidential election. Even if asked, therefore, he would not accept the nomination. Roosevelt, who saw MacArthur as his most dangerous potential opponent, was relieved.[28]

When Major Charles H. Morehouse, Egeberg's predecessor, returned to the United States to see his sick mother, he was asked by a local newspaper correspondent whether MacArthur wanted to run for president. Morehouse was said to have replied: "No, he is a soldier and desires to march on to Tokyo."[29] Because of this statement, Morehouse was, in effect, dismissed. The incident offers an indication of MacArthur's real thinking.

Since Roosevelt was planning to run for a fourth presidential term, he was careful not to alienate MacArthur and his supporters. He therefore arranged to meet MacArthur in Hawaii to discuss the strategy for invading Japan. Roosevelt traveled by heavy cruiser to Pearl Harbor, while MacArthur flew in the B-17 bomber *Bataan,* accompanied by no staff officers and just five adjutants. The conference, in which Nimitz and Admiral William D. Leahy also participated, was held at Pearl Harbor from July 26 to 28, 1944. Against Nimitz's idea of bypassing the Philippines to attack Formosa, MacArthur argued passionately that recapture of the Philippines would motivate the American and Philippine peoples and serve the national interest. Roosevelt gradually leaned toward MacArthur's position.[30] The JCS, as well, gave up on attacking Formosa. The Philippine Recapture Operation was formally approved, and it was decided that Nimitz would advance to Iwo Jima and Okinawa. MacArthur was delighted that, with this decision, his return to the Philippines became a possibility.[31]

"I Shall Return"

The Hawaii conference opened the way for the recapture of the Philippines, and that recapture was MacArthur's primary concern. It remained to be decided when and where to land. With its condition worsening, the Japanese army was focused only on defense, giving the United States a clear advantage in the choice of landing place. Based on useful information on the deployment of Japanese forces offered by local Filipino guerrillas, on September 21, 1944, MacArthur ordered a recapture of Leyte Island, southeast of Luzon. Leyte was the unforgettable place where he had worked when first assigned to the Philippines as a young officer.

Admiral Kinkade's 7th Fleet, which comprised forty-five ships (including six battleships and eighteen aircraft carriers), escorted 420 transport vessels carrying a total of sixty-five thousand 6th Army troops from Hollandia and Manus Island (one of New Guinea's Admiralty Islands) to the Philippines. At 6:00 a.m. on October 20 the troops began their landing at Tacloban on the northeast coast of Leyte and at Dulag Beach further to the south. The Japanese defense garrison was surely surprised at the sight of no fewer than five hundred ships lined up along the thirty or forty kilometer (about eighteen to twenty-four miles) of coastline. MacArthur was on board the flagship *Nashville*, and he had invited Sergio Osmena, who had become president of the Philippines following Quezon's death in Washington on August 1, 1944, to join the landing operation along with two members of his cabinet. MacArthur felt that their presence in the Philippines on the first day of the landing would signify to the Philippine people that their government had returned. According to Egeberg, MacArthur also placed great importance on the declaration he would make at the time of landing. He wrote the speech himself, and on the evening before the landing he rehearsed before Larry and Egeberg. Egeberg wrote: "He [MacArthur] felt that this was going to be a very important time, a time to rally the Philippine people, to reassure the guerrillas, to warn the Japanese, and to tell the world. There was no doubt that he was going to say, 'I have returned.'"[32]

At the time of the Hawaii conference in July, the Japanese Imperial General Headquarters made a firm decision to combine its army, navy, and air forces for an all-out attack on the Allies. Called the Shogo Sakusen (Winning Operation), this was thought to be the most crucial stage of the Pacific War. The Philippine theater in particular was termed Sho No. 1. Preparations for Sho No. 1 and Sho No. 2 (Formosa and Okinawa) were to be completed by the end of August. Preparations for Sho No.3 (the four main islands) and Sho No.4 (Hokkaido and the Kuril Islands) were to be completed by the end of October. For the Philippine theater, the 14th Army was upgraded to become the 14th Area Army. The 35th Army was newly organized with about 110,000 soldiers to defend the southern part of the Philippines including Leyte. At Luzon, the expected site of the decisive battle with the United States, about 130,000 troops of the 14th Area Army headquarters were to intercept the enemy. The headquarters of the Southern Area Army was moved to Manila.

In order to deal with U.S. air assaults on Okinawa, Formosa, and the Philippines, in October the Japanese navy attacked the mobile units of the 3rd Fleet under Halsey in a battle known in Japanese as the Taiwan Oki Kokusen (Air Battle Off Formosa). The headquarters announced big military gains but, in fact, damage on the U.S. side was light and no more than seventy-five aircraft were lost. By contrast, Japan suffered the loss of as many as 650 aircraft. This loss was to have an enormous impact on the Battle of Leyte Gulf, which was about to begin.[33]

On October 18 the Japanese Imperial General Headquarters issued the order to launch Sho No. 1 in the Philippine theater. Admiral Toyota Soemu, commander of the Combined Fleet, ordered the counterattack. The bold strategy of the Japanese was to use Vice Admiral Ozawa Jisaburo's First Mobile Fleet, comprising four aircraft carriers and two battleships, as a decoy to entice Halsey's 3rd Fleet. Meanwhile, the fleets of Kurita Takeo, Shima Kiyohide, and Nishimura Shoji would each burst into Leyte Gulf. On October 17, a large fleet of MacArthur's naval forces was approaching Leyte Gulf. On October 18, Leyte Bay was stormy, with winds blowing at thirty meters per second, but the fleet burst through the high waves into the bay. For several days a special U.S. team had been clearing the water of obstacles, including mines set by the Japanese. On the morning of October 20, the U.S. 7th Fleet opened naval gunfire in unison, and then four divisions of the 6th Army under Krueger's command landed at Tacloban and in the Dulag area. Since the Japanese had expected the decisive battle to take place on Luzon, only the 16th Division had been left to defend Leyte. Surprised by the sudden attack, the Japanese army was forced to retreat, making it easy for the Americans to land. Intelligence on Japanese movements obtained by guerrilla units was of great use to the U.S. side. MacArthur's army had completely outmaneuvered the Imperial General Headquarters and succeeded in seizing the advantage at the outset of the battle.

MacArthur watched the landing operation from the bridge of the *Nashville*. Just before 2:00 p.m. on October 23, he changed into a new military uniform, put on his Philippine field marshal's cap and Ray-Ban sunglasses, and boarded the landing craft. Picking up Osmena on the way, the boat headed for the landing point, called Red Beach, located some eight kilometers (five miles) south of the Tacloban Airfield. Because of dense fog and rain, the group had to wait in the landing craft for one or two hours. At last it ran ashore onto the beach, and the ramp was dropped. MacArthur was the first to disembark, walking through knee-high seawater. Osmena, Kenney, Sutherland, and Brigadier General Whitney followed him. Brigadier General Carlos P. Romulo of the Philippine army hurried to keep up with the taller Americans. Keen not to miss the good shots, cameramen clicked away as they walked.

MacArthur walked about quietly, exchanging comments with his officers. A signal officer handed him a portable microphone and the Voice of Freedom radio broadcast began. MacArthur took out his prepared notes and spoke: "People of the Philippines: I have returned. By the grace of Almighty God, our forces stand again on Philippine soil—soil consecrated by the blood of our two peoples. We have come, dedicated and committed to the task of destroying every vestige of enemy control over your daily lives, and restoring upon a foundation of indestructible strength, the liberties of your people.... The seat of your government is now, therefore, firmly re-established on Philippine soil."[34] The speech was partly modified to become shorter. MacArthur's voice and hand shook, overcome with emotion at having kept his "I shall return" promise two years and seven months after evacuating from Corregidor.

The Japanese Combined Fleet was successful in trapping Halsey's 3rd Fleet by using the Ozawa fleet as a decoy and, on October 24, the Japanese fleet of Admirals

Kurita, Shima, and Nishimura entered Leyte Gulf. MacArthur and Kinkaid guessed that the Japanese fleet would head for Leyte and attack the American transports. However, tricked by Ozawa's fleet, Admiral Halsey's fleet was far north of Leyte. MacArthur knew that the landing would have failed if even one Japanese battleship had entered the Gulf. Hundreds of ships were lined up like the proverbial ducks in a row. An enemy attack on the fleet would have caused grave losses in men and ships. It would have meant the end of the landing operation and the end of the counterattack on the Philippines.

Egeberg could easily sense MacArthur's deep concern, though he appeared to be calm. He wrote:

> There was more and quicker pacing than usual, more frequent pipe-lighting, and definite withdrawal from us....He stayed in his cabin much of this time. Finally he learned that the Japanese were using magnesium flares—those very bright and far-reaching lights sent up to come down by parachute. This obviously excited him, and he spoke with intensity: "If they're using flares they can't have radar, and without radar we'll get them in the dark. We'll get them!" he clenched his fist and his face emphasized his words. After that he seemed to relax a bit. This relaxation was a positive indication that he felt the outcome would be favorable and an indication that permeated the cabin with a feeling of relief.[35]

However, the movement of the Kurita fleet was the main reason for the Japanese defeat. Unable to receive the radio message from the Ozawa fleet that the decoy had succeeded, it turned back without carrying out the attack on the U.S. transport and cargo vessels, missing the prey before their eyes. As a result of this major miscalculation, the Battle of Leyte Gulf was, as MacArthur expected, a big victory for the U.S. Navy, which could use radar to attack the enemy, even at night. Halsey's 3rd Fleet was indeed far to the north, but once Nimitz realized that Kinkaid's 7th Fleet was in trouble, he ordered Halsey to turn south and pursue the Japanese fleet. Halsey sent shipboard planes to join the battle, even though he knew that the distance was too great for them to return to the carrier. Once the fighting was over, these planes made a forced landing on the former Japanese airfields at Tacloban and Dulag on Leyte. The shell-torn landing strips did not permit a normal landing and many of the planes were damaged.

The Battle of Leyte Gulf, which involved the full force of both the Japanese and the U.S. militaries, was one of the most bitterly fought naval battles in world history. Mistakenly believing that they held air supremacy, the Japanese suffered big losses, including three battleships, ten heavy cruisers, and four aircraft carriers, for a total of twenty-four ships including the *Musashi*, one of their newest and largest battleships. (By contrast, the Americans lost only three aircraft carriers and three destroyers.) With this defeat, the Japanese Combined Fleet was, in effect, destroyed. In addition, the Japanese lost 370 planes while the Americans lost ninety-nine. It was from this time that the navy introduced the kamikaze units whose suicide attacks would menace American forces. In the ground battle, Japanese mistakes accumulated. On October 22, the Southern Army Headquarters, which had advanced to Manila in order to carry out Sho No. 1, shifted the battle site from Luzon to Leyte and ordered the 14th Area Army to attack the U.S. Army on Leyte. However, General Yamashita Tomoyuki, the so-called Malayan Tiger, who had been commander of the 1st Area Army, was appointed commander of the 14th Area Army just two weeks before the American landing. Lieutenant General Muto Akira was named chief of staff of the 14th Area Army on the very day of the landing. By the time the 35th Army reinforcement forces, which consisted of the main part of the 30th Division and five infantry battalions of the 102nd Division, arrived at Ormoc on the west coast of Leyte on November 1, the 16th Division had already lost its organizational fighting power and soldiers were fleeing into the jungle.[36]

After the landing on Leyte, the U.S. military sent seven divisions as reinforcements in November and established a firm military base. MacArthur set up his headquarters at Tacloban and aimed to advance to Manila on Luzon and then to his final destination—Tokyo.

FROM THE PHILIPPINES TO JAPAN, OCTOBER 1944 TO AUGUST 1945

Control over Leyte Island

MacArthur's successful landing on Leyte meant that he had returned to the Philippines two years and seven months after his infamous withdrawal from Corregidor in March 1942. After setting up a military base at Tacloban on Leyte's northeast coast, he moved energetically around battlefields to free the entire Philippines from Japanese control. For MacArthur, retaking the Philippines was, of course, directed at securing a geographically important base for the advance on Japan. At a deeper level, however, it was also designed to wipe out the indignity of having deserted his men when he withdrew from Corregidor. MacArthur aimed to justify his actions to Roosevelt and to meet the expectations of the seventeen million Filipinos who were presumably awaiting his return. MacArthur wrote: "The Philippine Islands had constituted the main objective of my planning from the time of my departure from Corregidor in March 1942. From the very outset I regarded this strategic archipelago as the keystone of Japan's captured island empire, and, therefore, the ultimate goal of the plan of operations in the Southwest Pacific Area."[1]

MacArthur had now taken his first steps toward reaching the ultimate goal. Around Christmas 1944, when the deadly combat on Leyte had been continuing for more than two months, he declared that Japanese organized resistance had ebbed. (The announcement was made on December 26.) The declaration, written by MacArthur himself, evokes another one, written six years later, on the first Christmas after the outbreak of the Korean War, when he announced the end of hostilities. The statement at Leyte was also premature because the 8th Army under Robert L. Eichelberger would be mopping up the remnants of Japanese power for no less than four months thereafter. This declaration of victory, however, gave added glory to his promotion to general of the army. On December 15, ten days before the declaration, at the president's recommendation the U.S. Senate passed a bill to promote Richard J. Marshall, MacArthur, Dwight D. Eisenhower, and Henry H. Arnold to general of the army and William D. Leahy, Ernest J. King, and Chester W. Nimitz to fleet admiral. MacArthur's excessive self-awareness and overwhelming pride may have provoked the criticism against him.

MacArthur was eager to have the Philippine people fully understand that the Philippine government had returned to Leyte. With Osmena, he held a ceremony at the provincial capitol building at the southern end of Tacloban to mark the resumption of constitutional government. He wrote in his *Reminiscences:* "I believe that the civil power of government should be paramount to any power wielded by the military. I, therefore, restored to [*sic*] the duly elected Philippine government, in the person of President Osmena."[2] But MacArthur had by no means forgotten that Osmena had criticized his defense plans and had the budget reduced. The relationship between the two men cooled.

In the middle of the battle at Leyte, an incident almost claimed MacArthur's life. Brigadier General Burdette M. Fitch, the Southwest Pacific Area (SWPA) adjutant general recalled MacArthur's cool bravery:

> At Leyte a couple of days after the landing the Jap planes were coming in low, jumping over the mountain range, and were right down on us on the beach.... The antiaircraft gunners were so anxious to make good that they got a little careless in aiming their gun sights. One of these [American] shells went through General MacArthur's bedroom and landed on a couch across from his bed. The next morning he came into breakfast with us (we were a small staff there), and he brought the shell in and laid it down on a table in front of Marquat's place. He said, "Bill, ask your gunners to raise their sights just a little bit higher." But he was undisturbed and cool, and he was a courageous man.[3]

Fitch added that if the Japanese had been using napalm, they could have burned the Americans out in no time. Roger O. Egeberg's narrative was little different: "One night after the General had gone to bed, a Japanese plane flying very low strafed us. The tile on the roof shattered and danced, but two bullets came through a wall and landed in the beam about a foot-and-a-half from the General's head. The next morning he remarked on it—he hadn't gotten up—but suggested we take a look at it and possibly dig one out for him. He thought he might send it to Arthur."[4] MacArthur's luck had held.

According to Egeberg, MacArthur dined in a composed manner, even during the regular Japanese air raids. Usually he had breakfast alone. His deputy joined him for lunch. For dinner, he was usually joined by his adjutant and eight or ten of the Bataan Boys who knew him well. Almost every night the Japanese army bombing ritual would begin. Sometimes twice in an evening, Japanese aircraft would fly in low from an airfield in southern Luzon. MacArthur would be talking about the war in Europe, or some old Army story, or general U.S. political issues. (He never talked about the problems his own army was facing.) The officers would listen, and sometimes Sutherland might respond. Sometimes, however, the engine roar of the bombing aircraft would echo in their ears, and, as the American antiaircraft attacks became stronger, talking would be difficult: "As the firing mounted and the crescendo of the engine began to break through, I would usually light a cigarette to see if I could, and possibly to show that my hand wasn't shaking. One particular general would freeze with a petrified look on his face. He would stick out his tongue.... The General might stop talking, waiting for the plane to level off, or for noise to subside enough for them to hear each other."[5] Each time MacArthur was resolute and showed absolutely no sign of fear. Full of courage, he glared at those around him.

One problem that did bother MacArthur was Sutherland's relationship with Elaine Clarke, an Australian woman whose husband had served as an officer in the Middle East. Sutherland had Clarke enlist in the Women's Army Corps (WAC) as a captain, and brought her to Hollandia in New Guinea. MacArthur was surprised to learn that Clarke was serving drinks to the officers at the headquarters as if she were a hostess. He had been annoyed that an Australian woman was enlisted in the WAC, that her rank was too high, and that she was doing an unsuitable job, and he told Sutherland to send her back to Brisbane. But Clarke did not return, and had instead come to Leyte. Furthermore, Sutherland had ordered Colonel Jack Sverdrup, who was responsible for constructing the headquarters, to build a cottage for her at Tanauan. When MacArthur heard the story from Egeberg, his response was explosive. MacArthur was amazed and exclaimed, "I can't believe it!" He ordered "Get me Dick!" What MacArthur said to Sutherland was quite unusual. "General MacArthur had blown his top.... It was violent.... It continued for several minutes. Officers in the street below were plugging their ears."[6] Sutherland was ordered to have Clarke leave Leyte within forty-eight hours. Two days later, she loaded her belongings into a plane and departed for Brisbane.

Thus the affair was settled, but it had eroded MacArthur's trust in Sutherland. Although MacArthur was already aware that many of his men disliked Sutherland's arrogance and selfishness, he had given Sutherland preferential treatment as his closest aide for several reasons. First, MacArthur prided himself on having promoted Sutherland in the army. Sutherland was unusual in that he had joined the army after graduating from Yale University during World War I. He was not a graduate of West Point, usually favored by MacArthur. However, having worked alongside Sutherland several times, MacArthur recognized his ability, and finally promoted him to lieutenant general. Second, Sutherland had the ability to convert MacArthur's ideas into specific reports and concrete policies. He was skilled at handling the personnel matters and daily business that MacArthur was reluctant to become involved in. According to Egeberg, although Sutherland was a loner and had few friends, he was tough and combative and he could fire people in a calm and businesslike manner.[7] Third, even if MacArthur had dismissed Sutherland and sought someone in Washington to replace him, there was no certainty that a more capable person would have been available. There was, in short, a kind of father-son relationship between the two men. However, after fulfilling his wish to accompany MacArthur to Tokyo after the war, Sutherland left within half a year, probably because of the problem regarding Clarke.

Advance toward Manila

After MacArthur was promoted from general of the Philippines to five-star general of the U.S. Army, his next target was an attack on Luzon. Not until the capture of Manila would his "I shall return" promise be fulfilled. He assembled two hundred thousand (later 280,000) troops for the attack. On the Japanese side, the defense force led by General Yamashita Tomoyuki initially totaled 287,000 men in Luzon, but since forty thousand to forty-five thousand men had been lost on Leyte, its strength was declining. The 14th Area Army therefore developed its Ruson Jikyu Sakusen Keikaku (Attrition War Plan in Luzon). According to the plan, the Japanese army would avoid a war of annihilation against the Americans, withdrawing instead into the mountains in order to keep the massive U.S. forces tied down on Luzon as long as possible, thereby postponing their attack on the Japanese homeland. On January 4, 1945, the headquarters of the 14th Area Army was moved from Manila to the mountainous area of Baguio, north of the Lingayen Gulf, in preparation for the American landing.

On January 6, no less than eight hundred ships of the U.S. fleet appeared at Lingayen Gulf in Luzon. A navy aircraft telegraphed that the fleet was so expansive that the last line of vessels could not be recognized in the haze. Using every possible trick, MacArthur had drawn Japanese attention to the southern part of Luzon and then chosen as the landing area this spot in the north, where the Japanese army had once landed. For three days through January 8, fierce gunfire continued. Then, on January 9, some 190,000 fighters of the 6th Army began a landing from three sides. The Japanese 23rd Division intercepted them, but the U.S. forces immediately overwhelmed the Japanese coastal artillery base and easily established a bridgehead. Under MacArthur's orders, the U.S. landing forces rushed to get to the city of Manila, about two hundred kilometers (125 miles) to the south. Filipino civilians who were expecting an American victory welcomed the advancing troops and offered their cooperation. Yamashita attempted a counterattack by sending the 2nd Tank Division and the 3rd Brigade to help the 23rd Division, but they were no match for the heavily armored U.S. tanks. The 3rd Brigade was annihilated. The 23rd Division clashed with the enemy at night, but the situation simply worsened. Yamashita decided to withdraw his forces from Manila in order to avoid burning or destroying the city. By the end of January, his troops had at last retreated to their second base at the foot of Mt. Baguio. All the tanks were lost. Persistent bombardment of Clark Field, the largest airfield in the Philippines, destroyed the remaining Japanese aircraft, and Japanese air supremacy was completely lost.[8]

MacArthur had arrived at Lingayen Gulf in a heavy cruiser by dawn on January 9. He wrote of his feelings on the way, as he looked toward Manila, Corregidor, Marivales, and Bataan gleaming far off on the horizon: "I felt an indescribable sense of loss, of sorrow, of loneliness, and of solemn consecration."[9] He boarded the landing craft and headed for the beach, but right before the landing point he dismounted and once more took springing strides into the water.

The U.S. Army thus attempted to make a dash to Manila, but Japanese resistance was so fierce that the battle seesawed back and forth. MacArthur established his headquarters at Dagupan near the Gulf, and offered encouragement to General Walter Krueger, who was commanding the 6th Army at the front. MacArthur revealed his feelings to Egeberg: "Doc, I want to get in there early. Three years ago I was driven out of there—made it an open city to save it."[10] MacArthur joined the 1st Cavalry, which had the important role of fighting off enemy attacks and advancing straight into Manila. It also had the job of liberating Santo Tomas, the large civilian internment camp, and nearby Bilibid Prison. On February 5, MacArthur sat next to his driver as usual as his jeep pushed its way forward through the tanks, armored trucks, and other larger vehicles on the road. By the next morning, they had caught up with the 37th Infantry Division, which was making its way down Route 3. MacArthur's jeep took its place at the head of the group, indicating how strongly MacArthur wanted to get to Manila and free the imprisoned citizens. While they were in Dagupan, MacArthur had his sixty-fifth birthday. They had a little impromptu parade down the main street up to his house where he stood on the second story veranda while they serenaded him with "Happy Birthday."[11]

On February 3, a mixed troop, comprising a guerrilla force of the U.S. 6th Army as well as Filipino guerrillas, entered Manila and carried out a surprise attack. The Japanese army withdrew as the U.S. Army approached and, as noted, arranged to leave Manila an open city. However, the Manila defense forces, consisting of about sixteen thousand men, and the Noguchi troop, consisting of about four thousand men, engaged in a do-or-die fight under Rear Admiral Iwabuchi Sanji. A breakdown in communications because of the destruction of equipment meant that they had missed the chance of retreating from the surprise U.S. attack. On February 12, the U.S. Army crossed the Pasig River and, after completely surrounding the downtown Manila area, began an indiscriminate bombardment. On February 25, Iwabuchi committed suicide and, on March 3, the U.S. Army took control of the entire base in the city. As a result of intense downtown fighting that continued for about a month, much of the downtown area was reduced to rubble and about ninety thousand Philippine citizens caught up in the violence lost their lives. Anti-Japanese guerrilla activities prompted the Japanese army to engage in indiscriminate atrocities, adding to the number of casualties. Deaths caused by the U.S. bombing amounted to 30 percent of the total killed. Although the civilian casualties were unintended, it cannot be denied that Manila paid a high price for liberation.[12] At the Hawaii conference, MacArthur had stated confidently to Roosevelt that the Philippine route would result in fewer casualties on the Allied side, but the reality went beyond his assertion.

With the American military's entry into Manila, many Americans who had been imprisoned for two years and eight months were released, along with military prisoners in the Cabanatuan and Bilibid internment camps outside of Manila. MacArthur himself visited Bilibid camp. Entering a small hall, he saw an acquaintance, a general named Wilson, who had been captured on Bataan. With food supplies almost gone, he appeared to be on the point of death by starvation. MacArthur was informed that the number of deaths had radically increased in the past several months. He shook hands, put his hand on the prisoners' shoulders, leaned forward to catch their eyes, and spoke in a quiet, husky voice.[13] MacArthur had thus reached his goal after two and a half years and a sixty-four hundred kilometer (four thousand mile) journey from Australia.

Recapture of Bataan and Corregidor

At almost the same time as the Manila campaign, the U.S. Army began its recapture of Bataan and Corregidor, both unforgettable places for MacArthur. On February 16, 1945, MacArthur rose at 4:30, hours earlier than usual, and headed by jeep for Bataan via San Fernando. His expression was more serious than ever before. The 151st Regiment landed at Mariveles on the same day, and the 1st Infantry Regiment of the 6th Division was moving down the east coast of the Bataan Peninsula. MacArthur's party headed south along the eastern road where U.S. and Philippine prisoners had been forced to endure the Death March. They reached Pilar in the center of the peninsula, where the defense line had once been drawn, and advanced further. Brigadier General Clyde D. Edelman, who had joined them, asked MacArthur to turn back. But MacArthur reportedly said: "No, this is easing an ache that my heart has carried for three years. I'm going forward. I'll lead by personal patrol."[14] The dead bodies of Japanese soldiers lay on the roadside. The Japanese army had been repulsed just thirty minutes earlier and there was a possibility that those who survived might attack in retribution.

Egeberg recalled that, after fifteen or twenty minutes of advancing slowly through the jungle, the road suddenly opened out into an open space. They had reached a Japanese field camp, with the rice cooked, a kettle steaming, and a machine gun that had been set down. All indications pointed to a hasty Japanese departure. At this point, a P-38 aircraft passed overhead and soon set its sights on them as it descended. Egeberg realized that it was an American plane: "I started waving at the plane like mad as it came in sight. It—he—was only a few hundred feet up and he was aimed right at us, but he didn't pull the trigger and he didn't come back. I found a log on which I very much needed to sit. But not the General. He wandered around a bit with his hands in his pockets, distressed at our not being able to go farther."[15] Egeberg recalled MacArthur's mood that night: "That evening he [MacArthur] relived with relish the patrol on which he had taken us....'Doc, it's been a long time since I led a patrol into no-man's land. Makes you tingle a bit, doesn't it?'...This was a deeply emotional time for the General. Probably more than his return to the Philippines, this return to Bataan was the real cleansing of the old defeat, of the ignominy and the starvation and death of his earlier troops. He had said three times that day, 'You don't know what a leaden load this lifts from my heart.'"

On Corregidor, for half a month from January 23, the U.S. Army Air Forces used three thousand tons of explosives to inflict heavy losses on about forty-five hundred Japanese defense forces. Navy mine sweepers cleared mines laid all around the island by the Japanese. On February 16, the day MacArthur left for Bataan, the 503rd Parachute Infantry Regiment consisting of two thousand men dropped onto Corregidor to launch a surprise attack on the Japanese defense forces. Due to the heavy winds and narrow landing space, some 10 percent sustained injuries, but the parachute regiment succeeded in occupying Topside in the center of the island. Moreover, the regiment landed from the southern coast, instead of from the northern coast as the Japanese had expected. Compared with what had happened three years and three months earlier, defense and offense were reversed. The routed Japanese set off mines in Malinta Tunnel and tried to use the ensuing confusion to launch an assault on the U.S. Army. The plan failed, however, and with the exception of nineteen who were taken prisoners, all of the Japanese were killed. On March 2, after two weeks of fighting, the stronghold of Corregidor fell to the Americans. On the same day, in a series of events that exhibited his romantic personality, MacArthur made a triumphant return to Corregidor with several Bataan Boys in four PT boats. He immediately held a flag-raising ceremony in the central square, ordering the troops to raise the colors, saying, "Let no enemy ever haul them down."[16] It was a satisfying moment for MacArthur.

Meanwhile the U.S. 8th Army conducted mopping-up operations on the surrounding islands near Luzon. Against fierce Japanese resistance, it landed on Palawan at the end of February and on Mindanao, Panay, and Cebu in March.

In the case of Luzon, by contrast, the Japanese main troops withdrew from Manila and shifted to a war of attrition in the mountains. Their most important task was to transfer munitions from their supply base to the mountains, but they were blocked by U.S. aircraft and Philippine guerrillas and their defense capability was seriously weakened. On March 3, defense forces in Manila were all killed in battle; the remaining Japanese who were hiding in the mountains were bombed by the Americans and attacked by guerrillas. At the end of April, the 14th Army Headquarters in Baguio fell and Yamashita and his men were driven deep into the northern mountains. They suffered severe food shortages and disease until the war ended on August 15. About 631,000 Japanese troops participated in the defense the Philippines of whom 498,600 were killed in battle or died of hunger or disease. The losses constituted 79 percent of the whole, four out of every five men; they also constituted one-fifth of total losses in the Pacific War. The figures underscore just how heavy the casualties were in the Philippine war.

Osmena, who had entered Manila with MacArthur, took over as president of the Philippines and on March 21, Jose P. Laurel, president of the pro-Japanese puppet government, moved from Baguio to exile in Japan. His departure marked the actual end of the Japanese control of the Philippines.[17]

De-Japanization and Democratization of the Philippines

MacArthur set up his new headquarters in the former city government office building in Manila. It was a strong building and had survived the war with only partial damage. As soon as the engineering unit had repaired the building, MacArthur took over the mayor's office. This room became the base from which he examined ways of rebuilding the Philippines and from which he planned the invasion of Japan, his final target.

As security in Manila was gradually restored, MacArthur made arrangements to bring Jean and his family from Brisbane. He told his adjutants frankly how much he missed Jean and Arthur, now seven, and in March they arrived in Manila. The family had been separated for five months. In Brisbane, as in Manila and Corregidor, Jean had gained popularity as a charming, gentle, good-natured, and sociable woman. When shopping for groceries or other supplies, she refrained from moving to the head of the queue, preferring to chat with other women as she waited in line. Visitors to her home would sometimes try to lead her into conversation about the war in order to get information. Jean would always reply with a smile that she knew only what she read in the newspapers.[18] It is hard to estimate just how much MacArthur, who was seen as stiff and reserved, was helped by his wife, but it is clear that her return changed his everyday life. In contrast to life during the campaign, he could now follow a relaxed and settled routine. Up at seven in the morning, he would work at home until about nine-thirty, when he went to the office. He would return for lunch at about quarter to two in the afternoon, and then change and take a nap. He would return to the office at four and come home at seven-thirty. His one entertainment was watching movies in the basement with Jean several times a week.[19] For her part, Jean frequently visited wounded soldiers in hospital.

Many problems caused by the Japanese military control over the Philippines were brought to MacArthur. Osmena had returned to Manila only in February, and the political and economic foundation of the Philippine government was weak. Furthermore, the relationship between MacArthur and Osmena was a cool one. To most Filipinos, MacArthur was a symbol of hope and an almost godlike presence. Therefore, it was not to the Philippine government but to the U.S. Army that they brought their complaints about Japanese sympathizers and those who had worked for the Japanese army. Those who were accused were in fear of being executed by the Americans. MacArthur ordered four staff members to work on the de-Japanization and democratization of the Philippines: Colonel Elliott R. Thorpe, who led the Counter Intelligence Corps (CIC); Brigadier General Bonner F. Fellers, MacArthur's military secretary; Colonel Crawford F. Sams, who was in charge of health and welfare, and Colonel Courtney Whitney, who had gained a reputation for organizing Philippine guerrilla resistance against the Japanese.

Thorpe, who had experienced the Japanese attack while stationed in the Netherlands East Indies, was transferred to Australia at Sutherland's recommendation and thereafter was put in charge of CIC. In this position, he dealt with the Philippine administration. After the Japanese were swept out of Manila, the CIC and the Philippine Civil Administration Unit (PCAU) were stationed in the city and

tasked with securing order. Thorpe's next job was to abolish the censorship established under the Japanese military control system. He did this without obtaining authorization from the War Department. Thorpe wanted to act promptly
because there were many in Washington, including Secretary of the Interior Harold L. Ickes, who were critical of MacArthur, and Thorpe worried about when
and in what form they might interfere in the Philippine administration. In addition to the abolition of censorship, he wrote a declaration that guaranteed free
speech and MacArthur signed it. Thorpe recalled that MacArthur rested his hand
on Thorpe's shoulder and said, "Thorpe, you have a flaming pen."[20] Thorpe was
deeply impressed.

The biggest issue Thorpe faced was dealing with alleged collaborators. He
exposed more than five thousand people, and arrested and put in jail members
of the country's leading families. Since he finished the job late at night, he waited
until the following morning to report to MacArthur. MacArthur responded that,
although some Filipinos may have engaged in bribery or immoral acts to survive
under the Japanese control, this was a matter for the Philippine people to handle.
All that the U.S. military government could do was to punish those in local government and above who had collaborated with the Japanese in order to profit
financially. Although MacArthur's attitude may have been based on his humani-
tarianism and the principle of nonintervention, it may also have derived from his
sympathy for the upper-class Filipinos with whom he had long acquaintance and
deep connections. In his biography of MacArthur, William Manchester wrote:
"In the abstract MacArthur was humane, even compassionate....Yet he could
be wildly inconsistent when the oppressors were friends of his."[21] This tendency
could be seen in the case of Manuel Roxas, who defeated Osmena in the election
of July 1946 to become president of the Philippines. Roxas had worked for a
long time in MacArthur's headquarters as a staff officer and was treated warmly
by MacArthur but he was later criticized by the Philippine people for his close
association with José P. Laurel's pro-Japanese puppet government.

Thorpe, who had planned severe punishment of the pro-Japanese collaborators, had to shift to a more lenient policy in accordance with MacArthur's views.
He later commented that "knowing the Filipinos and Philippine history, I knew
that the minute that we left the Filipinos would wash it out. They'd bribe each
other, and that'd be the end of it."[22] On the afternoon of his conversation with
MacArthur, Thorpe visited his old acquaintance Osmena and reported his intention to hand over to the Philippine government the treatment of imprisoned
collaborators (about fifty-six hundred cases). Osmena had just appointed an
attorney general, however, and indicated that he could not make any sudden
decisions. In fact, the list of prisoners included the names of six mayors, and
Osmena was at a loss trying to decide how to deal with them. After waiting two

days, Thorpe took all the personal records and the prison keys and passed them to Osmena without comment. This was a last-ditch measure to avoid having the United States drawn into problems among Philippine citizens. MacArthur wrote in his *Reminiscences* that Ickes had interfered with Philippine sovereignty from above and had intended to shoot or hang all Filipinos who had associated with the pro-Japanese puppet government, but that Secretary of War Henry L. Stimson and Roosevelt had supported his stance.[23] Had Ickes been free to handle matters as he wished, the postwar Philippines would have been a place of great confusion.

The second person appointed to handle de-Japanization and democratization of the Philippines was Brigadier General Bonner F. Fellers. Born in Illinois in 1896, Fellers graduated from West Point and in 1922 attracted favorable attention from MacArthur in the Philippines. Based on this experience during his service on Corregidor from 1936 to 1938, he was appointed staff officer to MacArthur and worked as a liaison officer between MacArthur and Quezon. After a period of service in North Africa, Fellers once again became a staff officer for MacArthur in October 1943, when he was appointed chief of planning and chief of the psychological warfare section in the SWPA headquarters in Australia. During the New Guinea campaign, he clashed with his superior, Steven J. Chamberlin, chief of G-3, and was transferred to G-1 (personnel), but soon afterward he was selected as military secretary by MacArthur. His job was to keep MacArthur advised of problems in the area. The position filled the gap between adjutant and higher adjutant chief, but it was commonly viewed as an inquisitor's position.

The administrative reforms for Philippine democratization handled by Fellers included the important task of setting up a temporary government in each province to fill the gap created by the withdrawal of the Japanese. For this purpose, he needed to select anti-Japanese or pro-American personnel to replace those who had favored the Japanese. Fortunately, Fellers had lived in the Philippines for about five years and during that time gained knowledge of Philippine society by socializing with persons of importance. These personal relationships helped him carry out these difficult administrative reforms. He sent new qualified personnel to the various provincial governments, thus strengthening the organization of each government and laying a foundation for rebuilding and reform.[24] The organization and personnel in both national and local politics contributed greatly to America's control over the postwar nation.

The third person appointed to handle Philippine affairs was Brigadier General Crawford F. Sams, who was born in St. Louis, Missouri, and after graduating from the Medical School of Washington University became a military doctor. He served in the Middle East during World War II, and in May 1945 Sams was appointed to the military government staff of the Philippines GHQ, with responsibility for health, education, and welfare. His superior was Brigadier General William Crist, head of G-5 (public affairs and civilian-military relations) and in charge of military government. The entire Philippines had been damaged in the war. Facilities and houses were destroyed, the water supply had been disrupted, and disease was widespread. Sams began his work by getting a medical support team from the United States. Personnel were assembled and the team organized at training centers for military government staff at Monterey and at Yale University. Sams had to get food, clothing, and medical supplies shipped from the United States, competing for priority against weapons and ammunition. Insecticide and daily household goods were also necessary. When the Okinawa campaign began in April 1945, Sams was made responsible for the Philippines and Okinawa, and his workload reached a peak.

In the Philippines, Sams worked to control the spread of disease, in particular gastrointestinal disorders, typhoid, and smallpox. Many corpses lay untended. The deterioration of water systems produced an outbreak of fly-borne diseases. American teams sprayed the city of Manila with DDT from aircraft. They mobilized troops to help with water shortages by carrying water from the Pasig River. By late February 1945, heavy fighting had ended in Manila, but mopping-up operations continued. Public health activities had to be conducted with care around important facilities such as airfields and harbors.[25]

This series of administrative policies implemented in the Philippines offered effective models for the occupation of Japan that began immediately after its surrender.

The Rise of Whitney

The fourth officer responsible for the demilitarization and democratization of the Philippines was Colonel Courtney Whitney, whose role was incomparably more important than that of the other three. Whitney's outstanding administrative ability in the Philippines gained him MacArthur's strong confidence and, overcoming the high wall that surrounded the Bataan Boys, he gradually approached MacArthur's inner circle. After MacArthur's headquarters moved from Manila to Tokyo, Whitney would exercise enormous power in the occupation of Japan as MacArthur's closest aide after Sutherland and Marshall left Japan. Yet he was not one of the Bataan Boys who had risked their lives together. How did Whitney gain the trust and favor of MacArthur in just a few years?

Consider, first, Whitney's background. He was born in Maryland in 1897. When the United States entered World War I in 1917, he enlisted as a private in the 3rd Infantry of the District of Columbia National Guard and was inducted into the U.S. Army as a private in the newly formed aviation section of the Signal Corps Reserve. When he received his commission as a second lieutenant, he entered the Signal Corps Aviation School and in 1923 graduated from Columbia National Law School and received a Bachelor of Laws degree. (There is also some information that Whitney attended the night school of the Columbia National Law School, now George Washington University, and obtained a doctorate in law.) In 1925 he was assigned as first lieutenant to the U.S. Army Air Forces in the Philippines. At one point, he returned to Washington, where he became head of the publications section of the information division attached to the staff section of the Air Corps. In June 1927, Whitney resigned from the military and returned to Manila to establish a law practice. In 1940, as war with Japan approached, Whitney returned to active duty as a major and was appointed assistant chief of the legal division of the U.S. Army Air Forces. In April 1943, Whitney, now a colonel, was named chief of the Philippine Regional Section of the Allied Intelligence Bureau in the SWPA. For his exceptional organization and supervision of the guerrilla resistance in the Philippines, he was awarded the Distinguished Service Medal. In January 1945, Whitney was promoted to brigadier general. Early in 1946 he joined MacArthur's staff as chief of the Government Section of the supreme commander for the Allied Powers in Japan (GHQ/SCAP). Whitney became well known for his outstanding ability in demilitarizing and democratizing Japan through policies such as the enactment of a new constitution and the purge.[26]

How did Whitney become close to MacArthur? Whitney first met MacArthur when he was transferred to the U.S. Army Air Forces in the Philippines in 1925 and worked as a daredevil pilot stationed at Nichols Field on the outskirts of Manila. At this time MacArthur was commanding the Military District of Manila in his second tour of duty in the Philippines. However, Whitney resigned from the Army Air Forces after just two years and opened his law practice in Manila, while also becoming involved in mining and other enterprises. During his military service and his work as a lawyer, Whitney spent some fifteen years in the Philippines. This long experience worked to his advantage. In particular, through his work as a lawyer Whitney became well acquainted with the expatriate American community as well as with Philippine society and became friends with Manila's political and financial elite. Moreover, from 1935, when MacArthur returned for his fourth tour in the Philippines and became Quezon's military advisor, Whitney had various contacts with MacArthur's group. He often met MacArthur socially and he later recalled that he also had a close relationship with Sutherland. His appointment as chief of the legal division of the Army Air Forces immediately before the outbreak of war between the United States and Japan was largely owing to his relationships with MacArthur and Sutherland.[27]

Whitney used this position as a springboard to raise his reputation as a skillful practitioner of the law, gradually gaining the attention of Sutherland. He used this relationship with Sutherland to advance professionally.

Three years later, in 1943, Whitney got lucky. According to Manchester, the chance was connected with MacArthur's possible presidential candidacy. That year, as Arthur H. Vandenberg, an influential senator, was taking steps to set MacArthur up as a Republican candidate, Willoughby, chief of G-2 and Bataan Boy, was visiting Washington. He put Vandenberg in touch with Sutherland, Lloyd Lehrbas, and two new members of the Moresby staff, one of whom was Whitney.[28] Laurence E. Bunker, who was deputy chief of staff and aide to Brigadier General Richard Marshall from the time they were in Australia, stated that, when Sutherland came to Washington looking for somebody to take charge of the guerrilla operation in the Philippines, he noticed Whitney, who happened to be there.[29] Both statements, however, are clearly incorrect. As noted earlier, Whitney and Sutherland already had a close relationship from Whitney's days as a lawyer and, by April 1943, Whitney had already been appointed chief of MacArthur's intelligence section. Moreover, after returning to the military as a captain in 1940, Whitney had had the rare distinction of being promoted to colonel in less than three years. This quick promotion indicated that his legal knowledge, control of guerrilla forces, and particularly his anti-enemy propaganda, strengthening of intelligence networks, and organization of guerrilla activities to assist MacArthur's forces, were all highly regarded. These were the very qualities that MacArthur was looking for. It is difficult to think of other reasons for his unusually favorable treatment of Whitney.

In the end, it was Whitney's leadership of the guerrilla campaign against the Japanese that was the main factor in his rise to power. In this, he was probably able to make good use of social contacts he had made during his long residence in the Philippines. Samuel S. Auchincloss Jr., who worked under deputy chief Brigadier General Spencer B. Akin in intercepting and decoding Japanese military communications, recalled as follows:

> We had another responsibility and that was to provide signal supplies for the guerrilla network throughout the islands in the Western Pacific and in the Philippines. The actual guerrilla network was commanded by Colonel Whitney and by the Navy.…One of them, Colonel Fertig in Mindanao, also commanded the native guerrilla forces. On Mindanao there were about twelve thousand organized natives who were paid regularly during the war in gold and with trade goods like cigarettes, nylon stockings, chocolate bars and matchbooks inscribed with the message "I WILL RETURN." These people harassed the Japanese

and provided excellent information to us right up to the day we landed back on Leyte.[30]

Bunker disclosed the following fact:

> I don't know what the contact in Manila had been before the war between Sutherland and Whitney, but Sutherland brought him back to the SWPA headquarters on that job.... It was Sutherland's decision. MacArthur let Sutherland run the headquarters, particularly as far as subordinate personnel were concerned. Of course, Whitney came back in a subordinate position. He was supposed to be working under G-3, but, as time went on, Whitney gradually arranged it so that he was reporting directly to Sutherland rather than to [General Stephen] Chamberlin. Then when we went up into the Philippines, actually Whitney was an old hand. In the Philippines he had all kinds of contacts. When he went up to Leyte with the command, at that time there were various local problems.[31]

But according to Bunker he handled them all well. Bunker also described a key episode in which Whitney gained MacArthur's respect:

> It really started in the Philippines.... MacArthur had asked Sutherland to have a letter prepared. When Sutherland took it to the General, the General found it unsatisfactory. He said, "This is not what I want. This requires special understanding of the legal problems involved. You have to put somebody else on it." Sutherland said, "Well, why don't I get Whitney to do it?" Whitney took it and produced exactly what MacArthur wanted. From that time on, Whitney was drawn more and more into that relationship with the General. It was primarily because Whitney had an ability to understand more clearly some of the problems that the General faced with civilian authorities than the staff as a whole did.[32]

As Bunker's evidence makes clear, Whitney obtained MacArthur's unreserved trust because of his expertise in legal affairs. This expertise was indispensable for administration in the Philippines but, even though there were many military experts at GHQ, no one was better than Whitney in handling civilian administration. Taking advantage of this rare situation and ignoring his superior Chamberlin, Whitney raised his own profile by making a political approach to Sutherland, who was second in authority to MacArthur.

On the other hand, Whitney also drew criticism, as well as praise, from those around him for his self-made career and calculating personality, his willingness to use any means to achieve his goals, and his undisguised tendency to approach MacArthur intuitively. Major General (later Lieutenant General) Edward M. Almond, who served as chief of staff in Tokyo, criticized him severely: "Whitney was a smart, ruthless, and incisive lawyer. He realized early in his career the advantage of being a satellite to MacArthur, he made it his business to be agreeable with MacArthur, he would go to great lengths to obtain his purposes."[33] Brigadier General Burdette M. Fitch, the adjutant general, also reported: "Whitney had insinuated himself into the favor of the General." Fitch claimed: "His reputation as an attorney wasn't too bright and shining. I and a number of other staff heads never quite knew how to take Whitney....I think Sutherland knew that as an attorney Whitney would be valuable to him and MacArthur."[34] Brigadier General (later Lieutenant General) Alonzo P. Fox recalled: "He was a sharp man and I would say quite sensitive. His boiling point was very, very low on certain matters, especially if anyone infringed upon his particular domain. When somebody was either crossing him or getting into what he felt was his field, he could be a sharp and tough man to deal with. I've heard that said [about his vindictiveness]."[35] To the comment that Whitney brought back so many objects to his home in the United States that it looked like a museum, Fox responded that Whitney had considerable means in his own right from his mining interests in Manila.

Thorpe, chief of CIC, said:

> He [MacArthur] had some outstanding men....Dick Sutherland was a great soldier—ruthless but able. The only two sorry apples were Whitney and Willoughby....When we went back into Manila, General William Crist, who lived in Bradenton, was in charge of the military government for about three days. Then he was relieved, and Courtney Whitney was put in charge. Well, the people who had just gotten into Santo Tomas internment camp were foaming at the mouth....He was a slick operator...Whitney cultivated the Old Man [MacArthur] very assiduously. He didn't rush at this thing, little by little built it up, so that the Old Man was relying on him more.[36]

Egeberg described Whitney as "a slimy son-of-a-bitch." His criticism was based on Whitney's command of the guerrilla war. He claimed that, in order to use his position to best advantage, Whitney kept the guerrillas from establishing relationships with anyone but himself at headquarters. Egeberg was also critical of Whitney's actions in an incident that occurred in Manila. Whitney came to Egeberg's office, explained that he wanted to take a month's leave to return to Washington because of a family problem, and tearfully asked Egeberg to get MacArthur's special permission. On Egeberg's request, MacArthur gave Whitney permission to be away for six weeks. Two days later, however, Whitney told Egeberg that he had decided not to go home because MacArthur needed him too much. Egeberg was angry because Whitney had used him in a ruse to raise his profile with MacArthur. Even before this incident, Egeberg had once told MacArthur directly that Whitney was not appropriate as a staff officer, but MacArthur had thought for a moment and then changed the topic. He had already decided on Whitney's capability and helpfulness.[37]

Through his outstanding legal competence and careful but aggressive personality, Whitney had thus emerged as the number-one civil administrator of the Philippines and had secured MacArthur's trust. A glorious pathway to Tokyo was opening for him.

Japanese Surrender

With the expectation of Japan's defeat, planning for occupation was reaching a climax among U.S. government leaders in Washington. As early as 1943 the State Department had set up the Far East Area Committee (FEAC), and in early 1944 the Post-War Programs Committee (PWC), comprising officials of the ranks of secretary, undersecretary, and department chief, was established to discuss the demilitarization and democratization of Japan's politics, economy, military, and society. The original Office of Far Eastern Affairs was upgraded to the Far Eastern Section. Moreover, the Joint Chiefs of Staff, the War Department, the Navy Department, and the Department of the Treasury were each preparing occupation policies. At this point, however, it was necessary to finalize the overall policy by unifying the individual planning modified by each department. The State-War-Navy Coordinating Committee (SWNCC), established at the end of 1944, determined a series of important policies for the occupation of Japan.

In the international arena, in November 1943 Roosevelt, Winston Churchill, and Chiang Kai-shek, leaders of the United States, Great Britain, and China, respectively, held a conference in Cairo. At the conclusion of that conference, they issued the Cairo Declaration, which stated that the Allied Powers should secure the unconditional surrender of Japan, that Japan should be stripped of all the territory that it had seized or occupied since the beginning of the World War I, that Manchuria, Formosa, and the Pescadores should be returned to the Republic of China, and that in due course Korea should become independent. Following the conference, Roosevelt and Churchill met Josef Stalin for the first time in Teheran, where they agreed that the Soviet Union would enter the war against Japan within two or three months of Germany's surrender. In February 1945, when Japan and Germany were almost defeated, Roosevelt, Churchill, and Stalin met again, this time at Yalta. The Yalta Agreement, signed by Roosevelt and Stalin, stipulated the participation of the Soviet Union in the war against Japan and the handover to the USSR of the southern part of Sakhalin as well as the

Kurile Islands adjacent to it. Roosevelt died suddenly on April 12, 1945, and Vice President Harry S. Truman took over as president.

In Japan, Tojo Hideki, who had wielded power as prime minister and minister of war since the outbreak of the Pacific War, resigned in July 1944 to take responsibility for the fall of Saipan in the Mariana Islands, located some two thousand kilometers (1250 miles) from Tokyo. General Koiso Kuniaki, governor-general of Korea, was chosen as his successor and, with the support of Admiral Yonai Mitsumasa, the so-called Koiso-Yonai coalition cabinet was formed. The resignation of Tojo heightened the mood for peace domestically and, with the mediation of the Soviet Union, the new cabinet initiated peace negotiations with the Allied Powers as well as with China. However, defeat at Leyte Gulf, the U.S. landing on Luzon, and the B-29 air raids on major Japanese cities launched from the Mariana Islands meant that the war situation for Japan had deteriorated badly; and the negotiations with Chiang Kai-shek to end the war also failed. In this situation, the cabinet had no scope to maneuver. On April 1, 1945, immediately after the U.S. military landed on Okinawa, Admiral Suzuki Kantaro, former grand chamberlain, was appointed prime minister. He continued to seek peace negotiations through the Soviet Union, but before he could form a cabinet the Soviet Union sent notification that it would not extend the Soviet-Japanese Neutrality Pact. The policy of negotiation thus ended in failure. It was inconceivable that the Soviet Union, having promised participation in the war against Japan under the Yalta Agreement, would help Japan with peace negotiations.

On April 3, 1945, as Japan's defeat became imminent, MacArthur was named commander-in-chief of the United States Army Forces, Pacific (AFPAC). He reorganized the SWPA headquarters to establish the General Headquarters of United States Army Forces in the Pacific (GHQ/AFPAC). Under the new arrangement, all U.S. Army and Air Force units and resources in the Pacific were placed under MacArthur's command while all naval resources in the Pacific, except those in the southeastern region, were placed under the command of Admiral Nimitz. The B-29 air units based in the Marianas would be commanded by Major General Archibald V. Arnold as a third headquarters. MacArthur lost control of the excellent 7th Fleet, but gained control of a powerful ground force in Hawaii. The U.S. objective was to establish the strategy for and implementation of control over Japan—a control premised on military victory.

On April 20, MacArthur recommended to Chief of Staff George Marshall in Washington that the United States launch a direct attack on Kyushu, the southernmost island in the Japanese archipelago, and secure an air base there in order to support a ground battle on the main islands of Japan. On May 25, the JCS issued an order, code-named Operation Olympic, for an assault on Kyushu. MacArthur assumed responsibility for execution of the overall operation, which was code-named Downfall. Operation Olympic, which was set to begin on November 1, contained plans for a landing on northwestern Kyushu from the Ariake Sea. It would be followed by Operation Coronet, the invasion of Honshu, the main island of Japan, from Sagami Bay beginning on March 1, 1946. Operation Olympic was to be carried out by the 6th Army under Krueger; Operation Coronet was to be carried out by the 8th Army under Eichelberger. Regarding the atmosphere within the general headquarters at the time, Deputy Chief of Communications Auchincloss recalled that many believed that surrender might come as early as September because of the heavy and continued bombing of the Japanese Islands. On the other hand, others, including himself, thought that the Japanese would fight until the last man to defend the homeland: "They knew that massive defensive positions had been developed and large supplies of food and munitions stored. There had been many examples of suicidal actions, and the loyalty to the Emperor was fanatical."[38]

Meanwhile, following on his work in the Philippines, MacArthur began to plan for the military government of Japan. Two days after Germany signed its surrender on May 7, 1945, MacArthur assumed responsibility for the military government of mainland Japan. After searching for professional military government officers who were knowledgeable about the Far East, he selected Brigadier General William E. Crist, assistant chief of military government in Okinawa, and invited him to Manila. Responding to MacArthur's request, Crist recruited capable bureaucrats and scholars, including Charles Kades, Frank Rizzo, and Justin Williams. Rizzo (later chief of the Government Section GHQ in Japan) was scheduled for dispatch to China but was eventually persuaded by Crist to come to Tokyo. He left the United States on August 15, the day of Japan's surrender, and within five weeks of arriving in Manila had made a commitment to join the planning for the occupation of Japan.[39] Already having been instructed by JCS on June 14 to prepare for the sudden collapse and surrender of Japan, MacArthur had had a plan for peaceful occupation drawn up in his headquarters using the code name Blacklist. Completed on August 7, the final draft was entitled "Basic Plan for the Military Government—Blacklist Operation." Consisting of nine parts, it envisaged direct military rule of Japan while at the same time clearly stipulating the maximum use of existing Japanese administrative structures. On August 5, as the occupation policies solidified, MacArthur set up a new Military Government Section (MGS) as General Staff 5 (G-5) in General Headquarters; Crist was named section chief. Preparations for the occupation of Japan were under way.[40]

Meanwhile, in July, Truman, Churchill, and Stalin held the Potsdam Conference on the outskirts of Berlin, where they discussed final plans for the handling of postwar Europe and the defeat of Japan. On July 26, the Allied Powers issued the Potsdam Declaration, which called upon Japan to surrender unconditionally. The Declaration accorded with a document entitled United States Initial Post-Surrender Policy for Japan, which had been discussed in the SWNCC and bore the number SWNCC 150. However, the Declaration deliberately avoided reference to the most crucial point, that of the emperor's war responsibility and the future status of the imperial institution. On July 17, Truman received the important information that the first atomic bomb had been successfully detonated near Alamogordo, New Mexico, the previous day. Already harboring suspicions about Stalin and the Soviet Union, Truman switched to an aggressively negative stance toward Soviet entry into the war against Japan as envisaged in the Yalta Agreement. Truman agreed with Marshall that landing and ground operations on the main islands of Japan would claim as many as one million lives among the U.S. military. On July 25, the day before the Potsdam Declaration was issued, he approved the dropping of an atomic bomb on Japan in order to hasten the end of the war. After Prime Minister Suzuki's announced that Japan would "ignore" (*mokusatsu*) the Potsdam Declaration, atomic bombs were dropped over Hiroshima on August 6 and Nagasaki on August 9. Casualties included hundreds of thousands of Japanese civilians, mostly noncombatant women and children. At dawn on August 9, the Soviet military issued a declaration of war against Japan and advanced across the borders of Manchuria and Korea. Finally, on August 10, the Japanese government decided in an imperial conference to accept the Potsdam Declaration and formally notified the United States, Britain, and China through the offices of Switzerland, a neutral country.

MacArthur was surprised on hearing the news of the atomic bombs. He had no advance knowledge of either the Manhattan Project or the plan to drop the bombs. He commented to Egeberg: "This will end the war. It will seem superhuman—almost supernatural—and will give the Emperor and the Japanese people a face-saving opportunity to surrender. You watch, they'll ask for it pretty quick."[41] Events followed MacArthur's prediction. The atomic bombing took Casey by surprise as well: "We had not been made cognizant of the advances there nor of the plans, even though we were ordered to prepare special hardstandings [parking lots] for the planes that came over with the atomic bombs prior to the dropping of them on Japan."[42] Auchincloss later disclosed the following secret communication regarding the surrender:

> On August 12, President Truman suspended the B-29 raids against Japan and we learned that we should try to communicate with the Japanese government. At the Signal Center we attempted to break into the Tokyo-Saigon channel, which was one of the busiest in the Japanese net. We used the well known international signals to call them using their

own call signs and frequencies, but for forty eight hours we couldn't get them to answer. Finally they came back with the international signal meaning "Are you calling us?" We established that we would only communicate in English and then we had to wait for quite a while until they got English speaking operators at their transmitters. My copy of the Manila Signal Center log dated August 16th, 1945 states that: Beginning shortly after noon, 15 August 1945 Manila time, the Signal Corps began transmitting Message No. 1 on several frequencies....By 9 p.m. Manila time, an acknowledgement was received that Message No. 1 had been received.[43]

While Auchincloss was trying to contact the Japanese Imperial Headquarters, MacArthur was anxiously waiting to hear whether or not Washington had decided to appoint him supreme commander of the Allied Powers. On August 15, Japan formally accepted the surrender terms set by the Allies and Truman declared the end of the war. Auchincloss and other signals engineers set up a teletype machine to be fully operational at all times in the Manila headquarters, and MacArthur waited with Jean. Since almost all messages came in the "Eyes Only" cipher, no other work could be done. That night, MacArthur paced up and down the stairs outside his bedroom. Eventually, the officer on duty received a clear communication that MacArthur had been appointed supreme commander for the Allied Powers. Auchincloss's six-hour vigil had ended.[44] It was well after midnight, but MacArthur could not conceal his delight. Jean was happy, and congratulated him. On August 16, Manila was overflowing with celebrations of the victory over Japan. For MacArthur, his joy was twofold: in addition to the defeat of Japan, he had beaten Nimitz and the navy in the final race. The victory over Nimitz was connected with the death of Roosevelt, who had harbored deep suspicions about MacArthur. Had Roosevelt lived, would MacArthur have received the appointment? Once more, MacArthur's luck had held.

Arrival at Atsugi Airfield

On August 19, 1945, a delegation from Japan flew to the Philippines to discuss the surrender ceremony. Sixteen officials under Lieutenant General Kawabe Torashiro, deputy chief of staff, disembarked from a U.S. C-54 transport plane at Nichols Field on the outskirts of Manila. On the way, a U.S. P-38 combat plane had checked them in the air over Iye Jima, to confirm that they were a real delegation. After the Japanese flashed the signal "Bataan," as arranged in advance, the

U.S. aircraft instructed them to land at Iye Jima, where they transferred to the C-54 for Manila. The choice of the code word "Bataan" reflected MacArthur's sense of grievance. When the C-54 landed at 5:00 p.m., Nichols Field was filled with hundreds of officers and civilians who were hoping for even a glance at the delegation. MacArthur's aide Egeberg and his friends were among them. Like the others who waited, they wondered whether the Japanese would indeed emerge when the door of the aircraft was opened.[45]

Within GHQ discussions had been held on how to greet the delegation. Willoughby, chief of G-2, handled everything in a businesslike manner, refraining from shaking hands with Kawabe and the other group members or offering them greetings. Since Willoughby had the impression that Kawabe was nervous, he avoided coercive language in an effort to relieve the stress. At about 5:30, all members of the Japanese delegation got off the aircraft and hurriedly boarded the four or five vehicles that had been prepared. Some Filipinos began to throw stones, but the delegation was able to leave the airfield safely. Willoughby took them first to their accommodations at Rosary Apartment and, three hours later, to MacArthur's headquarters.[46]

Since MacArthur considered himself to be higher in authority than even the emperor, he did not speak with the delegation directly. The group visited Chief of Staff Sutherland and handed over the emperor's credentials. Willoughby was particularly bothered by the fact that they carried swords. From the Japanese point of view, this was formal attire, but to the Americans it was strange. Told to put their swords down, the Japanese complied. Auchincloss described the scene as follows:

> General Sutherland told the delegation that it was desired that the advance party should land on Atsugi Aerodrome [near Tokyo] in four days. The Japanese were shocked because Atsugi was a Kamikaze training field and was a hotbed of revolt [against surrender]. They said that it could not possibly be made safe for an Allied landing in so short time. Sutherland agreed to a five day delay, but insisted that the landing be at Atsugi and not another airport. They were then shown a draft of the surrender document starting out "I Hirohito, Emperor of Japan...." using the pronoun "Watakushi" for "I." The Japanese were horrified as the Emperor always referred to himself as "We." Colonel Sidney Mashbir, MacArthur's chief interpreter, made the change and the general later approved.[47]

Their difficult assignment over, the Japanese delegation returned to Tokyo on August 20. Willoughby handled the farewells.

Next it was the turn of the Americans to send an advance delegation. Chamberlin, chief of G-3, wanted Casey to send a team of engineers to Atsugi about a week before landing to ensure that U.S. military could land safely. Casey was excited at the prospect of being the first American to land on Japan since the end of the war. But MacArthur reportedly refused: "No, we will not send Pat nor any general officer nor anybody above the rank of colonel."[48] At heart, MacArthur may have been reluctant to lose such a congenial officer as Casey. As a result, it was decided to send a party of 150 engineers under Colonel Charles P. Tench to Atsugi. Auchincloss was chosen to command the Signals Section of the party. He later confessed his feelings of anxiety: "None of us were delighted with the assignment because we were not at all sure that the Japanese, even at the order of the emperor, could ensure our safety....Actually, at the time I don't think I thought much about the safety angle because I was delighted to be selected to be about the first American on Japanese soil."[49]

The advance party led by Tench left Manila for Okinawa on August 27. According to Auchincloss, they arrived at Iye Jima about noon and were able to look around the island before taking off in formation for Japan early the next morning in thirteen DC-3s. Auchincloss rode in the lead plane with Tench. Every plane was overloaded, and one crashed on takeoff, killing everyone on board. In addition to being overloaded, the planes carried enough gasoline for an eleven-hundred-mile flight. As they approached Tokyo, Auchincloss was lucky enough to see Mt. Fuji and declared it a memorable sight. By the time the planes reached Atsugi, they had almost no gasoline. They were forced to make a hurried landing, at 8:30 a.m., at the exact opposite end of the airstrip from the one the Japanese had expected and, moreover, not upwind as usual but in the more difficult downwind direction.[50] Viewing the landing, the Japanese suspected that the Americans had intentionally flown their planes in a downwind direction in case they needed to make a quick escape, but the truth was that they did not have enough gasoline to circle the field.

A few days before the arrival of the advance party, a group of Japanese officers had blown up their own combat planes in a suicide mission aimed at preventing the Americans from landing. By the time of the actual landing, however, the matter had been taken care of and not a shot was heard. Auchincloss and the rest were presumably much relieved. Lieutenant General Arisuye Seizo, chief of the Second General Staff Office of the Army, was in charge of the reception. Because of the unexpected landing place, he had to hurry the entire length of the field to meet them. Since he had lived in the United States, Arisuye spoke perfect English and was well equipped to handle the details of receiving MacArthur. A table and some chairs had been set up in a small tent on the field. Tench and Auchincloss took seats on one side and the Japanese sat opposite them. Arisuye asked what would be required to prepare for MacArthur's coming. The Americans handed over a list that included trucks, cars, drivers, bulldozers, accommodation in Yokohama, and access to radio and telephone facilities. After they had finished explaining these items, Arisuye asked how many geishas they would need. Knowing that MacArthur would never allow the use of geishas, Tench replied that they were not required.[51]

Preparations were thus in place for MacArthur's landing. MacArthur ordered the 8th Army under Eichelberger to be stationed in Japan, and said he and his staff would be with them. Eichelberger was astonished at the supreme commander's boldness in arriving in Japan with no more than a small defense force. Eichelberger was forced to send the 11th Airborne Division and the 27th Infantry Division from Okinawa to serve as a vanguard in the Japanese mainland, and he prepared three hundred transports to carry the troops. Fortunately, on the day MacArthur was scheduled to arrive, a typhoon threatened the main Japanese islands and made it impossible for aircraft to land or take off. This delay gave Tench's advance force enough time to complete preparations for the main party to arrive.

On August 29, MacArthur and his staff flew from Manila to Yomitan Airfield in Okinawa in a C-54 transport and cargo aircraft named *Bataan*. At 2:15 p.m. on August 30, following the arrival of Eichelberger, the *Bataan* landed at Atsugi Airport. When the door of the plane opened, MacArthur emerged with sunglasses and corncob pipe and, after pausing briefly to look around, he walked down the steps. With his strong sense of self-consciousness, he had imagined this scene of his personal glory, knowing it would endure as a historical moment. Churchill later commented that, among all the amazing deeds of the war, he regarded MacArthur's landing at Atsugi as the most courageous. MacArthur later recalled his words to Eichelberger: "Bob, from Melbourne to Tokyo is a long way, but this seems to be the end of the road."[52] However, the Occupation reforms had just started. History was to show that MacArthur would face hardships as he made the transition from hero of the battlefield to peacetime warrior.

THE DEMILITARIZATION OF JAPAN, AUGUST 1945 TO DECEMBER 1947

The Surrender of Japan and the Beginning of the Occupation

On August 30, 1945, MacArthur landed safely at his final destination and from Atsugi Airfield headed for his accommodation at the Hotel New Grand in Yokohama. Armed Japanese troops stood on guard at regular intervals on both sides of the road, their backs to MacArthur. It had been rumored that some fifty thousand so-called kamikaze pilots stood immediately behind them and that there were at least two million armed Japanese troops within a five or six kilometer (about three or four mile) radius. From this one can imagine the deep concern felt by staff officers and the twelve hundred 8th Army airborne troops as MacArthur arrived. But MacArthur had insisted on the use of Atsugi Airfield, asserting that the Japanese people were desperately short of food and that he had the emperor's word that nothing untoward would happen.[1] In fact, nothing did happen. The hotel at which MacArthur arrived two hours later was a nostalgic choice: he and Jean had stayed there in 1937 on their way back to the Philippines after their marriage in New York.

The U.S. Army had requisitioned the Yokohama Customs Building near the hotel and this became the Headquarters of the U.S. Army Forces in the Pacific (GHQ/AFPAC). The 3rd U.S. Pacific Fleet under Admiral William F. Halsey and the USS *Missouri* with 258 ships had entered Tokyo Bay, carefully avoiding mines and other obstacles as well as Japanese fishing boats. On August 30 Halsey landed at Yokosuka accompanied by Marines.

On August 31 two other generals arrived in Japan. One was Lieutenant General Arthur Percival, British commander at the fall of Singapore; the other was Lieutenant General Wainwright, who had surrendered at Corregidor. Both had been held for three years at the Mukden prisoner of war camp in Manchuria and had been flown to Tokyo to attend the surrender ceremony on the *Missouri*. That night an emotional reunion took place at the hotel. MacArthur's physician, Roger Egeberg, described the scene: "They all jumped up to welcome a very thin but well-looking older officer: Lieutenant General Jonathan M. 'Skinny' Wainwright…MacArthur was quoted as saying, 'Hang on and we'll be back to relieve you.'…MacArthur was on his feet and welcomed and embraced General Wainwright. His eyes were moist as he embraced him."[2]

On September 2, the formal ceremony of surrender was conducted on board the *Missouri* in Tokyo Bay. Why was the *Missouri* chosen? MacArthur had originally wanted to hold the ceremony on the plaza in front of the Imperial Palace. In fact, the infamous "Tokyo Rose," broadcaster of wartime Japanese propaganda, had once promised that MacArthur would be arrested and hanged in the square, and it is not impossible, given MacArthur's stubborn personality, that this story had provoked MacArthur's choice. But the *Missouri* was the final selection for three reasons. First, an onboard ceremony would remove the possibility of obstruction by militaristic Japanese soldiers. Second, the *Missouri* had been named by President Truman's daughter, after the state where he had been born. The third reason was to honor the Navy.

Thus, after half past eight in the morning of September 2, MacArthur boarded the *Missouri*, followed by Foreign Minister Shigemitsu Mamoru and Chief of the General Staff Umezu Yoshijiro, who headed the eleven-member Japanese delegation. The ceremony commenced at nine o'clock. MacArthur stood at a microphone and announced:

> …Nor is it for us here to meet, representing as we do a majority of the people of the earth, in a spirit of distrust, malice or hatred. But rather it is for us, both victors and vanquished, to rise to that higher dignity which alone befits the sacred purposes we are about to serve, committing all our people unreservedly to faithful compliance with the obligation they are here formally to assume. It is my earnest hope and indeed the hope of all mankind that from this solemn occasion a better world shall emerge out of the blood and carnage of the past—a world founded upon faith and understanding—a world dedicated to the dignity of man and the fulfillment of his most cherished wish—freedom, tolerance and justice.[3]

The sonorous speech was broadcast all over the world. The Stars and Stripes floating behind MacArthur was the very same flag that had flown over the USS *Susquehanna* when Commodore Matthew Perry had urged Japan to open its borders ninety-two years earlier and MacArthur got the flag carried over to the *Missouri*. Furthermore,

MacArthur had ordered the battleship *Missouri* to anchor off Yokohama, which was the very same place that Perry had anchored his ship. This was not simply a dramatic production created by MacArthur, a man well versed in history; MacArthur probably saw himself as a second Perry, charged with the opening of Japan. Shigemitsu, representing the emperor and the Japanese government, and Umezu, representing the Japanese military, signed the surrender document. Somehow their signatures left an impression of weakness. Fleet Admiral William Halsey, ever one to speak his mind, observed ironically that the "tiny eleven-man delegation of a tiny country signed as if they were chimpanzees in human costumes."[4]

General MacArthur, as commander of the Allied Powers, signed the surrender document, followed by Fleet Admiral Chester Nimitz, commander-in-chief of the U.S. Pacific Fleet and Pacific Ocean Areas (POA), representing the United States. A representative of each delegation of the Allied Powers signed in succession. Exercising careful consideration, MacArthur had Wainwright and Percival stand immediately behind him during the signing. As he moved to affix his own signature, MacArthur pulled five additional fountain pens from his pocket and used six pens to sign the two surrender documents. He then handed the first to Wainwright and the second to Percival. The third would to go West Point, his alma mater, and the fourth to the War College. MacArthur saved the fifth for himself.[5] MacArthur ended the ceremony with a short statement, introduced by the famous line: "Today the guns are silent."[6] Former Colonel Ralph E. Wilson, the officer in charge of arranging the ceremony, noted that, as commander of the Allied Powers, MacArthur had assumed the responsibility to rule Japan with the help of the emperor. Therefore he had to demonstrate to the Japanese people the dignity needed to rule over the emperor.[7]

While the surrender ceremony was in progress, MacArthur had ordered Colonel Sidney Mashbir, a Japanese language expert, to go into Tokyo with Egeberg to inspect the capital. They were accompanied by Major General Hugh J. Casey, chief engineer, Brigadier General Jack Sverdrup, Casey's deputy, and other civil engineers. Japanese Foreign Ministry staff and an interpreter completed the group.[8] The twenty-five miles from the Hotel New Grand in Yokohama to the center of Tokyo was, according to one Foreign Service officer, "a vast area of destruction. Between seventy and eighty percent of the buildings had been destroyed, burned, bombed."[9] As the group approached one station in the center of the city, they were surrounded by Japanese troops. About two million Japanese military personnel had not been disarmed and the city was still under Japanese control. Instinctively, Egeberg and his companions reached for their revolvers, but nothing happened. They were relieved to find the U.S. Embassy in good condition. Next, they paid the Swiss Embassy a courtesy call. Then, after inspecting the Dai-Ichi Mutual Life Insurance Building and the Imperial Hotel, they confirmed that the buildings were undamaged and could serve as the headquarters of the supreme commander for the Allied Powers (SCAP). After hearing their report on the morning of September 3, MacArthur decided to move into the embassy as soon as Tokyo was cleared of Japanese troops. He also decided to use the Imperial Hotel and other nearby buildings as residences for officers and noncommissioned officers and their families. Finally, MacArthur settled on the eight-floor Dai-Ichi Building as SCAP headquarters.[10]

On the morning of September 8, MacArthur and his staff left the Hotel New Grand and drove to Tokyo, reaching the U.S. Embassy in Toranomon an hour later. A ceremony of occupation was held in the garden, and the Stars and Stripes was raised over the embassy roof. This ceremony marked the beginning of the U.S.-led occupation of Japan. The embassy was to be home for MacArthur and his family for the next five years and eight months, until his departure from Japan in April 1951. Each day he left home by car at about nine or ten o'clock in the morning, rode along the same route to the Dai-Ichi Building, and worked until about 1:30 or 2:00, before returning to the embassy for lunch. After a short nap, he returned to the office by about four o'clock and worked again until about 8:00. He followed this routine every day, even on Sunday.

Around the time of MacArthur's move to Tokyo, Allied troops were dispatched to various regions to begin the occupation of the Japanese main islands: the 8th Army under Lieutenant General Robert Eichelberger occupied the northern and eastern regions, while the 6th Army under General Walter Krueger occupied the western and southern regions. The British army took control of the Chugoku and Shikoku regions. By the beginning of December 1945, with the initial Occupation forces in place, the total number of Allied troops had reached 430,000, including eighteen combat divisions. During 1946, however, the number of troops was steadily reduced to about 200,000, less than half of the initial total. Most of the 6th Army veterans, who had fought in the fierce campaigns in New Guinea and the Philippines, left Japan.

The Establishment of GHQ/SCAP and the Departure of Sutherland

After completing the formal occupation of the Japanese mainland, MacArthur's forces moved immediately to set up SCAP as the central organization for implementing Occupation policies. On September 17 the General Headquarters of the U.S. Army Forces in the Pacific (GHQ/AFPAC) was moved from Yokohama to Tokyo, and the Dai-Ichi Mutual Life Insurance Building located near the Imperial Palace in the center of Tokyo became MacArthur's headquarters. Additionally, some six hundred nearby buildings were requisitioned for use as offices. Already, on August 5, while MacArthur was still in Manila, a G-5 Military Government Section (MGS) had been set up within GHQ/AFPAC to take charge of the Occupation administration. However, on September 15 the Economic and Science Section (ESS) was set up independently of MGS, followed by the Civil Information and Education Section (CIE) on September 22. On October 2, MGS itself was dissolved and the General Headquarters of the supreme commander of the Allied Powers (GHQ/SCAP) was established. Within GHQ/SCAP were a total of nine sections: the Government Section (GS), the Civil Intelligence Section (CIS), the Legal Section (LS), the Public Health and Welfare Section (PHW), the Natural Resources Section (NRS), the Statistical and Reports Section (SRS), and the Civil Communications Section (CCS), as well as the previously established ESS and CIE. These so-called Special Staff Sections were placed in a different category from the General Staff Section (G-1–G-4), which primarily controlled military affairs. Both the Special Staff and the General Staff were headed by a chief of staff and deputy chief of staff, some of whom held posts concurrently in GHQ/AFPAC.[11]

Who was appointed to the top positions at the outset of the Occupation? Lieutenant General Richard Sutherland, who was closest to MacArthur and had served as chief of staff during the war, continued as MacArthur's chief of staff in the GHQ. Major General Richard Marshall was appointed deputy chief of staff for AFPAC, and Major General Stephen J. Chamberlin, chief of G-3, was promoted to deputy chief of staff for SCAP. With regard to the Special Staff Sections, Brigadier General William E. Crist, who had headed the MGS, moved across to chief of GS; Colonel Raymond Kramer, former company president and department store executive, became chief of ESS; Colonel Alva Carpenter headed LS; Brigadier General Elliott R. Thorpe, who had worked in the occupation of Manila, was appointed to CIS; Colonel Kenneth R. Dyke headed CIE; Brigadier General Crawford F. Sams, a military doctor, was transferred from the MGS in Manila to head PHW; and Lieutenant Colonel Hubert G. Schenck, formerly a professor of geology at Stanford University, became chief of NRS. Major General Spencer B. Akin, a Bataan Boy, was appointed chief of CCS. In addition to Akin, former Bataan Boys appointed to top positions included Major General Charles A. Willoughby, who was named chief of Intelligence (G-2); Major General William F. Marquat, who was appointed to the Anti Aircraft Section (AAS) of AFPAC; and Major General Hugh J. Casey, who became chief of the Signals Section (SS) of AFPAC. Harold George and Joseph P. Sherr had died in the war, Charles H. Morehouse and Joseph D. McMicking had left for the United States, and Charles P. Stivers did not come to Japan because of illness.

During this time of transition, fierce conflict erupted behind the closed doors at GHQ. It revolved around the exercise of authority by Crist, who had been appointed head of MGS. Crist was not a member of the Bataan Boys. Because it had been evident at the time of its formation that MGS would have an important role in the Japanese Occupation, a scramble for positions, power, and policies had ensued. Each section made a determined effort to prevent usurpation of its powers by the MSG. Captain Frank Rizzo, who had been recruited in Washington by Crist and became his aide in Manila, described the situation as follows:

> [In the whole headquarters] there was an awful scramble for position and power, and Crist was a lamb among those fellows. The section he had was the Military Government Section, conceived under the old army manual plan where he had the whole military government. The outcome wasn't that at all. The outcome was, first, there was no military government; and second, each of his divisions became an independent SCAP section....While I was still in Manila, they started tearing him apart. They were taking sections out of his Military Government Section. They were creating the new sections. I think Economic and Scientific was the first; it was under Cramer....Crist was too mild a man, too gentle of a man to run this kind of operation. He could run by the book with a strong chief of staff supporting him, but by himself where he had to do the job, he just couldn't do it. He couldn't complete. So Government Section almost went to sleep; in fact, it did go to sleep.[12]

Sams, who moved from Manila to head the Public Health and Welfare section, likewise recognized the scramble for power:

> This was quite a conflict. When you have a military staff that's been fighting a war, you've got G-1, G-2, G-3, and G-4, and signal officer, the chief engineer, and so on. They were not about to let go of their prerogatives and have another bunch come in and take over. So it can be pretty bitter, and it was in Tokyo. For a while we didn't know if we were going to swing it or not in organizing SCAP.[13]

Thorpe, concurrently chief both of the Civil Intelligence Section and the Counter Intelligence Corps, noted that although Crist was a man of mild personality, he was stubborn in making policy decisions, giving Sutherland an unfavorable impression.[14] In the end, it was Crist who was defeated in the power struggle with the Bataan Boys and he was forced to return to the United States at the end of 1945. His successor as head of GS was none other than Whitney.

On Whitney's appointment as head of GS, Lawrence E. Bunker, MacArthur's aide-de-camp, commented as follows:

> As the time came for the Japanese surrender, we ran into a real difficulty because the situation in Japan was entirely different from what it was in Germany. When we went into Japan, there was a functioning Japanese government; in all its ramifications at all levels the government was still there. In Germany a great deal of it had been wiped out.... So the technique that had to be used in Japan was totally different from the establishment of military government.[15]

Bunker noted that the unexpected circumstances in Japan made it necessary to switch the functioning of the newly established MGS from military occupation to supervision of the Japanese government. Once it became apparent that the officer in charge of the MGS was finding it impossible to readjust his thinking, personnel changes were unavoidable. As a result, the G-5 MGS was abolished and the GS was established. Whitney was made chief of GS because his work in the Philippines had involved establishing a variety of relationships with the Philippine government. He had established himself by that time as a capable and rather shrewd operator in handling certain types of problems for MacArthur. As Bunker remembered:

> When we actually moved up to Tokyo, he established himself pretty thoroughly in the entourage, but not without some expense in popularity with the other members of the staff. When they were setting up the office in the Dai-Ichi Building, Whitney insisted that his office be on the same floor with General MacArthur. He was the only one of the staff officers, aside from chief of staff, who was on that floor. It's obvious why he did it.[16]

In fact, Whitney was selected to head GS because his administrative competence in the process of reconstructing Manila had been evaluated highly by MacArthur. Among MacArthur's staff he was respected as a sharp, highly capable section chief who could adapt to the transition from wartime to postwar exigencies. Under Whitney's leadership, GS, located on the same sixth floor of the Dai-Ichi Building as MacArthur's and Sutherland's offices, became the most powerful of the Special Staff Sections and enjoyed the strong support of MacArthur.

Whitney's rise was also aided by the return to the United States of Chief of Staff Sutherland at the end of 1945. In addition to his wartime affair with the Australian Elaine Clarke, which had brought him into disfavor with MacArthur, Sutherland suffered from heart disease caused by high blood pressure. However, a further reason for his return to the United States concerned Whitney. From the time of MacArthur's triumphant return to the Philippines, Whitney's important role in its reconstruction had drawn him increasingly close to MacArthur.

Gradually, he came to threaten Sutherland's own position. Ironically, it was Sutherland who had highly recommended Whitney to MacArthur even before Whitney had returned to active service. After the Japanese surrender, the astute Sutherland probably recognized that the transition to postwar occupation marked a career end for a wartime-oriented officer such as himself. It can be no coincidence that he left his position just two days before Whitney assumed the top position at GS on December 12. Sutherland had gotten the better of Dwight Eisenhower in becoming chief of staff in prewar Manila, but in postwar Tokyo he was eased out of the same post by Whitney. His departure was symbolic not only of a membership change in MacArthur's inner circle but also of the beginning of the decline of the Bataan Boys. After returning home, Sutherland underwent a lengthy hospitalization and retired from the military. Deputy Chief of Staff Marshall, who had supported Sutherland, succeeded him as chief of staff, but he never attained the high prestige held by Sutherland.

The Disarmament of the Japanese Military and the Arrest of War Criminals

Although MacArthur assumed the responsibility for implementing Occupation policies, the basic goals for Japan had been drafted during the war by the State Department and the departments of the Army and the Navy in Washington, as well as by the Joint Chiefs of Staff, which directly oversaw the Occupation. In the process, three main points of controversy emerged: first, whether to retain or abolish the imperial institution; second, whether the Allied Occupation should govern Japan directly or indirectly; and third, whether there should be exclusive control by the United States or joint control shared with the rest of the allies.

The first controversy was closely related to the issue of the emperor's war responsibility. The so-called China Hands used the emperor's war responsibility to insist strongly on the abolition of the imperial institution. On the other hand, the "Japan Hands" led by former Ambassador to Japan Joseph C. Grew rejected the notion of the emperor's war responsibility and emphasized rather the need to take advantage of the emperor's prestige and Japanese respect and affection toward him in order to secure a complete end to the war. Aided by the realist views of President Harry S. Truman, the position of the Japan Hands won out, and even the Potsdam Declaration avoided a clear statement on the imperial problem. On the second point, it was decided, after consideration of the negative example of direct occupation in Germany, that indirect military occupation using existing Japanese government institutions would be more likely to secure smooth administration of the country. On the third point, a decision was reached that, since, in contrast with Europe, victory in the Pacific theater had been secured by the United States alone, the division of Japan into separate zones of occupation would not be appropriate. Thus, by the end of the war, the retention of the imperial institution and relinquishment of the emperor's war responsibility together with indirect government and unified control by the United States had been established as basic policies for the Occupation.

These policies were stipulated in documents such as the SWNCC 150/13 (U.S. Initial Post-Surrender Policy for Japan) of September 6 and the JCS 1380/15 (Basic Directive for Post-Surrender Military Government in Japan Proper) of November 3 and communicated to MacArthur. (Occupation officers referred to JCS 1380/15 as their "bible.") Accordingly, the GHQ/SCAP (hereafter GHQ) led by MacArthur was obliged to implement the Occupation on the basis of these directives. In fact, however, because of the postwar confusion in Japan and because of pressure to deal with actual problems as they cropped up, the Occupation was not necessarily implemented in accordance with official policies. On the contrary, some sections enforced their own measures in disregard of Washington; and GHQ gave priority to actual conditions.

Consider the actual activities of each GHQ section. In the initial months of September and October 1945, MacArthur and GHQ focused their attention on the release of prisoners detained in Japanese internment camps and on demilitarization, as ordered by Article 9 of the Potsdam Declaration ("The Japanese military forces, after being completely disarmed..."). In addition, they arrested political and military leaders such as Tojo Hideki as war criminals based on Article 6 of the Declaration ("There must be eliminated for all time the authority and influence of those who have deceived and misled the people of Japan into embarking on world conquest, for we insist that a new order of peace, security and justice will be impossible until irresponsible militarism is driven from the world.") MacArthur's own strong intentions were reflected in every measure.

Willoughby's intelligence unit (G-2) and Eichelberger's 8th Army played an active role in the release of prisoners of war. Within hours of their arrival at Atsugi, men detained at Omori and Shinagawa in Tokyo and Ofuna in Kanagawa were released; within two weeks all were on their way home. A bigger problem was securing the release of some thirty thousand prisoners from internment camps in inland Japan. Provisions and medicine were transported by air and dropped by parachute. With the successful release of the men soon afterward, the task of freeing prisoners of war was completed much sooner than expected.

The demobilization and disarmament of Japanese forces was expected to be difficult. At the time of surrender, the total strength of Japanese contingents at home and abroad was about seven million, organized in 154 army divisions. Of these, 2,576,000 soldiers organized in fifty-seven divisions were stationed in

Japan. This marked a sharp contrast with Germany, where 90 percent of military forces had been annihilated. The corresponding U.S. forces amounted to just two-and-a-half divisions, all recently arrived in Japan. This was clearly a risky gamble. Within a month, the 6th Army forces, with almost the same number as the 8th Army, arrived, allowing demilitarization to proceed. The G-2 under Willoughby, which had accumulated detailed knowledge of Japanese military organization during the war and had conducted successful surrender negotiations with the Japanese army in Manila, assumed a leading role. By October, the disarmament and demobilization of Japanese soldiers in the homeland had been completed, again with surprising speed.

However, the repatriation of Japanese troops from Manchuria and the Pacific Islands was a larger and more complex job. Japanese naval and army officers took charge of the practical work under the supervision of GHQ, the 8th Army, and the U.S. Navy. With the end of the war, the desire to repatriate soldiers immediately strengthened in the United States, and this stimulated the early repatriation of civilians as well as military personnel in Japan. Urged on by popular opinion, U.S. forces applied LSTs (tank landing ships) and smaller Liberty ships to the repatriation work. By the end of 1945, a total of 960,000 Japanese, 480,000 each of soldiers and civilians, had returned home from South Korea, the South Sea Islands, northern China, and Okinawa. By the end of 1976, the total number repatriated amounted to 6,290,000, including 3,110,000 military personnel and 3,180,000 civilians.[17]

As chief of Counter Intelligence Corps, Thorpe assumed the responsibility for arresting war criminals, as he had in the Philippines. On the very day he arrived at Atsugi, he was ordered verbally by MacArthur to arrest Tojo Hideki, and to draw up a list of other Class A war criminals. Thorpe had the staff of CIC (which included many Americans of Japanese descent) to conduct an investigation, and he ordered three lawyers to make a list of the accused. Although the work of compiling information on Japanese political leaders had begun while MacArthur was stationed in Australia, it was clear that any identification of war criminals would attract international attention. For this reason, prompt and careful work was required. Initially, twenty-five Class A war criminals were decided upon; an additional thirteen were included at the request of the State Department, for a total of thirty-eight. On September 11, Tojo and others accused were arrested.[18] Tojo's attempted suicide ended in failure; two others killed themselves by taking poison. The arrests were completed with careful attention to preventing suicides. Gifts and invitations flooded Thorpe's office from former Japanese leaders who feared that they would be arrested.

Among the conciliatory measures taken by the Japanese side, one was unforgettable for Thorpe. Admiral Nomura Kichisaburo had served as foreign minister and as ambassador to the United States until immediately before the outbreak of war. As a young man, Thorpe had been acquainted with Nomura. In the days following the war's end, as he worked to finalize the list of war criminals, Thorpe removed Nomura's name, convinced that he was not a military aggressor. Some correspondents on the Allied side became suspicious and reports of Nomura's possible arrest appeared in the newspapers. Fearing that Nomura might commit suicide, Thorpe sent a staff member to Nomura's residence in Kamakura to tell him that the news reports were mistaken. Several days later, around 11 p.m., Thorpe heard a rap on the door of his room at the Imperial Hotel. There stood the old admiral wearing striped trousers, formal morning coat, and top hat. There was a powerful odor of mothballs. With tearful eyes, Nomura thanked Thorpe for his message. By contrast, General Doihara Kenji, who had been chief of a special military organization in Hoten, Manchuria, was hanged as the correspondents demanded. Thorpe later confessed that he had doubts about the arrests of 108 Class A criminals because they were based on retroactive application of the law. Since Thorpe knew that MacArthur's father had once banished some anti-American Philippine leaders to Guam, he recommended that MacArthur exile the inmates of Sugamo Prison to the Ogasawara (or Bonin) Islands. But MacArthur replied that such a decision would exceed his power. The Allied Powers wanted blood. Accordingly, Thorpe's request was in vain.[19]

The Meeting between MacArthur and Emperor Hirohito

On September 27, 1945, the Showa Emperor visited MacArthur at the U.S. Embassy. The meeting took place not because MacArthur had invited the emperor but because the emperor had requested it. From the outset of the Occupation, MacArthur had directed that there should be no disrespect to the emperor and that he should be paid the honors appropriate to a sovereign. On the day of the emperor's visit, military police enforced strict security. According to Willoughby, MacArthur prepared nothing for the meeting and did nothing that might suggest the application of pressure. He dismissed everyone but the emperor's own interpreter so that they might converse in private. But there were witnesses to the meeting. Jean and Egeberg had hidden behind a curtain and listened to the conversation in the manner of children listening in on the conversation of adults:

> The tone of the talk, this first one between these two men, was friendly and as easy as a conversation carried out through interpreters could be....General MacArthur soon got down to the business of the first

cabinet. He was suggesting a cabinet of high military or war-office officials which could continue the complete demobilization of Japan; then
the dismantling of the Imperial Japanese staff corps was a little more
touchy. The General's tone was one to which agreement seemed appropriate, not the mere acceptance of an order from a conqueror.[20]

MacArthur himself reminisced favorably on the encounter as follows: "We sat
down before an open fire at one end of the long reception hall. I offered him an
American cigarette, which he took with thanks. I noticed how his hands shook
as I lighted it for him. I tried to make it as easy for him as I could, but I knew
how deep and dreadful must be his agony of humiliation. I had an uneasy feeling
he might plead his own cause against indictment as a war criminal."[21] Far from
pleading his case, however, the emperor stated that he bore sole responsibility
for the war. MacArthur was deeply impressed. Although the Russians and the
British had included the emperor in their initial list of war criminals, MacArthur
disagreed: "I had advised that I would need at least one million reinforcements,
should such action be taken. I believed that if the Emperor were indicted, and
perhaps hanged, as a war criminal, military government would have to be instituted throughout all Japan, and guerrilla warfare would probably break out."[22] In
fact, Egeberg recalled: "Not long after this first conversation between the General
and the Emperor, MacArthur said, 'They want me to arrest the Emperor and to
hold him for trial as a war criminal.' Deeply disturbed and angered, he talked to
himself [sic] and to me about this. 'They don't understand. He was a virtual prisoner of Tojo and the military clique.... I can't possibly accomplish the transition
without him.'"[23]

The first meeting between MacArthur and the emperor was thus successful.
They met frequently thereafter, and their conversations, ranging over various
world problems, played a major role in ensuring the smooth progress of the
Occupation. If MacArthur had rejected the imperial institution and arrested the
emperor as a war criminal, how would the Occupation have changed? His prediction of guerrilla warfare by as many as two million Japanese veterans may
not have been far-fetched. In this sense, given his positive feelings toward the
imperial institution and his use of the emperor to advance Occupation goals,
MacArthur's appointment as leader of the Occupation was significant in deciding the shape of postwar Japan.

On October 4, accompanying the demilitarization of the Japanese army and
navy, MacArthur issued his Civil Liberties Directive. All laws that restricted political, civil, and religious rights in Japan, including the Maintenance of Public Order
Act (Chian Iji Ho: a law that infringed freedom of speech and thought), were abolished; censorship of the press was ended; political prisoners were released; and the

infamous Kempeitai, or military police, who had threatened and abused Japanese citizens, was dissolved. In addition, the home minister, the top levels of the police force, and six thousand members of the Special Higher Police were purged. Lieutenant Colonel Carlos Marcum, who had been transferred from the CIC under Thorpe to GS, took the initiative. He forced implementation of the purge, arguing that democracy could not take root in Japan unless the Maintenance of Public Order Act and the Special Police Organization (Tokko, which was referred to in the United States as being similar to the Gestapo in Germany) were dissolved. This radical action forced the resignation of the Higashikuni cabinet. On October 9, Shidehara Kijuro, a former foreign minister who had promoted cooperative diplomacy with Britain and the United States, was installed as prime minister. Two days later, MacArthur verbally ordered Shidehara to implement a five-point reform for the protection of human rights. The five points were: (1) the emancipation of Japanese women by granting them the right to vote; (2) the encouragement of labor unions; (3) the liberalization of school education; (4) the abolition of repressive institutions; and (5) the democratization of Japanese economic institutions.

It was Thorpe, chief of CIS and CIC, who took charge of overseeing the democratization measures. Thorpe released four thousand people imprisoned for their political actions and views, including Tokuda Kyuichi, who had led the Communist movement, and abolished censorship and government control of the media. He led efforts to ensure the election of women candidates in the first postwar Diet election of April 1946. A curious episode relating to Thorpe indicates something of his character. During a ten-day period when Thorpe was serving as director of the Bank of Japan, he found a pile of diamonds and gold, along with the skull of an indigenous Javanese person that the Japanese had stolen from a museum in Java during the war and a Buddha's tooth, as large as a whale's tooth, that had been plundered from a statue in the Schwedagon Pagoda in Rangoon. Thorpe sent the skull back to the Dutch and returned the Buddha's tooth to the Burmese. Feeling the burden of handling money, Thorpe transferred to the Economic and Scientific Section (ESS), led by Marquat, its second chief. He handed all the bank keys to Marquat. Marquat later left an "M Fund" that would occupy a mysterious place in Japan's postwar history. It is unclear whether the M Fund had any connection to the Bank of Japan treasure originally discovered by Thorpe.

Disease and Food Shortages in Japan

Japanese social conditions in the months immediately following the end of the war were indescribably miserable. Sams, chief of Public Health and Welfare, aggressively confronted the difficult problems. Arriving at Yokohama from Manila early in the Occupation, Sams focused his efforts on disease and sanitation problems out of concern that the spread of disease would endanger the lives of the American soldiers soon to be stationed throughout Japan. Receiving reports of an epidemic in Tokyo of an illness being called "*ikiri*," Sams obtained MacArthur's authorization to travel the city to investigate. Upon investigation, it was determined that *ikiri* was not cholera, as had been thought. So many children were suffering diarrhea symptoms that Japanese doctors had wrongly diagnosed the illness as cholera.

Later detailed examinations by Sams's research group revealed that Japanese children typically suffered from calcium deficiencies because of the low levels of milk and other essentials in their diet and that many had contracted bacterial dysentery. Giving them protein, particularly in the form of powdered milk, was thus an urgent priority. The United States had a large surplus of skim milk, but it had been marked for shipment to Europe. The U.S. government paid businesses fifteen cents per pound for shipments to Europe, but for shipment to Japan the payment was just four cents per pound. Using the argument that many Japanese people were dying of starvation, Sams managed to secure fifty million dollars' worth of skim milk. The U.S. Army thus provided calcium for eighteen million malnourished Japanese children.

One epidemic that did present a challenge to the Occupation forces was smallpox. According to Sams, in one year alone some thirty-five thousand people died.[24] To deal with the situation, he ordered eighty-four million doses of smallpox vaccine to be sent from the Philippines. The next major public health problem was typhus, which spread throughout Japan as infected Korean laborers who had been working in Hokkaido coal mines traveled south to Shimonoseki for their journey home. Sams tried to bring shipments of DDT from the Philippines to the Tsugaru Straits to kill the lice that had infested the Korean workers. But the U.S. military placed priority on shipments of military equipment to Japan, and Sams was unsuccessful. In the end, it took two years for typhus to be eradicated. Besides smallpox and typhus, Sams's working group was engaged in painstaking efforts to deal with various intestinal and gastric illnesses caused by unsanitary conditions, including inadequate waste disposal, contaminated water, and contaminated food.

In this extraordinary situation MacArthur's attitude contrasted sharply with that of High Commissioner John J. McCloy, who controlled the occupation of western Germany. While McCloy's priority was the restoration of industry, MacArthur placed greater weight on the condition of the Japanese people themselves. In fact, McCloy invited Sams to work with him in Germany, but Sams declined the offer. Sams's decision to remain in Japan was based on his confidence in MacArthur's leadership. MacArthur's statement that his first concern was the Japanese people was backed by the support he offered Sams in prioritizing the delivery of necessary provisions. Sams took pride in the priority status enjoyed by PHW during the early, emergency phase of the Occupation.

In addition to the problems of disease, PHW also had to confront the shortage of food. Cities and towns had been destroyed in the war and about fourteen and a half million people were homeless. Although Sams's team considered the European practice of placing the homeless in camps and offering them food, in the end they adopted a different approach. They set up a nationwide organization with the aim of promoting the rehabilitation of refugees, established various new laws on which to base their operations, and provided food and constructed housing. Their positive efforts extended even to the supply of clothing and the alleviation of water shortages. Defeat had sapped the energy of the Japanese people and left them unwilling to cooperate. It took six years for Sams to achieve the goals of the rehabilitation project.

Sams later stated that he placed great pressure on himself to demonstrate his loyalty to MacArthur, who had so fully supported his efforts, and to achieve results that surpassed those of the German occupation. He repeatedly emphasized his accomplishments in improving Japanese nutrition. Daily food allowances for the occupied areas, determined in Washington, were set at eighteen hundred calories per person for Germany but at a minimal fifteen hundred per person for Japan. Compared with Germany, Japan did not have an adequate system of food provisioning. Sams reported the Japanese situation faithfully to MacArthur and, with MacArthur's backing, did his best to ameliorate conditions in Japan.[25]

THE DEMOCRATIZATION OF JAPAN, AUGUST 1945 TO APRIL 1950

The Purge

The policy of public purges was implemented on the basis of Article 6 of the Potsdam Declaration of July 26, 1945: "There must be eliminated for all time the authority and influence of those have deceived and misled the people of Japan into embarking on world conquest." It created a whirlwind in every aspect of postwar Japanese society.

Already during the war, the purge issue had been discussed in Washington as a tool for the demilitarization and democratization of Japan. Immediately after the war, U.S. policy document SWNCC 150/4, authorized on September 6, 1945, and communicated to MacArthur, ordered that persons who had actively promoted militarism or militant nationalism be removed and excluded from public office; ultranationalist or militarist societies and organizations were to be banned. In fact, MacArthur's headquarters in Manila had already made preparations for a purge. Operation Blacklist, completed on August 7, 1945, identified the purge targets as "racial terroristic secret patriotic associations or organizations such as the Political Association of Great Japan, the Imperial Rule Assistance Association, the Imperial Rule Assistance Political Society, the Women's Federation of Great Japan."[1] The documents prepared in Manila formed the basis of the purge directives later issued in Japan. Furthermore, the Joint Chiefs of Staff in Washington prepared their own document, JCS 1380, which confirmed the basic aims of the military occupation as the "elimination of militaristic and ultra-nationalistic ideology from every field," the "disarmament and demilitarization of Japan," the "revival and strengthening of democratic tendencies," and the "promotion and support of liberal thought."[2] JCS 1380 specified more detailed provisions for a public purge than either SWNCC 150/4 or Operation Blacklist. Although the JCS documents were known as the "bible" of the Occupation, each section of GHQ implemented the details of policy on the basis of its own decisions.

On October 2, 1945, the nine sections of GHQ were officially launched as the Occupation administration, and the allocation of responsibilities was finalized. GS and the Civil Intelligence Section were placed in charge of the public purges. In terms of policymaking, the key person was Colonel Charles L. Kades, chief of the Public Administration Division and later deputy chief of the Government Section. After graduating from Harvard Law School, Kades had worked in the Department of the Treasury as a progressive bureaucrat engaged in New Deal policies. After enlisting in the Army, he had seen active service in Europe and was transferred after the war to Japan via Washington. Kades had no knowledge of Japan, later noting that he had not read even Ruth Benedict's *Chrysanthemum and the Sword*. However, Kades landed on Japanese soil with the original JCS 1380 document in hand, an indication of the special job assigned to him. Aged just thirty-nine, Kades worked vigorously as the youthful chief of GS and as a leading voice among the New Dealers who aimed to transform Japan. He was both an outstanding member of the GHQ staff and a somewhat threatening figure from a Japanese point of view.

Captain Frank Rizzo, who assumed responsibility under Kades for conducting the purge (and went on to become chief of GS), recalled that he first became acquainted with Kades in the Pentagon and was impressed by his accomplishments and brilliance. According to Rizzo, Kades not only worked hard but also had the capacity to get others to work hard for him. He could easily cajole people into doing things, and the female staff gravitated toward him. Possessed of a warm personality and disarming popularity, he was intellectually sharp and skilled in organizing support around an idea. In Rizzo's assessment, if something needed to be done, "Chuck" [Kades] could be depended upon to come up with a response.[3]

Under Crist, the current chief of GS who had already lost his administrative authority, Kades took responsibility for formulating directives about the purge. In cooperation with Lieutenant Colonel Spencer Byard, a lawyer, as well as Marshall Goodsill and his friend Rizzo, Kades organized a team to prepare a draft order based on the JCS documents and on denazification policies developed for Germany. By the beginning of November, two important directives had been drafted. SCAPIN-548, the Abolition of Certain Political Parties, Associations, Societies and Other Organizations, set purge guidelines and clarified the names of organizations, including nationalistic, militaristic, and secret societies, that were to be dissolved. SCAPIN-550, the Removal and Exclusion of Undesirable

Personnel from Public Office, listed the names of alleged war criminals, political leaders, military leaders, and exponents of ultranationalist, terrorist, and secret patriotic societies who were to be removed from public service.

But the harsh proposal prompted strong criticism from a group of former military officers at the Chiefs of Staff of GHQ, led by Willoughby, of G-2. This group was broadly negative toward the Potsdam Declaration, because, anticipating that conflict would erupt between the United States and the Soviet Union in the near future, they believed it necessary to retain the support of Japan's conservative leadership not only from the former army and navy but also from government and business. Willoughby's group expressed intense opposition to a wholesale purge of Japan's former elites and called for modifications. Since Whitney had not yet taken over leadership of GS, Kades lacked the political power to resist Willoughby, and he was forced to compromise. A revised document submitted at the beginning of December reflected a considerable reduction in purge categories. Now category A was comprised of war criminals; B included army and navy career officers; C included leaders and influential members of ultranationalist, terrorist, or secret patriotic societies; D included leaders and influential members of the Political Association of Great Japan, the Imperial Rule Assistance Association, and the Imperial Rule Assistance Political Society; E included officers of financial and development organizations involved in Japanese expansion; F included administrators of the Japanese occupied areas; and G included any other militarists or ultranationalists. GS could deliberately make category G flexible in applying it to those who were in a gray zone.

The criteria in the original draft included persons from the rank of minister down to section chief in all ministries, but the revised draft referred only to the three ministries of army, navy, and munitions. Moreover, only "key persons" were to be subject to the purge. The applicable time period was shortened: the period "from the Manchurian Incident to the end of the Pacific War" (1931–45) in the original draft was modified to "from the Marco Polo Bridge Incident to the end of the Pacific War" (1937–45). However, the revised document did broaden the applicable rank categories: while the initial draft had proposed that only officers of the rank of "major or above" should automatically be purged, the revised document specified officers of the rank of "second lieutenant or above." This modification had been recommended to Kades by Chief of Staff Richard Marshall, who emphasized that those who had been most actively engaged in Japanese aggression were young officers.[4] Accordingly, all officer graduates of the Imperial Army Academy and the Imperial Navy Academy were designated as subjects of the purge. Furthermore, Kades succeeded in creating an additional purge category G, for "any other militarists and ultra-nationalists," who had not been included in the German purges. Because the terminology was vague, this category offered

GS considerable latitude in determining whether or not a particular individual should be purged. It later would bestow great power on Kades when he came to review proposed lists of purge subjects.

With the basic guidelines for the purge now decided, Kades wanted to communicate the directives to the Japanese government as soon as possible, but MacArthur ordered him to avoid the three-day new-year holiday, according to Kades.[5] On January 4, 1946, with the new-year mood still in the air, SCAP issued the purge directives to the Japanese government. Even though rumors of a purge had been circulating, the severe provisions took government officials by surprise. With no choice but to accept, they set to work on preparing legislation, including translation from English to Japanese. The work was completed in February: SCAPIN-548 became Imperial Ordinance 101; SCAPIN-550 became Imperial Ordinance 109; and the implementation of the purge began. During the next two-and-a-half years, until the purges ended in May 1948, approximately 210,000 individuals, led by former military personnel and extending to members of the political, bureaucratic, economic, media, and educational elite, were removed or barred from public office. If one includes those who retired early for fear of being purged and the families of those purged, more than one million people were affected by the effort to clean up the leadership of Japan. The purge was so severe that many people were chilled with fear.

The New Japanese Constitution

The enactment of a new constitution to replace the Meiji Constitution promulgated in 1889 can be seen as the ultimate symbol of the democratization of postwar Japan. And yet, ironically, the drafting of the Constitution was conducted in secret within the Government Section of GHQ. How did such a situation emerge?

The first step was taken on October 4, 1945, when MacArthur suggested the necessity of constitutional revision to former prime minister Konoe Fumimaro, who was serving as deputy prime minister in the cabinet of Higashikuni Naruhiko. However, as the Higashikuni cabinet was dissolved the next day, the order to revise the Constitution was communicated to Higashikuni's successor as prime minister, Shidehara Kijuro. Shidehara established the Kenpo Mondai Chosa Iinkai (Constitution Problem Investigation Committee) under the chairmanship of State Minister Matsumoto Joji, and by the beginning of February 1946 the committee had prepared a draft of a new constitution. But since the committee's draft proved to offer nothing more than a rewording of the Meiji Constitution, it did not gain MacArthur's approval.

The Far Eastern Committee (FEC), consisting of eleven (later thirteen) Allied Powers, was scheduled to hold its first meeting in Washington on February 26. If the FEC were to embark on real deliberations, it would surely intervene in GHQ Occupation policies. Among the FEC members, Britain and the Soviet Union held doubts about the continuance of the imperial institution. Anxious to bring the constitutional revision to an advanced stage before the FEC meeting, on February 3 MacArthur ordered Whitney, a lawyer who had contributed much to the democratization of the Philippines, to draft a new constitution. Whitney had arrived from the Philippines at the end of 1945 and had replaced the weakened Crist as chief of GS. Whitney was also already filling the vacuum left by the departure of Richard K. Sutherland, who as chief of staff had established a close relationship with MacArthur. Kades, who had labored under Crist's weak leadership, was excited to have the powerful Whitney appointed as his boss.

Kades's testimony reads as follows:

> As far as I know, it was his [MacArthur's] idea to write a new constitution....As far as the Government Section was concerned, we were busy with the purge, the dissolution of the ultra-nationalist societies, cutting off communications between Japan and Formosa. We had many projects in the fire. As far as I was concerned, the Constitution was on the back burner. The Far Eastern Commission asked me to appear as a witness, so to speak, at a briefing. I was quizzed very thoroughly on what we were doing about writing a new constitution, or changing the Japanese Constitution. I said we were changing the Constitution by various directives like the civil liberties directive, in October '45, saying that the women would be able to vote in the forthcoming elections. MacArthur had called for elections in March or April of '46. We were busy trying to define where the elections would be held at that time. I said we are not writing a new constitution, but we're reorganizing the Japanese government, we're abolishing the Ministry of East Asia, we're abolishing the position of Lordkeeper [sic]....They weren't a bit satisfied with that response. Afterward I sent an extract of the interchange to General Whitney, and General Whitney sent it to MacArthur.[6]

Within ten days, on Sunday, February 3—the same day that MacArthur issued his order to Whitney—Kades was ordered from his residence at the Imperial Hotel to meet Whitney in his office on the sixth floor of the Dai-Ichi Building. Also called to Whitney's office were Commander Alfred R. Hussey and Lieutenant Colonel Milo E. Rowell. Whitney told the three that MacArthur had ordered the GS to be convened as a constitutional assembly to write a new constitution for Japan. Whitney wanted them to make a plan for carrying out the order. He had already decided to call a meeting of GS staff the next morning to order the preparation of a constitutional draft within a week to ten days or, at the latest, two weeks. Whitney emphasized the urgency of the project. In response to the protests of Kades that GS had other things to do, Whitney insisted that all other work should be set aside. When Kades mentioned the possibility of interference from other staff sections, Whitney's response was: "Lock the doors. We're just going to go into executive session—the whole Government Section."[7]

Whitney handed Kades a note, written by hand and in pencil, that set out four basic principles for the new constitution. The items listed on this so-called MacArthur note were: first, there was to be a representative legislature; second, the emperor would exercise no political power; third, the budget was to be patterned after the British system; and, fourth, war and the possession of armed forces were to be renounced. Unsure of the meaning of the third item, Kades assigned that task to Rizzo. Although Kades could not recall the exact words later, he affirmed that the fourth item, the renunciation of war, was definitely included in the note. Although it has been suggested that the renunciation of war was Shidehara's proposal, Kades rejected that possibility. On the other hand, Kades was uncertain whether the note was actually written by MacArthur himself or by Whitney, since their handwriting was rather similar. Kades observed that there was a high possibility that MacArthur dictated the note to Whitney, who wrote it down. It is noteworthy that the order to revise the Japanese constitution did not come from the Joint Chiefs of Staff, MacArthur's direct superiors in Washington. Indeed, the decision to proceed with constitutional revision may have been MacArthur's alone.

On Monday, February 4, 1946, some twenty GS members were called into a large conference room. To the assembled group Whitney conveyed MacArthur's order that for the next week the GS would function as a constituent assembly charged with the drafting of a new constitution for Japan. Under the leadership of Kades, Hussey, and Rowell, the special working committee investigated the U.S., Weimar, and French constitutions as well as draft proposals from the Japanese government. Working day and night, they completed the draft of a constitution in nine days. Kades described the process as follows:

> We had a steering committee consisting of the three of us; Hussey, Rowell, and myself. We had a committee on civil liberties that was made up of others. We had a committee on the Emperor, a committee on the Diet, and a committee on local government. They would submit drafts to us, to the steering committee. The civil liberties draft provisions were three to five times as long as they are in the present Constitution. I kept making the point that we weren't writing a statute, that we

were writing a constitution, and so we eliminated a great deal....We had some discussions with the Japanese in regard to a new Constitution.... MacArthur read every provision as it was prepared and made various suggestions along the way.[8]

The deadline for completing the draft was set at February 12, Lincoln's birthday.

On February 13, the day after the GS draft was finalized, Whitney, Kades, and others on the GS side met a group of cabinet officials, including Foreign Minister Yoshida Shigeru and State Minister Matsumoto Joji. Unaware of the secret GS activities, the Japanese representatives presented copies of their own constitutional draft. Whitney rejected it, and in its place presented the GHQ draft. Whitney urged the Japanese representatives to accept the draft, reminding them that the FEC, along with public opinion in the United States, the Soviet Union, Australia, and other nations, was insisting on the execution of the emperor. Accordingly, Whitney asserted, if the principles contained in the constitutional draft, including the reform of national political ideology, the renunciation of war, and respect of human rights, should be rejected, it would be difficult to retain the imperial system or even to protect the emperor from trial as a war criminal. The Japanese representatives, particularly Yoshida, were astounded and troubled by Whitney's demand. They responded to the actions of GHQ with distrust and shock.

On February 21, Shidehara visited MacArthur to ask his real intention and learned the major points to be incorporated in the draft: sovereignty would be vested in the people; the emperor would become a symbol of the nation; and war would be renounced. In particular, the provision for the renunciation of war was specified: "The threat or use of force is forever renounced as a means for settling disputes with other nations. No army, navy, air force or other war potential forces will ever be authorized and no right of belligerency will be given to the nation" (Constitution Article 9). It is generally reported that although Shidehara agreed with the war renunciation clause, he objected to the unilateral abrogation of Japan's right to retain military forces and a right of belligerency. Persuaded by MacArthur, however, he reluctantly conceded on the article. On March 2, the Japanese government prepared a draft of the new constitution based on the GHQ document, and on March 4 submitted it to GHQ. The final version was settled on March 5. On March 6, the Kempo Kaisei Soan Yoko (Outline Draft of the Constitutional Revision), which stipulated popular sovereignty, the emperor as the symbol of the nation, and the renunciation of war, was announced under MacArthur's authorization.

In the process of establishing Article 9, the war renunciation clause, however, a proposal referred to as the "Ashida revision" was advanced in a special legislative committee of the Diet led by Ashida Hitoshi (later foreign minister and prime minister). At the beginning of the second clause of Article 9, Ashida inserted the words: "In order to accomplish the aim of the preceding paragraph, land, sea, and air forces, as well as other war potential, will never be maintained." With this addition, the original phrase, which stated unconditionally that no military forces would be maintained, was changed to a phrase meaning that armed forces with war potential would not be maintained. This revision was interpreted at the time as indicating that it would be permissible to maintain military forces for the purpose of defense. In its final form, Article 9 declared:

> Aspiring sincerely to an international peace based on justice and order, the Japanese people forever renounce war as a sovereign right of the nation and the threat or use of force as means of settling international disputes. (2) In order to accomplish the aim of the preceding paragraph, land, sea, and air forces, as well as other war potential, will never be maintained. The right of belligerency of the state will not be recognized.

The FEC did not ignore Japan's constitutional revision. Based on the historical fact that in the prewar era the Japanese military had interfered in politics and in order to prevent a recurrence, FEC insisted that all ministers of state, including the prime minister, should be civilians. This demand for a "civilian clause" was conveyed to MacArthur through Washington. MacArthur responded quickly, sending Whitney to Yoshida to request that the clause be inserted. Although the Japanese government was not pleased, it had no choice but to accept. Article 66 was amended to include as Clause 2: "The Prime Minister and other Ministers of State must be civilians." Additionally, in order to end the privileges of the nobility, Kades proposed that the House of Peers should be abolished. Whitney and MacArthur both considered the proposal, but since there was a strong request for a bicameral system from the Japanese side, they withdrew the idea. Kades later commented with some irony that he was surprised to find that there were no further revisions to the original draft. On November 3, 1946, the new Constitution of Japan was promulgated. It took effect six months later, on May 3, 1947.[9]

Dissolution of the Zaibatsu and Land Reform

The dissolution of the Zaibatsu, or financial cliques, was conducted from 1945 to 1948 as part of the effort to democratize the postwar Japanese economy. The reform policy aimed to dissolve the head offices of the holding companies that characterized the Zaibatsu and to purge or drive out the small group of top executives as a means of blocking their control over subsidiary companies and promoting economic decentralization.

Zaibatsu dissolution was first carried out by Colonel Raymond Kramer, chief of the Economic and Science Section (ESS), who viewed the Zaibatsu as prowar entities that had positively advanced the war. From about September 1945, when the U.S. Initial Post-Surrender Policy for Japan was announced, he had demanded the voluntary dissolution of the four largest Zaibatsu: Mitsui, Mitsubishi, Sumitomo, and Yasuda. Yasuda accepted Kramer's order, but Mitsui and Sumitomo resisted and Mitsubishi protested vehemently. The Zaibatsu had a strong sense of victimhood, asserting that during the war they had been obliged to cooperate with the military, but in the end they were forced to give in to government pressure.

In December 1945, Marquat, one of the Bataan Boys, replaced Kramer as chief of ESS. Like Crist, the first chief of GS, Kramer had been forced to withdraw because of lack of support from the Bataan Boys. Marquat was from the artillery and, lacking expertise in the economic field, he had to rely entirely on economic advisors such as Sherwood Fine. Fine, who obtained his doctorate from Columbia University, was transferred to Tokyo from the Department of the Treasury immediately after the war. He later stated that he was under the impression that Marquat was delicate, sensitive, and quite different from the typical soldier. The fact that he had not graduated from a military academy distinguished him from the other career soldiers, who viewed him as an outsider.

Although Marquat continued Kramer's policies, Washington considered the GHQ measures too lenient. It dispatched to Japan a group of antitrust specialists chosen from the State Department and the Department of Justice and headed by Corwin D. Edwards to investigate not only the dissolution of the Zaibatsu but also the possibility of broad-ranging antimonopoly policies. The Edwards Report, submitted in March 1946, recommended severe measures, including the dissolution of family combines, or Zaibatsu, as well as industrial combines that had monopolistic or extremely consolidated economic power. Even in ESS some opined that the Edwards Report was idealistic, but Washington ordered GHQ to pursue policies in accordance with its recommendations. Of necessity, GHQ had the Japanese government organize the Holding Company Liquidation Committee (HCLC). Already, Eleanor M. Hadley, a researcher on Zaibatsu, had arrived in Japan and assumed responsibility under Kades for dissolving the Zaibatsu. Her job was to check whether GHQ orders were being faithfully carried out or whether there were evasions on the Japanese side. Any irregularities were to be communicated from Hadley to Kades, to Whitney and then to MacArthur, who would then give instructions to Marquat. The ESS staff included a number of New Dealers such as James M. Henderson, head of the Anti Trust and Cartels Division, and Edward C. Welsh, who worked actively with the GS to dissolve the Zaibatsu. Through the operation of the HCLC, eighty-three small and medium-sized companies, including Asano, Ayukawa (Nissan Group), and Okura, were dissolved, along with the four largest Zaibatsu. At the same time, about eighteen hundred entrepreneurs were purged in accordance with the economic purge policy. Only younger businessmen survived.

The land reform, which aimed to transform tenants into independent farmers, was conducted from 1946 until 1950. MacArthur described it thus: "One of the most far-reaching accomplishments of the occupation was the program of land reform."[10]

The Japanese government began preparations for reform, fearing the rise of antigovernment movements and increasingly serious conflicts between landlords and tenant farmers caused by demands that farmers supply more rice after the war. In October 1945, the Nochi Seido Kaikaku An (Rural Land System Reform Plan), which took account of landlords' concerns, was discussed and finalized at the Cabinet Council. In December, the Nochi Kaikaku Hoan (Rural Land Reform Bill), which aimed to strengthen independent ownership in agriculture and the payment of farm rents in cash instead of in kind, was delivered to the Diet. But in the course of discussion the plan met fierce opposition from conservatives, including large landholders, as well as liberals. Just as the bill was about to be withdrawn, the GHQ, which had been watching silently, suddenly intervened. It handed the Japanese government a Memorandum of Land Reform it had drafted and ordered the government to submit a plan for rural land reform by March 1946. This memorandum was effective in undercutting opposition to the reform bill in the Diet. The bill passed, and the First Land Reform was implemented.

Land reform not only dissolved the feudal relationship between landlords and tenant farmers but also, by dissolving land ownership by landlords, it significantly raised agricultural productivity. Nevertheless, the Natural Resources Section (NRS), which handled agricultural issues in GHQ, considered that the land reform had not adequately released tenant-held farmland. It instructed the Japanese government to postpone indefinitely the election of a local agricultural land commission that was supposed to take charge of the reforms. Consequently, except for the monetization of tenant rents, the First Land Reform remained in stasis. The Japanese government proved incapable of creating a new land reform proposal and thereafter reforms were considered under the initiative of the Allies.

To be prudent, MacArthur referred the land reform issue to the Allied Council for Japan (ACJ), an advisory organ to the GHQ, which began discussions in April 1946. The ACJ adopted a British proposal and GHQ directed the Japanese government to undertake a second land reform. In October, the government drafted Nochi Choseiho Kaisei Hoan (Revision of the Agricultural Land Adjustment Law) and Jisakuno Sosetsu Tokubetsu Sochi Hoan (Law for Special Measures for

Establishing Owner-Farmers) as the Second Land Reform Law. Both bills were passed in the Diet. Kades described the situation as follows:

> Whitney and MacArthur were very anxious that the Land Reform Act go through the Diet. It was sticky; we had a hard time inducing the Diet to pass it. I knew that they would be gratified to learn that it had been enacted. So I went down to Colonel Herb Wheeler.... Whitney said, "Come in." I think actually that was when I was introduced to General MacArthur.... He leaned back in his chair.... I didn't see what he was looking at.... I said to Whitney later, "What was he looking at? Was he talking to his Father in heaven?" He said, "No. He was looking at a picture of his father."[11]

In fact, MacArthur's respected father Arthur had himself carried out land reform in the Philippines. According to Kades, in this little-known episode, MacArthur was not only looking at his father's photo but "talking" to his father to tell him that he had now accomplished land reform in Japan.

By 1950, when the Second Land Reform was completed, 1.942 million hectares, or 80 percent of all tenant land, had been released. Most was sold to the government and then resold to former tenant farmers. The proportion of land held in tenancy decreased dramatically, from 46 percent before the reform to 9 percent afterward. MacArthur claimed proudly: "The redistribution of farmland was a strong barrier against any introduction of Communism in rural Japan."[12] It is probably more accurate, however, to note the historical significance of the reform in advancing the modernization of agricultural management and laying the foundations for high-speed economic growth.[13]

Educational Reforms

The educational field in Japan also experienced the shock of Japan's defeat. The emperor-centered, nationalistic education of the prewar and wartime eras was completely destroyed. Instead, under the leadership of the Occupation, American democratic education was introduced.

In Washington during the war, it had mainly been the State Department that prepared educational reform plans for postwar Japan. The staff at State believed that the Japanese educational system cultivated totalitarianism, placed more value on the state and organizations than on individuals, and indoctrinated students in militarism and ultranationalism through thought control. The educational reforms were planned in accordance with the basic view that university entrance examination systems selected elites who were to serve national purposes, and primary education was intended to cultivate a general public that was fanatically loyal to the state. In brief, the reforms recommended by the State Department were as follows: introduction of the ideas and principles of democracy, pacifism, and internationalism; and suspension of the educational policy-making functions of the Ministry of Education and abolition of the ministry division of superintendents in charge of thought control. However, State officials also recommended the possible use of the Japanese educational bureaucracy for four further proposals: first, elimination of militarist and ultranationalist teachers from educational institutions; second, suspension of courses in morals, Japanese history and geography, and abolition of military training courses; third, appointment and dispatch of civilian educational advisors representing the Allied Powers to the Ministry of Education and to each prefecture; and fourth, reeducation of teachers and a drastic revision of the normal school education system.

In October 1945 MacArthur told Prime Minister Shidehara about "the Five Basic Reform Plans for Democratization," including democratization of the school system. By the end of 1945, GHQ had issued four directives on education to the Japanese government. The first one was SCAPIN-178, "Administration of the Educational System of Japan." Here and in the second directive, the educational purge was announced. All teachers and educational officials were screened. As a result, about six thousand teachers and officials were purged from educational institutions. The third and fourth directives, issued in December, banned State Shinto, indoctrination in the emperor cult, and ultranationalist ideas, as well as suspending courses in Shushin (morals), Japanese history and geography. One highlight in the evolution of policy during the early period of the Occupation was the report by the First U.S. Education Mission in March 1946. "Postwar Educational Reforms in Japan" criticized Japanese education as highly centralized, providing standardization of education for the masses. Furthermore, it emphasized the imperative need to recognize the dignity and worth of individual human beings. The education it recommended would foster freedom of inquiry and training in the ability to analyze critically. It recommended that schools be made coeducational. The school education system should work on 6-3-3 basis, with six-year primary schools and three-year lower secondary schools made compulsory, and three-year upper secondary schools recommended. Instead of the multiple ladder system, which was diversified by elite courses for higher education, technical education courses, and general public courses, the report suggested application of a single ladder education system. School education should be equally available to anyone who wished to receive it corresponding to his or her ability. Furthermore, to reduce the centralized administrative powers of the Ministry of Education, the report recommended an educational committee or agency in each prefecture. These committees, politically independent from the central government, would control public elementary and secondary education and should be composed of representative citizens elected by popular vote.

Under Civil Information and Education (CIE) instructions, new democratic projects were implemented one after another. In place of inking deleted textbooks to black out passages with objectionable content, stopgap textbooks and new versions of textbooks were published. In the school curriculum, social study courses were introduced to foster creativity and socialization, and to inculcate faith in rational discourse. Introduction of the course of study for the Core Curriculum, and world history for knowledge of international affairs, was recommended. Other reforms introduced were the Japan Teachers Union, organized on a nationwide scale, and an American-style Parent Teacher Association (PTA) that aimed at a cooperative relationship between schools and society—it penetrated 90 percent of the schools. Another significant feature was the establishment of the Japan Education Reform Council, a government think tank separated from both the Ministry of Education and the Occupation authority. The Council drafted a fundamental law of education to replace the Imperial Rescript on Education of 1890, and proposed a new education system, a 6–3–3–4 establishment that added four years of university study beyond senior high schools. In 1947 the Fundamental Law of Education and the School Education Law came into existence to reinforce the ideals embodied in the new constitution. The following year saw the Local Boards of Education Law, which codified a decentralized administration based on elected local school boards. Thus was the foundation of the postwar education system laid.[14]

The First Postwar General Election

During the first three or four months after the end of the war, the political parties that would engage Japanese politics began to emerge. At the beginning of November 1945 the Japan Liberal Party was formed under Hatoyama Ichiro as an offshoot of the Seiyukai (one of the two largest wartime parties). One week later, the Japan Progressive Party was established. It originated in the Minseito (another of the wartime parties), which was connected to the Dainihon Seijikai (Great Japan Political Party). As a counterweight to these conservative parties, progressives established the Japan Social Democratic Party under Nishio Suehiro; Katayama Tetsu was its first secretary-general. In December, the moderate People's Cooperative Party was formed to advance a cooperative ideology. The Japanese Communist Party, which had been suppressed as an illegal organization before the war, was reorganized as a legal party with GHQ support; Tokuda Kyuichi, who had been released from prison, became secretary-general.

At the end of November 1945, the 87th extraordinary session of the Diet was convoked as the first actual session of the postwar era, and several political parties made their debut in the Diet. The allocation of seats on the opening day was 272 for the Japan Progressive Party, ninety-two for the Nonpartisan Club, forty-five for the Japan Liberal Party, fifteen for the Japan Social Democratic Party, and two independents. Various bills aimed at the democratization of Japan, including election law revisions stipulated by GHQ, were presented to the Diet by the Shidehara cabinet. In accordance with MacArthur's orders, Kades insisted on revisions that included the granting of women's suffrage, lowering of the voting age to twenty (with eligibility for election set at twenty-five), the adoption of large election districts and a plural ballot system, and the freedom to conduct election campaigns. These revisions aimed at a complete changeover of Diet members, facilitation of entry by new members, and a broadening of the range of candidates. After partial modification, the law was promulgated on December 17. The Shidehara cabinet was then dissolved and a general election was announced for the end of January 1946.

GHQ, however, directed the Japanese government to postpone the general election. One reason was that preparation of the top-secret purge bill had reached a climax and GHQ intended to sweep Japanese conservative forces completely from the political field. A second reason was that constitutional revision was moving slowly on the Japanese side, and little progress could be detected. MacArthur was anxious to test the good and bad points of the new constitution in the first postwar general election but the Japanese attitude to revision was negative. As a result, MacArthur decided to postpone the election.

Purge directives communicated to the Japanese government on January 4, 1946, caused serious repercussions in the Japanese political world. Moreover, as the details of the purge were revealed, it became clear that the impact on each political party would be enormous. In particular, all persons who had stood as government-recommended candidates in the 1942 general election became subject to the purge under provision G of the purge directive in 1946. As a result, 260 out of 274 Diet members from the Progressive Party were barred from running for office, including party leader Machida Chuji and others in leadership positions; only fourteen members passed the screening and qualified as candidates. The Liberal Party had forty-three seats at the time of its foundation but thirty occupants were purged, leaving only thirteen. Ten of the Social Democratic Party's seventeen Diet members were purged, and so were all thirteen members of the People's Cooperative Party. The goal of Kades and the GS, to clear away conservative power before the election, was largely accomplished.

Postponed by the GS, the first postwar general election eventually took place on April 10, 1946, based on the new election law. The 2,770 candidates, including seventy-nine women, competed for 466 seats. Some 2,624 candidates, or 95 percent of the total, were competing for the first time. This sea change resulted from the purge of prewar politicians. Those who had been purged managed to exert only a bare minimum of influence through local members with whom they had connections or by having family members elected as their substitutes. In terms of candidate numbers and the number of first-time candidates, no later election would surpass this first postwar election, which became a symbol of Japan's postwar democracy. When the votes were tallied, 140 Diet seats went to the Liberal Party, ninety-four to the Progressive Party, ninety-two to the Social Democratic Party, fourteen to the People's Cooperative Party, five to the Communist Party, thirty-eight to other groups, and eighty-one to independents. No party secured a majority. Although conservatives constituted an overwhelming majority of those elected despite the revisions to the election law, 375 of the 464, including thirty-nine women, became Diet members for the first time. As the percentage of first-time winners accounted for 80 percent of the total, it was clear that the purge had succeeded in replacing an old generation of politicians with a new one.

Following the election, however, there were difficulties in forming a new cabinet and it was not until May 22, forty days after the election, that the Yoshida cabinet was established. The first reason for the delay was that Prime Minister Shidehara, who should have dissolved his cabinet, declared a desire to remain in office in order to take responsibility for constitutional revision. The second reason was that Hatoyama Ichiro, leader of the top vote-winning Liberal Party, was purged immediately before the emergence of a new cabinet in accordance with category G of the purge directives. His purging was the result of an explicit and intentional intervention by Whitney and Kades who aimed to prevent the conservatives from establishing a government. Subsequently, a secret and bitter power struggle was carried on between GS, which supported the Social Democratic Party and other progressives, and Yoshida's conservative faction, which had drawn close to G-2 under Willoughby. In fact, for an entire year the Yoshida cabinet faced various crises, such as food shortages, inflation, and labor disputes. Throughout, however, Yoshida ignored GS and appealed to MacArthur. He thus avoided GS opposition by taking advantage of Willoughby's political power, even though he frequently angered Whitney and Kades in doing so.

In that same May, Chief of Staff Marshall, successor to Sutherland, returned to the United States. He had turned down MacArthur's request to remain with GHQ because he had been offered a position as head of the Virginia Military Institute, his alma mater (his wife disliked living in Japan). Although Marshall did not exercise leadership as strong as Sutherland's, he had made good use of his leading position among the Bataan Boys and his fair and moderate personality to play an important role in balancing the deepening conflict between Whitney in GS and Willoughby in G-2. With Marshall's departure and in the absence of anyone to continue his balancing role, the power struggle in GHQ escalated. Laurence E. Bunker, MacArthur's aide, later testified as follows:

> The only officer in the headquarters who was in a position to exert any pressure on Whitney was Dick Marshall after Dick Sutherland left. They were the only two who could have done anything about trying to keep him in the normal staff relationship. So after Dick Marshall left, there was nobody who could speak with any authority to Whitney except MacArthur. By that time he [Whitney] had established a personal relationship where he had immediate access to the General, and he did it at the expense of a great deal of hard feeling. It made my job as aide extremely difficult. He ignored me in going into the General's office, regardless of who was there. He didn't check with me to see if the General was free. So my relationship with Whitney was anything but cordial.[15]

Immediately after MacArthur ordered the suspension of a general strike planned by labor unions for February 1, 1947, he instructed Yoshida to call a general election to resolve the political confusion. The House of Representatives was dissolved at the end of March, and on April 25 the second postwar general election was held. The Social Democratic Party won 143 seats, the Liberal Party 131, and the Democratic Party 124. (In addition, the People's Cooperative Party gained twenty-nine, the Communist Party four, and other minor parties and independents thirty-eight seats.) Since the Social Democratic Party had gained a majority, on May 23 the House of Representatives nominated Katayama Tetsu as prime minister. On June 1, a coalition cabinet consisting of the Social Democratic Party, the Democratic Party, and the People's Cooperative Party was formed. MacArthur commented that the Japanese had chosen a median line between the extreme right and the left, and he welcomed the emergence of a Christian prime minister in Katayama. The GS side led by Whitney and Kades had overturned the conservative Yoshida cabinet and had won the Japanese domestic power struggle by enabling the reformists to gain power. Furthermore, they dominated in the power struggle with Willoughby's conservative group within the GHQ.[16]

Dissolution of the Ministry of Home Affairs

Since the advent of the Meiji Restoration, the Ministry of Home Affairs had wielded more power than any other government ministry. Its political base was local administration and the police. Not only did the minister of Home Affairs have the power to appoint and remove prefectural governors but he also appointed the police chiefs in each prefecture. Since most governors were originally Home Affairs bureaucrats, the ministry's influence over them was enormous. Although some of its authority later shifted to the ministries of education, justice, and welfare, through the end of the war the Home Ministry exercised strong authority over internal administration through four main offices: the Local Affairs Bureau (Chihokyoku), the Police Bureau (Keihokyoku), the Public Works Bureau (Kokudokyoku), which was responsible for public works such as road construction and river works, and the Management Bureau, which handled Korea, Formosa, and Sakhalin.

Kades and his group paid special attention to this enormous organization. Although they used it to share some responsibility for the Occupation administration, they soon came to view the Ministry of Home Affairs as an obstruction to the demilitarization and democratization that formed the basis of Occupation policy. The first step toward dealing with it was the Civil Liberties Directive issued by MacArthur in October 1945. Not only was the Peace Preservation Law abolished and political prisoners released from prison but the Police Bureau, which handled these matters within the Ministry of Home Affairs, and the Special Higher Police (Tokko), notorious for political repression, were also abolished. Also dismissed were the minister of Home Affairs, the chief of the Police Bureau, the superintendent general of Police, the division heads of prefectural police offices, and all officers of the Special Higher Police and the Protection and Surveillance Commission (Hogo Kansatsu Chosatai) under the Ministry of Justice. In December a directive to end State Shinto was issued and the Board of Shrines, which administrated State Shinto affairs, was abolished.

On January 4, 1946, when GHQ issued its public purge directives, categories D and F were aimed directly at the Ministry of Home Affairs. Category D targeted the leaders and influential members of ultranationalist, terrorist, and secret patriotic societies as well as members of the Imperial Rule Assistance Association (IRAA), the Imperial Rule Assistance Political Society, the Political Association of Great Japan, and their affiliates. Category F identified chief administrators of occupied areas as persons to be purged. In fact, the head of the IRAA branch office in each prefecture had been held concurrently by the governor, who was also in most cases a former official of the Ministry of Home Affairs. The Ministry of Home Affairs may not have been directly targeted by the directive, but a large number of its higher officials were thus effectively purged. Moreover, many chiefs and superintendents of the Korea, Formosa, Kwantung, and South Seas jurisdictions were former officials of the Ministry. In addition to police chiefs, senior officials in local administration thus became targets of the purge.

Another blow to the Ministry of Home Affairs was the purge of the Dai Nippon Butokukai (Great Japan Military Virtue Society). Established in the late nineteenth century to promote Budo (Japanese fencing arts), the Butokukai was a powerful organization with branches at home and abroad. Although it was prominent enough that Prime Minister Tojo Hideki had served as its president during the war years, it was spared in the early stages of the purge. However, knowing that many of the prefectural and divisional heads of the Butokukai were governors and police heads who had come from the Ministry of Home Affairs, Kades and his group forced the Japanese government to classify the society as an undesirable organization and purge its main officeholders under the provisions of Category G. This was clearly a strategy aimed at the Ministry. At the same time, Whitney, Kades, and other GS officers were attempting to strike a blow at the Japanese police organization controlled by Willoughby and G-2. The Butokukai purge was thus a political scheme to kill two birds with one stone.

In April 1947 Whitney sent a memorandum to the Ministry of Home Affairs, stating a need to reform the centralized political system and inquiring how the Ministry planned to respond. The Ministry interpreted the memorandum as an instruction to decentralize and prepared to move ahead with its own reforms. It decided to transfer some responsibilities to other ministries and to local offices and to rename itself the Ministry of Public Administration (Minseisho). Cabinet approval for the changes was obtained in June. Kades, however, was angered by what he saw as a halfhearted reform and immediately accelerated his own plan to dissolve the Ministry. Immediately before this incident, in May 1947, Kades's hopes had been realized with the formation of the Katayama government founded on the Social Democratic Party, and the situation had become politically advantageous for the GS. The government cooperated with the GS, and an administrative review department under Katayama set about preparing for reorganization. Its final plan proposed radical changes: the Ministry of Home Affairs would be abolished; the functions of the Local Affairs Bureau would be transferred to a newly formed Self-Government Commission (Jichi Iinkai); a newly formed Construction Board (Kensetsuin) would take over functions formerly conducted by the War Damage Rehabilitation Board in the Home Ministry's Public Works Bureau; a newly formed Public Safety Commission (Kancho) would assume the functions of the Police Bureau and the Investigation Bureau; and these new bodies would be affiliated with the Cabinet Bureau. The reform proposal was approved immediately in cabinet discussions.

The proposal to abolish the Ministry of Home Affairs was thus prepared in July and, after GHQ discussion, was presented to the House of Representatives in August. Subsequently, an alternative plan was prepared for the local self-government commission and a new administrative system was launched based on specific functions, including the Local Police Headquarters (Kokka Chiho Keisatsu Honbu), the National Firefighting Bureau (Kokka Shobocho), and the Bureau of Justice (Homucho). After the bills passed the Diet, on December 31, 1947, the Ministry of Home Affairs was eliminated. Not only was this the end of a powerful government ministry, it also marked the historic peak of Japanese demilitarization and democratization by the GHQ, or, more specifically, the GS Potsdam group.[17]

WASHINGTON'S POLICY SHIFT ON JAPAN AND MACARTHUR'S RESISTANCE, JANUARY 1948 TO JUNE 1950

Failure of the Proposal for an Early Peace Treaty with Japan

On March 17, 1947, two-and-a-half months after the beginning of the second phase of public purges, which covered the economy, the press, and local administration, MacArthur used a press interview to call for an early peace treaty with Japan. At the time this was viewed as a sudden announcement, without any advance consultation with Washington. For MacArthur, however, it was no more than a restatement of his previous thinking. On February 20, for example, he had sent a message to the War Department, emphasizing that Japan had already achieved a democratic system and that people were enjoying its reality.[1] History, he suggested, had shown that long military occupations were unable to achieve a positive effect. In fact, MacArthur's argument for an early peace treaty was closely related to his desire to run in the 1948 presidential campaign. He dreamed of being nominated as the Republican Party candidate and being elected president.[2] Successful administration of the Japanese Occupation would be an important asset during any campaign. Furthermore, if he could conclude the peace treaty, he could expect hero status from the American public. MacArthur's aim was clear.

The timing of his announcement, however, brought MacArthur failure. His announcement of a possible early peace treaty was made only five days after the March 12, 1947, announcement of the Truman Doctrine had marked the beginning of the cold war. From the perspective of both ideology and power politics, a new containment policy had been proposed in Washington. As chief administrator of the Occupation, MacArthur should have been more careful in assessing the world situation. In addition, he should have paid attention to the domestic situation in the United States, where it was clear that President Truman was expecting to be reelected. MacArthur's poor timing was partly because his long tenure in Tokyo had made him insensitive to political movements far away in Washington, and partly because he had been planning his own presidential campaign. In practice, his announcement sparked conflict between Tokyo and Washington, and in particular, between Tokyo and the State and War departments.

MacArthur's treaty proposal was discussed in the Office of Far Eastern Affairs of the State Department. A preliminary draft of the response, prepared by department staff on August 5, and based on the punitive policies of the Potsdam Declaration, not only demanded heavy reparations from Japan and the maintenance of military bases but also opposed Japanese rearmament. It proposed to establish an observation committee consisting of ambassadors from the eleven countries of the Far Eastern Committee (FEC), which would keep a close watch over any violations of the demilitarization policy and secure its achievements for twenty-five years after conclusion of the peace.[3]

The State Department had already begun preparations for a peace treaty conference by opening discussions with related governments. In July, it sent invitations to the ten other FEC nations to urge them to participate in a preliminary treaty conference in Washington on August 19, 1947. However, there was disagreement between the United States, which proposed decision making by majority, and the Soviet Union, which demanded the right to a veto. The preliminary conference was affected by the cold war. In the summer of 1948 the conference meeting was aborted because of these procedural objections.

Washington's Review of the Japan Occupation Policy

In an international situation in which the cold war was gradually expanding into Asia, George F. Kennan, appointed in May 1947 as chief of the Policy Planning Staff (PPS) of the State Department, was critical of the early Japanese peace treaty drafted by the Office of Far Eastern Affairs. According to Kennan, the punitive draft paid too much attention to patient but firm and vigilant containment by the international powers, through which drastic demilitarization and democratization were to be achieved.[4] Kennan was doubtful that international vigilance by nations such as the Soviet Union would contribute to Japanese democratization. Moreover, considering the unstable political situation of the Chiang Kai-shek administration in mainland China, he considered Japan more important than China as a potential strategic factor in world politics. He emphasized, therefore, that promoting Japan's economic recovery and stabilization should be a primary U.S. objective. Kennan's view attracted attention at the highest levels of the State Department. In October he presented a long paper entitled "PPS Outcome concerning Issues of Japan's Peaceful Settlement" to Secretary of State George Marshall, and Undersecretary of State Robert A. Lovett. Kennan argued that in the new context of the cold war, the emphasis of Occupation policies should shift from demilitarization and democratization to economic recovery. The current purge policy, the antitrust program, and demands for war reparations should all be immediately terminated. Kennan's paper provided a foundation for the NSC-13 statement that would, in turn, become the basic document for the so-called reverse course in Occupation policy.[5]

Kennan anticipated MacArthur's veto over the proposal. The State Department had set up its Diplomatic Section within GHQ (reorganized from the Office of Political Advisors) as the U.S. representative, but it could not gain access to helping form Occupation policy because of MacArthur's mistrust of the State Department.[6] Not even President Truman had complete control. MacArthur's headquarters in Tokyo occupied a highly independent position. If its officers looked at all to Washington for guidance, it was to their immediate superiors in the Joint Chiefs of Staff (JCS) and the Civil Affairs Division (CAD). MacArthur was both commander in chief, Far East Command (CINCFE) and supreme commander for the Allied Powers (SCAP). As Kennan noted, "The commanders had, as a rule, two hats: an American one and an international one. In part, they executed American directives, and in part, they were the executors of international agreements among the allies."[7] They used the two roles strategically. If they received pressure from one side, they skillfully preserved their position by using reasons drawn from the other side. According to Kennan, this flexibility gave MacArthur unusual power to resist Washington-generated pressure and made the occupation of Japan very different from that of Germany.

Under these circumstances, on submitting his paper to the secretary of state and the undersecretary of state, Kennan proposed making MacArthur's agreement on these most important issues a prerequisite and suggested that a person should be dispatched to Tokyo to persuade MacArthur. In the spring of 1948, Kennan himself was to play this role. In September and October of 1947, the War Department sent William H. Draper Jr., who had been newly appointed as the undersecretary, to Tokyo. According to the Kauffman Report, in which James L. Kauffman excoriated its anti-Zaibatsu provision, Draper stressed the importance of Japanese economic recovery and pointed to the excessive nature of SCAP controls over the Japanese government. He also suggested that the purge of Japanese entrepreneurs was having a negative effect on Japan's economic revival. The War Department thus took the initiative, ahead of the State Department, in discussing a shift in Occupation policy in the context of the cold war. Since Kennan's proposals had attracted the support of the upper echelons of the State Department, there was a basic consensus between War and State regarding the shift in Occupation policy. In the end, the punitive conditions for an early peace treaty recommended by the Office of Far Eastern Affairs of the State Department were avoided. Kennan's emphasis on Japan's stability and economic revival in place of an early peace treaty was reflected in a modification of Occupation policy for Japan.

On January 6, 1948, Secretary of War Kenneth C. Royall delivered a well-publicized address in San Francisco. Royall stated that the original occupation goals had been largely realized, and that in determining Japan's future political stability the importance of a healthy and independent economy should be taken into account: "The United States cannot forever continue to pour hundreds of millions of dollars annually into relief funds for occupied areas....There has arisen an inevitable area of conflict between the original concept of broad demilitarization and the new purpose of building a self-supporting nation." He added, "We hold to an equally definite purpose of building in Japan a self-sufficient democracy, strong enough and stable enough to support itself and at the same time to serve as a deterrent against any other totalitarian war threats which might hereafter arise in the Far East."[8] Royall's speech reflected the change of political mood in Washington. Not only did it flag a shift in basic American policy toward Japan from demilitarization and democratization to economic independence, but it also noted publicly and for the first time the possibility of Japanese rearmament to oppose communism in Asia.

With regard to the rearmament of Japan, the Plans and Operations Division (POD) of the War Department heeded Royall's words and by May 1948 had completed a draft document entitled "Limited Military Armament for Japan." It offered the following arguments for a possible Japanese force: first, it would be a small, lightly equipped Japanese army of perhaps a few hundred thousand; second, it would be organized, trained, and supervised by the U.S. Army; third, it would be given adequate means in the form of limited military armament to help safeguard Japan's national security and enhance the country's regional defense against military threats from abroad; fourth, it would contribute to the recovery and enhancement of Japanese national dignity but never be a threat to neighboring countries; and fifth, it would allow a reduction in the numbers of U.S. military forces deployed in the defense of Japan. The document also noted that as many as one million Japanese nationals with military experience could form a pool from which recruits for this new military would come and thus offer a deterrent against the expanding Soviet threat.[9] Thus Washington, in an escalating cold war, saw Japan as a stronger and more dependable ally than China. It recognized that a policy shift regarding Japan was vital. As Kennan had pointed out, however, it was necessary to persuade MacArthur in Tokyo.

MacArthur's Opposition

After arriving in Japan on February 26, 1948, Kennan took immediate steps to meet MacArthur. As anticipated, MacArthur embarked on a monologue that lasted approximately two hours. Kennan, following Marshall's advice, simply listened to MacArthur's assertions about the significance of the Japanese Occupation, Chinese and Soviet reactions to the proposed peace treaty with Japan, and Japan's future. However, before their second meeting on March 5, Kennan was able to establish a procedure by which he would first present his views (identified as those of the secretary of state) and then hear MacArthur's position. Kennan noted, first, that since there was little likelihood that a peace treaty would be concluded and ratified in the near future, it would be necessary to deal with Japan for some time without a treaty. Second, the U.S. Occupation policy had been based on the Potsdam Declaration, but since the objectives of the Potsdam Declaration had been achieved, it was no longer useful as a guide to the future. Third, Kennan stated Washington's view that because of the changing world situation, the basic aim of future policy should be the stabilization of Japanese society so that Japan could stand on her own feet after Occupation forces withdrew. With these various points in mind, Kennan proposed several necessary conditions: a firm U.S. security policy in the Pacific; a Japanese defensive capability adequate to withstand future military pressures from the outside world; an intensive program of economic recovery; and the relaxation of Occupation control, in order to stimulate a sense of autonomy within the Japanese government.[10]

In his response, MacArthur pointed to the existence of the Far Eastern Commission (FEC) as an obstacle to the modification of Occupation policy, saying that any changes might be expected to encounter opposition on the part of Allies in the FEC. It was a misconception to think that the future could be discussed at the FEC on the premise of cooperative relations with the Soviet Union. He criticized Frank R. McCoy, the U.S. representative, for hesitating to use the veto in the FEC. With regard to the security of the Pacific, MacArthur outlined his views that the strategic boundaries of the United States lay along the eastern coastline of continental Asia, forming a U-shaped line that linked the Aleutians, Midway, the former Japanese-held islands, Clark Field in the Philippines, and Okinawa. Maintaining a military base in Okinawa was, MacArthur argued, the key point. If adequate forces were stationed there, the United States would no longer need military bases on the Japanese home islands. For this reason, securing long-term use of Okinawa as a military base was an urgent necessity.

Although MacArthur agreed that Japan's economic recovery was an important Occupation objective, he pointed out that negative attitudes on the part of other Far Eastern nations toward Japan were likely to impede Japan's development as a trading nation. He also argued that the control exerted by GHQ over the Japanese government was less than imagined in Washington. As for the Zaibatsu problem, MacArthur denied that the men who had been purged were necessarily persons of superior competence. Many Japanese citizens had written to GHQ thanking it for getting rid of those elderly incompetents. Although it was regrettable that the intelligent contributions that former Japanese military personnel could have made to public life had been eliminated by purges, the purge policy was one of the first directives embodied in the Potsdam Declaration. MacArthur emphasized that the economic purge, which involved no confiscation of property, was not as extreme as many people in Washington thought. On the other hand he realized that GHQ was home to some left-wing theorizers, and he was planning to announce a reduction in their numbers.[11]

Kennan was sympathetic about the difficulties MacArthur faced with regard to the FEC. There was, he said, no need for MacArthur to consult the FEC or to feel bound by views it had expressed at earlier dates with a view to implementing the terms of surrender—the surrender terms had already been implemented. MacArthur was greatly impressed with this interpretation. Furthermore, Kennan stated, "If the FEC could no longer serve as instrument of Allied policy, I thought the Russians would take a different view of the problem of a peace treaty. We would then have them over a barrel; for they would either have to agree to the type of treaty we liked or consent to see us remain indefinitely in Japan with our military forces."[12] MacArthur agreed. The conference ended with the question of reparations. MacArthur's surprising insistence that Kennan should meet him once more before leaving Japan was an indication that the meeting had gone well.

After returning to Tokyo from an inspection trip in Okinawa, Kennan was surprised to learn that Undersecretary Draper had arrived in Japan. The two men met on March 20, ahead of their meeting with MacArthur. On Japanese security, they shared the opinion that a FBI-type central organization should be established to confront the power of communism. In addition, Draper emphasized that there were just two security solutions: either station U.S. forces in Japan until the Soviet threat disappeared, or establish a Japanese self-defense force. Kennan agreed with Draper that they should adopt the latter solution, and noted that they would need to find reasons to justify Japanese rearmament. Having confirmed their shared views, Draper and Kennan met MacArthur on March 21.

Draper stated at the outset that there was a general trend in recent War Department thinking toward the early establishment of a small defensive force for Japan, which should be ready by the time that U.S. Occupation forces left the country. MacArthur expressed his outright opposition to any Japanese military force. His reasons were: first, that all the nations of the Far East were still mortally fearful of a remilitarized Japan; second, that Japanese rearmament was contrary to the fundamental principles of SCAP policy; third, that even the best efforts toward rearming Japan would produce no more than a fifth-rate military power; fourth, that Japanese economic recovery would be negatively affected; and, fifth, that the Japanese people themselves were no longer willing to support an armed force.[13] MacArthur argued further that once a peace treaty was signed, Occupation forces should withdraw from Japan completely, and that the peace treaty should prohibit the establishment of any military force in Japan with the exception of civilian police forces, a small-scale unit to maintain domestic order, and a small-scale coastal patrol to counteract smuggling. Air forces of any type would be prohibited. MacArthur was aiming at the demilitarization of the Japanese mainland and the establishment of Japan as a neutral nation. Washington's efforts to persuade MacArthur had failed.

Learning through this meeting with MacArthur of Kennan's interest in Japanese rearmament, Robert Eichelberger, commander of the 8th Army, prepared a proposal for using Japanese manpower as part of the U.S. military force. He submitted it to MacArthur through Chief of Staff Paul Mueller. MacArthur's reaction was, however, negative. Like Kennan and Draper, Eichelberger was confronted by the insurmountable barrier of MacArthur's opposition; all three had to hold back on their ideas for Japanese rearmament.[14]

NSC 13/2 and MacArthur's Resistance

Immediately after the conference with MacArthur, Kennan returned to the United States. Draper, who was accompanying an economic mission led by the banker Percy F. Johnston, made contact with newly elected Prime Minister Ashida Hitoshi and other high-ranking Japanese officials. They also interviewed some purged business leaders and used various means to send the message that the economic purge and Zaibatsu dissolution should be stopped immediately because they would prevent Japan from becoming self-supporting. MacArthur criticized Draper severely, saying that Washington elites opposed the purge and Zaibatsu dissolution because it would disadvantage their own business interests. MacArthur's remark was to the point. On the other hand, he did not hesitate to write to Secretary of the Army Royall that Japanese economic recovery was a necessary condition for economic restoration of the Far East. The Draper-Johnston Report, submitted to the War Department after the group returned to the United States, emphasized the importance of Japan's industrial revival, argued for the curtailment of reparations, and urged the implementation of a balanced financial policy to restrain inflation.

On March 25, 1948, following his return home, Kennan submitted to Secretary Marshall his "Recommendations with Respect to U.S. Policy toward Japan" (PPS 28). The document discussed Japanese domestic problems in view of the cold war and made the following proposals: first, postponement of conclusion of the peace treaty; second, permanent retention of U.S. military facilities in Okinawa; third, Japanese police to be strengthened by the reinforcement and reequipping of the present forces; fourth, termination of the purge; fifth, lightening of reparations; sixth, reduction of occupation costs and prioritization of economic recovery; and seventh, early termination of the war crimes trials of category "A" suspects.[15] Kennan criticized as inappropriate MacArthur's evaluation of diplomacy toward the Soviet Union. From the viewpoint of Kennan, who was knowledgeable about Soviet affairs, it was unthinkable that the Soviet Union would comply with its international moral obligation to maintain Japanese military neutrality. He thought, moreover, that MacArthur was exaggerating the anticommunist sentiments of the Japanese. Kennan's interpretation was, rather, that purged Japanese leaders had become antagonistic to the new order, raising the dangerous possibility that Communists might exploit the situation. He argued, therefore, that the United States should adopt a containment policy against the Soviet Union internationally and a preventive policy against communism domestically. From this perspective, it was important to end the purge not only of economic leaders but also of former army and navy personnel and politicians as soon as possible.[16]

On June 2 Kennan's paper was approved with revisions by the National Security Council (NSC) as NSC 13 under its original title, "Recommendations with Respect to U.S. Policy toward Japan." In this revised version, the section entitled "Limited Military Armament for Japan" was deleted. The phrase "along the lines of FBI" was deleted from the section on Japanese police forces and the recommendations were scaled back to reinforcing and reequipping the Japanese police, the establishment of a Maritime Safety Board (Coastal Patrol), and the strengthening of the central defense organization. This policy statement clearly reflected Washington's sensitivity to MacArthur's opposition to rearmament. But the sensitivity was lost on MacArthur. On June 12, he insisted in a memorandum to Draper that any reinforcement of the Japanese police forces, however slight, might meet stiff resistance from the Allied Council for Japan (ACJ) and the FEC.

Ignoring MacArthur's opposition, Washington made further modifications to the document in September and approved it under the new name of NSC 13/2 on October 7. President Truman signed the document on October 9. With this signature, the objectives of U.S. Occupation policies shifted from demilitariza-tion and democratization to economic autonomy for Japan. Moreover, against MacArthur's opposition, the policy of strengthening Japanese police forces was adopted. The so-called reverse course had begun.[17]

On December 4 MacArthur sent the following critical communication:

> Messages are addressed to Commander in Chief, Far East Command (CINCFE), (W 80453 and W 80454) seemingly under the misapprehen-sion that CINCFE as an executive agency of the United States Govern-ment has that authority over the non-military phases of the Japanese occupation which would permit him to implement the non-military features of NSC 13/2 ... SCAP is an international officer charged as "The sole executive authority in the occupation of Japan" with the imple-mentation of policy decisions of the eleven nations concerned acting through the Far Eastern Commission.[18]

On December 18, he wrote again that he could not understand the thinking behind NSC 13/2 and argued that, if implemented, it would certainly produce contradictions in the context of FEC directives.

With regard to the key issue of rearmament, MacArthur emphasized through Major General Paul. J. Mueller, his chief of staff, that complete and guaranteed neutrality was the ideal status for Japan following the peace treaty. The establish-ment of an inadequate armed force or a quasi-military alliance with the United States would destroy the purpose and character of the Occupation and thereby jeopardize the relationship with the Soviet Union. He asserted that the rearma-ment of Japan would make the present situation worse and would in turn neces-sitate the presence of a U.S. military force in the Far East. From the military point of view, Japanese rearmament was undesirable. MacArthur also argued:

> Visualization of a civil police force capable of expanding into an army appeared unrealistic....A sharp distinction should be drawn between a police force and defense force. By training and selection, police person-nel are unfitted to provide the nucleus for a field force capable of action beyond the requirement for maintenance of internal law and order.... The existence of this pool [of trained police] is the very factor which necessitates maintenance of the guarantees of complete neutrality until such time as hostilities actually begin. Apparently inspired press specu-lation on utilization of this experienced manpower pool has already

seriously jeopardized the strong United States moral position....Exploration of possibility of amending the present Japanese Constitution would not be in the best interests of the United States.[19]

In sum, MacArthur not only opposed the limited rearmament plan being considered in Washington but he totally rejected the idea of reinforcing the police force as a temporary expedient. The policy gulf between Washington and Tokyo had become too wide to be easily bridged, and another cold war was brewing.[20]

Conflict within GHQ/SCAP: GS vs. G-2

While MacArthur in Tokyo and the War and State departments in Washington were revealing their conflicts in 1948, antagonism between the Government Section (GS) and General Staff 2 (G-2; Intelligence) was gradually rising to white heat at GHQ. Whitney, chief of GS, had already secured his position as MacArthur's closest aide after Sutherland and Marshall departed in the spring of 1946. He was the only person who could meet MacArthur without an appointment. Whitney was surrounded by powerful brains such as Kades, deputy chief of the Government Section; Justin Williams, chief of the Parliamentary and Political Division; Special Assistant Frank Rizzo; and Jack P. Napier, chief of the Public Purge Screening Committee and later chief of GS. By controlling them, he carried out the policies of demilitarization and democratization. Although he was not a member of the Bataan Boys, his loyalty to MacArthur and his legal expertise satisfied MacArthur's needs. From the beginning of 1946 to the end of 1947, GS played a key role in a series of reforms including the drafting of the new constitution, the public purge, the establishment of a democratic election system, land reform, the democratization of local government, and dissolution of the Ministry of Home Affairs. Although Spencer B. Akin, chief of the Civil Communications Section, and Hugh Casey, chief of the Engineering Section, were both Bataan Boys, neither showed any great interest in politics, and William Marquat, chief of the Economic and Science Section, was a man of mild personality. None of these three could assume the authority wielded by Sutherland and Marshall. Thus, no staff remained in Tokyo who could remonstrate with Whitney. His power was unassailable.

It was Major General Willoughby, chief of G-2, who felt bitter hostility toward Whitney. His personality was eccentric, but with a prestigious background among the Bataan Boys, he controlled a group of men who had seen active military service. Willoughby's group was critical of the demilitarization and democratization policies of the GS.[21] Emphasizing the confrontation with the Soviet Union, they put up strong resistance against a purge policy that would eliminate the conservative forces of former army and navy men as well as politicians and business leaders. In February 1946, Willoughby consolidated his power by driving out the chief of the Civil Intelligence Section (CIS), Elliott Thorpe, his wartime rival. By taking over the leadership of Civil Censorship Detachment (CCD), which was attached to Counter Intelligence Corps (CIC), and by dominating the Allied Translation and Interpreters Service (ATIS), which had five hundred personnel, Willoughby controlled almost all aspects of military intelligence at GHQ. His direct and indirect control extended to more than one quarter of the entire GHQ staff.[22]

Taking advantage of his position as chief of the War History Editorial Section, Willoughby appointed Hattori Takushiro (former colonel, former secretary to Prime Minister Tojo, and chief of the operations section of the Imperial Headquarters), along with other prominent former military officers who were in line to be purged, to editorial positions relating to the war history. He gave all appointees special exemption from the political purge. The total of exemptions thus granted supposedly amounted to several hundred. Willoughby established a close liaison with important former members of the Japanese military while at the same time he was exerting influence on the organization of the Japanese police through the Public Safety Division (PSD) led by his subordinate Colonel H. E. Pulliam. In Japanese politics he cooperated with the conservative Liberal Party led by Yoshida Shigeru, thereby opposing the GS, which was strengthening its association with the moderate Socialist Party and the Democratic Party. During the early years of the Occupation, MacArthur's support for democratization lessened Willoughby's influence. Indeed, G-2 accumulated losses in its struggle against GS through its handling of the Butokukai (Military Virtue Society) purge and the police reform. However, even though Chief of Staff Mueller, who succeeded Sutherland and Marshall, enjoyed a high personal reputation, he exerted less authority than his predecessors. For this reason he was unable to mediate in the confrontation between G-2 and GS. Political strife continued unabated.

The Proxy War for GS vs. G-2: Ashida vs. Yoshida

The conflict between GS and G-2 deeply affected not only the GHQ but also the Japanese political world. The anticonservative stance of Kades was well known and exerted a great influence on the political purges of Hatoyama Ichiro, president of the Liberal Party, and Ishibashi Tanzan, minister of finance. Kades thought highly of the potential of Ashida Hitoshi (former minister of welfare and chief of the Constitution Amendment Committee), who had left the Liberal

Party and joined the Democratic Party. Kades helped Ashida gain political power. In a countermove, Yoshida carried out his so-called Item Y purge,[23] expelling Democratic Party members Narahashi Wataru, Inukai Takeru, and Hori Shigeru, who had supported Ashida. The trouble between Ashida and Yoshida was not simply a clash between former Foreign Ministry colleagues; it also signified a proxy war between GS and G-2. According to Hitotsumatsu Sadayoshi, minister of telephone and telegram in the Yoshida administration (later minister of welfare under Katayama and minister of construction in the Ashida administration), Ashida imposed his opinions on others and was so dominant that his colleagues felt unable to oppose them. Ashida said: "GHQ said you should be a political leader for the future Japan, recommending me to be President of Democratic Party. So I decided to do my best for the country."[24] Ashida had already fallen ultimately under GHQ control.

On April 25, 1947, the second postwar general election, and the first one under the new constitution, took place. The Democratic Party gained only 124 seats, falling behind the 143 seats won by the Socialist Party and 131 by the Liberal Party. The possibility of an Ashida premiership suffered a setback, and attention now focused on the formation of a coalition led by the Socialist Party. The issue ignited another struggle within the Democratic Party. The Ashida faction favored a coalition, but the Shidehara faction opposed it. After heated debate, the Ashida faction won out, giving Ashida the possibility of becoming a future prime minister. In this matter, as well, Kades and GS officials exerted great influence. A coalition government was formed with Katayama of the Socialist Party as prime minister on June 1, 1947, comprising the Socialist, Democratic, and People's Cooperative parties. During this time, the possibility survived of a coalition of the Liberal and Democratic parties, but excluding the Socialists. Finally, however, that possibility vanished due to internal strife among the three former diplomats, Ashida, Yoshida, and Shidehara. Ashida was appointed as foreign minister in the Katayama cabinet with the title senior vice minister.

As foreign minister, Ashida no longer encountered the diplomatic obstacles placed by military cliques, but he was forced to conduct his diplomatic business under the absolute power of the Occupation authority. The Japanese government could not expect to conduct diplomatic negotiations with the United States on an equal basis. Nevertheless, Ashida aimed at the future restoration of independence with two preparatory measures. One was his July 1947 submission to Whitney and George Atcheson Jr., chief of the Diplomatic Section, of his "Requests concerning a Peace Treaty," based on MacArthur's idea of an early peace treaty. The other was his "Viewpoints on Japanese Security," which was handed to Eichelberger, commander of the 8th Army, in September 1947 before Eichelberger's temporary return to the United States. The first bore no fruit, since the push for an early peace treaty was abandoned, but it was significant that a Japanese minister had taken an initial step to express a clear preference for a peace treaty. The second document presented a view of the U.S. military role in an emergency, which formed the basis of the later U.S.-Japan Security Treaty.

Despite the high expectations of MacArthur and the GS, the Katayama cabinet was unstable. The factors that added to its unpopularity included poor leadership by the prime minister and a fateful opposition between the left and right wings of the Socialist Party. In addition, there was a deepening antagonism between Nishio Suehiro, a leading right-wing figure, and Chief Cabinet Secretary and Agriculture Minister Hirano Rikizo that originated in a basic disagreement between the two. Nishio wanted to give Ashida an opportunity to form a government by strengthening ties with both the Socialist and the Democratic parties, whereas Hirano aimed to disrupt Nishio's plan by forming a new party with Yoshida's Liberal Party. Behind these two strategies was a rivalry between GS, which supported the Nishio-Ashida cooperative groups and G-2, which supported Yoshida and Hirano. In short, the political strife between the middle-of-the-road parties and the conservatives can be seen as a proxy for the conflict between GS and G-2. In the end, Hirano was purged, leaving Yoshida and Hirano at a strategic disadvantage and giving victory to Nishio and Ashida. The left wing of the Socialist Party took advantage of the split on the right, provoking dissent within the Democratic Party over the socialist bill for the National Control of Coal Mines. The Shidehara faction withdrew from the Democratic Party in opposition to the bill. Having lost its political base of support, the Katayama coalition cabinet was obliged to resign on February 10, 1948, after a mere eight months in office. Kades's expectation of a four-year cabinet was well off the mark.

For the next month, a bitter competition for power raged between Yoshida and Ashida. Yoshida, in support of Shidehara, insisted that in terms of "the principle of constitutional government," the Liberal Party, as the main opposition party, should form the next government. Ashida, on the other hand, with the support of the right wing of the Socialist Party and the People's Cooperative Party, continued his push for a middle-of-the-road regime. Ashida, of course, had obtained a guarantee of GS support. On February 21, the nomination of a prime minister took place in the Diet. Although he had lost to Yoshida by two votes in the House of Councilors ballot, Ashida defeated Yoshida in the House of Representatives ballot by thirty-six votes. In accordance with the priority given to the House of Representative by Article 67 of the Constitution, Ashida was declared prime minister. The press criticized these procedures as "a game of musical chairs," but Guy J. Swope, the GS official in charge of the central government, declared the process to be absolutely democratic and in accordance with Article 67 of the constitution. Ashida was pleased with Swope's support, but already newspapers were reporting allegations that two hundred million yen had been spent to ensure Ashida's nomination. Those allegations identified a hotbed of bribes in excessively generous loans from the Showa Electric Company, a scandal that was soon to erupt. Furthermore, it was not until March 10, 1948, after a long struggle for posts, that a coalition cabinet comprising members of the Democratic, Socialist, and People's Cooperative parties was formed. The *Asahi Shimbun* commented that the powerless cabinet that resulted controlled only about ninety seats (out of 466) in the Diet and would not last long. It dismissed the new cabinet as nothing but "an election control cabinet" for the next government, or "a liaison cabinet" that would only keep inflation down until foreign investments were introduced. A public opinion poll put support for the government at 30 percent and nonsupport at 31 percent, which showed the unpopularity of the government.[25] In order to prop up its weakened state, the Ashida cabinet, like the preceding Katayama cabinet, had to depend on GS support.

The first major problem confronting the Ashida cabinet was a dispute over the salaries of government employees. Dissatisfied with proposed salary levels, unions representing government employees in transportation, communications, and other services planned a general strike for the end of March 1948. Immediately before the planned strike, however, GHQ intervened to order that the strike be called off. GHQ's action offered temporary relief to the embattled government, but by June allegations about the acceptance of suspicious donations by Minister of State Nishio were causing further trouble. Within the government no agreement had been reached over the budget, requiring another GHQ intervention. The government barely managed to complete its budget in early July, but it was the target of heated public criticism.[26]

Meanwhile, within GHQ, a sharp disagreement broke out between GS and ESS over a proposed amendment to the National Public Service Law to prohibit strikes and collective bargaining by government employees. Blaine Hoover, chief of the Civil Service Division, GS, insisted that all such rights be rejected. Kades and Whitney both supported Hoover's position, even though it contradicted Kades's stance as a New Dealer. By contrast, James S. Killen, chief of the Labor Department, argued that the rights of workers should be protected, and strikes should not be suspended. Unfamiliar with labor issues, Marquat, chief of the ESS, was at a loss in attempting to resolve the problem. On July 21, Killen and Hoover had long hours of discussion with MacArthur. Kades recalled: "We went in MacArthur's office about 8:30 or 9:00 in the morning, and we recessed for lunch about 1:00 in the afternoon. We reconvened about 3:00 and went to 10:00 that night. MacArthur handled it just like a judge."[27] At the end of the discussion MacArthur said he would reveal his decision on the following morning but that his mind already was made up. On July 22, Whitney informed the GHQ staff that MacArthur supported the GS position. MacArthur had not been moved by Killen's arguments, and Killen then resigned his post and returned to the United States. Theodore Cohen, ESS advisor and former chief of the Labor Department, later commented that MacArthur was nervous about American public opinion.[28]

On the afternoon of that same day, Whitney handed Prime Minister Ashida a letter from MacArthur ordering the government to revise the National Public Service Law. Since the salary dispute with government workers had almost caused a general strike and so threatened the government, amending the law to deny the rights of collective bargaining and striking could be expected to stabilize the Ashida government. GHQ proposed that denial of collective bargaining and the right to strike of government employees be made on the basis of the Potsdam Ordinance. On July 31, the government enacted Government Ordinance 201 to deny these rights, and brought it into effect on the same day. Popular criticism of the cabinet as a "yes man cabinet" to GHQ intensified.

The Ashida cabinet faced a further serious issue: the introduction of foreign capital. Immediately after the formation of the Ashida cabinet in March 1948, Kennan from the State Department and Draper from the War Department visited Japan to report to MacArthur about Washington's policy shift regarding the Occupation, and to present a large-scale assistance plan. This plan offered positive support for the introduction of foreign capital. In his policy speech of March 20, the prime minister claimed that promoting the import of raw materials by inviting foreign investment was vital to the economic stabilization of Japan and the control of inflation. Although some concerns were raised about foreign investors gaining control over Japan or claiming special advantages, those prominent in financial circles were positive toward accepting foreign capital. However, the proposed U.S. financial aid package for Japan was scaled back so radically in congressional budget deliberations that, in the end, only a $150 million grant for the recovery of the Japanese textile industry was approved. Political, bureaucratic, and financial circles in Japan became wary of the foreign investment plan.

At this time the Showa Electric Scandal erupted. It was disclosed that the president of the Showa Electric Company had received 2.4 billion yen (about 6.7 million dollars) in financing from the government's Fukko Kinyu Kinko (Reconstruction Finance Bank), and had given part of it as political donations to political, bureaucratic, and business circles. In June the president and several others were arrested, and in September Kurusu Takeo, chief of the Economic Stabilization Headquarters and close advisor to Ashida, was detained. Although Ashida received personal encouragement from Whitney, former Vice Prime Minister Nishio was arrested on October 6 on suspicion of taking a bribe. Ashida announced the resignation of his cabinet the next day. It had lasted for just seven months.[29]

It is clear that interwoven with the Showa Electric incident were complex conflicts within GHQ. Since the affair dealt a blow to the GS, which had supported the moderate cabinets of Katayama and Ashida, it appeared that Willoughby and other G-2 officers who controlled information and public safety measures were hatching counterplots against the GS behind closed doors. (No documentation is, however, available to confirm such claims.) Moreover, Kades was in a difficult situation because of a personal scandal involving a Japanese woman. Also, the Democratic Liberal Party, formed in March 1948 after the Shidehara faction split off from the Democratic Party, was actively maneuvering to bring about a change of government. On the other hand, Kades in GS and Justin Williams, chief of the Diet Department, tried one last maneuver. Aiming to break up Yoshida's Democratic Liberal Party, which had a close relation with G-2, they suggested to Ashida that he should pull Yamazaki Takeshi, secretary-general of the Democratic Liberal Party, toward the three moderate parties and form a reshuffled cabinet from all four. This was Kades's last chance; he would concede the next regime to the Democratic Liberal Party, but with Yamazaki, rather than Yoshida, as prime minister. Kades's strategy was to prevent Yoshida from succeeding Ashida, and there seemed to be a consensus for this outcome within the Democratic Party. However, Yamazaki's choice was to resign his Diet seat, putting an end to the GS plot. On October 19, 1948, the second Yoshida cabinet was formed.

In December Kades returned to Washington. He said that his intention was not to run away from the Showa Electric Company scandal but to fulfill an important mission entrusted to him by MacArthur: persuading Washington to return to its original policies. He failed in this endeavor. He did not return to Tokyo, but at his request, MacArthur set his resignation for Constitution Day, May 3.[30] Dismissal of this influential New Dealer from the Occupation heralded the end of the Occupation reforms led by GS. It signified that the Occupation was to take a different course in the shadow of the cold war.

The "Cold War" between MacArthur and Washington

Once in a while history creates an unexpected coincidence. In October 1948, just as American Occupation policy was making the historic shift marked by NSC 13/2, the political leaning of the Japanese government changed from moderate to conservative, and the conservative second and third Yoshida cabinets launched a new policy aimed at restoring Japan's economic independence. The second Yoshida cabinet involved a single minority party, so asserting control over the Diet was difficult. Furthermore, it was viewed with disfavor by the GS. The one hope of survival for the Yoshida regime lay in dissolution of the Diet. Fearing disadvantage to themselves, the three moderate parties that had become the opposition resisted the ruling party's proposal of an early dissolution. As a compromise, Whitney presented a cozy resolution. On December 23, the day when the seven convicted Class A war criminals, including Tojo Hideki, were executed, the Diet was dissolved. In the third postwar general election on January 23, 1949, both the Democratic Party and the Socialist Party, which had forfeited public trust as a result of the Showa Electric scandal, lost badly. Thereafter, middle-of-the-road power vanished from the Japanese political world. The third Yoshida cabinet constituted a dominant government for the first time in the postwar era, marked by the emergence of Yoshida's "one man politics." His conservative government advanced Japan's progress toward economic independence.

In February 1949, Joseph M. Dodge, president of the Detroit Bank, and formulator of the successful currency reform instituted in West Germany, visited Japan. He demanded that the Yoshida government implement a strictly balanced budget based on his Nine-Point Economic Stabilization Program, the so-called Dodge Line. Dodge believed that rampant inflation in Japan had been provoked by two main factors: the U.S. government's financial assistance to Japan, and financial aid offered to Japanese businesses by the Japanese government. Both needed to be cut. Finance Minister Ikeda Hayato was forced to lay off as many as 285,000 government personnel, including one hundred thousand railway workers. Credit controls were tightened, especially by an end to easy loan practices for private enterprises. As a result, social unrest intensified, reflected in numerous bankruptcies among small and midsized businesses and strikes protesting the layoffs. The huge number of government layoffs in the summer of 1949 was a major cause of labor violence. This dark period for Japanese labor was characterized by three widely reported incidents.[31]

The international situation around Japan was uneasy as well. Already, 1948 had seen the Berlin Blockade begin in June, and the establishment of the Republic of Korea (South Korea) and the People's Democratic Republic of Korea (North Korea) in August and September, respectively. In 1949 the North Atlantic Treaty Organization (NATO) was formed in April, the Soviet Union successfully tested an atomic bomb in September, and October saw the births of the People's Republic of China and the German Democratic Republic (East Germany). All proved to be signifiers of an intensified "cold war."

At the same time the "cold war" between MacArthur in Tokyo and the War and Defense departments in Washington became more heated. In February 1949 Secretary of Army Royall confidently noted that, if Japan were attacked, the U.S. Army would fight and would defend Japan against the Soviet Union and other hostile powers. He argued that, although MacArthur was requesting an increase in U.S. Occupation forces, the current level was adequate to cope with any invasion. He insisted that the denial of MacArthur's request for reinforcements in no way implied plans for a withdrawal of U.S. troops. On the reinforcement of Japanese police forces, Royall pointed out that in certain situations Japanese police would be armed with pistols and other light weapons so that they could assist Occupation forces in maintaining domestic security.

On March 3, 1949, MacArthur expressed his opposition to Royall's ideas in an interview with the London *Daily Mail.* If a war should break out, the United States did not want Japan to fight. Japan was to become a neutral nation, a Switzerland of the Pacific. Second, in case Japan should be attacked, the United States would give strategic protection to Japan, but MacArthur did not foresee a Soviet attack. Third, the United States had no thought of taking advantage of the Japan-U.S. relationship to make strategic use of Japan. The United States wanted Japan to maintain her neutrality. Fourth, and despite the recent Communist victory in China, U.S. and British interests in the Pacific were secure. Fifth, the success of the Japanese Communist Party (JCP) in winning thirty-five Diet seat in the January election should cause no concern; MacArthur saw no possibility of direct contacts between the JCP and the Soviet Union. Sixth, any proposal to permit the establishment of Japanese defense forces was premature. Such a proposal could be considered only when a peace treaty was being drafted. Until that time, Occupation forces would be stationed in Japan. Seventh, there was no possibility that the police forces could become the core of Japanese military forces; the responsibility of the 125,000-strong police force was simply to maintain domestic order. No more than 20 percent of police officers carried pistols.[32] This declaration was simply a repetition of MacArthur's earlier positions, but it underscored once more the clear discrepancy between his thinking and that of Royall and other policy makers in Washington. At the same time it was clear that, holding firmly to his own ideas, MacArthur had no intention of yielding to the rearmament policy that Washington was proposing.

MacArthur's unwillingness to follow Washington was not limited to the rearmament issue. He was also adamant regarding the purge. Although he gave his consent to termination of the purge program, he opposed depurging those already purged and he flatly rejected the comeback of purged officials. MacArthur based his opposition on Article 6 of the Potsdam Declaration, JCS 1380/15, and the FEC 15 documents of March 11, 1946. He argued, moreover, that any shift in purge policy by Washington would invite severe criticism from other FEC countries.

Harry Kern, Far East Section chief of *Newsweek,* and Compton Pakenham, chief of the Tokyo office, were critical of GHQ's purge policy, and wrote in opposition to the purging of Hatoyama Ichiro and Ishibashi Tanzan. Japanese administrators of the screening committees who had obediently followed GHQ purge orders and carried it out felt uneasy, and were afraid that those they had purged would purge them in revenge if they ever regained power. MacArthur argued that any support for those who had been purged would spur strong feeling against the Occupation and possibly lead to a revival of ultranationalism. The United States, he believed, should discuss its proposed shift in policy openly in the FEC meeting to obtain the consent of the Allied nations, including the Soviet Union. If necessary, the shift should be carried out.[33]

MacArthur's criticism was far more trenchant than Washington had expected. The War Department, however, disregarded it, maintaining that he had given excessive weight to the authority of the FEC. In fact, in the NSC 13/3 document approved at the NSC on May 6, 1949, the wording on the purge was left unchanged from document 13/2. Similarly, with regard to MacArthur's criticism of rearmament, the War and the Defense departments initiated a strengthening of the Japanese police force and the coast guard. Washington was ignoring MacArthur's opinion and limiting his authority—a situation that MacArthur surely watched with bitterness. On July 26, the chief of the Diplomatic Section, William J. Sebald, who acted as representative of the State Department in communications with MacArthur, noted to the State Department: "He [MacArthur] thinks it unreasonable to expect the Japanese police to act as a constabulary as obviously they are not armed beyond pistols nor trained as troops."[34] On the other hand, on U.S. Independence Day, July 4, MacArthur declared Japan to be a bulwark against communism. Furthermore, in his New Year's statement for 1950, MacArthur asserted that the Japanese Constitution did not deny the right of self-defense. Such statements contradict his continuing opposition to the rearmament of Japan and his emphasis on Japan's neutrality in the Pacific. His real strategy was to secure his own position whatever circumstances he might face.

In the autumn of 1949, the State Department, Undersecretary of State Dean G. Acheson, resumed discussion of a peace treaty for Japan. In response, debate intensified within Japan from the beginning of 1950. By May opinion had divided along two lines: one in support of an overall peace treaty (*zenmen kowa*), the other in support of a separate treaty (*tandoku kowa*). Based on their view of Japan as an unarmed and neutral nation, the opposition parties, including the Socialist Party and the Communists, together with labor unions and progressive intellectuals, backed an overall peace treaty to be signed with all former enemy nations, including the Soviet Union. By contrast, the Yoshida administration and the ruling Liberal Party argued, in the context of the cold war, first for a separate peace treaty with the Western bloc that would allow an early end of the Occupation. Without informing MacArthur or GS, Yoshida dispatched his right-hand man, Minister of Finance Ikeda Hayato, to Washington to convey Yoshida's preferences confidentially to Dodge. These included Yoshida's hope for an early peace treaty, his intention to request the stationing of U.S. troops in Japan following an end to the Occupation, and his conviction that such measures were in compliance with the Japanese Constitution. Yoshida's message was passed to John Foster Dulles, who had been given responsibility for the peace treaty problem in April.

Dulles visited Japan on June 21, and conferred immediately with MacArthur on the peace treaty. On June 22, he had a meeting with Yoshida. Early in the morning of the 25th, however, Dulles was informed that the North Korean military had moved south, across the 38th Parallel that formed a boundary with South Korea. He cut his Japan visit short and returned immediately to the United States. It was a critical moment for both Japan and MacArthur.

13

THE KOREAN WAR AND THE DISMISSAL OF MACARTHUR, JUNE 1950 TO APRIL 1951

Outbreak of the Korean War and MacArthur's Appointment as Commander of the United Nations Command

On June 25, 1950, at 04:00 local time, the North Korean People's Army (later North Korean army) opened an assault along the 38th Parallel (38 degrees north latitude), which served as the boundary between the northern and southern portions of the Korean Peninsula. Shortly thereafter, seven infantry divisions and one brigade of tanks thrust into the south. These actions marked the beginning of the Korean War, which lasted three years and one month. This sudden invasion put the Republic of Korea (later South Korea) into utter turmoil, and its frontline troops completely collapsed. Seoul, the capital, fell in three days. At 2:00 p.m. on June 25 (2:00 a.m. on June 26, Korean time), the United Nations Security Council adopted a resolution that labeled the North Korean attack a "breach of the peace" and called for a cease-fire and a withdrawal of the North Koreans to the 38th Parallel.[1] The North Korean army ignored the resolution, and continued its advance.

How did MacArthur respond? At 6:00 p.m. on June 25, when MacArthur met with John Foster Dulles, who was visiting Tokyo, John M. Allison, a top aide, and William Sebald, chief of the Diplomatic Section, he expressed his view that the action of the North constituted simple armed reconnaissance. MacArthur asserted that the attack was not a total war; that the Soviet Union was not necessarily backing the attack; and that South Korea would win. In a report sent to

Washington soon after the outbreak of war, MacArthur estimated the size of the North Korean army at three divisions. In all, he presented an exceedingly optimistic outlook.

Sebald later described the background of events in Tokyo:

> The General did not appear unduly concerned by the reports of the fighting which had been received up to that hour, nightfall on the first day of the conflict....MacArthur expressed confidence in the ability of the South Korean Army to brace itself and hold, once the initial shock of the Communist attack had worn off. If anything, Dulles seemed more apprehensive....My wife told me later that she had been invited to tea by Col. and Mrs. Sidney Huff during the afternoon....My wife casually mentioned the North Korean attack of which she had heard from Suzu [Japanese maid]. Col. Huff, the personal aide to MacArthur, excitedly asked whether Edith [Sebald] was sure of her facts, and when he learned that the story had been broadcast over the Japanese radio, hurried off to inform General MacArthur.[2]

According to Allison, it was not until June 27, three days after the initial attack, that MacArthur admitted the situation in Korea was deteriorating rapidly, and that all he could do was to evacuate American citizens. He had never seen MacArthur so discouraged and depressed. Dulles's memorandum, submitted to the Department of State on June 29, noted critically that GHQ in Tokyo had not recognized the seriousness of the situation until Seoul fell to the enemy on June 27.[3]

It is clear from these accounts that it took time for MacArthur to realize that what had happened in Korea was the outbreak of war, and to take appropriate action. This slow realization calls to mind his response when he learned of the Pearl Harbor attack: he told those around him of his firm belief that the United States would win and Japan would suffer defeat. Common to both situations was MacArthur's confidence that the U.S. military could not be defeated and so by extension that the South Korean army would never flee. This confidence, based on set assumptions, resulted in his misunderstanding of the situation.

By contrast Truman's judgment was less colored by fixed ideas, and his actions were more flexible and immediate. MacArthur informed President Truman that the South Korean army was in a state of collapse, that President Syngman Rhee had requested U.S. assistance, and that the United Nations Commission on the Republic of Korea had called the North Korean attack a "planned invasion." Truman instructed the U.S. Navy and Far East Air Forces to attack the North Korean army south of the 38th Parallel. Truman explained his concern in his memoirs: "If the Communists were permitted to force their way into the Republic of Korea without opposition from the free world, no small nation would have the courage to resist threats and aggression by stronger Communist neighbors....If this was allowed to go unchallenged it would mean a third world war....It was also clear to me that the foundations and the principles of the United Nations were at stake unless this unprovoked attack on Korea could be stopped."[4]

At 3:00 p.m. (3:00 a.m. Korean time) on the 27th, in the absence of the Soviet Union, the United Nations Security Council in New York passed an important resolution that, in order to repel aggression by North Korea, required signatories to offer military aid to South Korea. Furthermore, it authorized the naval and air involvement already ordered by the United States. Washington was careful about the deployment of ground forces, however, for fear of provoking Soviet involvement. The crucial problem was the collapse of the Korean military and Korean fighting spirit. Inadequate military power could be reinforced, but in the absence of fighting spirit such reinforcements would be useless.

On June 29, MacArthur flew to the south bank of the Han River, where he could observe the recently fallen city of Seoul. Following that visit, he cabled Washington with the recommendation that U.S. ground troops be deployed. Sebald recalled:

> The General's plane took off early on the morning of June 29 for the relatively short flight to the battle area. It landed at Suwon Air field, twenty miles south of Seoul, and MacArthur immediately went into conference with Rhee, [John J.] Muccio [U.S. ambassador to South Korea], and with Brigadier General John H. Church....Muccio telephoned me.... He hoped the "bold plan" of MacArthur could be adopted. I assumed that this phrase, a necessarily obscure part of our almost telepathic conversations, meant the commitment of American forces in strength.[5]

MacArthur later explained his thinking: "Once again it looked like a forlorn hope....Once again it was Bataan—and Corregidor—and New Guinea." He added: "The scene along the Han was enough to convince me that the defensive potential of South Korea had already been exhausted....Even with air and naval support, the South Koreans could not stop the enemy's headlong rush south. Only the immediate commitment of ground troops could possibly do so....It would be desperate, but it was my only chance."[6] Despite his initial misstep, MacArthur had now recovered his stride and showed the indomitable courage and determination of a military hero.

Truman announced the dispatch of U.S. ground forces on June 30. Having already begun a full-scale air operation, U.S. Air Forces in the Far East soon overpowered the North Korean air force and gained air supremacy over Korea. The U.S. Navy attacked the east coast of the peninsula, and used naval gunfire to inflict damage on transportation thoroughfares, thereby delaying the North Korean army's advance south. Following the June 29 authorization of naval and air attacks on North Korea, U.S. and British planes launched their first attack on Inchon from aircraft carriers on July 3. From the next day onward, the coastline of the entire peninsula was blockaded. On the other hand the North Korean army, crossing the Han River south of Seoul at the end of June, launched a second operation to liberate the country beyond the 37th Parallel. South Korean forces could not prevent the North Korean army from crossing the river, and were forced to withdraw. North Korean tank units finally reached the southern bank of the Han River. In this situation the U.S. 24th Division based in Kyushu was deployed to Korea, despite inadequate preparation. In a battle that began on July 5, however, U.S. forces were badly defeated by the North Koreans, which repeated their earlier tactic of sending tanks in first ahead of the infantry.

On July 7, the UN Security Council passed a resolution to establish a unified military command under the United States and requested Truman to appoint the commander. On July 8, Truman named MacArthur to the position. With this appointment, MacArthur gained status unprecedented in U.S. military history: he was commander in chief of the Far East Command, supreme commander for the Allied Powers, and commander in chief of the United Nations Command (UNC). To assume these three positions at the age of seventy may well have strengthened his self-respect. MacArthur's current situation resembled that of July 1941, when he had made a sudden comeback from retirement as commander in chief of the Far East Command. Given his self-promotional tendencies, there must have been a pride and a sense of exhilaration at the thought that only he could fulfill this great mission. It was the moment when the first United Nations Command was born with MacArthur as its leader.

Although the United States had been entrusted with the general command of the U.N. forces, strictly speaking, the force was not stipulated in the Charter of the United Nations. However, the United States had the considerable advantage of being able to conduct operations independently. Since the South Korean army came under U.N. command, MacArthur placed the South Korean army, navy, and air force under the U.S. 8th Army (led by Lieutenant General Walton H. Walker), the U.N. Navy (Vice Admiral C. Turner Joy), and the U.N. Air Force (Lieutenant General George E. Stratemeyer), respectively. Thus, the U.N. chain of command was unified. As the forces of an additional sixteen countries joined the war effort, they were placed under command of the U.S. Army, Navy, and Air Force.[7]

MacArthur's Directive for Japan's Rearmament

When MacArthur was appointed as commander in chief of United Nations Command on July 8, 1950, he sent a letter to Prime Minister Yoshida, that read in part: "I authorize your government to take the necessary measures to establish a national police reserve of 75,000 men and expand the existing authorized strength of the personnel serving under the Maritime Safety Board by an additional 8,000."[8] This directive became famous as the first step toward Japan's rearmament. However, it is not well known that these words were simply added at the end of the letter and that MacArthur devoted the first two thirds of the document to an explanation of his opinions about domestic security and police power. He wrote in the last part of the letter: "To insure that this favorable condition will continue unchallenged by lawless minorities, here as elsewhere committed to the subversion of the due process of law and assaults of opportunity against the peace and public welfare, I believe that the police system has reached that degree of efficiency in organization and training which will permit its augmentation to a strength which will bring it within the limits experience has shown to be essential to the safeguard of the public welfare in a democratic society." He argued that "events disclose that safeguard of the long Japanese coastal line requires employment of a larger force under this agency than is presently provided for by law." This explanation formed the logical background to MacArthur's argument for the necessity of establishing a national police reserve and strengthening the Maritime Safety Board.

Why did MacArthur discuss the crucial issue of rearmament after referring to Japan's national security and the strengthening of police power? Why did he not simply demand rearmament? An important part of the answer is the friction, mentioned in chapter 12, that had developed between Truman and MacArthur on the issue of Japan's rearmament. MacArthur had strenuously objected to Japan's rearmament at the time NSC 13 was issued, but with the outbreak of war he was forced to recant his opposition. However, since he had advocated so strongly in favor of Japan as a peaceful country based on Article 9 of the Constitution, which stipulated Japanese disarmament, he could not simply reverse course and accept Washington's demand for rearmament. He thus concealed Washington's true intentions regarding rearmament, asserting that the aim of the directive was simply to reinforce the Japanese police forces and that he accepted the Japanese government's insistent demand for disarmament. This complicated logic reflects his stubbornness and the pride of a man who would not submit completely to Washington's demand for rearmament.

Such a contradictory politics was bound to disrupt future policy formation in the Japanese government. Although the government accepted at the beginning that the aim of the directive was literally to strengthen police power, it gradually realized that U.S. instructions and the provision of armaments extended far beyond the police and involved the formation of a small army and navy. The issue of Japanese rearmament was heavily influenced by the "cold war" between MacArthur and Washington.

Japanese rearmament was advanced to balance the dispatch of U.S. forces from Japan to Korea. The announced size of the new police reserve forces matched almost exactly the seventy-five thousand U.S. forces sent to Korea. The Police Reserve (later Security Forces and then Self-Defense Forces) had several noteworthy characteristics. First, its organization, training, equipment, and control were all overseen by the Military Assistance Advisory Group to Japan (MAAG-J) of the United States. One week after MacArthur's directive, GHQ Civil Affairs Section Annex (CASA) was established in the former Tokyo Higher Merchant School building in Echjima, downtown Tokyo. Colonel Frank Kowalski Jr., the first appointed chief of staff of MAAG-J, had arrived in Tokyo barely two months earlier, but he was ordered by Major General Witfield P. Shepard, chief of the Civil Affairs Section (CAS), to read repeatedly and memorize a manual that, he said, contained a fundamental project: the basis of a future Japanese army. Shepard had assumed responsibility for organizing the Police Reserve Forces. In fact, either the Chief of Staff 2 (G-2) under Willoughby or the Chief of Staff 3 (G-3) had been expected to undertake the project, but Whitney gave the responsibility to CAS because he was reluctant to expand Willoughby's power. Thus, some thirty MAAG-J members of CASA became engaged in the leadership and training of the Police Reserve.

Second, CASA members received strict orders to keep the Police Reserve secret. MacArthur planned to develop the force of seventy-five thousand men into a future four-division army but he believed that the planning to create his quasi-army should be carried out in confidence. Moreover, care should be taken to ensure no violation either of the Allied Powers Convention or of the Japanese Constitution, which renounced war and armed forces. Therefore, CASA members could not at first tell Japanese officials that the Police Reserve would become a future "army." Even in the initial organizational phase, MAAG-J members had to use misleading language. Many Reserve members who did not understand the situation were troubled by the artifice. In any case, despite the contradictions involved, the Police Reserve was put under the prime minister's direct control, and was organized as a national defense unit that could take immediate action in national emergencies.

Third, since the military advisory members of CASA under Shepard made great efforts in recruitment, preparation, education and training, they successfully established the Police Reserve. High salaries made it easy to attract recruits; job assignment, control, and training in each unit also went well. Some seventy-four thousand carbines were supplied. By the end of the year, the organization of the Reserve was complete, and various training schools had been established. As the Reserve gradually gained more autonomy, the role of MAAG-J changed from general leadership to support and advice for the individual units and schools. Nevertheless, inadequate leadership emerged as a problem. At the beginning there had been discussion regarding whether to recruit former army officers and professional military personnel. Although the inclusion of former officers would have had clear advantages, they had been purged in compliance with the purge directives based on the Potsdam Declaration. Their entry into the Police Reserve, it was decided, would not only violate SCAP policy but also invite criticism from countries such as the Philippines and Australia. The strong antiwar sentiment in Japan also had to be considered. As a result, those formerly concerned with military affairs were excluded from recruitment. This decision proved disadvantageous as the organization expanded.

To solve the problem, Willoughby recommended Hattori Takushiro, a former colonel, as commander (chief of staff) of the Police Reserve Forces. Willoughby had employed Hattori's group in G-2 to do editorial work on the war history, and gave them a special exemption from the public purge. At this time, GHQ had temporarily suspended the purge of former military officers (probably more than one thousand persons were affected) in order to deal with demobilization smoothly, but Willoughby's action was clearly a political maneuver. Whitney, who belonged to the anti-Willoughby faction, opposed Hattori's assignment as chief of staff. Also opposed was Prime Minister Yoshida, who wanted to avoid the empowerment of former military personnel. In the end MacArthur decided not to allow Hattori's appointment.[9]

Although employment of former elite officers in the Police Reserve was prevented, the problem of leadership of the organization remained unsettled. When Shepard met Assistant Secretary of Army Earl D. Johnson in February 1951, he emphasized that lack of leadership was a serious weakness of the Police Reserve. The only way to cope with the problem was to employ purged military officers, particularly those of the rank of colonel and above. Shepard argued, moreover, that police bureaucrats (from the former Ministry of Home Affairs) who occupied important positions in the Police Reserve Forces should be removed.[10] Since the beginning of the Korean War the release from the public purge, including former army and navy personnel, had rapidly been in process. MacArthur and Whitney had gradually loosened their strict attitude toward the purge and, as a result, starting in August 1951 former army and navy officers below the rank of colonel were gradually depurged. That fall, all but a few military officers were released. Former military, including senior officers, were encouraged to enter the Police Reserve. The leadership problem was finally solved.

Secret Activities of Japanese Minesweepers

In light of the Korean situation MacArthur ordered an increase of eight thousand in the strength of the Maritime Safety Board (known as the Coast Guard in America). In May 1948 it had been established as an affiliated office of the Ministry of Transportation. Duties of the Maritime Safety Board had been undertaken by twenty-eight vessels of the former Japanese navy to prevent illegal entries and smuggling, and to protect Japanese fishing boats from capture by Korean or Soviet forces. At the same time, about 350 minesweepers had been clearing mines placed by the Japanese during the war. The Korean War changed the situation. On July 23, 1950, MacArthur sent a telegram to the Defense Department, requesting approval for the Maritime Safety Board to use forty PC and SC type cutters from the idle U.S. fleet. Washington responded positively, authorizing the establishment of the police reserve and an increase of strength for the Maritime Safety Board.[11]

After the UNC's successful landing at Inchon in September 1950, the tide of war turned. Next came the Wonsan landing on the east coast of the peninsula, an operation authorized by JCS on September 27, with an agreed date of October 2. To meet the schedule it became an urgent necessity to clear mines sown by the enemy in the eastern coastal area. The U.S. Navy, however, had only ten minesweeping vessels, with no chance of reinforcement. Major General Arleigh Burke, deputy chief of staff of U.S. Naval Forces Far East (USNFFE), requested that MacArthur suspend the Wonsan landing because the U.S minesweeping corps was undependable and he knew the danger posed by Soviet-made mines. MacArthur rejected any change in his orders. Knowing the sophisticated minesweeping capabilities of the former Japanese navy, Burke asked Okubo Takeo, chief of the MSA, to dispatch Japanese minesweeping forces. Although Okubo was persuaded of the importance of the landing operation, he hesitated to accept the request because any sweep along the Korean coastline would in fact be a combat operation, and would therefore violate the constitution. Under the condition of strict secrecy, Prime Minister Yoshida made the final decision to agree to the U.S. request.[12]

On October 6 a special sweepers group was organized with twenty minesweeping vessels, four patrol vessels, and one inspection boat under the command of former navy captain Tamura Kyuzo. After forming up at Shimonoseki, the Japanese sweeper force participated in the operation under the command of the 7th U.S. Navy. Divided into four groups, Japanese minesweepers worked from mid-October until early December at entrances to five ports: Wonsan on the east coast, and Kunsan, Inchon, Haeju, and Nampo on the west. Most of the vessels were old and wooden, and had been built hurriedly during the war, making it difficult to conduct repairs. Furthermore, they had to work amid fierce tides and severe cold. During this dangerous work one minesweeper hit a mine and sank. Another was stranded, leading to the death of one crewman and injuries to eight others. The operation covered some 327 kilometers (204 miles) of ocean waterway and 606 square kilometers (378.75 square miles) of water. They cleared twenty-seven mines successfully before they returned home.[13]

On December 9, Okubo welcomed the crews at Shimonoseki with an expression of pleasure at their success. He passed along a message of commendation from Admiral C. Turner Joy, commander in chief of the Far East Navy. Okubo said that "your movement in Korea has shown the future path to be taken by Japan.... Our great undertaking, indeed, should be recorded permanently on the history of the newly-born Japan."[14] In particular the U.S. Far East Navy gave the highest praise. Deputy Chief of Staff Burke was surprised at the unexpected level of achievement. He later developed a strong interest in secret Japanese rearmament by former Japanese navy personnel, and made great efforts to realize it.

Thus the independence of the Maritime Security Force from the Maritime Safety Board was achieved, furthermore creating a connection with the birth of the Japan Naval Defense Force. The activity of the Japanese minesweepers was closely related to postwar Japan's rearmament.

The Sneak Landing Operation on Inchon

After the North Korean army advanced southward in July 1950, MacArthur began to examine the possibility of a surprise attack on the rear of the North Korean front line. According to MacArthur he already had in mind the idea of the Inchon Landing Operation when he made his risky inspection visit to Seoul immediately after the outbreak of hostilities. However, the tidal range at Inchon was great. At low tide, there was only one waterway, two kilometers (1.25 miles) wide and 90 kilometers (56.25 miles) long, and there was no beach except for a muddy sandbar, making it difficult for landing vessels to reach the shore. Even if attacking forces managed to approach a landing spot through the narrow waterway, they would be in range of batteries on Walmi-do. Not only were they thus restricted to a high-tide landing but the day and hour of the landing were also limited, making an Inchon landing extremely difficult. Lieutenant General Walker, commander of the 8th Army, proposed an attack in the south from Gunsan, which was not occupied by North Korean troops, against surrounding North Korean forces. However, MacArthur persisted with his plan for a landing at Inchon, located north of Seoul, and thus an early recapture of Seoul. MacArthur finalized the plan by personally persuading the top U.S. leadership, including Major General Joseph Lawton Collins, U.S. Army chief of staff; Admiral Forrest Sherman, chief of Naval Operations; President Truman; and Secretary of Defense Louis A. Johnson. On August 30 he ordered the Inchon landing to be carried out by the newly organized X Corps, consisting of the U.S 1st Marine Division, the 7th Infantry Division, and a part of the South Korean forces.[15]

Major General (later Lieutenant General) Edward Almond, GHQ chief of staff, assumed the key role. At the end of 1948 when General Mueller, who had been chief of staff for three years, decided that to return to the States for health reasons, he had recommended Almond as his replacement. It was unusual for a GHQ chief of staff to take a field command. Almond was engaged not only in the planning of the Inchon landing but also in the secret task of organizing the X Corps. Almond later described the process as follows:

> MacArthur thought that by a saber-like thrust at Inchon and the capture of Seoul he could throw these North Koreans into thorough confusion. Anybody who knows anything at all about this operation knows for a fact that this was exactly what happened. He always thought that this operation would only take a short time—two or three weeks. He had the idea that he could assemble a couple of divisions since he knew that the Marines [the 1st Marine Division] were prepared, but it was very difficult to get them.... Problems of assembling and forming the invasion force, which was later named the X Corps, arose in securing equipment and allocations of personnel of various kinds and so on.... I went in to General MacArthur and told him that whenever we put in a requisition that they wanted to know what unit we were drawing from in the States. We would reply, "This is no regular unit." They'd say, "Well, you can't get anything until we know what kind of unit is going to be issued this equipment." General MacArthur recognized that so we decided to call it the X So Corps. The X Corps was formed in a most expeditious matter and was first called the "X Force."
>
> The staff met in the motor pool of the headquarters of the service group in Tokyo, and not even the correspondents knew that it existed. They had no idea that the X Corps was being assembled or that plans were being made for the Inchon landing.[16]

However, William Sebald, chief of the Diplomatic Section, stated: "The fact that Inchon was the target became almost an open secret in Tokyo. It was miraculous that the network of spies, which North Korea was known to maintain in Japan, did not alert the Communist capital of Pyongyang."[17] This statement suggests that

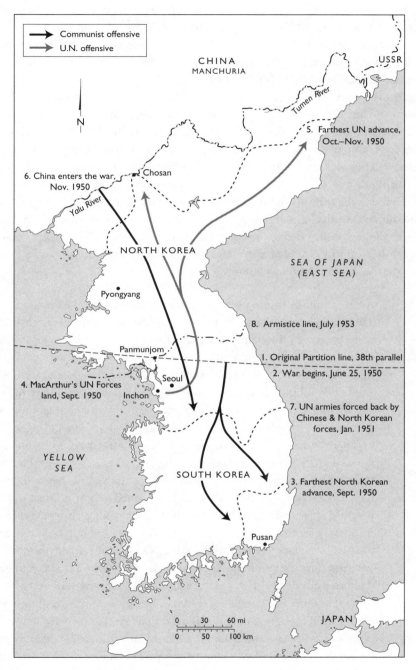

- → Communist offensive
- → U.N. offensive

CHINA
MANCHURIA

USSR

Tumen River

5. Farthest UN advance,
   Oct.–Nov. 1950

6. China enters the war,
   Nov. 1950

Chosan

Yalu River

NORTH KOREA

SEA OF JAPAN
(EAST SEA)

Pyongyang

8. Armistice line, July 1953

Panmunjom

1. Original Partition line, 38th parallel

2. War begins, June 25, 1950

4. MacArthur's UN Forces
   land, Sept. 1950

Seoul

Inchon

7. UN armies forced back by
   Chinese & North Korean
   forces, Jan. 1951

YELLOW
SEA

SOUTH KOREA

3. Farthest North Korean
   advance, Sept. 1950

Pusan

0   30   60 mi
0   50   100 km

JAPAN

MAP 5.   The Korean War, 1950–1953

secrecy was not as strict as Almond proudly claimed. On September 1, Almond reported to MacArthur that the X Corps had been formed and the staff officers were rehearsing the landing operation. He asked who would be the commander. MacArthur looked at him piercingly and said it would be Almond himself. Surprised, Almond hesitated saying, "I am the chief of staff here in Tokyo. I can't do two jobs at once." MacArthur's response was, "We'll all be back in two weeks. You can turn your job over to Hickey and let him be acting chief of staff while you are in command of this force"[18] Knowing that MacArthur had thought about this appointment carefully, Almond accepted it, leaving Major General Doyle O. Hickey to replace him as GHQ chief of staff. Almond became commander of the X Corps.

How was the Inchon landing operation carried out? As noted, the geographic situation was difficult. In addition, there was the threat of a typhoon, given that the landing was scheduled for typhoon season in September. The problem could be resolved only by careful preparation. Admiral Arleigh Burke, commanding the 1st Marine Division, wrote as follows:

> An amphibious landing is a very complicated and detailed operation. This one had a peculiarity in it in that the tide was high, and they had to arrive at exactly the right time. You always have to arrive at exactly the right time, because your artillery, your gun fire, your air support and those things come in on you. If you're two minutes early, you're dead. If you're two minutes late, you've lost the effect of it. They all have to be exactly timed. My particular job was to make sure that that landing at Inchon was properly conducted. I was to give a "go" or "no go" signal.
>
> There was a typhoon building up in the South China Sea. Nobody knows exactly where a typhoon is going to go. There was a possibility that that typhoon would come up through the East China Sea and perhaps go west of Korea. If it did, and if it happened to be timed just right, it would raise all kinds of hell with the Inchon landing. It would make it impossible to conduct the operation. This was a young typhoon. In the Navy you have to start avoiding things a long time before they happen. You can't wait until the last minute and then make a decision to do it and have it done. I checked back and found that the way we had to avoid that thing was to make sure that our ships were at sea and west of the position that the typhoon was in so that the chances were that the typhoon, if it came, would not hit so many ships and would delay them so that they couldn't meet their rendezvous. That meant that MacArthur had to board his ship a day early. There were a lot of elements involved in all of this. A lot of other loading operations had to be speeded up, too.[19]

Burke went to GHQ in the hope of discussing the landing operation problem with MacArthur, but Almond refused to allow the meeting, telling Burke that MacArthur was too busy to see him. Almond said he would convey to MacArthur Burke's ideas about the landing operation. But Burke wanted to talk to MacArthur in person. Told again that MacArthur was busy, Burke left a message for MacArthur: "This landing might fail, and if MacArthur wants to see me, I'm available."[20] Shortly afterward Burke received a call from Almond calling him back to speak to MacArthur. Using charts, Burke explained the details of the problem to MacArthur for about fifteen minutes. In response to MacArthur's questions, he stated that the operation needed to be moved forward with all speed. The General replied: "All right. Do what's needed."

What did Almond conclude as a result of this new information? He stated:

> Before the Inchon landing the matter was touch-and-go between the Navy, Army, Marines, and Air Forces as to just how this remarkable strategic operation could be carried out....But doubts arose in the minds of the various armed services when the plans were being made....The Inchon landing was set for the 15th of September, and everybody who knows the coastline of Korea knows that the tide range at Inchon is the second highest in the world....This range of thirty-one feet, when the tide goes out, leaves all boats in the Inchon harbor merely sitting ducks on the sand until the next tide comes in and floats them again.
>
> We had a warning around the first of September that a typhoon was generating in the Philippine area and would be expected to reach Japan about the middle of September. This threat was duck soup for those who objected to Inchon being selected as a landing point.
>
> But the real reason MacArthur chose Inchon was that in spite of the difficulties, it was only eighteen miles from the sea to Seoul. If we came into the Korean area from the east side—the Sea of Japan and Wonsan area—we would have been separated from Seoul by a great mountain range. There would have been one road that we could have depended upon using. It was a distance of 135 miles from the east coast to Seoul. Therefore Inchon was the logical strategic spot to select for the invasion in spite of the difficulties.
>
> Knowing the typhoon threat, I, as chief of staff, had our staff prepare a history of typhoons and their courses as to when they approached Japan or Korea and where they went to from there. In the previous twenty-five year period, one typhoon had ever turned westward into the Yellow Sea [the sea on Korea's west coast at Inchon], all others had turned Eastward into the sea of Japan....The Navy began to plan all the

possible typhoon threats. I went in to General MacArthur and indicated that Admiral Joy [*sic,* actually Burke] had asked for a conference with him.... He said, "Well, it's about the typhoon threat."

Whereupon I took to MacArthur my staff study on typhoons of the past twenty-five years, and I said in no uncertain terms, "General, this conference is for the purpose of persuading you against Inchon as the landing point. I strongly urge you that you do not let them counter persuade you." His response to that was "Don't worry, Ned. Inchon is the spot."[21]

On the morning of September 15, nearly 260 landing craft assembled off Inchon. At 5:00 a.m. rear supporting fire began. At 6:30 the U.S. 5th Marine Regiment landing team began the Inchon landing. The main regiment followed at high tide. From the north side of Inchon harbor the rest of the 5th marine regiment and the Korean marine forces succeeded in getting to the targeted point without facing any counterattacks. The next day the 1st Marine Division landed, advanced, and beat back the North Korean army. Sebald described the battle thus:

> The Inchon landings—there were two of them—became one of the most incredible operations.... With the tide in at dawn on D day, September 15, a battalion of Marines went ashore at Wolmi Island, a small wooded and rocky, triangular-shaped islet guarding the entrance to the harbor and on which the North Koreans maintained artillery.... The enemy then knew that a second landing would be made at sunset, when the tide next was at flood, in order to capture Inchon itself and surrounding area. Within three days, supply operations were well in hand, and with the end of the spring tides on D plus 3, adequate logistic support was assured through superb organization and teamwork.
>
> Despite staggering difficulties, the operation was a complete success, and the port was quickly secured by U.S. Marines, supported by a vast array of naval gunfire and airpower.[22]

Although it was carried out not at night but in daytime, the Inchon landing was successful and MacArthur's prestige once again flourished.

China's Entry into the War

After the 1st Marine Division succeeded in landing at Inchon, the 7th Division followed, allowing the main forces of X Corp to begin the push inland. On September 20 the advance combat group, the 5th Marine Regiment, crossed the Han River. On the morning of the 26th, breaking down the stiffening resistance of the North Korean 25th Brigade, the 5th Marine Regiment occupied the western side of Seoul. The 1st Marine Regiment also crossed the Han River, captured Namsan to the south of Seoul, and poured into the city. After a fierce eight-day battle, it completed mopping up operations inside the city on the 28th, causing the North Korean army to flee north. At the time of the X Corps' Inchon landing, the 8th Army, which had continued a defensive campaign around Pusan, turned to the offensive. Another amphibious assault by the I Corps, commanded by Lieutenant General Walker, which consisted of the U.S. 1st Infantry Division, the 24th Division, and Korean 1st Division, advanced along Taegu, Kunchon, Taejonhit, and Suwon and in cooperation with X Corps, hit the North Korean troops directly. On the 22nd Walker ordered an all-out attack toward the 38th Parallel. In response, North Korean troops began a disorderly retreat northward. More than nine thousand North Koreans were captured. The United Nation Command could not, however, totally defeat the main North Korean army, which was one hundred thousand strong.[23]

At the outset of the Korean War, the initial purpose of the United States, based on the Security Council resolution of June 27, was to repel the North Korean army north of the 38th Parallel. But that had been an emergency decision, and there was from the beginning no clear idea on when to end the war. As events unfolded, differences of opinion arose within the U.S. government about operations after the North Korean army was repulsed. Even within the State Department, there were two contesting views. One, advanced by the Office of Far Eastern Affairs, was that since halting operation at the 38th Parallel would invite the North Koreans to resume hostilities, the aim should be unification of the Korean Peninsula in cooperation with the United Nations Command. The other view, advanced by the Policy Planning Staff, was that, since going farther north would invite the involvement of the Soviet Union and Communist China, military operations should end at the 38th Parallel and a political solution be pursued thereafter.

As commander in chief of the United Nations Command (UNC), MacArthur was primarily of the opinion that the North Korean army should be destroyed, and for that purpose an advance beyond the 38th Parallel was unavoidable. Influenced by MacArthur's opinion, the secretary of defense and the Joint Chiefs of Staff were inclined to accept the argument for a northward advance. Because of these differences of opinion, the National Security Council could not reach an agreement. It was not until September 11, immediately before the Inchon landing, that President Truman approved NSC 81/1, a crucial statement of policy. According to the document, UNC forces would be authorized to move across the 38th Parallel in order to force the withdrawal of the North Korean army from the south, but only in the case that the Soviet Union or Communist China should intervene in the dispute. Thus was the plan for a northward advance finalized.

On September 28, MacArthur sent operation plans to the JCS. On the 29th, the JCS approved the plans, and instructed MacArthur to implement them. Advance beyond the 38th Parallel was viewed as a crucial issue because it implied a shift in the objective of the war. Essentially, the government had reached a decision and the military had been ordered to make it happen. The fact that the judgment regarding Soviet or Chinese involvement had been left to a military commander was a matter of no little significance.

In fact, on South Korean president Syngman Rhee's order, the Korean 3rd Division began moving in force across the 38th Parallel on October 1. Rhee judged that once North Korea had crossed the 38th Parallel, the border became meaningless. After the success of the Inchon landing he aimed to achieve Korean unification by means of a U.N. military offensive in the north. On the same day MacArthur urged the North Korean army to surrender, but there was no reaction. On October 2 the UNC issued a general order to advance beyond the parallel. However, each time the resolution was debated in the Security Council it was vetoed by Soviet Union. Consequently, the United States submitted it to the General Assembly. After heated discussions the resolution to advance beyond the 38th Parallel was approved by a large majority on October 7. Based on this resolution MacArthur ordered an offensive northward on the morning of October 10.

Even before the resolution, MacArthur had already decided the plan for a northward advance. In principle the plan was as follows. First, the 8th Army would advance northwest from Seoul, crossing the 38th Parallel to advance on the North Korean capitol of Pyongyang. Second, the X Corps would board ships at Inchon and Busan, land at Wonsan, and then proceed to Pyongyang. The plan thus envisaged a pincer attack on Pyongyang that would annihilate the main North Korean army. The 8th Army opposed this plan on the grounds that the South Korean army, advancing north, would have occupied Wonsan even before the X Corps arrived there, and capture of Pyongyang by the Corps would simply be delayed. Buoyed by the success at Inchon, however, MacArthur kept to his plan. As the 8th Army had predicted, the Wonsan Landing operation was unsuccessful.[24] At this very time, the Japanese special minesweeping unit was, at Burke's demand, engaged in its operations along the coast of Wonsan.

On October 12 MacArthur received a message from Secretary of Defense George C. Marshall. It conveyed President Truman's request for a conference with MacArthur at Honolulu, Hawaii. In fact, because of the Korean situation, the meeting was held on Wake Island nearer Korea, on October 15. The President's party arrived with thirty-five reporters and photographers, while only three adjutants accompanied MacArthur. Truman described the meeting:

We talked for more than an hour alone. We discussed the Japanese and the Korean situations. The general assured me that the victory was won in Korea. He also informed me that the Chinese Communists would not attack and that Japan was ready for a peace treaty....He said he wanted me to understand that he was not in politics in any way—that he had allowed the politicians to make a "chump" (his word) of him in 1948 and that it would not happen again....He was sure it would be possible to send one division from Korea to Europe in January 1951. He repeated that the Korean conflict was won and that there was little possibility of the Chinese Communists coming in.[25]

MacArthur's reminiscences offer a different version of events:

The conference itself was innocuous enough....They dealt with such matters as the administration of Korea when united, its rehabilitation, the treatment of prisoners of war, the economic situation in the Philippines, security of Indo-China, the progress of a treaty of peace with Japan, routine details of supply logistics for Japan and Korea,... Formosa was not on the agenda. Near the end of the conference, the possibility of Chinese intervention was brought up almost casually. It was the general consensus of all present that Red China had no intention of intervening....The entire conference lasted only an hour and thirty-six minutes, and I then drove with the President to the air field to see him off....Rather impertinently, I asked him if he intended to run for re-election....[He] immediately countered by asking me if I had any political ambitions along such lines. I had no need to duck the question, and I replied: "None whatsoever. If you have any general running against you, his name will be Eisenhower, not MacArthur."[26]

Thus, interpretations about an intervention by Red China were far apart. Truman reported that MacArthur flatly denied a possibility of Chinese intervention, and assured him that enemy resistance would be over by Easter (on March 25 that year). MacArthur, however, defended himself by declaring that most opinion leaders had reached a consensus that China had no intention of intervening and commented that the question of Chinese intervention had been brought up almost casually at the end of the conference. However, MacArthur's testimony was unconvincing and undeniably misleading. Rather, with the midterm elections coming up just two weeks later, MacArthur's indifference was probably a reaction to Truman's political strategy. He suspected that Truman would use the success at Inchon to secure a victory for the Democratic Party. As a Republican, and one who had experienced a sense of frustration in the 1948 presidential election, MacArthur had naturally no intention of sharing the victory with Truman. His participation in the meeting was nothing but reluctant.

Sebald explained the political feud between the two men as follows:

> Fundamental differences of viewpoint over the Korean conflict remained. In particular, they disagreed over the relative importance of Europe and Asia in global strategy, a controversy held over from World War II. MacArthur firmly believed that the Communists would conquer Europe through Asia unless stopped in the Far East. He believed also that both Europe and the United States were shortsighted in failing to accept this premise. The Administration, on the other hand, clearly was following a global strategy. Despite the demands of the Korean War, Washington was increasing and strengthening United States forces in Europe.[27]

For this reason, Truman shared Washington's view that the Korean War was localized and limited, and wanted MacArthur to conform to fundamental policy. MacArthur, on the other hand, attended the conference reluctantly, and regarded the Wake Island trip as merely a political junket. Sebald wrote, as well: "MacArthur had also brushed aside the probability that the Chinese would enter the Korean conflict in force… [He] expressed the belief that they [the Russians] would be unable to spare ground troops for Korea; there was the possibility, however, that Russian air strength could support Chinese ground troops."[28] MacArthur was too optimistic. It may be said that his preconceived notions about Russian and Chinese intentions prevented an accurate evaluation.

Meanwhile in the east of the peninsula, the Korean force was making steady progress. The Korean 1st Division, part of the 1st Army stationed in the west, aimed to be first to capture Pyongyang. On October 19, they crossed the Daedong River, which flows through the city of Pyongyang, and achieved the goal of entering the old city. The U.S. Army arrived later. At this point MacArthur had the end of the assault in sight, and on October 24 he ordered a slashing attack in the direction of the Yalu River, which formed the border with China. However, the successful advance of the UNC now confronted problems. The supply line was stretched, and as troops moved north their front line widened and their military force became dispersed. Between the 8th Army in the west and X Corps in the east lay a wide mountain range, making it difficult for the two to coordinate. Exacerbating the problem was personal antagonism between both commanders, Walker and Almond. Based on the chain of command, Almond's X Corps was subordinate to Walker's 8th Army. MacArthur had ignored this situation, and there was no one who could speak to him about it. Moreover, very few foresaw any dangers. Most of them optimistically anticipated that once they reached the

Yalu River, the war would end. Both the U.S. Army and the UNC had directed their attention to the postwar Korean problem. Each unit was interested only in its plan of attack and absorbed in advancing toward the border.

On October 25 the Korean 1st Division met sudden fierce resistance from Chinese forces. Since the 18th, the Communist Chinese People's Voluntary Forces of 260,000 under the command of Peng Dehuai had been crossing the Yalu River and secretly advancing through the mountainous area along the border. On October 1, North Korean Communist leader Kim Il Sung's request for help had reached the Chinese government. When the Chinese leadership learned on the same day that South Korean forces had crossed the 38th Parallel, Communist China regarded this as a northern offensive by the UNC and decided to enter the war. On October 9 the Chinese foreign minister, Zhou Enlai, flew to Moscow to inform the Soviet government of China's decision to intervene and to ask for Soviet air support. But the Soviet Union, reluctant to engage directly in hostilities against the United States, rejected the proposal. Mao Zedong was perplexed. The Chinese leaders regarded U.S. intervention on the Korean Peninsula as an invasion of Asia, and they believed that if the United States took control of Korea, China would be in a difficult situation. For this reason, China decided to enter the war without the support of the Soviet Union.[29]

The 8th Army, however, had not grasped the reality of the Chinese intervention. They did not use Chinese prisoners as informants, thinking of them as part of a volunteer army who participated in the war of their own free will. Chinese forces kept their movements strictly secret. Furthermore, MacArthur and the U.S. leaders did not consider the possibility that Beijing would enter the war. However, as Sebald later pointed out, "From August through October, 1950, antiaircraft fire from the Manchurian side of the Yalu River and captured prisoners within Korea indicated involvement of Chinese Communist forces. By October 30 it was clear from all available intelligence that Eighth Army was faced by major Chinese Communist forces in North Korea. In retrospect, however, I cannot recall that MacArthur showed concern during this period over the possibility that Peking would enter the war."[30] MacArthur had clearly been unwary.

Burke placed the responsibility on Willoughby, the chief of intelligence. He had been told by four intelligence officers in September that there were Chinese in North Korea and had met Willoughby to pass on the information. During intelligence briefings, Willoughby said that the information amounted only to fragments, and that he did not think the Chinese were in North Korea, because they would be very foolish to do so. He made a basic mistake. A few days later Burke received further information from the intelligence staff and passed it to Willoughby. Again Willoughby listened to him, and talked with his superiors, but the superiors did not believe there were Chinese in Korea. Convinced that the intelligence was correct, Burke sent the information to Admiral Forrest Sherman, the chief of Naval Operations. Sherman ordered that many ships be prepared for U.S. troops in case they were obliged to withdraw, but the army thought "it was silly as all hell."[31] Immediately thereafter the Chinese army rushed in, and the UNC was pushed back with heavy losses by a sudden onslaught by Communist forces. As Burke had predicted, there was a struggle for transport vessels.

Because of the sudden intervention of the Chinese Communist forces, the UNC was halted just before the Yalu River. MacArthur's immediate objective was to destroy the bridge across the Yalu to obstruct the Chinese advance and their supply lines. The proposal was suspended because of opposition from Washington, but later Washington was persuaded to approve it by MacArthur's strenuous arguments. Bombing began on November 8. MacArthur saw no alternative to the bombing of key points in Manchuria, but Washington refused to authorize it. Even after the Chinese attack, the UNC underestimated the size of the Chinese force, placing it at about seventy thousand, and believing that its objectives were limited. The UNC forces made another advance on the Yalu River on November 24. At this time, too, MacArthur boasted to one of the commanding officers that he could tell his men that they would be back home by Christmas. But on the following day, thirty-six divisions of Chinese forces, with large reinforcements, launched a major assault. The Chinese forces mobilized a new corps in the mountain area and began a frontal attack. The Korean 2nd Corps of the right wing of the 8th Army was annihilated. By early December the entire UNC had fallen into danger and MacArthur decided to withdraw to the 38th Parallel. X Corps retreated by sea, the 8th Army by land. They reached a point south of the 38th Parallel on December 15. Immediately afterward, Walker, commander of the 8th Army, died of an accident in the field. Lieutenant General Matthew B. Ridgway, assistant to the chief of staff, succeeded to the post. Thus the war went into a new phase.[32]

The Dismissal of MacArthur

In order to react to these new developments in the war, MacArthur needed a new political decision from Washington. He demanded the right to attack all Chinese territory with naval and air forces. He also requested permission to use a Taiwanese force of thirty-three thousand troops in Korea. Washington rejected his requests. Truman wrote in his memoir:

> No one is blaming General MacArthur, and certainly I never did, for the failure of the November offensive....I do blame General MacArthur

for the manner in which he tried to excuse his failure....MacArthur had many times in World War II announced victory while his troops still faced the stiffest part of the battle. But there was no excuse for the statements he began to make to certain people as soon as the offensive had failed. Within a matter of four days he found time to publicize in four different ways his view that the only reason for his troubles was the order from Washington to limit the hostilities to Korea.[33]

Truman did not hide his anger. The deep misunderstanding and distrust between MacArthur and Washington that had been accumulating since World War II had now resurfaced.

At this time Beijing, confident of military success, embarked on a change in operational approach. From the front lines, Peng Dehuai complained about shortages of provisions and troop fatigue. But Mao Zedong insisted that he advance south across the 38th Parallel, so as not to risk the chance of victory. For both the United States and China, there were disputes between political and military leaders and between the front and rear lines of the war. On December 31, a joint Chinese and North Korean force launched the so-called New Year's Offensive across all battlefields. Fleeing in disorder or surrounded by enemies, the UNC seemed fated for annihilation. On January 4, 1951, it abandoned Seoul and retreated to the 37th Parallel. Finally, Western European countries proposed an immediate cease-fire resolution at the U.N. Their objective was to use a break in fighting to resolve the Korean issue. After foreign forces were withdrawn, the Western European countries planned to establish a council to discuss the Formosa problem and the problem of Chinese representation at the U.N. The European move meant a humiliating defeat for the United States, but Washington reluctantly agreed. By contrast, China, taking advantage of battlefield success, demanded an immediate approval of its participation in the United Nations as a condition of agreeing to the cease-fire. This was not a proposal the United States could accept. It proposed that the U.N. General Assembly label China an invader and pass a resolution reaffirming the initial objective of expelling invaders from Korea. Despite vigorous resistance from the enemy, the UNC had been making steady northward progress since February. The Korean 1st Division succeeded in recapturing Seoul on March 15.

In the meantime, relations between MacArthur and Washington reached a critical stage because of conflicting interpretations over what the "territory of Korea" meant. Persuaded by MacArthur's view, Washington had originally seen the whole peninsula as Korean territory, but it later retreated to the position that "Korea" referred only to the area south of the 38th Parallel. By limiting the combat area Washington believed it could concentrate negotiations on a political solution. MacArthur, on the other hand, emphasized that only military victory could achieve a political solution. He seemed to have been under the impression that Washington wanted to place many restraints on his military activities. Thus, the conflict between Truman and MacArthur over the 38th Parallel intensified until some sort of resolution became unavoidable. According to Truman, to restore the border on the 38th Parallel was the final fulfillment of the mission. Any further advance northward would increase the danger of being drawn into a quagmire. Moreover, bombing mainland China, using an atomic bomb, or allowing Formosa to enter the war would invite serious problems such as the disaffection of the Western bloc, opposition from the Soviet Union, or even the outbreak of a third world war. Accordingly, Washington believed success would come from forcing China to abandon its military actions and encouraging it to sit down at the negotiation table. Truman instructed the State Department to draft a presidential statement to call for an armistice. However, on March 24, without prior discussion with Washington, MacArthur issued a statement that claimed that, absent the restrictions imposed on the UNC by the United Nations, China's military collapse would have been possible. MacArthur's claim was the exact reverse of the statement being prepared by Truman. It was at this point that Truman decided to dismiss MacArthur. On April 11, at 1 p.m. Washington time, Truman announced at an emergency press conference that he was removing MacArthur from his position as commander in chief. He named Lieutenant General Matthew Ridgway as MacArthur's successor.[34]

It has generally been said that MacArthur's dismissal arose from differences between his interpretation of Korea and that of Truman, but Sebald argued that the basic issue concerned Formosa. In other words, a serious misunderstanding between MacArthur and Washington probably began with the General's unannounced journey to Formosa on July 31, 1950, and his meeting with Chiang Kai-shek. Immediately afterward, on August 3, Secretary of State Acheson instructed Sebald to gather detailed information on the Formosa trip. When Sebald contacted MacArthur, he noted that their talk was on military matters and was limited to military cooperation between the Formosan government and himself as regional commander; for this reason, the trip and his military conversations were his own responsibility and none of the State Department's business. When Sebald insisted that this kind of military response would upset the delicate balance of diplomacy, MacArthur responded angrily that Formosan policy had been established with Truman's June 28 order, which had instructed the 7th Fleet to prevent Communist Chinese attacks on Formosa as well as Formosan acts of aggression against the mainland. He stressed Taipei's belief that the State Department had antagonistic feelings toward it.

This was clearly a diplomatic issue and outside the competence of a military commander. MacArthur' belief that the defense of Formosa was his responsibility upset the State Department. Truman dispatched W. Averell Harriman to Tokyo as ambassador-at-large to notify MacArthur that he was to refrain from using Formosa as an operational base for confronting Communist China. Sebald wrote as follows:

> The abrupt dismissal of General MacArthur from all his commands in April 1951 was a climax which had been developing slowly for five and one-half years....MacArthur handled his various command responsibilities and the innumerable challenges of the situation in a characteristic way, long familiar to Washington. With his sense of history, experience, seniority, reputation, and temperament, he did not easily compromise when his judgment or his decisions were questioned. Although he knew when to conform to specific superior authority, he did not hesitate to advance his views vigorously. He was never reluctant to interpret his authority broadly or to make decisions and act quickly—arguing the matter later. Many in Washington remembered these same qualities from World War II and resented them even more in the semipeace of the postwar era.[35]

Two months before MacArthur's dismissal, Dean Rusk, deputy undersecretary of state, had warned Sebald that MacArthur seemed to be forgetting that he was appointed by the president of the United States. He was not an international government official, but an American military general. But MacArthur had argued to Sebald that SCAP was an international position, and that he could be called to account only with the consent of the eleven countries of the Far Eastern Commission.[36] He was too confident of his international status to listen to advice.

Sebald wrote about the decisive occasion as follows: "On April 5, Washington time, Representative Joseph W. Martin threw gasoline on the public flames of the controversy by revealing a letter to him from General MacArthur, dated March 19. Martin was Republican leader in the House of Representatives and an active critic of President Truman's Korean policies....He [MacArthur] agreed with Martin's contention that Nationalist Chinese [Taiwanese] troops should be allowed to enter the conflict by establishing a front on the Chinese Mainland."[37]

Almond described a meeting he had held with MacArthur two days before the dismissal:

> I went to tell General MacArthur good-bye, and he said, "Ned, this may be the last time you see me over here." I said, "Oh, no. I'll be coming back from time to time." He said, "No, I don't mean that. I may be relieved." I

said, "That's incredible! I can't conceive of you being relieved." He said, "You know the President has been angered by the exposure of my letter to Congressman Joe Martin, which was read in Congress. He claims that I have introduced politics into this, and so my use is at an end."[38]

MacArthur sensed his impending dismissal at least two days in advance. Thus, MacArthur's half-century long military career came to an end

"Old Soldiers Just Fade Away"

The news of MacArthur's dismissal shocked the world. Conservatives at home were angry, and, irritated by the chaotic situation in Korea, many Americans resented President Truman's dismissal of the war hero. The majority of Japanese people were also bewildered by news of the dismissal. During the Occupation era MacArthur had been a godlike figure, surpassing even the emperor in his invincibility and utmost authority. The *Asahi Shimbun* gave the highest praise to him, reporting that he had been a great commander who had taught the Japanese people the value of peace and democracy. His dismissal was greatly regretted.

As a diplomat representing the U.S. government, Sebald was busy. He recalled that when he visited the general, MacArthur displayed a dispassionate expression, nevertheless expressing irony and bitterness that he had been "publicly humiliated after fifty-two years of service in the Army." He added somberly, as Sebald recounted it, that "as a soldier he would have retired without protest, if the President had given the slightest intimation that he wished him to do so."[39] On visiting Prime Minister Yoshida, Sebald found Yoshida tensely awaiting his report. As Sebald conveyed a message from the secretary of state, Yoshida nodded slightly. Regarding Yoshida's own responsibility, Sebald expressed his hope that neither the prime minister nor his cabinet would resign because of the incident. In view of Yoshida's close association with MacArthur, Sebald feared that Yoshida might act impetuously in support of MacArthur.[40]

Early in the morning of April 16, just four days after his dismissal, MacArthur left the U.S. Embassy for Haneda Airport with Mrs. MacArthur, his son Arthur, Whitney, and four others. As many as two hundred thousand Japanese lined the route from the Embassy to the airport. Waiting at the airport was Lieutenant General (later General) Ridgway, together with U.S. Army leaders, an imperial deputy, the prime minister and his cabinet and Diet members, and representatives of various countries. MacArthur boarded his plane *Bataan,* waving silently. At 7:23 a.m. *Bataan* took off. It was the end of the MacArthur era in Japan.

MacArthur did not lose his fighting spirit. In words that challenged the Truman administration, he declared that he was returning home to tell people the truth. The American people enthusiastically welcomed the war hero's homecoming after fourteen years. On April 17, the day after his return, in San Francisco a crowd of no fewer than five hundred thousand people welcomed MacArthur. On April 19, before a joint session of Congress, MacArthur made a dramatic address that was televised for millions. The words "old soldiers never die, they just fade away" in the closing lines of the address were to become symbolic of MacArthur's legacy. Many sentimental listeners, both Japanese and Americans, were moved by the phrase.

MacArthur stated in this speech that "I do not stand here as advocate for any partisan cause,... but [with] one purpose in mind—to serve my country."[41] The speech opened up a new wave of attacks on Truman, and the following week more than one million spectators gathered for parades in Washington, D.C., New York, Chicago, and Milwaukee, where MacArthur was honored. Taking advantage of MacArthur's popularity, the Republican Party used radio and TV broadcasts to call for an inquiry into the military situation in Korea and the reason for MacArthur's dismissal. But the Democrats, who held a majority in Congress, kept the committee hearings on MacArthur secret. MacArthur's testimony gradually prompted criticisms of his actions, and, contrary to the expectation of Republicans, a public fuss about MacArthur's recall ensued.

MacArthur had, nevertheless, shown an interest in contesting the 1952 presidential election. Through July 1952, he appeared many times before Republican Party meetings and attracted attention for his partisan denunciations of the Truman administration. But he could no longer exert his influence on the national party. The Republican National Convention to nominate presidential candidates held in Chicago on July 8 was MacArthur's last public appearance. When his former subordinate Dwight D. Eisenhower won the presidential nomination, MacArthur's dream of becoming president came to a complete end.[42]

MacArthur spent the rest of his life in a suite at the Waldorf-Astoria Hotel in New York. On April 5, 1964, one of the most distinguished soldiers in the history of the United States died at the age of eighty-four. He is buried alongside Mrs. Jean MacArthur at the MacArthur Memorial in Norfolk, Virginia.

Conclusion

MacArthur's military career occupied more than a half century of the eighty-four years of his life. It lasted for fifty-two years, starting in 1899 with his entrance into the U.S. Military Academy at West Point, and ending in April 1951 with his dismissal from the positions of supreme commander for the Allied Powers, commander of the United Nations Command, commander of U.S. Army Forces in the Far East, and chief of the U.S. Ryukyu Civil Government. MacArthur's life was a military life, and his history is the history of war from World War I through World War II to the Korean War. This book has focused on MacArthur from the outbreak of war between the United States and Japan through the occupation of Japan until the middle of the Korean War. It has aimed to depict a true image of MacArthur through the prism of his immediate staff.

What were the factors that enabled MacArthur to win unprecedented admiration as a hero? MacArthur's personal qualities as a hero in war and in peace can be summed up under seven headings: courage, decisiveness, loyalty, dignity, intelligence, leadership, and conviction.

MacArthur was, above all, courageous. Standing outside in the middle of an air raid or landing on enemy soil amid a shower of bullets, MacArthur always behaved calmly. He deliberately exposed himself to danger, covering his head with nothing more protective than a military cap that could easily become a target for enemy fire. Immediately after the Japanese surrender, he landed at Atsugi Airfield in enemy territory, where as many as two million Japanese military personnel remained armed. Such actions demonstrated a fearless attitude toward danger that astonished British prime minister Winston Churchill. Immediately after the outbreak of the Korean War, while the South Korean forces were fleeing, MacArthur led a few subordinates to the front at Seoul and conducted a military inspection despite fierce attacks by North Korean troops in the area. His courageous and confident actions inspired admiration and respect from his subordinates. In such incidents was the myth of MacArthur's invulnerability.

Second, MacArthur was decisive. Although he listened to staff members and raised questions at operations conferences, it was MacArthur who made the final decisions on operational strategy. For the withdrawal from Corregidor to Australia, his firm decision was to use the speedy PT boats, contrary to the assumption among his staff and top figures in Washington that submarines would be used. MacArthur never relied solely on advice from others. Accordingly, when

MacArthur sought his opinion in connection with whether or not to proceed by submarine, Hugh J. Casey recalled: "I was sort of surprised at that because he was a man of decision and he usually did not ask for suggestions or advice such as that."[1] Casey's comment underscores the point that MacArthur rarely sought advice from others.

After reaching Australia, MacArthur moved the Australian defense line north as far as New Guinea, and devised the "leapfrogging" strategy that proved to be effective against Japan in the southwest Pacific. In the early years of the Occupation, MacArthur's personal decisions formed the basis for the establishment of a new constitution that stipulated government by popular sovereignty and the renunciation of war. Similarly, his decisions saw the establishment of reserve police forces after the outbreak of the Korean War. During the Korean War, MacArthur boldly undertook the landing at Inchon and led it to success, ignoring opposition from General Headquarters and the U.S. Navy, which warned of possible dangers. No one at GHQ could match MacArthur as a decision maker.

Third, MacArthur placed high importance on loyalty—indeed, he placed it first in the list of qualities required from soldiers. By loyalty, he meant loyalty to superiors, loyalty to the idea of justice that the military works for, and loyalty to superiors and subordinates. Even those in superior positions had to cultivate the spirit of loyalty. LeGrande A. Diller, one of the Bataan Boys, said of MacArthur: "He was totally loyal to his men and to his officers. He gave loyalty before he asked for it and he never asked for it. And so you gave it back because he was loyal to you; if you got in a jam with somebody or something he was always there to help you out."[2] In this sense, MacArthur was a dependable leader. Those who showed loyalty he rewarded, with decorations or promotions. It was typical of MacArthur that on the first day of his arrival in Australia after the life-or-death escape from Corregidor he named Diller and Sidney Huff full colonels.[3]

On the other hand, if a close aide proved to be disloyal, he suffered the full force of MacArthur's anger and was never allowed to return to the inner circle. When Charles H. Morehouse, one of the Bataan Boys, commented during a trip to the United States that there was no possibility of MacArthur's running in a presidential election, MacArthur immediately relieved him of his post as aide. Even Richard K. Sutherland, who had long served loyally, invited MacArthur's anger because of his affair with a woman and could not restore his close relationship with MacArthur. As a result, Sutherland was obliged to leave Tokyo.

Fourth, MacArthur was a man of dignity. From his youth, his charismatic personality spontaneously attracted others and they were eager to serve with him and follow his leadership. MacArthur was tall and had chiseled features. Son of a lieutenant general, he was from a prestigious military family. His personal appearance and style of dress made him something of a dandy and he wore his military uniform with perfect style. He possessed characteristics that endowed him with unusually high dignity, including a calm and clear mind, an impeccably logical writing style, and speech that may have been overly dramatic but eloquent. For these reasons, many officers wanted to be MacArthur's aide, and, having gained such a position, could be proud of being close to him. When that close relationship became known to others, it sometimes invited envy. For example, when Courtney Whitney, who was not one of the Bataan Boys, was offered an important position, Charles Willoughby and others became jealous. In the background of the fierce power struggle between GS and G-2 was a struggle to gain MacArthur's favor.

MacArthur adopted various measures to maintain his lofty dignity. For example, he did not easily grant interviews. He had a succession of chiefs of staff, including Sutherland, Richard J. Marshall, Paul J. Mueller, and Edward M. Almond, act as barriers and emphasized his status by distancing himself from others. During the Occupation period, Prime Minister Yoshida Shigeru was the only Japanese person who could meet MacArthur frequently. Few Japanese officials other than the emperor met him more than twice.[4] For this reason, Japanese people felt a sense of awe and veneration toward MacArthur. One might well say that MacArthur had mastered the psychology and culture of the Japanese people.

Moreover, through his experience as press liaison for the military just before World War I, MacArthur was adept at manipulating the media. In particular, during the war with Japan he put Diller in charge of media affairs, and through him reported the bravery of MacArthur's army to newspapers and magazines in the United States. He was thus able to manipulate the media into creating a heroic legend both at home and abroad. In fact, during the week between his withdrawal from Corregidor and his safe arrival in Australia, MacArthur played the leading role in an action drama that was widely reported. In addition to raising the fighting spirit of the Allied forces, this had the effect of turning MacArthur into a "miracle hero." Marshall, deputy chief of staff at this time and one of the Bataan Boys, acknowledged MacArthur's efforts to gain prominence. At the landing on Leyte Island and again during the landing in the shallows of Lingayen Gulf in the northern Philippines, MacArthur was aware that he was being photographed by the press and made sure that he remained in front. Before he actually arrived at Atsugi Airfield after the war, he probably imagined several times the scene of his descending the ramp of his plane *Bataan* and was picturing in his mind the image of himself that would be sent all over the world. Marshall commented on MacArthur's thinking: "He felt he had to sell himself to the public all the time … he just felt he had to make the gesture."[5]

A fifth factor is MacArthur's intelligence. He entered West Point with the highest grade level in the school's history and continued to gain unprecedentedly high grades, demonstrating superior intellectual and physical talents that placed him at the top of his graduating class. Among career soldiers, it was common to aim for mastery of a particular specialty, such as military history or strategy and tactics. MacArthur was exceptional. Not only did he excel in military subjects but he also excelled in many other fields, such as history, arts, politics, economics, and sports. He presented himself as a man of learning equal to persons of high reputation, offering a wealth of topics for conversation in meetings with famous people around the world. His broad knowledge and deep learning enabled him to function well as an administrator, even after war had turned to peace.

MacArthur was endowed with an excellent memory. He would surprise people by instantly recalling names, family lineages, and even the scores of past American football matches. Casey commented: "He could react almost instinctively to any given situation.…He also had a marvelous memory. He could read a telegram of several paragraphs and put it down."[6] MacArthur's sharp mind and photographic memory were probably acquired naturally. Frank Rizzo, who worked in GS during the Occupation, did not hide his surprise: "I presented the Government Section solution, and he just asked a couple of questions, 'Why?' I pointed out to him why. He just said, 'Yes,' and that's all there was to it."[7] Rizzo was also impressed by MacArthur's penetratingly bright mind. MacArthur's high intelligence was one element in his status as a hero.

Sixth, MacArthur displayed able leadership. Grasping the essence of problems accurately and from a broad perspective, he had an outstanding ability to set goals after ascertaining what needed to be done and then exert all of his energies in their implementation. Moreover, he was mentally and physically tough, was always patient, and never gave up. Because of these qualities, he exercised vigorous leadership.

However, in order to lead effectively, MacArthur needed capable and thoughtful aides. Dwight D. Eisenhower, Sutherland, and Whitney were probably his best. The qualities they shared were the ability to catch quickly what MacArthur had in mind and the ability to convert MacArthur's ideas into concrete action by communicating them effectively to others. Once in a while, they had to take on unpleasant duties, but they devoted themselves to MacArthur and worked to meet his needs twenty-four hours a day. MacArthur had the capacity to select subordinates who could meet his demands. MacArthur was never ambiguous; he communicated clearly, even when instructing subordinates. For example, when ordering his aide Sidney L. Huff to convince President Manuel Quezon to move from Manila to Corregidor, MacArthur told him not to return until he had succeeded in the mission. On another occasion, he ordered Robert L. Eichelberger, commander of the 8th Army, not to show his face until he had defeated the Japanese. MacArthur's attitude was tough to the point of being merciless but this quality that created serious tensions within GHQ also contributed to his leadership.

Finally, MacArthur was a man of conviction, and he communicated his ideas strenuously, even when serving in remote locations far from Washington. On the verge of total defeat by the Japanese attack on Bataan Peninsula, he continued to push his own convictions and ideas, insisting that he would remain and fight to the end with his soldiers, despite messages from Washington urging him to retreat from Corregidor. At the July 1944 meeting held with President Roosevelt in Hawaii, he used his fiery eloquence to overturn the U.S. Navy's operational plan of breaking through the central Pacific to capture Formosa. In its place, the meeting agreed to adopt MacArthur's strategy of advancing northward from the southwest Pacific islands to the Philippines. Based on the "I shall return" pledge made at the time of his shameful escape from the Philippines, MacArthur held the firm conviction that he would personally free the Philippine nation from the Japanese. Following severe hardships, he had the satisfaction of fulfilling that pledge two years later. These examples point to MacArthur as a man of conviction.

On the other hand, MacArthur was opposed to the "Europe first" policy of the U.S. government and he often criticized Washington for overlooking Asia. During and after the war with Japan, and even during the Korean War, his attitude was unchanged. This was because he believed firmly that the United States should adopt an "Asia first" policy and viewed its basic policy as problematic. Crawford F. Sams, who worked to improve Japanese sanitation and public health during the occupation of Japan, explained MacArthur's thinking: "The people in America are always looking backward over their shoulders to the countries from whence their ancestors came, and this is not necessarily good for the future of this country.... He believed that the center of our principal interest is the Pacific, not this year, but in the long run."[8] MacArthur sincerely believed that postwar Japan should renounce war and aim to become a neutral country, like a Switzerland in Asia. This reflects his sincere belief based on his Christian faith.

These various personal qualities made MacArthur a hero. However, the MacArthur who can be glimpsed from daily life reveals many of the same weaknesses as other humans.

Sams described MacArthur as follows: "He was just not the kind of man to be informal around. He was introverted. In contrast, Eisenhower was the outgoing man; you could call him 'Ike'.... MacArthur was just a different kind of man.... He would meet you in reception lines and greet you warmly, but he wasn't one to slap you on the back and say, 'Hi, Bill.'"[9] As Sams observed, there was an introverted and unsociable side to MacArthur's disposition. Egeberg, who served as MacArthur's physician and deputy, described him as self-conscious and shy. Egeberg noted that MacArthur would end up canceling dinners on cruisers during the war because he was reluctant to dine with officers he did not know. He preferred to dine with those he knew well, and at the battlefield headquarters he took his meals in the officers' dining room. Egeberg concluded that MacArthur "felt responsible for the conversation."[10]

MacArthur showed a sensitivity toward others that suggested an empathetic temperament. Marshall recalled that during military operations he was concerned about casualties: "He didn't want to go into the Admiralty Islands until he was assured that the Japs weren't going to slaughter a lot of our men there."[11] William J. Sebald, head of MacArthur's Diplomatic Section during the Occupation, wrote: "For all of his long combat record, the General was a deeply sentimental and sensitive man. He did not always attempt to hide his feelings publicly, and he seldom did so in private."[12] Egeberg, too, described MacArthur's sensitive consideration in matters as detailed as the wearing of a cap. MacArthur said to Egeberg: "Doc, I noticed you were wearing an officer's cap while we were ashore. You probably took a look at me and put it on. Well, I wear this cap with all the braid. I feel in a way that I have to. It's my trademark…a trademark that many of our soldiers know by now, so I'll keep on wearing it, but with the risk we take in a landing I would suggest that you wear a helmet from now on."[13] At the same time, according to Diller, MacArthur was a prudent planner. When he was offered no less than five hundred thousand dollars from Quezon immediately before the withdrawal from Corregidor, MacArthur took great pains to ensure that he was not violating military rules. Clearly, he was prudent and somewhat nervous.

MacArthur had the habit of completely rejecting any attack, criticism, or defamation directed at him while at the same time transferring the responsibility to others. When U.S. Army Air Forces planes were destroyed by the Japanese surprise attack on Clark Field immediately after the outbreak of the war between the two countries, it was clear that the cause of the defeat was MacArthur's own hesitation over attacking Formosa. Nevertheless, he refused to acknowledge this point, instead criticizing the uncooperative attitudes of Washington and the U.S. Navy. When fierce Japanese attacks led MacArthur to abandon Manila and move to Bataan, he failed to take sufficient provisions and supplies. Although this failure indirectly caused hunger and suffering among his troops, he ignored his own mistake and instead complained that the Japanese military had adopted the inhuman strategy of intentionally driving several tens of thousands of Philippine people onto the peninsula, thereby causing food shortages and worsening starvation among his troops.

In the middle of the occupation of Japan, a group of conservative journalists in Washington, led by Harry Kern, organized the American Council on Japan (not to be confused with the Allied Council for Japan) to oppose the GHQ/SCAP policies of demilitarization and democratization, including Zaibatsu dissolution, reparations, and the public purges. Officials of the State Department and the War Department as well as Robert L. Eichelberger, who had retired as commander of the 8th Army, joined the group, and a campaign to criticize MacArthur was launched. MacArthur demonstrated his intention to confront the group by writing a public rebuttal.[14] His obstinate objections, however, had the effect of complicating the problem. It may have been better if he had simply shrugged off the criticism.

MacArthur's decision making tended to be arbitrary. After he succeeded in landing on Leyte Island, thus fulfilling his "I shall return" pledge, he urged Philippine president Sergio Osmena to declare that independence had been regained, even though resistance in the surrounding areas had not been mopped up. This kind of hasty arbitrariness, directed at securing his own honor, was repeated often enough that it formed a pattern of behavior. For example, during the occupation of Japan, he embarrassed Washington by suddenly announcing, without any prior consultation with the State Department, that the peace treaty was ready. After the outbreak of the Korean War, he angered the State Department by flying to Taiwan without permission from Washington and meeting President Chiang Kai-shek to discuss the possibility of Taiwanese troops joining the South Korean army. Furthermore, after successfully landing on Inchon and forcing North Korean troops well above the 38th Parallel, MacArthur boasted that the United Nations troops could go home by Christmas—a boast foiled by China's unexpected entry into the war. These examples demonstrate some negative aspects of MacArthur's arbitrary behavior.

MacArthur tended to shift his decisions suddenly. After repeated defeats by the Japanese in the Philippines, he ordered his troops to retreat to the Bataan Peninsula. Previously, he had rejected as impractical the Orange Plan, which specified a strategy of holding out on the Bataan Peninsula in the case of Japanese attacks. Instead of the Orange Plan, MacArthur had advocated a new military strategy, a defense of the entire Philippine coastline with PT boats to repel any Japanese attack. However, when his strategy collapsed under a powerful Japanese offensive, MacArthur did not hesitate to revive the Bataan defense strategy laid out in the Orange Plan. He made no excuses for such contradictions. Again, when Washington initiated a policy of Japanese rearmament in the immediate postwar years, MacArthur bitterly and repeatedly opposed it, but with the outbreak of the Korean War he unceremoniously switched sides to advocate for rearmament. This shift constituted a complete turnaround.

In the background of such contradictions lay MacArthur's unconscious prejudices. He felt sure that the U.S. military could not lose at the time of Pearl Harbor and in the various Philippine campaigns. In the case of Korea, he firmly believed that there was no possibility of war, and then no possibility of a South Korean defeat by North Korea. Accordingly, he failed to recognize the North Korean attack as the outbreak of war, regarding it as nothing more than a reconnaissance mission to demonstrate the North's power. MacArthur's fixed ideas and prejudices distorted his judgment and the misjudgments resulted in sudden changes of direction.

MacArthur was, however, abstemious and self-controlled. A specific example was his refusal to drink alcohol during wartime. As a young man, MacArthur had liked to drink. When he was commandant of West Point he had, on occasion, been drunk to the point of collapse with Assistant Secretary of the Navy Franklin D. Roosevelt (later to become President Roosevelt). After the war broke out, however, he abstained from alcohol. He later explained to Egeberg that his decision was made out of his sense of responsibility for the lives of the officers serving under his leadership and concern for the mothers, wives, and girlfriends who were worrying about their safety.[15] He made one exception: he had a glass of bourbon in February 1943 to mark his satisfaction with the success of a reconnaissance landing on the Admiralty Islands.

MacArthur seldom became angry. According to Marshall, he became very angry if he learned that someone had used his name to obtain a special benefit, such as an airline ticket.[16] Marshall commented that MacArthur would become enraged at any possible stain on his honor because he was nervous about his public image. Of course, he reacted in a similar fashion to breaches of loyalty. On the other hand, MacArthur did not often laugh. Sams wrote: "His sense of humor was limited to some extent. He had no interest in what was usually called barracks-room jokes, he had no gift for small talk."[17] Sams, Marshall, and Laurence E. Bunker all testified that they had no memory of seeing MacArthur laugh loudly.

The general maintained a healthy and consistent daily routine. From the time of his arrival in Manila and through consecutive moves under wartime conditions to Brisbane, Port Moresby, and Hollandia, back to Manila, and then to Tokyo, MacArthur maintained his daily routine. According to Marshall, at Brisbane he regularly stayed at home until 10:00 a.m. reading urgent messages and newspapers before heading off for the day's work at the office. However, between 1:00 p.m. and 3:00 p.m. he left the office for lunch and a nap. MacArthur's daily naps were famous, and whether in Manila or Tokyo, he maintained his routine. Naturally, his staff adjusted. Especially when the fighting became intense, they worked without reprieve from ten in the morning until late at night. Brigadier General Bonner F. Fellers, military secretary, recalled that they never thought their job was hard, noting: "Nobody ever knew when it was Sunday."[18]

Almond, chief of staff in Tokyo, testified as follows: "He would get in the office at a quarter till 11:00 and leave at 2:30 in the afternoon. He would get back at 5:00 or 5:30 and then leave whenever his work was through, which was sometimes midnight. Normally though, it was about 8:30 or 9:00. When I became chief of staff and he walked up to my desk, he said, 'You know my hours. Don't let them disturb you.'"[19] Alonzo P. Fox, deputy chief of staff, recalled: "General MacArthur didn't go out socially at all. The only entertaining he did was luncheons at his place. The only time there was any entertaining at their house was an official luncheon, which would happen several times a week, depending upon visitors passing through. People from the United States, members of the staff, and people of that sort would be invited.... There was never anybody that really got in close that I could remember, except in an official way. His normal work day was very unusual."[20]

MacArthur's healthy physical condition surprised those around him. When the elevator in the Dai-Ichi Building did not open immediately, MacArthur would not wait but would climb the entire six flights of stairs. It was usually the accompanying guard, and not MacArthur, who was out of breath on arrival. Bunker recalled: "All during the war and especially during the Occupation, a matter of amazement to all of us was the physical vitality of the man."[21] Egeberg estimated that on an average day MacArthur walked about five miles a day just in pacing up and down in his office. Sebald wrote: "The perennial Occupation question was how this man of action, who passed his seventieth birthday in harness, renewed himself for the enormous energy he used in his job.... MacArthur and a few of his key officers plodded ahead, month after month, on a seven-day week and often, a ten- or twelve-hour day.... He had no hobbies, except his reading, and few diversions, except movies at his embassy home."[22]

Elliott R. Thorpe, who was in charge of civil intelligence and counterintelligence, concluded that the key factor in MacArthur's good health was his indoor walking. His office had to be large enough for him to pace. He walked at a deliberate pace. Those who visited MacArthur's office to talk first learned that they had to walk slowly with him. But there were signs of aging. Thorpe disclosed some little-known facts: "Sometimes when he spoke he had to hold on to the rostrum, and when he wrote his hand shook."[23] Bunker recalled that MacArthur had many different kinds of pipes in his office but he rarely smoked. Since his pipe became something of a trademark, he sometimes posed with it at the request of photographers, for example in the famous image of him descending the steps of the airplane at Atsugi Airfield. But that was not what MacArthur would normally do himself.[24]

Finally, MacArthur was a good family man. Although his first marriage ended in failure, his dramatic onboard encounter with Jean led to a second marriage, and MacArthur was supported by a devoted wife's love both in his private and in his official life. At the age of fifty-eight, he became a father for the first time. He doted on his son Arthur, just as his own mother had once doted on him. He had deep respect for his parents. Diller commented: "I found that General

MacArthur admired his father deeply. His father was an outstanding officer during the Civil War and during his service in the regular army.... The General's mother was a Virginian, she was born near the Memorial in Norfolk and he loved his mother deeply, during her senior years she lived with him until she died. And he always spoke of his mother with the greatest of love and respect."[25] When Charles L. Kades, deputy chief of GS, met MacArthur for the first time at GHQ, he was looking at a picture of his deceased father and talking to him. Kades said: "It made an impression on me."[26] In this sense, MacArthur might be called an ordinary family man.

Some little-known aspects of MacArthur's human and physical qualities have already been outlined. What conclusions can we draw by comparing MacArthur the person with MacArthur the distinguished military hero depicted in earlier chapters of this book?

MacArthur was both a brilliant wartime commander and a man of outstanding peacetime gifts. Revolutions are accomplished by both destruction and construction. Through the war against Japan, MacArthur made extraordinary efforts to destroy the militaristic institutions of imperial Japan. Subsequently, he made an enormous contribution, under difficult circumstances, to construct a peaceful nation through the demilitarization and democratization of postwar Japan. It is no exaggeration to call this transformation a Japanese revolution, and MacArthur was the single most important person to influence both the destructive and constructive aspects of change in Japan.

MacArthur, like other human beings, had his weaknesses and failings. One finds excesses in the Occupation administration. Looking broadly, however, and particularly at MacArthur as commander of the Allied forces in the unusual circumstances of indirect occupation, one finds no one who surpassed MacArthur in dignity, knowledge, coordination, decision making, and control. MacArthur was an accurate observer of Japanese history, politics, economics, and society, and by observing the affection of the Japanese people for the emperor, he assured the continuation of the imperial institution. Moreover, by placing his authority and that of GHQ above that of the emperor, he drew both government and people to his ground and successfully conducted the administration of Japan. Specifically, MacArthur's use of his close relationship with the Showa Emperor as an invisible pillar in the Occupation administration was a key to his success. Sebald rightly concluded:

> I think he was a great man as far as the Occupation of Japan was concerned.... He managed to get the respect of the Japanese people. Without the accommodation, assistance, and cooperation of the Japanese people, the Occupation would have been impossible.... It was primarily

because of the image of MacArthur as a fair and just person who was doing his job as he was told to do it even though it meant hardship for the people. I think the Japanese people respected him, and thus they cooperated. The Emperor guided the Japanese people also. If the Emperor hadn't cooperated with MacArthur, MacArthur may have mishandled the situation. Apparently he did the right thing.[27]

However, the unexpected emergence of the cold war, the accompanying changes in Washington, and the shift in U.S. government policy from a hard to a soft occupation of Japan were all unlucky for MacArthur. He was angered by the changes and opposed the U.S. government's new policies by using various arguments, such as the violation of the new constitution, the nonnecessity of Japanese rearmament, and the impossibility of a Soviet invasion of Japan. Furthermore, he insisted that the purges, reparations, and Zaibatsu dissolutions had all been ordered by Washington and imposed on Tokyo. MacArthur utterly refused to accept any policy that contradicted the Japanese peace constitution that he had built. If he had observed the transformation of international politics a little more calmly and had shown some flexibly regarding Washington's basic policy as commander on the ground, MacArthur might have avoided his sudden and tragic dismissal. However, he was a hero of the Pacific War and had been discussed more than once as a possible presidential candidate; his pride and dignity did not permit him to negotiate or make concessions. The result was his unhappy dismissal.

Charles Bulkeley, who experienced the desperate retreat from Corregidor with MacArthur, testified as follows:

> MacArthur, again, not from my own personal opinion but from up close observation of the man, not only in war but also in peace there and also in the occupation of Japan, he's the greatest general of this century, probably the greatest general…this country's ever had….MacArthur was not only a great general, field general, but also a tactician, a strategist, and also a statesman when occupying Japan.[28]

Bulkeley's words reveal the "positive" image of MacArthur. But it is MacArthur's own words, "Old soldiers never die; they just fade away," that could be interpreted as a negative image of the last stage of his life.

Notes

CHAPTER 1

1. Taiheiyo Senso Kenkyukai, ed., *Zusetsu Makkasah* [Illustrated history of MacArthur] (Tokyo: Kawadeshobo Shinsha, 2003), 14–15, 148.

2. Ibid., 16–18; Carol Morris Petillo, *Douglas MacArthur: Philippine Years* (Bloomington: Indiana University Press, 1981), 144–45; Michael Schaller, *Douglas MacArthur: The Far Eastern General* (New York: Oxford University Press, 1989), 3–10.

3. Mary Pinkney ("Pinkie") Hardy MacArthur was the daughter of an aristocratic and wealthy cotton merchant from Virginia. Her brother and relatives fought for the South in the Civil War. She and Arthur had three sons, Arthur III, Malcolm, and Douglas. Malcolm died young and Arthur III died at the age of forty as a colonel, leaving Douglas as the focus of Pinkie's deep affection. Among the many episodes that showed her strong attachment, Pinkie took up residence at a hotel on the edge of the West Point campus while Douglas was a student there. For his part, Douglas appeared to be influenced more by his mother than by his father. Pinkie headed for Manila with MacArthur in 1935, but died in December of that year from a cerebral thrombosis. She is buried in Norfolk, Virginia.

4. John Jacob Beck, *MacArthur and Wainwright: Sacrifice of the Philippines* (Albuquerque: University of New Mexico Press, 1974), 2.

5. Schaller, *Douglas MacArthur*, 145–56.

6. Taiheiyo Senso Kenkyukai, *Zusetsu Makkasah*, 19–20; Schaller, *Douglas MacArthur*, 21.

7. Robert Wood, MacArthur's classmate at West Point and later chairman of Sears, Roebuck and Co. and leader of an anti–New Deal business lobbying group, took his old friend under his wing (Schaller, *Douglas MacArthur*, 21). Eisenhower testified that after the honeymoon between Roosevelt and MacArthur ended, Roosevelt took steps to keep MacArthur in the Philippines in order to avoid a disadvantageous situation. See Dwight D. Eisenhower, *The Eisenhower Diaries*, ed. Robert H. Ferrell (London: W. W. Norton and Company, 1981), 7; Petillo, *Douglas MacArthur*, 158–60, 167.

8. Schaller, *Douglas MacArthur*, 13.

9. Ibid., 14–21, 25–27.

10. Jean Faircloth was born in Tennessee in 1898. Her father was a wealthy flour-mill owner. Following the divorce of her parents, Jean grew up with her mother and two brothers in her grandfather's house in Murfreesboro, Tennessee. Her mother's family was well known in Tennessee politics and her grandfather was a leader in Confederate veterans' affairs. Having grown up listening to stories of relatives who fought in the Civil War and the Spanish-American War, Jean was, according to MacArthur's aide, Sidney L. Huff, "the flag-wavingest girl in town" (Sidney L. Huff, with Joe Alex Morris, *My Fifteen Years with General MacArthur* (New York: Harper, 1964).

After receiving her inheritance, Jean set out on a world cruise at the age of thirty-seven, boarding the SS *President Hoover* to visit a friend in Shanghai. The captain of the ship introduced her to MacArthur and his sister-in-law, Mary MacArthur. Mary MacArthur seemed to like Jean, and they became friendly. Persuaded by Mary to cut short her visit in Shanghai, Jean moved to a hotel in Manila. MacArthur and Jean had a wedding ceremony in New York. The next year their son, Arthur, was born. Jean enjoyed a high reputation as a devoted wife. In January 2000 she died at the age of 101. She is buried next to her husband in the MacArthur Memorial, Norfolk, Virginia. Huff, *My Fifteen Years with General MacArthur* 13; Papers of Jean MacArthur, Oral History, Transcript #6, RG13, June 19, 1984.

11. Beck, *MacArthur and Wainwright,* 3.

12. RG32, Oral Histories, Box 6, Folder 19, Admiral Charles Bulkeley, October 5, 1982, in Washington, D.C.

13. Engineer Memoirs, Major General Hugh J. Casey, U.S. Army, ed. Office of History, U.S. Army Corps of Engineers, September 25–29, 1979, 126–27.

14. Schaller, *Douglas MacArthur,* 28–29.

15. Ibid., 27–28, 31, 36.

16. Beck, *MacArthur and Wainwright,* 4.

CHAPTER 2

1. Engineer Memoirs, Major General Hugh J. Casey, U.S. Army, 125; according to Eisenhower's testimony, MacArthur had been unaware of deterioration of his reputation. Eisenhower, *Eisenhower Diaries,* 37.

2. Paper of Lieutenant General Richard K. Sutherland, USA (Retired), RG46.

3. Charles A. Willoughby, Biographical Sketches of Persons Interviewed: MacArthur Oral History Project compiled by Judy R. Hotard; Oral Reminiscences of Major Charles A. Willoughby. August 28, 1967, Interview D. Clayton James.

4. Oral Reminiscences of Major General Charles A. Willoughby, July 30,1971.

5. Oral Reminiscences of Major General Richard J. Marshall, July 27, 1971.

6. Excerpts from Oral Reminiscences of Major General Courtney Whitney, August 28, 1967.

7. Engineer Memoirs, Major General Hugh J. Casey, U.S. Army.

8. MacArthur Memorial Library Collection.

9. *Kyodo Kenkyu—Nihon Senryo* [Cooperative studies—the occupation of Japan], ed. Shiso no Kagaku Kenkyukai (Tokyo: Tokuma Shoten, 1972), 441.

10. Takemae Eiji, ed., *Nihon Senryo: GHQ Kokan no Shogen* [Occupation of Japan—GHQ high-ranking officers' testimony] (Tokyo: Chuokoronsha, 1988), 167.

11. Author's interview with Cappy Harada, September 14, 1984.

12. MacArthur Memorial Library Collection.

13. Engineer Memoirs, Major General Hugh. J. Casey, U.S. Army, 178–79.

14. *Sun News,* May 1, 1942; *Argus,* Melbourne, May 1, 1942.

15. Oral Reminiscences of Major General Richard J. Marshall, July 27, 1971.

16. MacArthur Memorial Library Collection.

17. Oral Reminiscences of Major General Charles A. Willoughby, July 30, 1971.

18. Ibid.

19. Oral Reminiscences of Major General Richard J. Marshall. July 27, 1971.

20. MacArthur Memorial Library Collection. Author's interview with James W. Zobel, librarian of MacArthur Memorial

21. Schaller, *Douglas MacArthur,* 121.

22. MacArthur Memorial Library Collection.

23. Oral Reminiscences of General LeGrande Diller, September 26, 1982.

24. *Washington Post,* September 5, 1987.

25. Huff, *My Fifteen Years with General MacArthur; New York Times,* November 12, 1962.

26. MacArthur Memorial Library Collection.

27. Ibid.

28. Papers of Jean MacArthur, Oral History. Transcript #7, RG13, August 17, 1984.

29. Papers of Lieutenant Paul P. Rogers, USA. RG46.

30. Papers of Jean MacArthur, Oral History. Transcript #7.

31. Author interview with Admiral Charles Bulkeley, October 5, 1982.

CHAPTER 3

1. Memo for the Sec. of War, Subj.: Strategic Concept of the Philippine Islands, L. T. Gerow, October 8, 1941, RG 46.

2. [SEC] Memorandum for the President, Subj.: Estimate of Ground forces required, Chief of Staff, October 21, 1941, RG46. The abbreviation [SEC] stands for secret.

3. [SEC] Memorandum for the Secretary, General President, Subj.: Estimate of Ground forces required, Chief of Staff, October 21, 1941, RG46. Staff, Subj.: Air Offensive Against Japan, War Dept., Office of the Chief of Staff, L. S. K., November 21, 1941.

4. [SEC] Conf. In the Office of the Chief of Staff, Present: Gen. Marshall, Gen. Arnold, Gen. Gerow, Col. Bundy, WPD, Col. Handy, WPD, 10:40 A.M. November 26, 1941. Conf. stands for confidential.

5. Ibid.

6. [SEC] Memorandum for the President, Subj.: Far Eastern Situation, H. R. Stark, November 27, 1941.

7. Ibid.

8. War Dept. Office Chief of Staff, December 1, 1941 (handwritten memo).

9. Beck, *MacArthur and Wainwright,* 6.

10. Oral Reminiscences of Brigadier General Clifford Bluemel, July 8, 1971.

11. *Senshi Sosho, Hito Koryaku Sakusen* [The operation to capture the Philippines], ed. War History Department of the Institute of the Defense Agency (Tokyo: Asagumo Shimbunsha, 1966), 29, 33, 39–40.

12. Beck, *MacArthur and Wainwright,* 5–6.

13. Engineer Memoirs, Major General Hugh J. Casey, U.S. Army, 146.

14. Beck, *MacArthur and Wainwright,* 7.

15. Ibid., 9.

16. Ibid., 9.

17. Oral Reminiscences of Brigadier General Clifford Bluemel, July 8, 1971.

18. Beck, *MacArthur and Wainwright,* 6–10.

19. Engineer Memoirs, Major General Hugh. J. Casey, U.S. Army, 143.

20. [SEC] From Adams to USA Forces Far East Manila, P. I., December 7, 1941, RG30.

21. Beck, *MacArthur and Wainwright,* 11–15.

22. Record of telephone conversation between Gen. Gerow, WPD, and Gen. MacArthur in Manila, P. I., December 7, 1941.

23. Douglas MacArthur, *Reminiscences* (New York: Fawcett World Library, 1964), 126.

24. This part of the description is not in the English version of the *Reminiscences.* It is quoted from the Japanese version, *Makkasah Kaisoki* [MacArthur reminiscences], vol. 1, trans. Tsushima Kazuo (Tokyo: Asahi Shimbunsha, 1964), 190. Where the information came from is unknown.

25. MacArthur, *Reminiscences,* 127.

26. *Senshi Sosho, Hito Koryaku Sakusen,* 114–15.

27. MacArthur, *Reminiscences,* 127.

28. Oral Reminiscences of Benson Guyton, August 5, 1971.

29. Engineer Memoirs, Major General Hugh J. Casey, U.S. Army, 149–50.

30. Huff, *My Fifteen Years with General MacArthur,* 33–34.

31. Taiheiyo Senso Kenkyukai, *Zusetsu Makkasah,* 27. Immediately before opening hostilities, information that the Japanese air force obtained showed forty-seven naval vessels (two heavy cruisers, one light cruiser, four aircraft carriers, fifteen destroyers, twenty-five submarines): *Senshi Sosho, Hito Koryaku Sakusen,* 111.

32. MacArthur, *Reminiscences,* 127.

33. Beck, *MacArthur and Wainwright,* 18.

34. MacArthur, *Reminiscences,* 130.

35. King might be a mistake in the original document. Stark is correct.

36. MacArthur, *Reminiscences,* 130.

37. Ibid., 131.

38. [SEC] From the Chief of Naval Operations to Chief of Staff, U.S. Army, Subj: The Dangerous Strategic Situation in the Pacific Ocean, H. R. Stark, December 11, 1941.

39. [SEC] From the Chief of Staff to the Chief of Naval Operations, Subj.: Defense of Oahu, December 12, 1941.

40. [SEC] General Strategic Review, Draft of WPD Study, about December 21, 1941.

41. Beck, *MacArthur and Wainwright,* 24.

42. Ibid., 24.

43. *Senshi Sosho Hito Koryaku Sakusen,* 76.

44. Imoto Kumao, *Daitowa Senso Sakusen Nisshi* [Operational diary of the Pacific war] (Tokyo: Fuyo Shobo Shuppan, 1998), 86.

45. *Senshi Sosho, Hito Koryaku Sakusen,* 87–90.The southern troops beside the 14th Army were General Headquarters (Tokyo), the 3rd Air Group (four fighter regiments), the 15th Army (three divisions), the 25th Army (two divisions), Kawaguchi unit and the 16th Army (one division and one brigade), *Senshi Sosho, Firipin Koryaku Sakusen,* 82.

46. Ibid., 91, 101, 114, 115–16; Imoto, *Daitowa Senso Sakusen Nisshi,* 88.

47. Ban Hachizo, "Eirei no Gojyukkaiki Hoyo o Itonami, Tatakatta ano Sento no Kioku o Tadoru" [The 50th memorial service for dead soldiers and memoirs of the war], *Heiwa no Ishizue Onketsuhen* [Foundation of Peace, Collection of Witnesses of Unentitled Military Pensioners], vol. 3, ed. Public Foundation for Peace and Consolation Incorporated Administrative Agency (Tokyo: Exhibition and Reference Library for Peace and Consolation, 1993), 2-3.

48. Kishimoto Eitaro, "Hito Batan Koryakusen" *Heiwa no Ishizue Onketsuhen,* vol. 5, 178.

49. *Senshi Sosho, Hito Koryaku Sakusen,* 156.

50. Ibid., 144.

51. Imoto, *Daitowa Senso Sakusen Nisshi,* 88.

52. Huff, *My Fifteen Years with General MacArthur,* 36.

53. Beck, *MacArthur and Wainwright,* 25.

54. Ibid., 25.

55. Huff, *My Fifteen Years with General MacArthur,* 36.

56. Beck, *MacArthur and Wainwright,* 32.

57. Ibid., 34.

58. Ibid., 36.

59. Ibid., 38.

60. Huff, *My Fifteen Years with General MacArthur,* 37–38.

61. Ibid., 38.

62. Papers of Jean MacArthur, Oral History, Transcript #5, RG13. This interview took place at the Waldorf Towers Apartments on June 19, 1984.

63. Beck, *MacArthur and Wainwright,* 39.

CHAPTER 4

1. Beck, *MacArthur and Wainwright,* 56–57.

2. Huff, *My Fifteen Years with General MacArthur,* 42.

3. Ibid., 43.

4. *Asahi Shimbun,* January 3, 1942.

5. Huff, *My Fifteen Years with General MacArthur,* 41; Papers of Jean MacArthur, Oral History, Transcript #5. According to the Japanese document collection *Hito Firipin Koryaku Sakusen* [The operation to capture the Philippines], "The full force of bombers struck the Corregidor Fortress from 12:00 to 12:40, and inflicted great damage on the military installations" despite antiaircraft fire (187). Regarding the discrepancy in the duration of the air raid, the Japanese estimate is probably correct.

6. Huff, *My Fifteen Years with General MacArthur,* 41, 45.

7. MacArthur, *Reminiscences,* 142.

8. Memo for the Adjutant Gen. Marshall, December 24, 1941; [SEC] Memo for the Adjutant Gen. Marshall, December 26, 1941.

9. MacArthur, *Reminiscences,* 139.

10. Beck, *MacArthur and Wainwright,* 42–43; MacArthur, *Reminiscences,* 139.

11. MacArthur, *Reminiscences,* 134.

12. Ibid., 134–35.

13. Ibid., 143. A Japanese soldier who was in the 16th Division, the field artillery platoon and the 22nd Regiment, testified, "The U.S. army caught our formation by radar. The tricky mechanism was set up: the moment we touched the wire strung through the trees, guns went off at the target. It was a really difficult position from which to attack. They aimed at targets from above the trees, and their fortress was secure. Steep hills prevented us from attacking them." Nishimura Yorio, "Hito Batanhanto no Tatakai" [The battle of Bataan Peninsula in the Philippines], *Heiwa no Ishizue,* vol. 15 (2005): 356–57.

14. *Senshi Sosho, Firipin Koryaku Sakusen,* 168.

15. Ibid., 178.

16. Ibid., 179–81.

17. Ibid., 182–84, 191.

18. Ibid., 186–89.

19. Ibid.

20. Casey said that the mining engineers volunteered to participate in these dangerous demolition jobs. Engineer Memoirs, Major General Hugh J. Casey, U.S. Army, 161; Beck, *MacArthur and Wainwright,* 56–57.

21. *Senshi Sosho, Hito Koryaku Sakusen,* 191.

22. Beck, *MacArthur and Wainwright,* 56–58. Takeuchi Kaneo, *Makkasah Gensui to Sono Bakuryo* [General MacArthur and his staff officers], vol. 1 (Tokyo: Jinji Koshinjyo, 1946).

23. MacArthur, *Reminiscences,* 135–36.

24. Schaller, *Douglas MacArthur,* 56.

25. William Manchester, *American Caesar: Douglas MacArthur 1880–1964* (Boston: Little Brown, 1978), 242.

26. Oral Reminiscences of Benson Guyton, August 5, 1971.

27. MacArthur, *Reminiscences,* 137.

28. *Senshi Sosho, Hito Koryaku Sakusen,* 193–95, 208–9; Terashima Sadatsugu, "Manira Ichibannori no Michi wa Kewashiku" [The first step to Manila was difficult], *Heiwa no Ishizue,* vol. 1 (1991): 121.

29. Imoto, *Daitoa Senso Sakusen Nisshi,* 90–91.

30. Ibid., 89–90.

31. *Senshi Sosho, Hito Koryaku Sakusen,* 104, 204.

32. Kishimoto Eitaro "Hito Firipin Batan Koryakusen," *Heiwa no Ishizue Onketsuhen,* [The Foundation of Peace, collection of witnesses of unentitled pensioners], vol. 5, Exhibition and Reference Library for Peace and Consolation, Tokyo, 1993–2005, 179.

33. Ibid., 179–80; *Daihonei Rikugunbu Senso Shidohan Kimitsu Senso Nisshi* [The secret diary of the War Instruction Department of Army Headquarters], vol. 1, ed. Military History Society (Tokyo: Kinseisha, 1998), 213.

34. Imoto, *Daitoa Senso Sakusen Nisshi,* 91.

35. Beck, *MacArthur and Wainwright,* 56.

36. MacArthur, *Reminiscences,* 140.

37. Ibid., 143. Since the Japanese sent only five thousand replacements from the 16th Detachment to defend Manila, "100,000 replacements" is incorrect.

38. Engineer Memoirs, Major General Hugh J. Casey, U.S. Army, 163.

39. MacArthur, *Reminiscences,* 141.

40. Papers of Lieutenant Paul P. Rogers.

41. Oral Reminiscences of Admiral Charles Bulkeley, October 5, 1982.

42. Manchester, *American Caesar,* 256.

43. Papers of Jean MacArthur, Oral History Transcript #5.

44. MacArthur, *Reminiscences,* 141.

45. Imoto, *Daitoa Senso Sakusen Nisshi,* 137.

46. Ibid., 137–38.

47. [SEC] From Marshall to Gen. MacArthur, January 23, 1942.

48. Schaller, *Douglas MacArthur,* 57.

49. Ibid., 56–57, 61.

50. Papers of Lieutenant Paul P. Rogers.

51. MacArthur, *Reminiscences,* 139. Part of this quotation is from the Japanese version of *Reminiscences, Makkasah Kaisoki.*

52. [SEC, Priority] MacArthur to AGWAR, January 24, 1942.

53. [SEC] MacArthur to Roosevelt, no date.

54. Engineer Memoirs, Major General Hugh J. Casey, U.S. Army, 174.

55. J. M. Wainwright, given to Col. Traywick verbally at Gen. Wainwright's CP, 4:30 P.M., January 27, 1942. Memo for Gen. MacArthur, February 7, 1942.

56. Eisenhower, *Eisenhower Diaries,* 44, 46.

CHAPTER 5

1. Manchester, *American Caesar,* 248.

2. *Senshi Sosho Hito Koryaku Sakusen* [War history series, The operation to capture the Philippines], ed. The War History Department of the Institute of the Defense Agency. Tokyo: Asagumo Shuppansha, 1966.

3. *Asahi Shimbun,* December 27, 1941.

4. [STRICTLY CONF] From Cabot Coville, Foreign Affairs Adviser to the US High Commissioner, Ft. Mills P. I., John K. Davis, January 11, 1942; [SEC] From Marshall to Gen. MacArthur, Jan. 16, 1942; Huff, *My Fifteen Years with General MacArthur,* 49; Beck, *MacArthur and Wainwright,* 89.

5. Schaller, *Douglas MacArthur,* 59.

6. *Asahi Shimbun,* January 8, 11, 22, 1942.

7. Beck, *MacArthur and Wainwright,* 92. Practically all members of Quezon's Commonwealth Cabinet, and those who attended the supreme national conference, decided to take a job in the Philippine administrative committee and the puppet republican government supported by the Japanese army. Some fourteen out of twenty-four members from the Upper House, and thirty-five out of ninety-eight from the Lower House cooperated with the Japanese army. See Renato Constantino and Letizia Constantino, *Firipin Minshu no Rekishi III* [History of the Philippine people, vol. 3], trans. Tsurumi Yoshiyuki (Tokyo: Imura Bunka Jigyosha, 1979), 745.

8. Beck, *MacArthur and Wainwright,* 92–94; excerpts from Oral Reminiscences of Major General Charles A. Willoughby.

9. [SEC] From Ft. Mills to Gen. Marshall, MacArthur, February 8, 1942; Beck, *MacArthur and Wainwright,* 97–99.

10. Beck, *MacArthur and Wainwright*, 99.

11. [SEC] From Ft. Mills to Gen. Marshall, MacArthur, February 8, 1942; Beck, *MacArthur and Wainwright*, 99.

12. MacArthur, *Reminiscences*, 148.

13. Ibid., 150.

14. Beck, *MacArthur and Wainwright*, 100; Eisenhower, *Eisenhower Diaries*, 46–47.

15. [SEC] Memorandum for the Adjutant Gen., Subj.: Far Eastern Situation, Franklin D. Roosevelt, February 9, 1942; Copy of Message sent by Gen. Marshall to MacArthur, February 9, 1942; [SEC] From Ft. Mills to Gen. George C. Marshall, MacArthur, February 10, 1942.

16. Manchester, *American Caesar*, 282–83; [SEC] From Ft. Mills to Gen. George C. Marshall, MacArthur, February 12, 1942.

17. [SEC] Draft of Proposed Cablegram to Gen. MacArthur, Marshall, December 31, 1941.

18. Beck, *MacArthur and Wainwright*, 58–59.

19. [STRICTLY CONF] From Babot Coville, Foreign Affairs Adviser to the U.S. High Commissioner, Ft. Mills P. I., John K. Davis, January 11, 1942.

20. Proposed Cable to Gen. MacArthur Written Last Night by Mr. McCloy, January 18, 1942.

21. [STRICTLY CONF] Memorandum for the President, January 27, 1942.

22. [SEC] From Fort Mills to Gen. Marshall, MacArthur, February 2, 1942.

23. [SEC] From Marshall to Gen MacArthur, February 2, 1942.

24. [SEC] Memorandum for the Adjutant Gen., Subj.: Far Eastern Situation, Franklin D. Roosevelt, February 9, 1942.

25. Copy of Message sent by General Marshall to General MacArthur, February 9, 1942.

26. [SEC] From Ft. Mills CK to the Adj. Gen., MacArthur, February 11, 1942.

27. [SEC] From Ft. Mills to Gen. George C. Marshall, MacArthur, February 16, 1942. [SEC] Memorandum for the Adjutant Gen., Subj.: Far Eastern Situation, Marshall, February 16, 1942.

28. [SEC] From Ft. Mills to the Adj. Gen., MacArthur, February 13, 1942; [SEC] Memorandum for the Adjutant Gen., Subj.: Far Eastern Situation, Franklin D. Roosevelt, February 14, 1942; [SEC] From Fort Mills to AGO, MacArthur, February 17, 1942.

29. [CONF] From Ft. Mills CK to AGWAR, MacArthur, February 15, 1942.

30. MacArthur and Quezon: Executive Order Number One.

31. One rumor suggests that MacArthur may have taken the assets out, but this is unlikely. Rather, it is more probable that the cash award was used for Quezon's daily expenses. Because no details have been made public, the matter remains unclear.

32. Constantino, *Firipin Minshu no Rekishi III*, 832; Adm. Glassford to Gen. MacArthur, February 17, 1942; [SEC] MacArthur to Adm. Glassford, February 17, 1942. The statement in the *Reminiscences* (152) that "Sayre left first, and then Quezon did" is incorrect.

33. [STRICTLY CONF] Memorandum for the President, January 27, 1942.

34. [SEC] From Marshall to Gen. MacArthur, February 2, 1942.

35. MacArthur, *Reminiscences*, 151–52.

36. Papers of Jean MacArthur, Oral History, Transcript #5.

37. [SEC] Secret Radio for Gen. MacArthur, L. T. Gerow, Brig. Gen., February 4, 1942.

38. [SEC] Memorandum for Adjutant General, Subj.: Far Eastern Situation, Franklin D. Roosevelt, February 9, 1942.

39. [SEC] From Ft. Mills CK to the Adj. Gen., MacArthur, February 11, 1942; MacArthur, *Reminiscences*, 152.

40. [SEC] Memorandum for the Adjutant General, Subj.: Far Eastern Situation, Marshall, February 14, 1942.

41. [SEC] Memorandum for the Adjutant General, Subj.: Far Eastern Situation, Franklin D. Roosevelt, February 14, 1942; RG-46: Papers of Lieutenant Paul P. Rogers, MacArthur and Quezon, Executive Order Number One.

42. [CONF] From Ft. Mills CK to AGWAR, MacArthur, February 15, 1942; [SEC] From Hq. Philippine Dept. in the Field to Adjutant General, February 15, 1942; [CONF] Memorandum for the Adjutant General, J. R. Deane, February 15, 1942.

43. Schaller, *Douglas MacArthur,* 60–61.

44. Papers of Lieutenant Paul P. Rogers, MacArthur and Quezon, Executive Order Number One.

45. Papers of Lieutenant Paul P. Rogers, Corregidor Diary and Selected Letters.

46. Papers of Lieutenant Paul P. Rogers, Corregidor Diary and Selected Letters. The reference to $50,000 is mistaken; the correct amount was $500,000.

47. Paper of Lieutenant Paul P. Rogers; MacArthur and Quezon, Executive Order Number One.

48. [SEC] From Gen. Marshall to Gen. MacArthur, 1942.

49. [SEC] Memorandum for Officer in Charge of Message Center, Marshall, Dwight D. Eisenhower, Brig. Gen., February 21, 1942.

50. MacArthur, *Reminiscences,* 152.

51. Ibid., 152–53.

52. Memorandum for the President, Marshall, February 24, 1942; [SEC] From FT Mills P. I. to George C. Marshall, MacArthur, February 24, 1942; MacArthur, *Reminiscences,* 153.

53. Eisenhower, *Eisenhower Diaries,* 49.

54. [SEC] Secret radiogram to Gen. MacArthur, Marshall, Dwight D. Eisenhower, Brig. Gen., February 25, 1942; [SEC] From Ft. Mills P. I. to Gen. George C. Marshall, MacArthur, February 26, 1942.

CHAPTER 6

1. The word "evacuation" was not used.

2. Manchester, *American Caesar,* 289–90.

3. [SEC] From Ft. Mills P. I. to Gen. George C. Marshall, MacArthur, February 24, 1942.

4. [SEC] From Ft. Mills P. I. to Gen. George C. Marshall, MacArthur, February 26, 1942.

5. Huff, *My Fifteen Years with General MacArthur,* 51–52.

6. Bulkeley, RG32, Oral Histories, Box 6, Folder 19. Bulkeley testified that the Japanese had surrounded Manila Bay with twenty-two to twenty-seven ships, but the Japanese forces left no record to support this claim.

7. Bulkeley, Oral History.

8. Ibid.; Papers of Jean MacArthur, Oral History, Transcript #31, RG 13, September 28, 1984.

9. MacArthur, *Reminiscences,* 153.

10. Papers of Lieutenant Paul P. Rogers.

11. Engineer Memoirs, Major General Hugh J. Casey, U.S. Army, 179–80.

12. Huff, *My Fifteen Years with General MacArthur,* 50.

13. General LeGrande Diller, RG32 Oral Histories, Box 6, Folder 23.

14. MacArthur, *Reminiscences,* 153–54.

15. Huff, *My Fifteen Years with General MacArthur,* 53–54.

16. Memo for the President, Marshall, February 24, 1942; [SEC] From Ft. Mills P. I. to Gen. George C. Marshall, MacArthur, February 24, 1942; [SEC] Secret radiogram to Gen. MacArthur, Marshall, Dwight D. Eisenhower, Brig. Gen., February 25, 1942; [SEC] From Ft. Mills P. I. to Gen. George C. Marshall, MacArthur, February 26, 1942; [SEC] Memo for

the Adjutant Gen., Subj.: Far Eastern Situation, Marshall, Dwight D. Eisenhower, February 26, 1942.

17. Huff, *My Fifteen Years with General MacArthur,* 52–54.

18. Admiral Charles Bulkeley, Oral History.

19. Huff, *My Fifteen Years with General MacArthur,* 54.

20. Ibid., 52.

21. [SEC] The Commandant, Sixteenth Naval District, to the Commander, Motor Boat Squadron Three, Subj.: Operation Order, March 10, 1942.

22. Papers of Lieutenant Paul P. Rogers.

23. Admiral Charles Bulkeley, Oral History.

24. General LeGrande Diller, Oral History.

25. MacArthur, *Reminiscences,* 153.

26. Papers of Jean MacArthur Oral History, Transcript #6.

27. Huff, *My Fifteen Years with General MacArthur,* 54.

28. Jean MacArthur, Oral History, Transcript #6.

29. Huff, *My Fifteen Years with General MacArthur,* 55.

30. MacArthur, *Reminiscences,* 154–55.

31. Admiral Charles Bulkeley, Oral History.

32. Ibid.

33. MacArthur, *Reminiscences,* 156.

34. Ibid.

35. General LeGrande Diller, Oral History.

36. Papers of Lieutenant Paul P. Rogers (Letter to His Mother, April 4, 1942).

37. Engineer Memoirs, Major General Hugh J. Casey, U.S. Army, 180.

38. Huff, *My Fifteen Years with General MacArthur,* 56–57.

39. MacArthur, *Reminiscences,* 156.

40. Huff, *My Fifteen Years with General MacArthur,* 61.

41. Jean MacArthur, Oral History, Transcript #6.

42. Engineer Memoirs Major General Hugh J. Casey, U.S. Army, 180.

43. Ibid., 181.

44. Huff, *My Fifteen Years with General MacArthur,* 60–61.

45. Engineer Memoirs, Major General Hugh J. Casey, U.S. Army, 182.

46. Jean MacArthur, Oral History, Transcript #6.

47. MacArthur, *Reminiscences,* 157.

48. Huff, *My Fifteen Years with General MacArthur,* 62.

49. Engineer Memoirs, Major General Hugh J. Casey, U.S. Army, 181.

50. Admiral Charles Bulkeley, Oral History.

51. Jean MacArthur, Oral History, Transcript #6.

52. Huff, *My Fifteen Years with General MacArthur,* 63-64.

53. MacArthur, *Reminiscences,* 157.

54. Admiral Charles Bulkeley, Oral History.

55. Ibid.

56. Papers of Lieutenant Paul P. Rogers (Corregidor Diary and Selected Letters).

57. [SEC] From Melbourne to AGWAR, Brett, February 28, 1942; [SEC] Memo for the Adjutant Gen., Subj.: Far Eastern Situation, Marshall, March 6, 1942; [SEC] Memo for the Adjutant Gen., Subj.: Far Eastern Situation, Marshall, Dwight D. Eisenhower, March 10, 1942; [SEC] From Australia to Adjutant Gen. Brett, March 12, 1942.

58. [SEC] From Ft. Mills P.I. to Gen. George C. Marshall, MacArthur, March 13, 1942.

59. Engineer Memoirs, Major General Hugh J. Casey, U.S. Army, 183.

60. [SEC] Memo for the Adjutant General: Subject: Far Eastern Situation, March 14, 1942.

61. Papers of Lieutenant Paul P. Rogers (Corregidor Diary and Selected Letters).

62. Jean MacArthur, Oral History, Transcript #6.

63. Ibid.

64. MacArthur, *Reminiscences,* 157–58.

65. Jean MacArthur, Oral History, Transcript #6.

66. Huff, *My Fifteen Years with General MacArthur,* 71–72.

67. [SEC CODE] March 17, 1942.

68. [SEC CODE] From President Roosevelt to the Former Naval Person, March 17, 1942.

69. Memorandum for the Adjutant General Marshall, March 17, 1942.

70. MacArthur, *Reminiscences,* 158.

71. Ibid., 158.

CHAPTER 7

1. *Daihonei Rikugunbu Senso Shidohan Kimitsu Senso Nisshi.*

2. Imoto, *Daitoa Senso Sakusen Nisshi,* 92–93; *Senshi Sosho, Hito Koryaku Sakusen,* 229; *Daihonei Rikugunbu Senso Shidohan Kimitsu Senso Nisshi,* 222, 232.

3. *Senshi Sosho, Hito Firipin Koryaku Sakusen,* 331, 334, 337.

4. Ibid., 315–16, 318–19.

5. Taiheiyo Senso Kenkyukai, *Zusetsu Makkasah,* 28–29; Engineer Memoirs, Major General Hugh J. Casey, U.S. Army.

6. MacArthur, *Reminiscences,* 153.

7. Ibid.

8. [SEC, PRIO] From MacArthur to AGWAR, February 27, 1942, and February 28, 1942.

9. Oral Reminiscences, General LeGrande Diller, 9.

10. From Ft. Mills to the Adjutant Gen. MacArthur, March 6, 1942; [SEC] From Ft. Mills P. I. to Gen. George C. Marshall, MacArthur, March 8, 1942.

11. [SEC, PRIO] MacArthur to AGWAR, March 4, 1942.

12. Ibid., March 5, 1942.

13. Ibid., March 6, 1942.

14. *Senshi Sosho, Hito Koryaku Sakusen,* 322, 339.

15. Ibid., 339, 350.

16. Ibid, 355.

17. Ibid., 355, 367, 377.

18. Ibid., 381–411.

19. Kawanami Toichi and Ban Hachizo, "Batan Shi no Koshin " [The Bataan death march], *Heiwa no Ishizue, Onketsuhen,* vol.1 (1991).

20. Katsuya Fukushige, "Korehidoru eno Michi wa Nagakatta!" [It was a long way to Corregidor], in *Mokugekisha ga Kataru Showashi* [Witness to Showa History], vol. 6, Taiheiyo Senso [Pacific War], ed. Inose Naoki (Tokyo: Shin Jinbutsu Ohraisha, 1989), 221–22.

21. Engineer Memoirs, Major General Hugh J. Casey, U.S. Army, 172.

22. Oral History, Admiral Charles Bulkeley.

23. [SEC] Memo for the Adjutant Gen., Subj.: Far Eastern Situation, Marshall, March 24, 1942.

24. Beck, *MacArthur and Wainwright,* 180.

25. Ibid., 192.

26. Memo for the President, Subj.: Situation in Bataan, Joseph T. McNarney, April 8, 1942.

27. Memo for the Chief of Staff, Subj.: Relief of Philippines, Dwight D. Eisenhower, Major Gen., April 8, 1942.

28. Memorandum for the President, Subj.: Bataan Situation from acting chief of staff, April 8, 1942.

29. Ibid.

30. Proposed dispatch to General Wainwright from Franklin D. Roosevelt; [SEC] Memo for the War Dept. Classified Message Center, Subj.: Message to Commanding General, United States Forces, Great Britain, Acting Chief of Staff McNarney, Dwight. D. Eisenhower Assistant Chief of Staff, April 8, 1942; [SEC] Memo for the President, Subj.: Bataan Situation, April 8, 1942; [SEC] Memo for Gen. Watson, Acting Chief of Staff McNarney, Franklin D. Roosevelt, April 8, 1942.

31. Memo for Sec War (handwritten).

32. *Daihonei Rikugunbu Senso Shidohan Kimitsu Senso Nisshi*, 234; *Senshi Sosho*, Hito *Koryaku Sakusen*, 426.

33. Ban Hachizo, "Eirei no Gohtykkaiki Hoyo o Itonami, Tatakatta ano Sento no Kioku o Tadoru" [The 50th commemoration service for dead soldiers and memories of the war], *Heiwa no Ishizue, Onketsuhen*, vol. 3 (1993), 7.

34. *Senshi Sosho Hito Koryaku Sakusen*, 427.

35. Message from General Wainwright, April 9, 1942.

36. Memorandum for the Classified Message Center, War Department, McNarney, April 9, 1942.

37. Memorandum for the Adjutant General, McNarney, April 9, 1942.

38. [SEC] Memo for President, Joseph T. McNarney, April 10, 1942.

39. [SEC] Southwest Pacific, Com. 16 to OPNAV [Office of the Chief of Naval Operations], April 14, 1942.

40. Engineer Memoirs, Major General Hugh J. Casey, U.S. Army, 145.

41. Oral Reminiscences of Benson Guyton.

42. [SEC] Memo for the War Dept. Classified Message Center, J. R. Dean, May 4, 1942.

43. Memorandum for the War Department Classified Message Center, Subject: Far Eastern Situation, May 4, 1942.

44. From Ft. Mills to Chief of Staff U.S. Army, Wainwright, May 5, 1942.

45. Kawashima Masuzo, "Batan Hanto Korehidoruto Jyugunki" [Bataan Peninsula and Corregidor campaign memoir], *Heiwa no Ishizue, Onketsuhen*, vol. 6 (1996), 218–19.

46. [SEC] From Ft. Mills to Chief of Staff, No Sig., May 6, 1942.

47. Taiheiyo Senso Kenkyukai, *Zusetsu Makkasah*, 32–33; Katsuya, "Korehidoru eno Michi wa Nagakatta!" 224–25.

48. Radiogram to Major General William F. Sharp, Jr., CO Visayan-Mindanao Force, Subject: Surrender, May 7, 1942.

49. Radiogram from Sharp to General Chynoweth, May 10, 1942.

50. Radiogram from Christie to Sharp, May 10, 1942.

51. Radiogram from MacArthur, May 11, 1942.

52. Radiogram from Sharp to Christie, May 11, 1942.

53. Radiogram from Christie to Sharp, May 12, 1942.

54. Letter to Christie from Sharp, May 12, 1942.

55. Radiogram from Sharp to Christie, May 19, 1942.

56. Eisenhower, *Eisenhower Diaries*, 54.

57. MacArthur, *Reminiscences*, 159.

58. This statement is quoted from the Japanese version, since it has been deleted from the English version. MacArthur, *Makkasah Kaisoki*, 243.

59. MacArthur, *Reminiscences*, 159.

60. Lester I. Tenney, *My Hitch in Hell: The Bataan Death March* (Dulles, Va.: Potomac Books, 2007), 46–61.

61. Kawanami and Ban, "Batan Shi no Koshin," 282–83.

62. Kotani Teruo, "Bukan Korehidoru Koryaku to Hito Haitai o Taikenshi" [The capture of Wuhan and Corregidor and the defeat of the Philippines], *Heiwa no Ishizue, Onketsuhen,* vol. 5 (1995), 252.

63. *Senshi Sosho, Hito Koryaku Sakusen,* 432–33. There was discrimination in the U.S. and Filipino force. There were big differences between Americans and Filipinos in terms of salary and food rations. In Bataan, the Filipino soldiers were placed in the front lines while most of the U.S. soldiers were used as reserves. As a result, relatively more Filipinos than Americans died or were injured and relatively more were taken prisoner. Of the approximately fifty thousand Filipino soldiers who were taken prisoner, some twenty-six thousand, or roughly half, died. Of the nine thousand U.S. soldiers who were taken prisoner, fifteen hundred, or one-sixth, died. Constantino, *Firipin Minshu no Rekishi III* [History of the Philippine people, vol. 3], 670–71.

64. Katsuya, "Korehidoru eno Michi wa Nagakatta!" 223.

65. [SEC] Southwest Pacific Com. 16 to OPNAV, April 14, 1942.

66. The National Institute for Defense Studies holds, "Furyoni kansuru Shorui Tsuzuri, 31–35" [Documents file on an investigation concerning prisoners in the Philippines, file nos. 31–35].

67. Tenney, *My Hitch in Hell,* 44.

68. Katsuya, "Korehidoru eno Michi wa Nagakatta!" 82–83. Among recent studies, Tachikawa Kyoichi, "Senshi no Kyokun-Naniga Horyo Mondai o Unda no ka: Nihongun no Hoshin to Haikei" [Lessons from military history: What caused the prisoner problems? The policy and background of the Japanese army], *MAMOR* (September 2008): 46–47, points to the influences, first, of the Doolittle Raid of April 18, 1942 (see Shibata Takehiko and Hara Katsuhiro, *Dorittoru Kushu Hiroku* [The secret record of the Doolittle air raid] (Tokyo: Ariadone Project, 2003), 189–91, and, second, of the instructions of Prime Minister and Minister of the Army Tojo Hideki, read by the chief of the Prisoner Information Bureau in June and July 1942. Regarding the first point, during the Doolittle Raid, two U.S. bombers made forced landings in a Japanese occupied area of China. The crew were not treated as prisoners but were executed as war criminals. Regarding the second point, Tojo's instructions on the treatment of prisoners stated that they should not be allowed to do nothing, but rather, so long as their human rights were not infringed, their skill and labor should be used productively in order to advance the Japanese war effort. Both points exerted influence on the subsequent treatment of prisoners by the Japanese army.

69. Oral Reminiscences of Benson Guyton.

70. MacArthur, *Reminiscences,* 159.

71. *New York Times,* January 28 and 29, 1944. Further articles on February 6, 8, 11, and on April 18, 25, 30 referred to the events in Bataan, each containing the expressions "march of death" or "death march."

72. GHQ/SCAP Records Box no. 1906, Sheet no. LS-35484; Hando Kazutoshi, "Soshireikan Makkasah no Fukushu" [The revenge of General MacArthur], *Ohru Yomimono* (September 1988). Similar examples may be found in the joint publication of *The Tragedy of Manila* (Military Intelligence Division, GHQ/SCAP) and Nagai Takashi, *Nagasaki no Kane* [The bells of Nagasaki] (Hibiya Shuppansha, 1949). In other words, when Nagai originally attempted to clarify the tragedy caused by the bombing of Nagasaki from a Japanese point of view, GHQ suppressed the publication. Nagai's book was later approved for publication on the condition that it was published jointly with *The Tragedy of Manila.* GHQ/SCAP aimed to justify the atomic bombing by emphasizing Japanese wartime atrocities.

73. MacArthur, *Reminiscences,* 160.

74. U. Alexis Johnson, later ambassador to Japan (1967–69) and undersecretary of state, had once met Homma when he served as an official of the U.S. State Department

in Tianjin, China. Johnson recalled that "Homma, on the other hand, always spoke softly and treated his subordinates well; he even spoke passable English. When I described the harassments Americans were suffering from his troops, Homma promised to investigate this and invited me to return should I have any need to. When Homma was executed after World War II as a war criminal charged in effect with responsibility for the Bataan Death March, I was saddened. Homma's responsibility was only nominal. Some American generals thought the verdict too harsh, and I had difficulty believing that the only gentleman I ever knew in the Japanese Army could have been so deliberately callous." U. Alexis Johnson and Jeff Odivarius McAllester, *The Right Hand of Power, the Memoir of an American Diplomat* (Prentice Hall Japan, 1984), 42.

CHAPTER 8

1. Taiheiyo Senso Kenkyukai, *Zusetsu Makkasa,* 34.
2. Oral Reminiscences of Brigadier General Burdette M. Fitch, August 28, 1971.
3. Takemae Eiji, *GHQ* (Tokyo: Iwanami Shinsho, 1983), 3–4.
4. Taiheiyo Senso Kenkyukai, *Zusetsu Makkasa,* 35–36; MacArthur, *Reminiscences,* 163–64.
5. Nomura Minoru, *Nihon Kaigun no Rekishi* [History of the Japanese Navy] (Yoshikawa Kobunkan, 2002), 195–96; Mizokawa Tokuji, ed., *Senso Jihen* [War and incidents] (Kyoikusha, 1991), 273–78; Shibata Takehiko and Hara Katsuhiro, *Dorittoru, Kushu Hiroku* [Secret records of the Doolittle air raid] (Tokyo: Ariadone Kikaku, 2003), see chaps. 2–4.
6. Taiheiyo Senso Kenkyukai, *Zusetsu Makkasa,* 37–38; MacArthur, *Reminiscences,* 177.
7. MacArthur, *Reminiscences,* 168.
8. Ibid.
9. Engineer Memoirs, General Hugh J. Casey, U.S. Army, 255.
10. Oral Reminiscences Roger O. Egeberg, June 30, 1971.
11. Oral Reminiscences Charles A. Willoughby, July 30, 1971.
12. Roger O. Egeberg, *The General: MacArthur and the Man He Called "Doc"* (New York: Hippocrene Books, 1983), 21.
13. Paul P. Rogers, MacArthur and Sutherland, RG30.
14. Engineer Memoirs, General Hugh J. Casey, U.S. Army, 53.
15. Oral Reminiscences Charles A.Willoughby, July 30, 1971.
16. George C. Kenney, *General Kenney Reports* (New York: Duell, Sloan & Pearce, 1949); General George C. Kenney, The War in the Pacific—December 8, 1941–September 2, 1945.
17. George C. Kenney, *General Kenney Reports.*
18. Oral Reminiscences of Admiral Arleigh A. Burke, July 2, 1971.
19. Ibid.
20. MacArthur, *Reminiscences,* 187.
21. Ibid.,178; Taiheiyo Senso Kenkyukai, *Zusetsu Makkasa,* 38–39; Mizokawa, *Senso Jihen,* 277–78.
22. Egeberg, *The General,* 25.
23. Ibid., 30, 33.
24. Ibid., 34–35.
25. Ibid., 45–46, 48.
26. Ibid, 53–54; Manchester, *American Caesar,* 405–6.
27. Mizokawa, *Senso Jihen,* 286–88.
28. John Gunther, *Makkasah no Nazo* [The riddle of MacArthur], trans. Kinoshita Hideo and Yasuho Nagaharu (Tokyo: Jijitsushinsha, 1951), 96–100; James Burns, *Ruzuberuto to Dainiji Sekaitaisen* [Roosevelt and World War II], vol. 2, trans. Inoue Isamu and Ito Takuichi (Tokyo: Jijitsushinsha, 1972), 304–6.

29. Manchester, *American Caesar*, 414.

30. Egeberg, *The General*, 54.

31. Taiheiyo Senso Kenkyukai, *Zusetsu Makkasa*, 40–41.

32. Egeberg, *The General*, 62, 66.

33. Mizokawa, *Senso Jihen*, 289.

34. Egeberg, *The General*, 69; Samuel Sloan Auchincloss Jr., *The Memoirs of Samuel Sloan Auchincloss Jr., October 12, 1903 to November 5, 1991*, 210 (this book was privately published by the family. No publication details are available); MacArthur, *Reminiscences*, 252.

35. Egeberg, *The General*, 73–74.

36. *Ichiokunin no Showashi: Nihon no Senshi*, vol. 10, *Taiheiyo Senso, part 4* [Showa history for one hundred million people: Japanese war history vol.10, the Pacific War 4], ed. Mainichi Shimbunsha (Tokyo: Mainichi Shimbunsha, 1980), 154–69; Mizokawa, *Senso Jihen*, 289–90.

CHAPTER 9

1. MacArthur, *Reminiscences*, 244; Constantino, *Firipin Minshu no Rekishi*, vol. 3, 637–827.

2. MacArthur, *Reminiscences*, 271.

3. Oral Reminiscences of Brigadier General Burdette M. Fitch, August 28, 1971.

4. Egeberg, *The General*, 82.

5. Ibid., 87–88.

6. Ibid., 90–93.

7. Ibid., 41.

8. *Ichiokunin no Showashi*, 170–75; MacArthur, *Reminiscences*, 276.

9. MacArthur, *Reminiscences*, 278.

10. Egeberg, *The General*, 131–32.

11. Memoirs of Samuel Sloan Auchincloss Jr., 214.

12. Taiheiyo Senso Kenkyukai, *Zusetsu Makkasah*, 44; *Ichiokunin no Showashi*, 178–84. Alfonso J. Aluit, *Corregidor* (Manila: Galleon, 2003), 112–23; *Ichiokunin no Showashi*, 176–77; MacArthur, *Reminiscences*, 289.

13. Egeberg, *The General*, 135–36; MacArthur, *Reminiscences*, 286.

14. Egeberg, *The General*, 146.

15. Ibid., 148–51.

16. MacArthur, *Reminiscences*, 289.

17. *Ichiokunin no Showashi*, 185–87; Taiheiyo Senso Kenkyukai, *Zusetsu Makkasah*, 43–45.

18. Egeberg, *The General: MacArthur and the Man He Called 'Doc,'* 185–86.

19. Ibid., 163.

20. Oral Reminiscences of Brigadier General Elliott R. Thorpe, May 29, 1977.

21. Manchester, *American Caesar*, 489.

22. Oral Reminiscences of Brigadier General Elliott R. Thorpe, May 29, 1977.

23. MacArthur, *Reminiscences*, 272–73.

24. Oral Reminiscences of Brigadier General Bonner F. Fellers, June 26, 1971.

25. Oral Reminiscences of Brigadier General Crawford F. Sams, August 25, 1971.

26. Biography: Papers of Major General Courtney Whitney, USA, in RG30.

27. Excerpts from Oral Reminiscences of Major General Courtney Whitney.

28. Manchester, *American Caesar*, 410.

29. Oral Reminiscences of Colonel Laurence E. Bunker, July 12, 1971.

30. Memoirs of Samuel Sloan Auchincloss Jr., 193.

31. Oral Reminiscences of Colonel Laurence E. Bunker, July 12, 1971.

32. Ibid.

33. Oral Reminiscences of Lieutenant General Edward M. Almond, August 4, 1971.

34. Oral Reminiscences of Brigadier General Burdette M. Fitch, August 28, 1971.

35. Oral Reminiscences of Lieutenant General Alonzo P. Fox, June 26, 1971.
36. Oral Reminiscences of Brigadier General Elliott R. Thorpe, May 29, 1977.
37. Oral Reminiscences of Dr. Roger O. Egeberg, June 30, 1971.
38. Memoirs of Samuel Sloan Auchincloss Jr., 217.
39. Oral Reminiscences of Frank Rizzo, August 8, 1977.
40. Masuda Hiroshi, *Koshoku Tsuihoron* [The public purge] (Tokyo: Iwanami Shoten, 1998), 29–31.
41. Egeberg, *The General,* 192.
42. Engineer Memoirs, Major General Hugh J. Casey, 263.
43. Memoirs of Samuel Sloan Auchincloss Jr., 217–18.
44. Ibid., 218–19.
45. Egeberg, *The General,* 193–94.
46. Charles A. Willoughby, *Shirarezaru Nihon Senryo* [Unknown occupation of Japan], trans. En Tei (Tokyo: Banchoshobo, 1973), 34–37.
47. Memoirs of Samuel Sloan Auchincloss Jr., 220.
48. Engineer Memoirs, Major General Hugh J. Casey, 264.
49. Memoirs of Samuel Sloan Auchincloss Jr., 221.
50. Ibid.
51. Ibid., 222.
52. MacArthur, *Reminiscences,* 310.

CHAPTER 10

1. Egeberg, *The General,* 205.
2. Ibid., 205–6.
3. MacArthur, *Reminiscences,* 314–15.
4. *Makkasah no Nihon* [MacArthur's Japan], vol. 1, ed. Shukanshincho Henshubu (Tokyo: Shinchoshasha, 1970), 27.
5. Egeberg, *The General,* 212, 215. According to records at the MacArthur Memorial Archives, there were six pens: one went to Wainwright, and is now at West Point; one went to Percival, and is now at his regiment's museum in England; two were kept by MacArthur and are now part of the MacArthur Archives collection; one went to Whitney, and is held by his family; and one went to Jean (Mail from archivist to author, August 14, 2009).
6. MacArthur, *Reminiscences,* 315.
7. *Makkasah no Nihon,* 35.
8. Egeberg, *The General,* 202–3.
9. Ibid., 203.
10. Ibid., 205; Oral Reminiscences of Dr. Roger O. Egeberg, June 30, 1971.
11. Takemae, *GHQ,* 88–91.
12. Oral Reminiscences of Frank Rizzo, August 8, 1977.
13. Oral Reminiscences of Brigadier General Crawford F. Sams (M.D.), August 25, 1971.
14. Oral Reminiscences of Brigadier General Elliott R. Thorpe, May 29, 1977.
15. Oral Reminiscences of Colonel Laurence E. Bunker, July 12, 1971.
16. Oral Reminiscences of Colonel Laurence E. Bunker.
17. Willoughby, *Shirarezaru Nihon Senryo,* 67–75. Repatriation from the Pacific Area was finished earlier, but it was 1976 when repatriation was completed from China and the Soviet Union.
18. The *Asahi* newspaper reported that the initial number of Class A war criminals totaled thirty-nine, but in fact the breakdown was twenty-three Japanese, fifteen foreigners, and one unclear. The unclear person is thought to have been former prime minister Abe Nobuyuki, but in the end he was not arrested. One other person was arrested but not sent to a detention center. Another, Homma Masaharu, former commander of the 14th Army, was reclassified from Class A to Class B and executed. Class A criminals Itagaki

Seishiro, Kimura Heitaro, and Muto Akira were abroad on the day of the arrests. Given these circumstances, an accurate count of the number of the criminals is difficult.

19. Oral Reminiscences of Brigadier General Elliott R. Thorpe.

20. Egeberg, *The General,* 227.

21. MacArthur, *Reminiscences,* 329.

22. Ibid., 330.

23. Egeberg, *The General,* 227; Oral Reminiscences of Brigadier General Elliott R. Thorpe.

24. Crawford F. Sams, *DDT Kakumei* [The DDT innovation], ed. and trans. Takemae Eiji (Tokyo: Iwanami Shoten, 1986), gives the number as seventeen thousand.

25. Oral Reminiscences of Brigadier General Crawford F. Sams (M.D.).

CHAPTER 11

1. [TOP SECRET] E.G. Crossman, FA, Memo for the Commander in Chief, U.S. Army Forces, Pacific, Subj.: Basic Plan for Institution of Military Government. Blacklist Operations.

2. [TOP SECRET] Initial Post-Defeat Policy Relating to Japan, JCS1380, 12 June 1945.

3. Oral Reminiscences of Frank Risso, August 8, 1977.

4. Masuda, *Koshoku Tsuihoron,* 17–62; Testimony by Kades to the author (August 15, 1995) at Kades's residence and correspondence from Kades to author.

5. Oral Reminiscences of Charles L. Kades.

6. Ibid.

7. Ibid.

8. Ibid.

9. Testimony by Kades to the author (August 15, 1995); Oral Reminiscences of Colonel Charles L. Kades, July 7, 1977; Narita Norihiko, "Nihonkoku Kempo to Kokkai" [The Japanese Constitution and the Diet], *Nihon Gikaishiroku,* vol. 4 [The historical record of the Japanese Diet], vol. 4, ed. Uchida Kenzo, Kimbara Samon, and Furuya Tetsuo (Tokyo: Daiichihoki, 1990), 3–75; Nishi Osamu, "Nihonkoku Kempo Seitei" [Enactment of Japanese Constitution], *Jitsuroku Nihon Senryo* [Documents on the occupation of Japan] (Tokyo: Gakken, 2005), 78–83; Takemae, *GHQ,* 158–67.

10. MacArthur, *Reminiscences,* 358.

11. Oral Reminiscences of Charles L. Kades.

12. MacArthur, *Reminiscences,* 359.

13. Masuda Hiroshi, "Zaibatsu Kaitai, Nochi Kaikaku" [Dissolution of the Zaibatsu and land reform], *Jitsuroku Nihon Senryo* [Documents on the occupation of Japan] (Tokyo: Gakken, 2005), 90–93.

14. Masuda Hiroshi, "Kyoiku Kaikaku" [Educational reforms], *Jitsuroku Nihon Senryo* [Documents on the Occupation of Japan] (Tokyo: Gakken, 2005), 94–95.

15. Oral Reminiscences of Colonel Laurence E. Bunker.

16. Kanesashi Masao, "Dai 1 sho, Gaikan Senryo Seiji kara 55nen Taisei e" [Chapter 1 overview: from political administration under the occupation to the 55 system], *Gendai Nihon Seito Shiroku* [Modern Japanese political party records], vol. 2, ed. Kitamura Kimihiko, et al. (Tokyo: Daiichihoki, 2003), 3–18; Oral Reminiscences of Major General Richard Marshall.

17. Masuda Hiroshi, "Naimusho Kaitai" [Dissolution of the Home Ministry], *Jitsuroku Nihon Senryo* [Documents on the occupation of Japan] (Tokyo: Gakken, 2005), 88–89.

CHAPTER 12

1. Shinobu Seizaburo, *Sengo Nihon Seijishi II* [Postwar Japanese political history], vol. 2 (Tokyo: Keiso Shobo, 1966), 517–19.

2. Howard B. Schonberger, *Senryo 1945–1952—Sengo Nihon o Tsukuriageta Hachinin no Amerikajin* [Occupation 1945–1952—eight Americans who created postwar Japan], trans. Miyazaki Akira (Tokyo: Jiji Tsushinsha, 1994), chap. 2, Douglas MacArthur.

3. Igarashi Takeshi, *Tainichi Kowa to Reisen* [The peace treaty with Japan and the cold war] (Tokyo: Tokyo Daigaku Shuppankai, 1986), 72.

4. Masuda, *Koshoku Tsuihoron*, 192.

5. [SEC] PPS Thirty-Ninth Meeting in Records of the PPS; Memo by the Director of the Policy Planning Staff (Kennan) to the Undersecretary of State (Lovett), Aug. 12, 1947.

6. Sebald, chief of Foreign Service officers, noted that the reason for the conflict between the State Department and MacArthur was, in part, "I think he went ahead of the Department of State business on his own very much. It was May 1950 when the Diplomatic Section could send its own secret telegram to Washington without MacArthur's censorship. It took four years and nine months to realize it." Oral Reminiscences of Ambassador William J. Sebald, July 30, 1971.

7. George F. Kennan, *Memoirs 1925–1950* (Boston: Little Brown, 1967), 369–70.

8. Masuda Hiroshi, *Rearmament of Japan, Part One: 1947–1952* (Washington, D.C.: Congressional Information Service; and Tokyo: Maruzen Company, 1998), 5-D-1.

9. Masuda, *Rearmament of Japan,* 1-A-46; Masuda Hiroshi, "Chosen Senso Izenniokeru Amerika no Nihon Saigunbi Koso, Part 1" [U.S. policy toward Japanese rearmament before the Korean War, part 1], *Hogaku Kenkyu*, vol. 72 (Tokyo: Keio University Press, 1999), 20–21.

10. Masuda, *Rearmament of Japan,* 2-F-36.

11. Ibid.

12. Ibid.; Masuda, *Koshoku Tsuihoron*, 224–27.

13. Masuda, *Rearmament of Japan,* 2-F-36.

14. Masuda, "Chosen Senso Izenniokeru Amerika no Nihon Saigunbi Koso Part 1," 22–25.

15. Masuda, *Rearmament of Japan,* 2-F-39.

16. Ibid., 5-A-30; Masuda, *Koshoku Tsuihoron* 229–30.

17. Masuda, *Rearmament of Japan,* 1-A-46.

18. Ibid., 5-A-30.

19. Ibid., 3-A-1.

20. Masuda, "Chosen Senso Izenniokeru Amerika no Nihon Saigunbi Koso Part 1," 26–31.

21. Rizzo, talking about Willoughby, said, "He admired himself. … It [his Prussian air] was his dramatization of self to an extent or his 'romantization' of self. For example, if you saw him in his room, he would have a beautiful robe on." Oral Reminiscences of Frank Rizzo, August 8, 1977.

22. Theodore Cohen, *Nihon Senryo Kakumei, GHQ karano Shogen* [The occupation and rebirth of Japan, testimonies from GHQ], vol.1 and 2, trans. Ohmae Masaomi (Tokyo: TBS Britannica, 1983), 150–51.

23. Political purges by Prime Minister Yoshida were called "the Item Y purge" from his initial. Masuda Hiroshi, *Seijika Tsuiho* [Purges of politicians] (Tokyo: Chuokoronshinsha, 2001), part 2.

24. Masuda Hiroshi, "Ashida Hitoshi," *Sengo Nihon no Saisho Tachi* [Prime ministers of postwar Japan], ed. Akio Watanabe (Tokyo: Chuokoronshinsha, 2001), 94–95.

25. Masumi Junnosuke, *Sengo Seiji 1945–1955* [Postwar politics, 1945–1955] (Tokyo: Tokyo University Press, 1983).

26. Masuda, "Ashida Hitoshi," 96–98.

27. Oral Reminiscences of Frank Rizzo; Oral Reminiscences of Colonel Charles L. Kades.

28. Theodore Cohen, *Nihon Senryo Kakumei*, vol. 2, 261.

29. Masuda, "Ashida Hitoshi," *Sengo Nihon no Saisho Tachi*, 98–101.

30. In an interview with the author at his residence on August 15, 1995, Kades compared his return home to the death of a bee immediately after it has stung. Masuda, *Koshoku Tsuihoron*, 277–78.

31. The murder of Shimoyama Sadanori, president of the Japanese National Railways, occurred during the tense period of austerity layoffs of workers; at Mitaka Station, unmanned train cars ran out of control; between Matsukawa Station and Kanayagawa Station, a railroad obstruction was created by removing rails.

32. Masuda, "Chosen Senso Izenniokeru Amerika no Nihon Saigunbi Koso Part 1," 33–34.

33. Masuda, *Rearmament of Japan*, 2-F-39; Masuda, *Koshoku Tsuihoron*, 229–30.

34. Masuda, *Rearmament of Japan*, 2-B-202.

CHAPTER 13

1. *Chosen Senso—Soru Kishu to Jinsen Jyoriku* [The Korean War—from the surprise attack on Seoul to the Inchon Landing], vol.1, ed. by Gakken (Tokyo: Gakken, 1999), 60, 74, 75.

2. W. J. Sebald, *With MacArthur in Japan, a Personal History of the Occupation* (New York: W. W. Norton and Company, 1965), 184.

3. Okonogi Masao, *Chosen Senso* [The Korean War] (Tokyo: Chuokoronsha, 1966), 104–5.

4. Harry S. Truman, *Memoirs of Harry S. Truman* (New York: Konecky & Konecky, 1955), 333.

5. Sebald, *With MacArthur in Japan*, 187–88.

6. MacArthur, *Reminiscences*, 377–78.

7. *Chosen Senso—Souru Kishu to Jinsen Jyoriku*, 75–77.

8. Sodei Rinjiro, ed., *Yoshida Shigeru–Makkasah Ofuku Shokanshu, 1945–1951* [Yoshida, MacArthur correspondence, 1945–1951], trans. Sodei Rinjiro (Tokyo: Hosei Daigaku Shuppan, 2000), 203–4.

9. Masuda Hiroshi, *Jieitai no Tanjyo* [The formation of Japan's self-defense forces] (Tokyo: Chuokoronshinsha 2004), 18–29; *Boeicho Jieitai Jyunen Shi* [Ten-year history of Japan's self-defense forces], ed. Defense Agency Ten-Year History of Japan's Self-Defense Forces editorial committee (Tokyo: Okurasho Insatsu Kyoku [Finance Ministry Printing Bureau], 1961), 372; Frank Kowalski, *Nihon Saigunbi* [The Rearmament of Japan], trans. Katsuyama Kinjiro (Tokyo: Saimaru Shuppankai, 1969), 24–33, 68–72.

10. Earl D. Johnson, assistant Sec. of the Army, National Police Reserve Notes on Conference with Maj. Gen. W. P. Shepard, Feb. 7, 1951; Masuda, *Rearmament of Japan, Part One: 1947–1952*, 1-C-144.

11. Masuda, *Jieitai no Tanjyo*, 107–9; James E. Auer, *Yomigaeru Nihon Kaigun* [The revival of the Japanese Navy], vol. 1, trans. Senoo Sadao (Jiji Tsushinsha, 1972), 106; Joint Strategic Plans Committee (JSPC), subj.: Japanese Maritime Police, JSPC959; 1-A-109 in *Rearmament of Japan Part One: 1947–1952*.

12. Masuda, *Jieitai no Tanjyo*, 109; Auer, *Yomigaeru Nihon Kaigun*, 119–25.

13. "Chosen Sokai no Ippankeika, dai 2 setsu " [Chapter 2, The general process of minesweeping in Korea], in *Chosen Doran Tokubetsu Sokaishi* [The Korean War special minesweeping history], preserved in the Defense Bureau Library.

14. Masuda, *Rearmament of Japan, Part One: 1947–1952*, 1-D-109.

15. MacArthur, *Reminiscences*, 394.

16. Oral Reminiscences of Lieutenant General Edward M. Almond.

17. Sebald, *With MacArthur in Japan*, 196.

18. Oral Reminiscences of Lieutenant General Edward M. Almond.

19. Oral Reminiscences of Admiral Arleigh A. Burke.

20. Ibid.

21. Oral Reminiscences of Lieutenant General Edward M. Almond.

22. Sebald, *With MacArthur in Japan*, 196–97.

23. *Chosen Senso—Soru Kishu to Jinsen Jyoriku*, 131.

24. Ibid., 138–40.

25. Truman, *Memoirs of Harry S. Truman*, 365.

26. MacArthur, *Reminiscences*, 411–12.

27. Sebald, *With MacArthur in Japan*, 216.

28. Ibid., 218.

29. *Chosen Senso—Soru Kishu to Jinsen Jyoriku*, 141–43, 148–49; *Chosen Senso, Chugokugun Sansen to Fumo no Taijisen* [The Korean War—Chinese entry into the war and fruitless confrontation], vol. 2, ed. Gakken (Tokyo: Gakken, 1999), 58–60.

30. Sebald, *With MacArthur in Japan*, 202.

31. Oral Reminiscences of Admiral Arleigh A. Burke.

32. *Chosen Senso, Chugokugun Sansen to Fumo no Taijisen*, 62–64.

33. Truman, *Memoirs of Harry S. Truman*, 381–82.

34. *Chosen Senso, Chugokugun Sansen to Fumo no Taijisen*, 64–81.

35. Sebald, *With MacArthur in Japan*, 211–12.

36. Ibid., 221–22.

37. Ibid., 225.

38. Oral Reminiscences of Lieutenant General Edward M. Almond.

39. Sebald, *With MacArthur in Japan*, 229.

40. Ibid., 228.

41. MacArthur, *Reminiscences*, 454.

42. Schonberger, *Senryo 1945–1952—Sengo Nihon o Tsukuriageta 8 nin no Amerikajin*, 110–12; Taiheiyo Senso Kenkyukai *Zusetsu Makkahsah*, 132–41.

CONCLUSION

1. Engineer Memoirs, Major General Hugh J. Casey, U.S. Army, 182.

2. Oral Reminiscences of General LeGrande Diller.

3. Huff, *My Fifteen Years with General MacArthur*, 64.

4. Richard B. Finn, *Makkasah to Yoshida Shigeru* [MacArthur and Yoshida Shigeru] vol. 1 and 2., ed. by Uchida Kenzo (Tokyo: Dobunshoin, 1993), states that Yoshida met MacArthur seventy-five times.

5. Oral Reminiscences of Major General Richard J. Marshall.

6. Engineer Memoirs, Major General Hugh J. Casey, U.S. Army, 274.

7. Oral Reminiscences of Frank Rizzo.

8. Oral Reminiscences of Brigadier General Crawford F. Sams.

9. Ibid.

10. Egeberg, *The General*, 35.

11. Oral Reminiscences of Major General Richard J. Marshall.

12. William Sebald, *With MacArthur in Japan*, 59.

13. Egeberg, *The General*, 33.

14. Masuda, *Koshoku Tsuihoron*, 216–22.

15. Egeberg, *The General*, 34.

16. Oral Reminiscences of Major General Richard J. Marshall.

17. Oral Reminiscences of Brigadier General Crawford F. Sams; Oral Reminiscences of Colonel Laurence E. Bunker.

18. Oral Reminiscences of Major General Richard J. Marshall; Oral Reminiscences of Brigadier General Bonner F. Fellers.

19. Oral Reminiscences of Lieutenant General Edward M. Almond.
20. Oral Reminiscences of Lieutenant General Alonzo O. Fox.
21. Oral Reminiscences of Colonel Laurence E. Bunker.
22. Sebald, *With MacArthur in Japan,* 105.
23. Oral Reminiscences of Brigadier General Elliott R. Thorpe.
24. Oral Reminiscences of Colonel Laurence E. Bunker.
25. Oral Reminiscences of General LeGrande Diller.
26. Oral Reminiscences of Charles L. Kades.
27. Oral Reminiscences of Ambassador William J. Sebald.
28. Oral Reminiscences of Admiral Charles Bulkeley.

U.S. Published Sources

Beck, John Jacob. *MacArthur and Wainwright: Sacrifice of the Philippines.* Albuquerque: University of New Mexico Press, 1974.

Breuer, William. *MacArthur's Undercover War: Spies, Saboteurs, Guerrillas, and Secret Missions.* New York: John Wiley and Sons, 1995.

Connaughton, Richard. *MacArthur and Defeat in the Philippines.* New York: Overlook Press, 2001.

Eisenhower, Dwight D. *The Eisenhower Diaries.* Edited by Robert H. Ferrell. New York: W. W. Norton, 1981.

Hunt, Frazier. *The Untold Story of Douglas MacArthur.* New York: Devin-Adair Company, 1954.

Huff, Sidney L., with Joe Alex Morris. *My Fifteen Years with General MacArthur.* New York: Harper, 1964.

James, D. Clayton. *The Years of MacArthur: 1880–1964.* 3 vols. Boston: Houghton Mifflin, 1970–85.

MacArthur, Douglas. *Reminiscences.* New York: Fawcett World Library, 1964.

Manchester, William. *American Caesar: Douglas MacArthur 1880–1964.* Boston: Little Brown, 1978.

Petillo, Carol Morris. *Douglas MacArthur: Philippine Years.* Bloomington: Indiana University Press, 1981.

Schaller, Michael. *Douglas MacArthur: The Far Eastern General.* New York: Oxford University Press, 1989.

U.S. Manuscripts

The holdings of MacArthur Memorial Bureau of Archives, the National Archives Record Center, and the Japanese National Diet Library provide coverage of MacArthur's activities. Some of the following manuscripts are from RG (Record Group). Sources held in these archives are used in this book.

Aluit, Alfonso J., *Corregidor.* Manila: Galleon, 2003.

Auchincloss, Samuel Sloan Jr. The Memoirs of Samuel Sloan Auchincloss Jr.: October 12, 1903 to November 5, 1991.

Masuda Hiroshi, ed. *Rearmament of Japan Part One: 1947–1952.* Washington, D.C.: Congressional Information Service; and Tokyo: Maruzen Company, 1998.

Report of General MacArthur: The Campaigns of MacArthur in the Pacific. GHQ G-2 MacArthur Report. Vol. 4 Tokyo: Gendai Shiryo Shuppan, 1998.

Rogers, Paul P. *The Good Years, MacArthur and Sutherland.* New York: Praeger, 1980.

——. Papers of Lieutenant Paul P. Rogers. USA, Box 1, Folder #1, RG46.

Sutherland, Richard Kerens. Papers of Lieutenant General Richard Kerens Sutherland. USA, 1941–1945, RG46.

Oral Histories and Interviews

Almond, Edward M. Oral Reminiscences of Lieutenant General Edward M. Almond. Interviewed by D. Clayton James. Anniston, August 4, 1971.

Bluemel, Clifford. Oral Reminiscences of Brigadier General Clifford Bluemel. Interviewed by D. Clayton James. Yardley, Pennsylvania, July 8, 1971.

Bulkeley, Charles. Oral Reminiscences of Admiral Charles Bulkeley. Washington, D.C., October 5, 1982, RG32: oral histories, Box 6.

Bunker, Laurence E. Oral Reminiscences of Colonel Laurence E. Bunker. Interviewed by D. Clayton James. Wellesley Hills, Massachusetts, July 12, 1971.

Burke, Arleigh A. Oral Reminiscences of Admiral Arleigh A. Burke. Interviewed by D. Clayton James. Washington, D.C., July 2, 1971.

Casey, Hugh J. Engineer Memoirs, Major General Hugh J. Casey, U.S. Army. Office of History, U.S. Army Corps of Engineers, Washington, D.C., September 25–29, 1979.

Diller, LeGrande. Oral Reminiscences of General LeGrande Diller. September 26, 1982. RG32: oral histories, Box 6.

Egeberg, Roger O. Oral Reminiscences of Dr. Roger O. Egeberg. Interviewed by D. Clayton James. Washington, D.C., June 30, 1971.

Fellers, Bonner F. Oral Reminiscences of Brigadier General Bonner F. Fellers. Interviewed by D. Clayton James. Washington, D.C., June 26, 1971.

Fitch, Burdette M. Oral Reminiscences of Brigadier General Burdette M. Fitch. Interviewed by D. Clayton James. San Francisco, California, August 28, 1971.

Fox, Alonzo P. Oral Reminiscences of Lieutenant General Alonzo P. Fox. Interviewed by D. Clayton James. Washington, D.C., June 26, 1971.

Guyton, Benson. Oral Reminiscences of Benson Guyton. Interviewed by D. Clayton James. Decatur, Alabama, August 5, 1971.

Hara, Cappy. Interview with Cappy Hara at the Athletic Club. Interviewed by Masuda Hiroshi. New York City, September 14, 1984.

Kades, Charles L. Interview with Charles L. Kades, at his residence. Interviewed by Masuda Hiroshi. August 15, 1995.

——. Oral Reminiscences of Colonel Charles L. Kades. Interviewed by D. Clayton James. New York City, July 7, 1977.

Kenney, George C. *General Kenney Reports: A Personal History of the Pacific War.* New York: Duell, Sloan, & Pearce, 1949.

——. Oral Reminiscences of General George C. Kenney. Interviewed by D. Clayton James. July 16, 1971.

MacArthur, Jean. Papers of Jean MacArthur, Oral History, Transcript #5, RG13, June 19, 1984.

——. Papers of Jean MacArthur, Oral History, Transcript #6, RG13, June 19, 1984.

——. Papers of Jean MacArthur, Oral History, Transcript #7, RG13, August 17, 1984.

——. Papers of Jean MacArthur, Oral History, Transcript #31, RG13, September 28, 1984.

Marshall, Richard J. Oral Reminiscences of Major General Richard J. Marshall. Interviewed by D. Clayton James. Leesburg, Florida, July 27, 1971.

Rizzo, Frank. Oral Reminiscences of Frank Rizzo. Interviewed by D. Clayton James. Tokyo, Japan, August 8, 1977.

Sams, Crawford F. Oral Reminiscences of Brigadier General Crawford F. Sams (M.D.). Interviewed by D. Clayton James. Atherton, California, August 25, 1971.

Sebald, William J. Oral Reminiscences of Ambassador William J. Sebald. Interviewed by D. Clayton James. Naples, Florida, July 30, 1971.

Thorpe, Elliott R. Oral Reminiscences of Brigadier General Elliott R. Thorpe. Interviewed by D. Clayton James. Sarasota, Florida, May 29, 1977.

Whitney, Courtney. Biography: Papers of Major General Courtney Whitney. RG30.

——. Excerpts from Oral Reminiscences of Major General Courtney Whitney. Interviewed by D. Clayton James. Washington, D.C., August 28, 1967.

Willoughby, Charles A. Biographical Sketches of Persons Interviewed: MacArthur Oral History Project compiled by Judy R. Hotard.

——. Oral Reminiscences of Major General Charles A. Willoughby. Interviewed by D. Clayton James. Naples, Florida, July 30, 1971.

Official Publications

"Chosen Sokai no Ippankeika, Dai 2 setsu" [The general process of minesweeping in Korea, chapter 2], in *Chosen Doran Tokubetsu Sokaishi* [The Korean War special minesweeping history], preserved in the Defense Bureau Library.

Daihonei Rikugunbu Senso Shidohan Kimitsu Senso Nisshi [The secret diary of the War Instruction Department of Army Headquarters], vol. 1. Edited by the Military History Society. Tokyo: Kinseisha, 1998.

Hando Kazutoshi. "Soshireikan Makkasah no Fukushu" [The revenge of Commander MacArthur]. *Ohru Yomimono,* September 1988.

Furyo ni kansuru Shorui Tsuzuri No.31–35 [Document Files on prisoners no. 31–35]. Preserved in the National Institute for Defense Studies.

Military Intelligence Division, SCAP. "Manila no Higeki" [The tragedy of Manila]. *Ohru Yomimono,* September 1988.

Japanese Editions of American Histories

Auer, James E. *Yomigaeru Nihon Kaigun* [The revival of the Japanese Navy], vols. 1 and 2, translated by Senoo Sadao. Tokyo: Jijitsushinsha, 1972.

Burns, James. *Ruzuberuto to Dainiji Sekaitaisen* [Roosevelt and World War II], vol. 2. Translated by Inoue Isamu and Ito Takuichi. Tokyo: Jijitsushinsha, 1972.

Cohen, Theodore. *Nihon Senryo Kakumei, GHQ karano Shogen* [The occupation and rebirth of Japan, testimonies from GHQ] vols.1 and 2. Translated by Ohmae Masaomi. Tokyo: TBS Britannica, 1983.

Constantino, Renato, and Letizia Constantino. *Firipin Minshu no Rekishi III* [History of the Philippine people], vol. 3. Translated by Tsurumi Yoshiyuki. Tokyo: Imura Bunka Jigyosha, 1979.

Egeberg, Roger O., M.D. *Hadakano Makkasah* [The general]. Translated by Hayashi Shigeo and Kitamura Tetsuo. Tokyo: Tosho Shuppansha, 1995.

Finn, Richard B. *Makkasah to Yoshida Shigeru* [MacArthur and Yoshida Shigeru], vols. 1 and 2. Supervised by Uchida Kenzo. Tokyo: Dobunshoin, 1993.

Gunther, John. *Makkasah no Nazo* [The riddle of MacArthur]. Translated by Kinoshita Hideo and Yasuo Nagaharu. Tokyo: Jijitsushinsha, 1951.

Johnson, U. Alexis. *Jyonson Bei Taishi no Nihon Kaiso* [The memoirs of Ambassador Johnson]. Translated by Masuda Hiroshi. Tokyo: Soshisha, 1989.

Kennan, George F. *Jyoji F. Kenan Kaikoroku* [The memoirs of George F. Kennan], vol. 1. Translated by Shimizu Toshio. Tokyo: Yomiuri Shimbunsha, 1973.

Kowalski, Frank. *Nihon Saigunbi* [The rearmament of Japan]. Translated by Katsuyama Kinjiro. Tokyo: Saimaru Shuppankai, 1969. Reprint, Tokyo: Chuokoronshinsha, 1999.

MacArthur, Douglas. *Makkasah Kaisoki* [MacArthur reminiscences]. Translated by Tsushima Kazuo. Tokyo: Asahi Shimbunsha, 1964.

Sams, Crawford F. *DDT Kakumei* [DDT innovation]. Edited and translated by Takemae Eiji. Tokyo: Iwanamishoten, 1986.

Schonberger, Howard B. *Senryo 1945–1952—Sengo Nihon o Tsukuriageta 8 nin no Amerikajin* [Occupation 1945–1952—Eight Americans who created postwar Japan]. Translated by Miyazaki Akira. Tokyo: Jijitsushinsha, 1994.

Sebald, William J. *Nihon Senryo Gaiko no Kaiso* [Memoirs of diplomacy during the occupation of Japan]. Translated by Nozue Kenzo. Tokyo: Asahi Shimbunsha, 1966.

Tenney, Lester I. *Batan: Tooi Michinorino Sakini* [My hitch in hell: The Bataan Death March]. Translated by Ibuki Yukako and others. Tokyo: Nashinokisha, 2003.

Truman, Harry S. *Toruman Kaikoroku* [Truman memoirs], vol. 2. Supervised by Kase Shunichi. Translated by Horie Yoshitaka. Tokyo: Kobunsha, 1966.

Willoughby, Charles A. *Shirarezaru Nihon Senryo* [The unknown occupation of Japan]. Translated by En Tei. Tokyo: Banchoshobo, 1973.

Japanese Published Sources

Ban Hachizo. "Eirei no Gojyukkaiki Hoyo o Itonami, Tatakatta ano Sento no Kioku o Tadoru" [The 50th commemoration service for dead soldiers and memories of the war]. *Heiwa no Ishizue, Onketsuhen* [The Foundation of Peace, Collection of Witnesses of Unentitled Military Pensioners]. Edited by the Public Foundation for Peace and Consolation, Incorporated Administrative Agency. Vol. 3, 1993. Tokyo: Exhibition and Reference Library for Peace and Consolation, 1993–2005.

Imoto Kumao. *Daitoa Senso Sakusen Nisshi* [Operational diary of the Pacific War]. Tokyo: Fuyoshobo Shuppan, 1998.

Katsuya Fukushige. "Korehidoru eno Michi wa Nagakatta!" [It was a long way to Corregidor], *Mokugekisha ga Kataru Showashi vol. 6, Taiheiyo Senso* [Witnesses to Showa history, vol. 6, Pacific war]. Supervised by Inose Naoki. Tokyo: Shin Jinbutsu Oraisha, 1989.

Kawanami Toichi and Ban Hachizo. "Batan Shi no Koshin" [The Bataan death march]. *Heiwa no Ishizue, Onketsuhen* [The Foundation of Peace, Collection of Witnesses of Unentitled Military Pensioners]. Edited by the Public Foundation for Peace and Consolation Incorporated Administrative Agency, vol. 1, 1991. Exhibition and Reference Library for Peace and Consolation, Tokyo, 1993–2005.

Kawashima Masuzo. "Batanhanto Korehidoruto Jyugunki" [Bataan Peninsula and Corregidor campaign memoir]. *Heiwa no Ishizue, Onketsuhen* [The Foundation of Peace, Collection of Witnesses of Unentitled Military Pensioners]. Edited by the Public Foundation for Peace and Consolation Incorporated Administrative Agency, vol. 6, 1996. Exhibition and Reference Library for Peace and Consolation, Tokyo, 1993–2005.

Kishimoto Eitaro. "Hito Batan Koryakusen" [The capture of Bataan in the Philippines]. *Heiwa no Ishizue, Onketsuhen* [The Foundation of Peace, Collection of Witnesses of Unentitled Military Pensioners], vol. 5, 1995. Exhibition and Reference Library for Peace and Consolation, Tokyo, 1993–2005.

Kotani Teruo. "Bukan Korehidoru Koryaku to Hito Haitai o Taikenshi" [The capture of Wuhan and Corregidor and defeat in the Philippines]. *Heiwa no Ishizue, Onketsuhen* [The Foundation of Peace, Collection of Witnesses of Unentitled Military Pensioners], vol. 5, 1995. Exhibition and Reference Library for Peace and Consolation, Tokyo, 1993–2005.

Nishimura Yorio." Hito Batanhanto no Tatakai" [The battle of Bataan Peninsula in the Philippines]. *Heiwa no Ishizue, Onketsuhen* [The Foundation of Peace, Collection of Witnesses of Unentitled Military Pensioners], vol. 15, 2005. Exhibition and Reference Library for Peace and Consolation, Tokyo, 1993–2005.

Senshi Sosho, Hito Koryaku Sakusen [War history series, The operation to capture the Philippines]. Edited by the War History Department of the Institute of the Defense Agency. Tokyo: Asagumo Shimbunsha, 1966.

Sodei Rinjiro, ed. and trans. *Yoshida Shigeru·Makkasah Ofuku Shokanshu, 1945–1951* [Yoshida, MacArthur correspondence, 1945–1951]. Tokyo: Hosei Daigaku Shuppan, 2000.

Takemae Eiji, ed. *Nihon Senryo: GHQ Kokan no Shogen* [Occupation of Japan—GHQ high-ranking officers' testimony]. Tokyo: Chuokoronsha, 1988.

Takeuchi Kaneo. *Makkasah Gensui to Sono Bakuryo* [General MacArthur and His Staff Officers], vol. 1. Tokyo: Jinji Koshinjyo, 1946.

Terashima Sadatsugu. "Manira Ichibannori no Michi wa Kewashiku" [The first step to Manila was difficult]. *Heiwa no Ishizue, Onketsuhen* [The Foundation of Peace, Collection of Witnesses of Unentitled Military Pensioner], vol. 1, 1991. Exhibition and Reference Library for Peace and Consolation, Tokyo, 1993–2005.

Other Japanese Publications

Boeicho Jieitai 10 nen Shi [Ten-year history of Japan's self-defense forces]. Edited by the Defense Agency editorial committee. Tokyo: Okurasho Insatsukyoku [Finance Ministry Printing Bureau], 1961.

Chosen Senso, vol. 1—Souru Kishu to Jinsen Jyoriku [The Korean War—from the surprise attack on Seoul to the Inchon landing], vol. 1, edited by Gakken. Tokyo: Gakken, 1999.

Chosen Senso—Chugokugun Sansen to Fumo no Taijisen [The Korean War—the Chinese entry into the war and fruitless confrontation], vol. 2, edited by Gakken. Tokyo: Gakken, 1999.

Ichiokunin no Showashi ·Nihon no Senshi, vol. 10, *Taiheiyo Senso,* part. 4 [Showa history for one hundred million people: Japanese war history, vol.10, Pacific war, part 4]. Edited by Mainichi Shimbunsha. Tokyo: Mainichi Shimbunsha, 1980.

Igarashi Takeshi. *Tainichi Kowa to Reisen* [The peace treaty with Japan and the cold war]. Tokyo: Tokyo Daigaku Shuppankai, 1986.

Kanesashi Masao. "Gaikan Senryo Seiji kara 55 nen Taisei e" [Overview—from political administration under the occupation to 55 system]. *Gendai Nihon Seito Shiroku* [Modern Japanese political party records], vol. 2. Edited by Kitamura Kimihito and others. Tokyo: Daiichihoki, 2003.

Kyodo Kenkyu—Nihon Senryo [Collaborative studies—the occupation of Japan]. Edited by Institute of Shiso no Kagaku Kenkyukai. Tokyo: Tokuma Shoten, 1972.

Makkasah no Nihon [MacArthur's Japan]. Edited by Shukan Shincho Editorial Section. Tokyo: Shinchosha, 1970.

Masuda Hiroshi. "Ashida Hitoshi." *Sengo Nihon no Saisho Tachi* [Prime ministers of postwar Japan], edited by Akio Watanabe. Tokyo: Chuokoronshinsha 2001.

——. "Chosen Senso Izenniokeru Amerika no Nihon Saigunbi Koso, part 1" [U.S. policy toward Japanese rearmament before the Korean War, part 1]. *Hogaku Kenkyu,* vol. 72. Tokyo: Keio University Press, 1999.

——. *Jieitai no Tanjyo* [The formation of Japan's self-defense forces]. Tokyo: Chuokoronshinsha, 2004.

——. *Koshoku Tsuihoron* [The Public purge]. Tokyo: Iwanamishoten, 1998.

——. "Kyoiku Kaikaku" [Educational reforms]. In *Jitsuroku Nihon Senryo* [Documents on the occupation of Japan]. Tokyo: Gakken, 2005.

——. "Naimusho Kaitai" [The dissolution of the Home Ministry]. In *Jitsuroku Nihon Senryo* [Documents on the occupation of Japan]. Tokyo: Gakken, 2005.

——. *Seijika Tsuiho* [Purges of politicians]. Tokyo: Chuokoronshinsha, 2001.

——. "Zaibatsu Kaitai, Nochi Kaikaku" [Dissolution of Zaibatsu and land reform]. In *Jitsuroku Nihon Senryo* [Documents on the occupation of Japan]. Tokyo: Gakken, 2005.

Masumi Jyunnosuke, *Sengo Seiji 1945-1955,* [Postwar politics, 1945-1955]. Tokyo: Tokyo University Press, 1983.

Mizokawa Tokuji, ed. *Senso·Jihen* [War incidents]. Tokyo: Kyoikusha, 1991.

Narita Norihiko. "Nihonkoku Kempo to Kokkai" [The Japanese Constitution and the Diet]. In *Nihon Gikaishiroku* [The Historical Record of the Japanese Diet], vol. 4. Edited by Uchida Kenzo, Kimbara Samon, and Furuya Tetsuo. Tokyo: Daiichihoki, 1990.

Nishi Osamu. "Nihonkoku Kempo Seitei" [The enactment of the Japanese Constitution]. In *Jitsuroku Nihon Senryo* [Documents on the occupation of Japan]. Tokyo: Gakken, 2005.

Nomura Minoru. *Nihon Kaigun no Rekishi* [History of the Japanese Navy]. Tokyo: Yoshikawa Kobunkan, 2002.

Okonogi Masao. *Chosen Senso* [The Korean War]. Tokyo: Chuokoronsha, 1966.

Shibata Takehiko and Hara Katsuhiro. *Dorittoru Kushu Hiroku* [History of the Doolittle air raid]. Tokyo: Ariadone Project, 2003.

Shinobu Seizaburo. *Sengo Nihon Seijishi* II [A postwar political history of Japan II]. Tokyo: Keiso Shobo, 1966.

Tachikawa Kyoichi. "Senshi no Kyokun—Naniga Horyomondai o Undanoka, Nihongun no Hoshin to Haikei" [Lessons from military history—what caused prisoner problems? The policy and background of the Japanese army], vol. 2. In *MAMOR,* September 2008.

Taiheiyo Senso Kenkyukai, ed. *Zusetsu Makkasah* [Illustrated history of MacArthur]. Tokyo: Kawade Shobo Shinsha, 2003.

Takemae Eiji. *GHQ.* Tokyo: Iwanami Shoten, 1983.

Yamamoto Reiko, *Beikoku Tainichi Senryokaniokeru "Kyoshoku Tsuiho" to Kyoshoku Tekikakushinsa* [Educational purge under the U.S. occupation of Japan and its screening committees]. Tokyo: Gakujyutsu Shuppankai, 2007.

Index

Pages numbers followed by n or nn indicate notes. *Italicized* page numbers indicate maps.

Acheson, Dean G., 247, 270
Adachi Hanazo, 153
Adversario, Domingo, 52
Aguinaldo, Emilio, 75
Ah Cheu (nanny), 48–49, 53, 85, 98, 105, 106,
    109, 112, 116, 117
Aitape, Battle of, 155
Akagi, 154
Akers, A. B., 106
Akiyama Monjiro, 56
Akin, Spencer B., 33, 158, 182, 197, 238
   background, 14–15, 22
   evacuation from Corregidor, 97, 107,
     109, 111
Allison, John M., 249, 250
Almond, Edward M.
   Korean War and, 258, 260, 261, 266, 271–72,
    277
   quoted on MacArthur, 282–83
   quoted on Whitney, 183–84
Arao Osakatsu, 122
Arisuye Seizo, 191–92
Arnold, Archibald V., 186
Arnold, Henry H., 29, 33, 38, 170
Arnold, William H., 163
Asahi Shimbun, 52, 73–74, 126, 132, 242, 272
Ashida Hitoshi, 215–16, 235, 239–44
Atcheson, George, Jr., 240
Atomic bomb, 188
Auchincloss, Samuel S., Jr., 182–83, 187–92
Australia
   MacArthur's arrival in, 117–19
   plans for defense of, 149–51, 152

Ban Hachizo, 140–41
Bataan "Death March," 137–47, 298nn63, 68
Bataan Peninsula
   first battle of, 61–65, *62*, 121, 123
   MacArthur's withdrawal to, 58–61
   recapture of, 174–76
   second battle of, 126–32
   second battle of, Japanese preparation for,
    121–23, 125–26

Beck, John Jacob, 32–33
Beebe, Lewis C., 125, 129
Bilibid Prison, 173, 174
Blamey, Thomas, 152, 155, 158
Bluemel, Clifford, 33
Brady, Francis M., 37
Brereton, Lewis H., 17, 54
   Clark Field attack and, 34–37
   Pearl Harbor attack and, 32, 34
   Philippine defense plans and, 28, 31
Brett, George H., 54, 150
   MacArthur's arrival in Mindanao and, 92,
    114–15, 117
   MacArthur's evacuation from Corregidor
    and, 98–99
Bulkeley, Charles, 6, 285
Bulkeley, John D., 17
   background, 24–25
   MacArthur's evacuation from Corregidor
    and, 67, 95, 96, 99, 103–4, 106–7, 110–14
Bundy, Charles W., 29
Bunker, Laurence E., 182–83, 198–99, 224,
    282, 283
Burke, Arleigh A., 158–59, 256, 257, 260–62,
    267–68
Byard, Spencer, 210

Cairo Declaration, 185
Carmichael, Richard H., 116
Carpenter, Alva C., 146, 197
Casey, Hugh J.
   atomic bomb and, 188
   background, 12–14
   Bataan and, 66, 124
   Clark Field attack and, 37
   Corregidor and, 48, 58–59, 70, 132
   Corregidor evacuation and, 97, 108, 109–10,
    111, 112
   counterattack in Pacific and, 154
   Japanese surrender and, 191
   MacArthur's arrival in Mindanao, 116
   MacArthur's inner circle and, 156, 157
   occupation of Japan and, 195, 197, 238

Casey, Hugh J. *(continued)*
    Pearl Harbor attack and, 33
    Philippine defense plans and, 32
    quoted on George, 17
    quoted on MacArthur, 276, 278
    quoted on second Bataan battle, 128
Chamberlin, Stephen J.
    counterattack in Pacific and, 150, 162, 183
    Japanese surrender and, 191
    MacArthur's inner circle and, 155–56, 158, 179
    occupation of Japan and, 197
Chiang Kai-shek, 185–86, 230–31, 270, 281
China, entry into Korean War, 262–69
Christie, Albert F., 136–37
Churchill, Winston, 150, 153, 160, 185–86, 187, 192, 275
Chynoweth (general), 137
Clark Field, Japanese attack on, 34–39
Clarke, Elaine, 171–72, 199
Cohen, Theodore, 243
Cold War, effects on Occupation policies and, 211, 213, 215, 230–31, 236–38, 245–47
Collins, Joseph Lawton, 258
Constitution, writing of new Japanese, 212–16
Coral Sea, Battle of, 153
Corregidor Island, 63
    fall of, 132–37, 145
    MacArthur on, 49, 51–54, 65–71
    MacArthur's evacuation from, 93–114
    MacArthur's evacuation from, authorized, 85–92
    Quezon's evacuation from, 79–85, 80
    recapture of, 174–76
Counterattack, in Pacific
    Japanese conquests and, 149–51, 151
    MacArthur's inner circle and, 150, 152, 155–59
    New Guinea and, 152–55
    planning for, 149–52
    plans to return to Philippines, 164–68
    strategy conflicts between Army and Navy, 159–64
Crist, William, 180
    occupation of Japan and, 187, 197, 198, 210, 213

Dai Nippon Butokukai, 226, 239
Daily Mail, MacArthur's statement to, 246
Davis, John K., 74
Davis, T. J., 137
Diller, LeGrande
    background, 20–21
    Bataan and, 124
    Corregidor and, 52, 68

Corregidor evacuation and, 89, 97, 98, 104, 106, 108, 111, 114
    MacArthur and, 276, 277, 280, 283–84
Dodge, Joseph M., 245, 248
Doihara Kenji, 203
Doolittle, James H., 154
Draper, William H., Jr., 231–32, 234–35
Dulles, John Foster, 248, 249–50
Dyess, William E., 146
Dyke, Kenneth R., 197

Eather, Kenneth W., 155
Edelman, Clyde D., 175
Education reforms, in post-war Japan, 219–21
Edwards, Corwin D., 217
Egeberg, Roger O., 172, 282, 283
    counterattack in Pacific and, 165, 167
    Japanese surrender and, 190, 194
    MacArthur's inner circle and, 156
    MacArthur's meeting with Hirohito, 203
    occupation of Japan and, 195
    quoted on MacArthur, 170–71, 279–80
    quoted on Whitney, 184–85
    return to Philippines, 173, 175
Eichelberger, Robert L., 278, 281
    counterattack in Pacific and, 170
    Japanese surrender and, 192
    MacArthur's inner circle and, 155, 156, 157
    occupation of Japan and, 187, 196, 201, 235, 240
    Sutherland and, 11
Eisenhower, Dwight D., 200, 273
    as aide to MacArthur, 5, 6, 7, 10, 278
    Bataan and, 129
    named general of the army, 170
    quoted, 71, 78, 92, 137, 287n7

Fellers, Bonner F., 177, 179, 282
Fine, Sherwood, 16, 217
Finschhafen, Battle of, 155
Fitch, Burdette M., 150, 170, 184
Formosa
    Korean War strategy and, 270–71
    plans to defend Philippines and, 34–37, 280
    plans to reach Japan and, 160, 163–65, 279
Fox, Alonzo P., 184, 283
Funk, Arnold J., 129

Garing, William H., 155
George, Harold H.
    in Australia, 118
    background, 16–17
    Clark Field attack and, 38
    counterattack in Pacific and, 152

evacuation from Corregidor, 97, 107, 111
occupation of Japan and, 197
Gerow, Leonard T., 27–29, 34, 86, 93
Glassford, William A., 38
Goodsill, Marshall, 210
Grew, Joseph C., 200
Grunert, George, 19, 30
Guyton, Benson, 36–37, 60, 132–33, 145

Hadley, Eleanor M., 217
Halsey, William F., 15, 160, 165, 166–67,
    193, 195
Handy, Thomas T., 29
Harriman, Averell W., 271
Hart, Thomas C., 24, 25, 32, 34, 54, 160
Hatoyama Ichiro, 221, 223, 239, 246–47
Hattori Takushiro, 126, 239, 255
Henderson, James M., 217
Herring, Edmund F., 155
Hickey, Doyle O., 260
Higashikuni Naruhiko, 212
Hirano Rikizo, 241
Hirohito, emperor, 203–4
Hiroshima, bombing of, 188
Hiryu, 154
Hitotsumatsu Sadayoshi, 240
Hollandia, landing at, 161, 162–63
Homma Masaharu, 135, 301n18
    attack on Philippines and, 42, 43, 55, 57
    Bataan and, 63, 65, 121, 127
    Bataan "Death March" and, 142, 146–47,
        298n74
Hoover, Blaine, 242
Hoover, Herbert C., 4
Hori Shigeru, 240
Huff, Sidney L., 105, 118, 124, 250, 278
    background, 21
    Clark Field attack and, 37
    Corregidor and, 47, 49, 52, 53, 66
    Corregidor evacuation and, 94, 96, 97–98,
        99, 104–5, 106, 108–9, 110, 111–12, 113
    counterattack in Pacific and, 161
    MacArthur's arrival in Mindanao, 116
    Philippine treasury assets and, 74
    Quezon's evacuation from Corregidor, 79
    Quezon's payment to, 74, 83, 89
Hull, Cordell, 29, 43, 81, 93
Hurley, Patrick J., 118
Hussey, Alfred R., 213, 214

Ickes, Harold L., 178, 179
Ikeda Hayato, 245, 247–48
Imoto Kumao, 63, 126
Inagaki Seiji, 122
Inchon, landing at, 257–58, 260–62

Inukai Takeru, 240
Ishibashi Tanzan, 239, 246–47
Itagaki Seishiro, 301n18
Iwabuchi Sanji, 174

Japan
    Allied plans for occupation of, 185–89
    Korean War and MacArthur's authorization
        for rearmament of, 253–55
    Korean War and minesweeping activities,
        256–57
    surrender of, 189–92, 193–95, 301n5
    U.S. bombing of, 188
Japan, U.S. occupation of
    disarmament of military and arrest of war
        criminals, 200–205, 301n18
    disease and food shortages in Japan, 205–7
    dissolution of Ministry of Home
        Affairs, 224–27
    dissolution of Zaibatsu, 216–18, 234,
        235, 285
    education reforms, 219–21
    efforts toward peace treaty with Japan,
        229–30
    establishment of Occupation administra-
        tion, 195–200
    general election, 221–24
    land reform, 218–19
    MacArthur's meeting with Hirohito, 203–4
    purge of militant nationalism, 209–12, 222,
        226, 239, 246
    writing of new constitution, 212–16
Japan, U.S. occupation of, policy changes
        toward economic recovery, 230–33
    MacArthur's opposition to, 233–38, 244–48
    U.S. government section differences and
        Japanese political reactions to, 238–44
Johns, Albert M., 132
Johnson, Earl D., 255
Johnson, Harold K., 60
Johnson, Louis A., 258
Johnson, U. Alexis, 298n74
Johnston, Percy F., 235–36
Jones, Albert M., 125
Jones, Dwight F., 55
Joy, C. Turner, 252, 257

Kades, Charles L.
    MacArthur and, 284
    occupation of Japan, 187, 210–16, 219, 222,
        223–24, 225, 226, 238
    occupation of Japan, and Japanese politics,
        239–44
Kaga, 154
Katayama Tetsu, 221, 224, 240–42

Kauffman, James L., 231
Kawabe Torashiro, 189, 190
Kawanami Tichi, 140–41
Kelly, Robert B., 106
Kennan, George F., 230–36, 243
Kenney, George C., 152, 155, 156, 157–58, 166
Kern, Harry, 246, 280
Killen, James S., 242–43
Kim Il Sung, 267
Kimitsu Senso Nisshi (Secret War Diary), 122, 130
Kimmel, Husband E., 68
Kimura Heitaro, 301n18
King, Edward P., Jr., 129–31
King, Ernest J., 39, 78, 85, 159–60, 163, 170
Kinkaid, Thomas C., 159, 164, 167
Koiso Kuniaki, 186
Kondo Nobutake, 159
Konoe Fumimaro, 212
Korean War, 245, 248, 249–73, *259*
  China's entry into, 262–69
  Japanese rearmament and, 253–57
  landing at Inchon, 257–58, 260–62
  MacArthur's dismissal and, 268–73
  MacArthur's reactions to start of, 249–51
  outbreak and MacArthur's appointment to UN command, 249–52
Kotani Teruo, 141
Kowalski, Frank, Jr., 254
Kramer, Raymond, 16, 197, 217
Krueger, Walter
  counterattack in Pacific and, 166
  MacArthur's inner circle and, 157
  occupation of Japan and, 187, 196
  return to Philippines, 173
  Sutherland and, 11
Kurita Takeo, 165, 167
Kurusu Takeo, 243

Land reform, in post-war Japan, 218–19
Laurel, José P., 85, 176, 178
Leahy, William D., 164, 170
Leary, Herbert F., 152, 158
Lehrbas, Lloyd, 182
Leyte Gulf, Battle of, 164–68, 169–70
Lovett, Robert A., 231

MacArthur, Arthur III (brother), 287n3
MacArthur, Arthur, Jr. (father), 1, 2, 4, 49, 219
MacArthur, Arthur (son), 21, 283, 287–88n10
  Corregidor and, 48–49, 52–53, 90
  Corregidor evacuation and, 22, 93, 96, 98, 105, 106, 109, 112, 116, 117
  return to U.S., 272–73

MacArthur, Douglas, 287n3
  atomic bomb and, 188
  Bataan and, 55, 59–61, 124, 128–29
  Bataan "Death March" and, 138, 145–47
  Clark Field attack and, 35–36, 38–39
  as commander of Southwest Pacific Area, 150
  as commander in chief of United States Army Forces, Pacific, 186
  defense of Australia and, 149–51, 152
  as "Dugout Doug," 133
  Japanese surrender and, 189–95, 301n5
  marriage to Jean Faircloth, 5
  marriage to Louise Brooks, 2, 3
  meeting with Hirohito, 203–4
  Pearl Harbor attack and, 32–34
  personal strengths and weaknesses, 275–85
  Philippine defense plans and, 28, 30–31, 125
  presidential ambitions of, 163–64, 182, 229–30, 273
  Quezon and Sayre's evacuation from Corregidor, 79–85
  Quezon's demand for neutrality and, 77–79
  Quezon's payment to, 74–75, 83–84, 88–90, 94
  before World War II, 1–8
  see also Corregidor Island; Counterattack, in Pacific; *Japan entries*
MacArthur, Jean Faircloth, 21, 24, 189, 203
  in Australia, 118, 177
  background and marriage, 5, 193, 283, 287n10
  Corregidor and, 48–49, 52–53, 67, 85
  Corregidor evacuation and, 22, 85–86, 93, 96, 98, 104–6, 109, 111, 112–13
  in Mindanao, 116–17
  quoted on McMicking, 23
  quoted on Wainwright, 105
  return to Philippines, 177
  return to U.S., 272–73
MacArthur, Malcolm (brother), 287n3
MacArthur, Mary Pinkney Hardy (mother), 3, 4, 5, 287n3
MacArthur, Mary (sister-in-law), 287n10
MacArthur and Wainwright (Beck), 32–33
Machida Chji, 222
Maeda Masami, 43, 56–57, 121, 122
Maki Tatsuo, 122
Manchester, William, 60, 93–94, 111, 178, 182
Mao Zedong, 267, 269
Marcum, Carlos, 205
Marquat, William F.
  background, 15–16
  Corregidor and, 66

Corregidor evacuation and, 97, 107, 111
occupation of Japan and, 197, 205, 217,
   238, 242
Marshall, George C.
   Bataan and, 124, 128–29
   Corregidor and, 54, 68
   Corregidor's fall and, 48, 133, 135
   Japanese attacks and, 39
   Korean War and, 264
   MacArthur's arrival in Mindanao, 114,
      115, 116
   MacArthur's evacuation from Corregidor
      and, 87, 89–92, 93, 94, 96, 98, 119
   Occupation plans and, 186
   Occupation policy changes and, 231
   Philippine defense plans and, 8, 28–31
   Philippine treasury assets and, 74
   post-Japanese attack defense plan
      changes, 41
   Quezon's anti-Americanism and demand
      for neutrality, 76, 78
   Quezon's evacuation from Corregidor,
      79, 81–83
Marshall, Richard J., 157, 182, 277
   background, 11–12
   Corregidor and, 59
   Corregidor evacuation and, 97, 106,
      110, 111
   democratization of Japan and, 211
   named general of the army, 170
   occupation of Japan and, 197
   Pearl Harbor attack and, 33
   Quezon's payment to, 74, 83
   quoted on MacArthur, 280, 282
   quoted on Stivers, 17
   quoted on Willoughby, 19
   return to U.S., 223–24
   Sutherland and, 11–12
Martin, Joseph W., 271, 272
Mashbir, Sidney, 195
Matsumoto Joji, 212, 215
McCloy, John J., 206
McCoy, Frank R., 233
McMicking, Joseph D., 22–23, 97, 106, 197
McNarney, Joseph T., 129–32
McNutt, Paul V., 7
M-Fund, 16, 205
Midway, Battle of, 154, 159
Mindanao Island, 113–14
Ministry of Home Affairs, dissolution of
   Japan's, 224–27
Moore, George F., 52
Morehouse, Charles H., 22, 97, 106, 164,
   197, 276

Mueller, Paul J., 235, 237, 239, 258, 277
Murphy, Frank, 7
Muto Akira, 168, 301n18

Nagasaki, bombing of, 188
Nagumo Chuichi, 159
Nakayama Motoo, 57, 121, 122, 131
Napier, Jack P., 238
Nara Akira, 63
Narahashi Wataru, 240
New Guinea, Battle of, 152–55
Nimitz, Chester W.
   as commander of Pacific Ocean Area, 150
   counterattack in Pacific and, 163, 164, 167
   Japanese surrender and, 186, 189, 195
   MacArthur and, 158–59
   named fleet admiral, 170
Nishimura Shoji, 165, 167
Nishio Suehiro, 221, 241, 242, 243
Nomura Kichisaburo, 202–3
North Korea. See Korean War

Okubo Takeo, 256, 257
Ord, James B., 6, 7, 10
Osmena, Sergio, 1, 5, 76, 125, 165
   Corregidor evacuation and, 79, 81
   de-Japanization of Philippines and,
      178–79
   return to Philippines, 166, 170, 176, 177, 281
Ozawa Jisaburo, 165

Pakenham, Compton, 246
Parker, George M., Jr., 32, 46, 59, 129
Pearl Harbor, Japanese attack on, 33–34
Peng Dehuai, 267, 269
Percival, Arthur, 194, 195
Perry, Matthew, 195
Philippine Scouts, 2–3, 8, 30–31, 60
Philippines
   Clark Field attack and, 34–39
   de-Japanization and democratization
      of, 176–80
   Japanese landing on and occupation of
      Manila, 42–46, 44, 54–58, 61–62
   MacArthur's evacuation to Corregi-
      dor, 46–49
   MacArthur's plan to return to, 164–68
   MacArthur's return to, 169–74
   other attacks, 38
   Pearl Harbor attack and, 33–34
   post-attack defense plan changes, 40–41
   pre-World War II defense plans, 3–8,
      27–33
   treasury assets of, 74, 83–84, 87–88

Political parties, formation in post-war
    Japan, 221–24
Potsdam Declaration, 187–88, 200, 201, 209,
    210, 230, 233, 234, 246
Prisoners of war, release of allied, 201
PT boats, 13–14, 24–25, 94–95, 106
Pulliam, H. E., 239

Quezon, Manuel L., 1, 3, 125, 278
    anti-Americanism and demand for neutral-
        ity, 75–79
    Corregidor and, 53, 67–68
    Corregidor evacuation and, 46–47, 48, 73,
        79–85, *80*, 87
    death of, 165
    defense of Philippines and, 4
    health of, 74, 81, 84
    Philippine independence and, 5–6

Ray, Herbert James., 24, 97, 99, 106, 110
Reminiscences (MacArthur), 35, 38–39, 77, 85,
    90, 96–97, 124, 138, 147, 170
Rhee, Syngman, 250, 264
Ridgway, Matthew B., 268, 270, 272
Rizzo, Frank, 187, 198, 210, 214, 238, 278
Rockwell, Francis W., 24, 54
    Corregidor evacuation and, 96, 97, 99,
        106, 111
Rogers, Paul P.
    background, 23
    Corregidor and, 52, 67, 69, 70, 83, 84
    Corregidor evacuation and, 97, 103, 106,
        108, 114
    MacArthur's arrival in Mindanao, 116
    MacArthur's inner circle and, 156
    Quezon's payments to MacArthur's staff
        and, 75, 87–89, 94
Romulo, Carlos P., 166
Roosevelt, Franklin D., 7, 39
    Corregidor and, 68, 71, 133–35
    counterattack in Pacific and, 153, 160
    death of, 189
    de-Japanization of Philippines and, 179
    MacArthur and, 5, 118, 279, 282
    MacArthur's evacuation from Corregidor,
        86–89, 96, 98
    MacArthur's presidential ambitions and,
        163, 164
    plans for occupation of Japan, 185–86
    post-attack Philippine defense plan
        changes, 41
    Quezon's anti-Americanism and demand
        for neutrality, 78

Quezon's evacuation from Corregidor,
    82, 84–85
Rowell, Milo E., 213, 214
Roxas, Manuel A., 76, 85, 88, 89, 125, 178
Royall, Kenneth C., 232, 235–36, 245–46
Rusk, Dean, 271

Salamaua, Battle of, 155
Sams, Crawford F.
    de-Japanization of Philippines and,
        177, 179–80
    occupation of Japan and, 197, 198, 206–7
    quoted on MacArthur, 279, 282
Santos, José Abad, 83
Sayre, Francis B.
    Clark Field attack and, 35
    Corregidor and, 48, 53
    Corregidor evacuation and, 78, 79–85, *80*,
        87, 126
    Pearl Harbor attack and, 32
    Philippine treasury assets and, 74
    quoted on Quezon, 77
Schaller, Michael, 60, 68, 75, 88
Schenck, Hubert G, 197
Schumacher, V. E., 107
Sebald, William J., 247, 270
    quoted on Inchon, 262
    quoted on Korean War, 249, 250, 251, 258,
        260, 267
    quoted on MacArthur, 266, 271, 272, 280,
        283, 284–85
Sejima Ryuzo, 58
Sharp, William F., 113, 115, 135–37
Shepard, Witfield P., 254, 255
Sherman, Forrest, 258, 268
Sherr, Joseph P., 21–22, 97, 107, 111, 197
Shidehara Kijuro, 205, 212, 214, 215, 220, 223,
    240, 241
Shigemitsu Mamoru, 194, 195
Shima Kiyohide, 165, 167
Shoho, 153
Showa Electric Company scandal, 242–45
Solomon Sea, Battle of, 154, 159
Soryu, 154
South Korea. *See* Korean War
Soviet Union
    Korean War and, 249, 251, 263–64,
        267, 270
    occupation of Japan and Cold War, 211, 213,
        215, 230–31, 236–38, 245–47
    World War II and, 185–86, 188
Stalin, Josef, 185, 187
Stark, Harold R.

Japanese attacks and, 32, 39
Philippine defense plans and, 29
post-attack Philippine defense plan
  changes, 40–41
Quezon's anti-Americanism and demand
  for neutrality, 78
Stimson, Henry
  Corregidor and, 48, 68, 82, 88–89, 93
  de-Japanization of Philippines and, 179
  Philippine defense plans and, 27, 31
  post-attack defense plan changes, 41
  Quezon's anti-Americanism and demand
    for neutrality, 76, 78
Stivers, Charles P., 17–18, 106, 158, 197
Stivers, Paul, 97
Stratemeyer, George E., 252
Sugiyama Gen, 42
Sutherland, Richard K., 71, 118, 190, 277, 278
  Akin and, 14
  background, 10–11
  Clark Field attack and, 34–38
  Clarke and, 171–72, 199
  Corregidor and, 48, 49, 52, 66, 71
  Corregidor evacuation and, 79, 90, 96,
    97–98, 99, 106, 126
  counterattack in Pacific and, 150, 155, 162
  MacArthur's inner circle and, 156, 158
  McMicking and, 23
  Morehouse and, 22
  occupation of Japan and, 197
  Pearl Harbor attack and, 33, 34
  Quezon's evacuation from Corregidor, 79
  Quezon's payment to, 74, 83, 89–90
  quoted on MacArthur, 276
  return to Philippines, 166
  return to U.S., 199–200, 213
  Stivers and, 17
  Whitney and, 181–82, 183
  Willoughby and, 19
Suzuki Kantaro, 186, 188
Sverdrup, Jack, 171, 195
Swope, Guy J., 241

Taft, William Howard, 1
Tamura Kyuzo, 256
Tench, Charles P., 191–92
Tenney, Lester I., 138–40
Terauchi Hisaichi, 43
Thorpe, Elliott R., 146, 239
  counterattack in Pacific and, 150, 152
  de-Japanization of Philippines, 177
  Nomura and, 202–3
  occupation of Japan and, 197, 202

quoted on MacArthur, 283
quoted on Whitney, 184
Tojo Hideki, 73, 201, 202, 226, 239, 245
Tokuda Kyuichi, 205, 221
Tokyo Rose, 194
Toyoda Soemu, 165
Truman, Harry S.
  Japanese surrender and 186, 187–89
  Korean War and, 250–52, 258, 263, 264–65,
    268–69, 273
  MacArthur's presidential ambitions
    and, 230
  occupation of Japan and, 200, 231, 237,
    253
Truman Doctrine, 229
Tsuchihashi Yuichi, 57
Tsuji Masanobu, 122
Tydings-McDuffie Act, 4, 7

Ueshima Yoshio, 45–46
Umezu Yoshijiro, 194, 195
USS Hornet, 154, 159
USS Lexington, 153
USS Mississippi, 195
USS Missouri, 193–94

Vandenburg, Arthur H., 163, 182
Vargas, Jorge B., 75
Vasey, George A., 155
Vial Island, Battle of, 155

Wachi Takaji, 122, 142
Wainwright, Jonathan M.
  Bataan and, 55, 59, 60, 126, 128–32
  Corregidor and, 71, 105, 132–37, 149
  Japanese landing in Philippines and, 46
  Japanese surrender and, 194, 195
  MacArthur's contingency plans and, 125
  Philippine defense plans and, 31
Walker, Kenneth N., 155
Walker, Walton H., 252, 257, 263, 266, 268
War criminals, arrest of Japanese, 202–3,
  301n18
Watson, Edwin "Pa," 92
Welsh, Edward C., 217
Wheeler, Herb, 219
Whitehead, Ennis C., 155
Whitlock, Lester J., 150, 158
Whitney, Courtney
  background, 180–82, 277, 278
  de-Japanization of Philippines and, 177,
    180, 183–85
  Korean War and Japanese rearmament, 254

Whitney, Courtney *(continued)*
  occupation of Japan, 198–200, 213–16, 219,
    223–24, 226, 238, 240
  occupation of Japan, and Japanese politics,
    242–43, 245
  quoted, 12, 18
  return to Philippines, 166
Williams, Justin, 187, 238
Willoughby, Charles A., 14, 15, 75, 89–90, 277
  background, 16, 18–19
  Corregidor evacuation and, 97, 106, 110,
    111, 114
  counterattack in Pacific and, 152, 155
  democratization of Japan and, 211
  Japanese surrender and, 190
  Korean War and, 254, 255, 267–68
  MacArthur's inner circle and, 156, 157
  MacArthur's meeting with Hirohito, 203
  occupation of Japan and, 197, 201, 223,
    238–39, 244

Quezon's evacuation from Corregidor, 79
  quoted, 10–11, 18
Wilson, Francis H., 19–20, 52, 53, 97, 106, 114
Wilson, Ralph E., 195
Wood, Robert, 287n7
Wootten, George F., 155

Yalta Agreement, 185, 188
Yamamoto Isoroku, 152, 154, 160
Yamashita Tomoyuki, 168, 172, 173
Yamazaki Takeshi, 244
Yonai Mitsumasa, 186
Yoshida Shigeru, 19, 272, 277
  Korean War and, 253, 255, 256
  U.S. occupation of Japan and, 215, 216, 223,
    224, 240–45, 247–48

Zaibatsu, dissolution of, 216–18, 234, 235,
  285
Zhou Enlai, 267